Praise for *Work and Play*

"Via an original analysis of toys and play, David Hamlin beautifully reconstructs the meaning of consumption, production, modernity, and individualism in Germany. Similar to toys, this book is full of surprises and insights!"
—Alon Confino, Professor of Modern German and European History, University of Virginia

"Exciting in the scope of its analytic purview, *Work and Play* explores not only the traditional business history of the toy industry in the Second Empire but also the cultural history of toys as well as the intellectual debates about the place of play in the cultivation of bourgeois individuals. In each arena, Hamlin makes extremely valuable contributions."
—Andrew Stuart Bergerson, Associate Professor of History at the University of Missouri–Kansas City, and author of *Ordinary Germans in Extraordinary Times: The Nazi Revolution in Hildesheim*

"A creative, groundbreaking study. By using the toy industry to explore the 'reciprocal relationship between economics and culture,' Hamlin shows how imperial Germany was transformed by the evolving structures and practices of mass retailing and consumption."
—Dennis Sweeney, Associate Professor of History and Classics, University of Alberta

Work and Play

Recent Titles

Work and Play: The Production and Consumption of Toys in Germany, 1870–1914, David D. Hamlin
The Cosmopolitan Screen: German Cinema and the Global Imaginary, 1945 to the Present, edited by Stephan K. Schindler and Lutz Koepnick
Germans on Drugs: The Complications of Modernization in Hamburg, Robert P. Stephens
Gender in Transition: Discourse and Practice in German-Speaking Europe, 1750–1830, edited by Ulrike Gleixner and Marion W. Gray
Growing Up Female in Nazi Germany, Dagmar Reese
Justice Imperiled: The Anti-Nazi Lawyer Max Hirschberg in Weimar Germany, Douglas G. Morris
The Heimat Abroad: The Boundaries of Germanness, edited by Krista O'Donnell, Renate Bridenthal, and Nancy Reagin
Modern German Art for Thirties Paris, Prague, and London: Resistance and Acquiescence in a Democratic Public Sphere, Keith Holz
The War against Catholicism: Liberalism and the Anti-Catholic Imagination in Nineteenth-Century Germany, Michael B. Gross
German Pop Culture: How "American" Is It? edited by Agnes C. Mueller
Character Is Destiny: The Autobiography of Alice Salomon, edited by Andrew Lees
Other Germans: Black Germans and the Politics of Race, Gender, and Memory in the Third Reich, Tina M. Campt
State of Virginity: Gender, Religion, and Politics in an Early Modern Catholic State, Ulrike Strasser
Worldly Provincialism: German Anthropology in the Age of Empire, edited by H. Glenn Penny and Matti Bunzl
Ethnic Drag: Performing Race, Nation, Sexuality in West Germany, Katrin Sieg
Projecting History: German Nonfiction Cinema, 1967–2000, Nora M. Alter
Cities, Sin, and Social Reform in Imperial Germany, Andrew Lees
The Challenge of Modernity: German Social and Cultural Studies, 1890–1960, Adelheid von Saldern
Exclusionary Violence: Antisemitic Riots in Modern German History, edited by Christhard Hoffman, Werner Bergmann, and Helmut Walser Smith
Languages of Labor and Gender: Female Factory Work in Germany, 1850–1914, Kathleen Canning
That Was the Wild East: Film Culture, Unification and the "New" Germany, Leonie Naughton
Anna Seghers: The Mythic Dimension, Helen Fehervary
Staging Philanthropy: Patriotic Women and the National Imagination in Dynastic Germany, 1813–1916, Jean H. Quataert
Truth to Tell: German Women's Autobiographies and Turn-of-the-Century Culture, Katharina Gerstenberger

For a complete list of titles, please see www.press.umich.edu

Work and Play

The Production and Consumption of Toys in Germany, 1870–1914

David D. Hamlin

The University of Michigan Press *Ann Arbor*

Published in the United States of America by
The University of Michigan Press
Manufactured in the United States of America
⊗ Printed on acid-free paper

2010 2009 2008 2007 4 3 2 1

A CIP catalog record for this book is available from the British Library.

Library of Congress Cataloging-in-Publication Data

Hamlin, David D., 1970–
Work and play : the production and consumption of toys in Germany, 1870–1914 / David D. Hamlin.
p. cm. — (Social history, popular culture, and politics in Germany)
Includes bibliographical references and index.
ISBN-13: 978-0-472-11588-4 (cloth : alk. paper)
ISBN-10: 0-472-11588-X (cloth : alk. paper)
1. Toy industry—Germany—History. I. Title.

HD9993.T693G3 2007
338.4'768872097309034—dc22 2006103237

For my wife, Karen, without whom this would be unimaginable;
and for my father, David Hamlin Jr., semper fidelis

Contents

Acknowledgments

A work developed over many years owes much to many people. It is impossible to conceive how this book would ever have been completed without the aid and intervention of others. As a result, my ideas have been challenged, and my vision has been extended. From the beginning of this project, Volker Berghahn has been a careful and thoughtful guide. He has read innumerable drafts, always with good humor and to my great profit. He has been equal parts a coach, critic, and cheerleader. I also had the good fortune to work with Mary Gluck, Carolyn Dean, and Omer Bartov as a graduate student at Brown. Mary Gluck in particular was untiring in her time and advice, for which I am deeply thankful. In addition, Andy Bell and David Rubin both read sections of this book when it was a dissertation in preparation.

My research would have gone nowhere had I not received the material support of the Deutsche Akademische Austauschdient as well as Brown University. While in Germany, the staff of the Staatsbibliothek in Munich was extremely helpful in locating an enormous variety of texts. I also would like to thank the highly solicitous staff at the Bayerische Wirtschaftsarchiv, as well as the Stadtsarchiv München, the Stadtsarchiv Nürnberg, the Staatsarchiv Nürnberg, and the Geheimes Staatsarchiv, Preussischer Kulturbesitz.

In the difficult process of transforming a dissertation into a manuscript, I have benefited from the aid of many. Colleagues from my brief stint as a visiting professor at Brown—Joan Richards, Seth Rockman, and Deborah Cohen—each took great interest in the revision of early chapters. Celia Applegate very kindly agreed to read an early draft, commenting thoughtfully on the cultural side. Jonathan Wiesen was extremely helpful in transforming the structure and thrust of the business chapters. Portions of this manuscript (identified in the text) appeared previously in the *Journal of Social History, Central European History,* and *Social History.* My colleagues at Fordham have been exceptionally helpful in putting the final touches on the manuscript. In particular, Kirsten Swinth has read the whole of the manuscript, sections of it twice. Her comments have been lucid, insightful, and always exceedingly helpful. Perhaps most valuable of all were the anonymous readers for the University of Michigan Press and Geoff Eley. The lengthy and detailed comments of the readers, coupled with Geoff's vision, have been enormously helpful in bringing the disparate parts of this monograph together and hammering it into proper shape.

Finally, this project would have gone nowhere had I not received the remarkable and unstinting support of my wife and family. The wandering life of an academic is not always easy. My way has been infinitely eased by the understanding, care, and heartless editing of Karen Hamlin. She has been at the center of everything I have ventured over the last decade, this book is but one small example of that. In addition, my parents have been enthusiastic supporters of a passion that has taken me a long way from the farm. Thank you, all.

Introduction

San Francisco was to have a world's fair. The opening of the Panama Canal had brought California's leading city closer to Europe, and it was time to celebrate the falling barriers between peoples. Ernst Jäckh, the managing director of the Deutscher Werkbund and intimate of the German foreign ministry, was excited. He wrote in Germany's premier cultural journal, *Der Kunstwart,* that San Francisco was to be the opening battle between, on one hand, the new German "taste industry" (which was being nurtured by *Der Kunstwart* and the Werkbund among others) and, on the other hand, the reigning champions of taste, the French consumer industries.[1] For Jäckh, San Francisco was to begin the conquest of the global market that would ensure Germany's long-term wealth and power—the triumph of *Weltpolitik.*[2] Beyond the moral and aesthetic critiques of commercial form offered by some of his colleagues in the Werkbund,[3] Jäckh saw form as central to cultivating consumers and therefore to dynamic economic growth. Authorized consumer products held the key to Germany's future.

Representatives of the doll industry in the Sonneberg *Handelskammer* (chamber of commerce) saw San Francisco in related, albeit more prosaic, terms—as a tremendous sales opportunity. The stakes were high. The Japanese were planning on a substantial effort to establish themselves in the American market, including using six hundred thousand dollars in state money to organize a Japanese exhibit. The toy industry was increasingly concerned about Japanese[4] and American competition in the all-important U.S. market (in 1913, over one-third of all German toy exports went to the United States). The Sonneberg *Handelskammer* emphasized that if Germany truly aspired to "a place in the sun," it simply could not surrender so important a market as the American West. State support for a German exhibition, a sort of socialized marketing, was urgently required.[5]

The German government wavered in that critical support. Considerable opposition to such participation came from within the business community, particularly from heavy industry, which exported very little to the United States. The foreign ministry was alleged to have opposed participation for fear of annoying Great Britain.[6] When added to the touchy finances that always plagued the *Reich* in these years,[7] there seemed little reason to officially participate. The business community was not fully behind the project, and both financial considerations and the diplomatic efforts made after the Second Moroccan Crisis in order to improve relations with Britain militated against it, so why do it?

That attitude provoked the fury of the *Rundschau über Spielwaren,* one of the two new trade journals for the toy industry. In early September 1913, it led with an article filled with seething anger against the government and heavy industry.

> **It is irresponsible of the German government,** that it has absolutely no understanding and no interest for branches of industry that do not simply rain iron, steel, and machinery. **In Germany one recognizes only iron and related things.** That must be said once open and frankly. In the circles of the toy industry and also other branches that permanently suffer from this one-sidedness of our leaders predominates **great and justified bitterness** . . . about the prospects of our circles for the World's Fair.[8]

The San Francisco World's Fair led the next issue of the *Rundschau* as well: "[I]t is undoubtedly not merely a question of whether Germany should officially participate in the World's Fair. Rather, next to it is the principal question, which at this opportunity would be finally brought to a decision, of whether it is permissible that in a matter so critical for the light and finishing industries, these industries may be simply ignored by the government. This is undoubtedly a trial of strength."[9]

The tone of the toy industry, as reflected in both the *Rundschau* and *Deutsche Spielwaren-Zeitung* (the other new trade journal), soon cooled. The *Rundschau* reported not long after its September explosions that not all toy makers were interested in participation and that a certain exhibition exhaustion existed among the highest profile firms in Nuremberg.[10] The *Deutsche Spielwaren-Zeitung* had maintained throughout a more even tone, while still actively advocating official participation in the World's Fair. It never hinted that there might be discord among toy makers on the issue of participation. It preferred to maintain an air of unity but refused to raise the emotional temperature on the issue. This is no doubt related to the fact that it was very closely tied to the largest Nuremberg toy-making firms and, through them, to the Verband bayerischer Metallindustrieller and the Maschinenfabrik Augsburg-Nürnberg (MAN), one of those firms that "rained iron, steel, and machines." These toy makers were not about to countenance any attack that could damage MAN, particularly since MAN and its chairman, Anton Rieppel, were among the most politically influential industrialists in Germany.[11] The San Francisco exhibition was in no way so important that the larger toy makers should endanger their link with Rieppel and, through him, with the Centralverband deutscher Industrieller (the principal industrial lobbying group in Germany) and the German government. There would be other battles to fight. Thus, when the prospect of official participation quietly died, the *Deutsche Spielwaren-Zeitung* reported so in its "Sundry Reports" section, though it still found the decision "unintelligible."[12]

The ultimately futile debate over the San Francisco World's Fair was about more than a toy industry at loggerheads with its own government or emerging divides within the industry. It concerned more than an effort to negotiate a position in an increasingly competitive international market. Toy makers and advocates of consumer industries genuinely believed that they had crucial roles to play in the nation. They were sources of prosperity and power because they were able to appeal to consumers across the globe. The *Deutsche Spielwaren-Zeitung* declared, "The German toy industry has become an important factor in German economic life; however, it's cultural significance stretches across the globe."[13] The failure of the government to properly appreciate what seemed stunningly self-evident to them activated the frustration and anger of the trade journals. Consumer products and proper form mattered for the German economy and therefore the state.

The emergence of such self-confident consumer industries as the German toy industry was one facet of a larger, though gradual, transformation of German society. Toy makers did not exist in a vacuum. The rapid development of toy makers depended on a previous reconceptualization of the individual and of public culture, changes that legitimized consumption generally and toys specifically. Toy consumers had to be made. Coupled with rapidly improving technologies of production and distribution, this development ensured a mass market for toys. To understand the dynamics of economic growth, therefore, implies a commitment to understand the dynamics of cultural change. That cultural change, moreover, made consumer objects into lightning rods for debates over modernity.

In *Work and Play,* I will explore these dynamics to consider three levels of argument. First, I shall demonstrate the rapidly increasing social, economic, and cultural significance of mass production and mass consumption in Germany before World War I. Second, I will analyze how production and consumption, economics and culture, mutually constructed the marketplace. Third, I shall assert that a set of common norms underwrote both liberal economics and consumerism and were intrinsic to modernity; therefore, examination of mass production and mass consumption shed considerable light on the nature of Wilhelmine society and German modernity.

Work and Play is centrally concerned with the significance of mass consumption and mass production for German society in the decades preceding World War I. The first argument *Work and Play* makes regards the extent to which a mass market based on cross-class consumption reordered sections of the economy, the geography of cities, the means of expressing values and ideals, and how intellectuals perceived their own societies. It is often suggested, however, that mass consumption emerged only after the Great War. Michael Geyer contrasts the "high consumption and luxury" of Wilhelmine Germany to the democratized consumption of the Federal Republic of Germany.[14] Victoria de Grazia sees the emergence of Fordist mass consumption only in the aftermath of World War I. Before, Europe had been dominated by a class-bound, elitist regime of consumption.[15] "Weimar was different," assert Alon Confino and Rudy Koshar. Before then, consumption was merely "an important subject of expert and even parliamentary debate in Imperial Germany."[16]

On the face of it, it would seem counterintuitive to argue that only after the massive destruction of wealth in World War I would consumerism suddenly and powerfully bloom. One might guess it more likely that, in patterns of consumption as in culture more generally, Peter Gay was correct that the Weimar Republic was the child of the German Empire.[17] Indeed, on the most immediate level, we can see precisely this in advertising before the war. Richly designed invitations to enjoy shoes, lightbulbs, cigarettes, and mouthwash were plastered across the newspapers and building walls of Germany.[18] Clearly, as David Ciarlo argues, "foundation for a consumer-oriented visuality had been laid at the *fin de siecle.*" Ciarlo demonstrates that, by the beginning of the war, consumer visuality permeated German culture.[19]

This transformation of scopic systems was important. Wilhelmine public culture was being refigured to reflect and promote an emerging consumerism. The Fordist system of broadly-based consumption emerged gradually, product by product, family by family, starting in the decades before the guns of August. Using toys as a heuristic device, *Work and Play* will make clear that Germany was becoming a consumer society even before the famed Weimar Republic and its many gifted analysts of consumerism.

Toys represent a perhaps surprising, but nonetheless extremely valuable, tool to access the growing influence of consumerism in late nineteenth-century Germany. They were generally quite inexpensive, making early cross-class consumption possible. They had definite forms that lent themselves to elaborating and negotiating meaning. The perceived role of toys in education provided a firm base from which to offer more incisive critiques of commercialism and consumer norms than any attack on parvenu ostentation. Moreover, the varied structures of production prompted very different analyses of the social implications of consumerism. Finally, there seems little reason to assume toys were wholly unique items of consumption.

The impact of the growing mass market in Germany was in some, limited respects eminently quantifiable. For example, government statistics suggest that employment in the Nuremberg toy industry grew at an annualized pace in excess of 18 percent between 1895 and 1907.[20] German toy exports by value grew 7.8 percent a year between 1898 and 1913.[21] According to one observer, the number of "independent" toy and doll makers in the Sonneberg region expanded by 746 percent between 1880 and 1899.[22] Taken together, these figures show an industry growing considerably faster than the general economy. These are, then, measurable signs of rapid expansion and the emergence of increasingly significant sectors dependent on consumer behavior.

Less quantifiable was the impact outside the economy. Proliferating retail purchasing and window-shopping shaped a new urban culture of spectacle. Objects (consumer goods) became axes on which parental love and identity turned. Toys became a means of exploring human development and the possibilities of freedom. Discussions of social policy had to address the consequences of consumerism. Consumption was reordering German culture and the terms of public debate. The world Germans saw and how they discussed that world were reshaped by the penetration of the systems and norms of consumerism.

In exploring the piecemeal emergence of mass consumption in the

Kaiserreich, I am inescapably broaching a wider issue. Historians have only in the last two decades begun to question the impact of consumption in German history. These inquiries have generally focused on the twentieth century—the Weimar, Nazi, and, above all, post–World War II eras.[23] The inquiries have used consumption to explore the relation between the provision of material things and political attitudes, the construction of gender and race, or the possibilities of *Eigensinn* (individual self-assertion) in liberal or fascist consumer societies. From the insight that consumerism is fundamental to modernity, historians have proceeded to consider the impact of commerce and form on the German understanding of "Germanness" and the modern. In extending the inquiry back to the imperial period, I am joining a variety of quite recent works that examine the role of consumption in the Wilhelmine era.[24] To argue that Wilhelmine Germany harbored a growing consumer society inevitably asserts the modernity of Germany before World War I—that it was not a semifeudal society dominated by preindustrial norms. As we extend our area of examination from the political economy of iron, steel, agriculture, and other primary products to explore the interaction between culture and economics in consumer products, doubt is raised about the sustainability—indeed, the logical consistency—of the old picture of a modern economy and premodern society. The emergence of light, consumer industries as dynamic, forceful, and modern sectors of Germany's industrial economy was deeply imbricated in the gradual emergence of a modern, consumerist society. Moreover, the assertion that the articulate concerns of many observers regarding the emergence of consumer norms were simple expressions of cultural pessimists attacking modernity seems unjustified. Many critics interrogated consumer capitalism to preserve the normative aspirations of modern individualism from an overreliance on spectacle and visuality. Imperial Germany was becoming increasingly modern and commercial, much like the other European nations.

Closely allied to the assertion that consumption mattered in the *Kaiserreich* is a methodological point and my second argument: the market cannot be properly understood by considering only economic calculations, nor can products be viewed as cultural registers alone. The full impact of consumerism can only be realized by tying together analyses of production and consumption. The influence of consumerism is a subtle thing. The place of commercial things in a culture and an economy can be simultaneously self-evident and virtually imperceptible. To properly assess the role of consumption, therefore, we must cast a wide net. Neither the complex negotiation of a consumer product nor the manifold influence of consumerism can be fully understood without bringing the whole market together. In *Work and Play,* therefore, an analysis of the interpenetration of cultural and economic factors in constructing a market is wound together with a discussion of the impact the creation of that market had on German society.

The difficulties in bringing production and consumption into the same narrative are manifest in the rarity with which it is attempted. Kenneth Brown's review of the British toy industry, for example, dwells a great deal on the business side, tracing how toys were made, by whom, and the competitive pressures felt in the business. It is, however, notably weak on what motivated consumers—why they bothered to buy such trifles or what meanings they attached to their toys.[25] Gary Cross's examination of toys in the United States, in comparison, is an excellent treatment of the cultural importance of toys—of why consumers would want such playthings. Above all, he examines how the web of meaning around toys has changed, how those meanings have been manipulated by toy companies, and what those changes have meant for the broader culture. But Cross pays little attention to the purely economic challenges faced by toy makers—to how a changing marketplace may have favored certain producers and certain products over others, independent of the desires of consumers.[26]

To overcome the artificial divide between the logically connected, *Work and Play* builds on the analysis of the economist Ben Fine and his sometime collaborator Ellen Leopold. Fine has noted the conceptual difficulty of theorizing about both production and consumption, observing that "[i]n the literature, it has usually been unwittingly avoided by an analytical separation between how commodities are provided (roughly what has been the terrain of political economy) and how they have been received as items of consumption (often the subject matter of other disciplines)."[27] Fine then suggests why theories of production and consumption have had such difficulty coming to terms with what lies on the other side of the cash nexus. He argues that a—perhaps *the*—major dilemma stems from the effort to generalize from an investigation of one part of one commodity chain to explain all aspects of all commodities. Such "horizontal" analysis must wipe away all the particularities—the multiple social, economic, and cultural factors—that shape the real fields of production and consumption that we habitually term "the market." Studies of producers tend to take consumption as a given (at best, a price-sensitive given). Histories of consumption too often treat products exclusively as mirrors of cultural trends. Because the market is a field of economic and cultural interaction and exchange, we must grasp a wide variety of conflicts and interconnections if we are to understand any consumer product. Each commodity is trapped in a multilayered web of specific incentives, structures, and meanings—a web that changes for each product.

Fine proposes a "vertical" analysis that moves from production to consumption for a specific commodity. In this type of analysis, the rich and contingent context that determines the form and success of a commodity emerges most fully. Fine and Leopold refer to this as a "system of provision."[28] This framework allows for the dialectical development of a consumer good. The structures that shape production and distribution—and therefore price and availability—are permitted to interact with the value systems and social structures shaping consumer preferences. Only by considering this mutually constitutive process of negotiation between business and consumers can we hope to grasp one of the most fundamental forces shaping modern society. *Work and Play* attempts this vertical analysis, exploring toys and the toy industry through the lenses of producers, distributors, retailers, consumers, pedagogues, and cultural and social reformers. In this fashion, the factors shaping increasing supply and demand, the negotiation of form, and the many unintended outcomes become both richer and clearer. It becomes obvious that the demands of consumers for inexpensive and novel toys were critical factors determining the structure of the toy industry. Toy makers also sought to respond to the specific thematic and discursive impulses of their buyers—"gaming" the forms that their products would take. Meanwhile, some toys became more attractive to consumers because particular production technologies enabled deeper cuts in factory costs and therefore in the end price for consumers.

Exploring the fullness of consumption allows a more complete examination of its role in—and therefore a richer analysis of—modernity. The third argument of *Work and Play* revolves around the claim that a critical component of the modern was the emergence of an ideal of the individual—as an agent capable of rational action, self-definition, and moral reflection and, simultaneously, as the object of continuous state and social pressure. This is certainly not the only means of examining the modern, but it is a particularly useful analytical approach for the study of the interconnections between consumption and production. The idealized autonomous individual lays at the conceptual heart of both liberal capitalism and consumerism. Nevertheless, a modern society constructed to elaborate and serve autonomous individuals suffered from a variety of conflicts—both internal to its ideals and resulting from its implementation. Before turning to the implications for modernity, let us first explore the justification for linking liberal capitalism and consumerism to one another and to the modern more generally.

Scholars of consumption tend to agree that the eighteenth century and perhaps the late seventeenth century marked a critical juncture for the emergence of consumerism.[29] They argue that critical cultural norms emerged in this time period: objects became useful for elaborating ideas about oneself beyond status claims; ephemeral styles were consciously cultivated by businesspeople; advertising began to spread. Although consumerism was then far from the dominant force it has become in contemporary society, the discursive structures developed in the eighteenth century authorized consumerism for the next two centuries.

The emergence of consumerism in this time period should not be surprising. The construction of a consumerist ethos was part and parcel of elaborating a new model of individualism. The "disembedding" of the individual—the creation of moral imperatives toward individual equality and identity—created an internal logic favoring the intensified use of material objects as tools of individual identity construction. The origins of a consumer society were written into bourgeois society; consumerism was "embedded" in the ideals and practices of middle-class life.

Consumerism should not be viewed, therefore, as a "product" of some new technology of marketing or of Henry Ford. In this respect, I am taking issue with the analyses of writers as disparate as Daniel Bell[30] and Frederic Jameson.[31] The perceived antithesis between modern capitalism and modern consumerism was present well before the 1920s (contra Bell), nor did consumerism arise as a result of a transformed postwar capitalism (contra Jameson). Consumer goods performed very important cultural labor within bourgeois society throughout the nineteenth century. Colin Campbell ties this role of consumer goods to the emergence of a Romantic ethic in the late eighteenth century that emphasized imaginative self-construction and self-representation. Not coincidently, that is roughly the period in which Peter Stearns, Niel McKendrick, John Brewer, and J. H. Plumb detect the emergence of consumerist norms. Daniel Roche likewise sees the basic transformation before industrialization. These norms were central to individualism generally and grew out of a broad, gradual transformation of Western culture. Thus, consumerism is not the dependent outcome of specific phases of industrial capitalism. At issue is not the "contradictions" between capitalism and modern culture but, rather, the multiple authentic outcomes of a social imaginary based on an idealized vision of the "emancipated" individual. Sociologist Don Slater explains, "The consumer . . . is one example or one aspect of the private and enterprising individual who stands at the centre of the very notion of modernity."[32]

The seventeenth and eighteenth centuries are widely recognized as critical moments in the construction of modern norms of individualism and rationality. The emergence of modern science, the radical reformation, the Enlightenment, and the emergence of a capitalist middle class and modern state structures all played very substantial roles in reconceptualizing the individual and his or her relation to society.[33] The philosopher Charles Taylor points to several important trends in this time period. Taylor argues that an "idea of moral order" based on individual autonomy emerged in the early modern period and has been expanded both in extension (by which he means more people live according to that idea) and intensity, an indication that the moral vision has made increasingly heavy demands. In Taylor's reading, individualism is not a simple removal of social or moral restraints, nor is it the invention of a novel psychological structure or the sudden discovery of rationality; instead, the moral norms of society change both to enable more individual freedom and to demand more of the individuals, particularly more self-control.[34] According to Taylor, the emergence of a "spirit of capitalism" can be seen as one particularly important aspect of an exceedingly broad transformation of Western civilization: the possibility of mutual benefit emerging from the pursuit of private interests, the heart of capitalism, emerged as one element of the disembedding of the individual.[35]

Taylor very usefully emphasizes the element of identity in this process. The emergence of modern individualism was not a dependent function of increasing rationality, of markets and secularizing states. Rather, individuals were learning to define themselves in new fashions, relying less on traditional elements based on caste and locale. In this fashion, Taylor effectively ties the emergence of market capitalism, individual liberty, civility, and the public sphere into a coherent whole.

By suggesting that the emergence of modern individualism was not a negative process of simply "liberating" the underlying individual, Taylor also opens an important additional vista. The creation of the autonomous individual was not the result of simply dissolving ties, of destroying connections. Rather, it was the outcome of proliferating connections.[36] Potential ties and identities grew with the expanding market and deepening civil society. The modern individual emerged not in contradistinction to a single, monolithic "Society" but in multiple and growing social interactions. This opportunity to choose was coupled with a gradual breakdown in supraindividual social norms capable of imposing values and identity. Rather than unthinking (and therefore unproblematic) inclusion in a single cultural system, posttraditional individuals were increasingly exposed to multiple value systems, implying a necessary choice. Even when not all choices in lifestyle are available, the recognition of multiplicity generates an awareness of possibility. Lifestyle, in this case, is taken to mean not the superficial set of styles a shopper purchases but, rather, "a more or less integrated set of practices which an individual embraces . . . because they give material form to a particular narrative of self-identity."[37] The modern self that emerged in small circles approximately during the eighteenth century is reflexively organized and negotiated. The individual, as Anthony Giddens argues, not only must choose but must define himself or herself as one who chooses[38]—a construction that encompasses many irreconcilable models of the "authentic" individual.

For those with the material and experiential horizons to choose between roles—and therefore to choose something of their identity—material objects became a means of representing that choice to oneself and to others. The reappropriation of that choice through consuming signs of it solidified the identity.[39] Consumption also extended and renewed the chosen roles by requiring a reaffirmation in the moment of purchase, as well as in every moment thereafter when the material object is seen. The reflexive, modern self constantly reexamines and often reaffirms lifestyle choices, whether through self-examination or through consumption. Giddens also points out that lifestyles are not necessarily unitary. Individuals may pursue different sets of practices at different times and places. These "lifestyle sectors" represent "a time-space 'slice' of an individual's overall activities," raising the possibility of conflicting styles and choices.[40] These sectors may be more easily managed and coordinated by the externalization of values and styles—that is, through consumption.

Contrary to the assumptions of market economics and utilitarian philosophers, then, human needs are not intrinsically insatiable. Demand for material products was not simply "liberated" in the course of the eighteenth century; rather, it represented a means for coping with and managing the strains of an individualistic social system.[41] The slow decline of "traditional society" did not release pent-up "natural" appetites but, rather, created opportunities and demand for new systems of status, identity, and representation.

The great project of modernity was to elaborate a society that maximized the freedom and dignity of the individual. That project, however, had some paradoxical consequences. Just as the greater specialization and interdependence of the capitalist economy tended to undermine the autonomy of "rational economic man," trapping the individual in hierarchical organizations of control, the efforts of individuals to define themselves through consumption tended to call into question the very possibility of an autonomous, authentic identity. The apparatus developed to deliver pleasure and identity—the production, distribution, retailing, and marketing systems of modern consumer capitalism—sought to identify and satisfy every partial enthusiasm, desire, or association. By the close of the nineteenth century, this apparatus already had developed several implications. On the one hand, the scale and intensity of the consumerist apparatus took on a life of its own. It proposed and articulated images and meanings for individuals. Individuals were put in the position of attempting to construct self-identity through images and styles elaborated by others. As a result, the expression of self-identity threatened to become an exercise in homogenization, as selves were organized around the consumption of images and motifs elaborated by industry, the press, and advertising; that is, society was constructed as revolving around spectacle.[42] On the other hand, a world mediated by things became a world fragmented and ephemeral. In the place of a collective tradition that would ground meaning and identity, consumer capitalism was one part of a "privatization" of meaning, in which individuals attempted to narrate their own significance, often by identifying and satisfying momentary and partial enthusiasms. The resulting "infinite nuances"[43] of modern life rendered society increasingly fractal and indeterminate. The apparatus of consumption can be portrayed thus as either a ham-fisted tool of compulsion or as an entropic agent of hypertrophic individualism. *Work and Play* assumes a sort of "double movement," to borrow a phrase from Karl Polanyi. Individuals lived in a heterogeneous social world of constant movement and disruption. At the same moment, the apparatus of consumerism guided individuals toward authorized forms, forms that were infinitely reiterated with only the most superficial variations. Modernity—like its habitus, the city—"put into question delusions of order and fantasies of disorder alike."[44]

Toys mirrored these movements. Toys instantiated the diversity of the human world and the human imagination and put it on display, creating a dizzying effect in which medieval knights, walking bears, Chinese mandarins, and antizeppelin guns rubbed elbows. One Berlin store window sought to distinguish itself in the eyes of distracted Germans by constructing a scene occupied by dolls representing Chinese, Japanese, and African children.[45] The impossible mixture of images thrown up by the toy world was then raided and reordered in the homes of children. The production forms and retail outlets developed to deliver this fractured vision of the world was itself a sort of molten apparatus—shifting forms and relations to react to the otherwise invisible movements of consumer demand.

The improbable social world constructed by toys was not, however, capricious. Toys became a negotiated product between the imaginations of children, producers, and retailers. The lingua franca that made this negotiation possible was the press. The press informed parents of significant events, presenting them with visual forms to associate with those events. When parents sought to educate their children, they mobilized the visual vocabulary provided by the press in their effort to discern valuable forms. Producers, too, had to find some means of generating forms, forms that would appeal to consumers. Often this was simply copying other toys, raiding an established system of visual representation. Forms were, however, also introduced by the press. On the strength of the popular press, toy ships were designed by men who had never seen the sea. Shoppers would construct stories about the toys they saw on the street, integrating them into narratives of their own choosing, but narratives ultimately constructed for them by the press. When General Boulanger was in the news, dolls became "Madame Boulanger"; when the Reichstag debated pensions, a mechanical mouse became an *Altersversorgungsmaus* (a "pensions mouse"). Similarly, retailers sought to construct narratives around their toy displays to ensure that they appeared not as simple, alienated things but, rather, as cultural objects. The press formed a sort of sign economy, creating a liquid reservoir of common images and associations, which producers, consumers, and retailers could all dip into to transform objects into markers. In this fashion, the dominant norms of German society were perpetually renewed. This ordering of signs can be clearly seen in the hegemonic position of dolls. The perpetual reinscription of the exclusive maternal mission of women left little room in the world of toys for girls' playthings other than dolls. As a result, the equation of women and motherhood was further reinforced.

The instability of the modern was even written into its foundations. "Individualism," for example, is and was a concept subject to debate and contest. For that reason, Georg Simmel suggested that the "external and internal history of our time takes its course within the struggle and in the changing entanglements of [differing] ways of defining the individual's role."[46]

In *Work and Play,* individualism will be invoked both as a social condition and as an ideological aspiration—a fact imposed by a given social system, or a moral norm that informs decision making and from which actions may be critiqued. Individualism may be seen through the eyes of Michel Foucault as a process of exposing individuals to constant observation and restraint: the individual is constructed by forces from outside in an effort to secure social tranquility and economic productivity—the modern individual as "an effect of power."[47] The Romantics, by contrast, saw the individual as a developmental project, some unique essence that must be allowed to grow according to the demands and inclinations internal to its own nature.[48] Alternatively, we may see the individual as an independent, rational calculator, the "rational economic man" of liberal economics. Such "rational actors" do not need cultivation so much as they need data, the material that allows them to calculate their interests and desires and strategize their behavior in society. They also must possess the drive and self-discipline to pursue those interests.[49] Marx and Polanyi, in their respective fashions, would take more jaundiced views of this rationalized individualism, an individualism that left laborers *vogelfrei* (free and rightless). In their analyses, a central characteristic of capitalist modernity is the collapse of traditional collective ties, the embeddedness of the economy in society, in favor of the individual capitalist and the "free" laborer.[50] While "individualism" may be central to modernity, the nature and implications of individualism are open to contest.

These representations of the individual are in part efforts to narrate what, if anything, defines human nature and the social condition and, therefore, the proper ambitions and desires of individuals. The various constructions of individualism thus shaped the aspirations and goals of individuals for themselves and for others (in this case, especially children). The tensions between these visions of modern individualism, as well as between vision and practice, opened intriguing fault lines in

German society, fault lines critical to the toy industry and toy consumers. Parents, for example, were caught between a Foucauldian mission to discipline their children and a Romantic demand to allow them to develop into the individuals nature intended. Pedagogues disputed whether toys should cultivate the imagination necessary for Romantic individualism or present the data and training desirable for a liberal, positivistic vision of humanity. These tensions within the emerging norms of modernity—intrinsic conflicts—could raise fundamental issues that could merely be managed, not resolved.

The portrait of Wilhelmine culture that emerges is that of something divided internally between several ideals and aspirations for modernity and frustrated in the achievement of any of those ideals. The upshot was predictable. Heinrich Driesmans remarked in 1902, "Reform is the catchword of our age."[51] Rather than dispense with the ideals of modernity (the autonomous, authentic individual variously defined), Germans organized. Given the various definitions and the multitude of paths toward them, Germans organized many competing and overlapping reform programs. Germans organized to change their eating habits, exercise plans, clothing, and housing. They sought to change landholdings, labor relations, and women's status. For our purposes, this reform impulse manifests itself most clearly in efforts to improve and discipline both product forms and production systems. Form was to be a key to both the elaboration of proper subjectivities and the promotion of material well-being. The effort to leverage form into a sort of social improvement program overlapped with the drive to create legitimate and illegitimate structures of production, specifically by eliminating domestic industry in favor of mechanized factories. Many of those who saw form as a central issue in developing and manifesting the self, however, feared the overemphasis on industrial capitalism. Indeed, they saw the cultural impact of a utilitarian ethic of self-interest as the central threat to the autonomous individual. In its efforts to heal the wounds of the modern, the reform impulse thus merely recapitulated the intrinsic conflicts of German modernity itself. Instability and conflict were written into the very foundations of Wilhelmine society.

"Consumer society is the product of a long historical evolution, at once material and mental," argues Rosalind Williams.[52] *Work and Play* seeks to understand and explain a portion of that evolution, both material and mental. Chronologically, this study explores the emergence of certain ideas in the late eighteenth and early nineteenth centuries, such as the ideal of bourgeois domesticity or the legitimization of play as educational. These ideas authorized toy consumption, creating a critical foundation for later mass consumption. The combined weight of liberalization, expanding markets, and industrialization from the 1860s through the 1880s enabled a dramatic expansion of toy production. Costs were cut dramatically, and toys became increasingly accessible to a cross-class audience. That audience was not created by the cost cutting of industry. The preceding transformation of cultural norms created a ready potential market, which liberal capitalism tapped. As a result, the number of toy producers and the quantity of toys produced grew enormously from the 1870s. The gradual emergence of mass consumption became increasingly self-evident in the 1890s and 1900s. Rapidly expanding urban retail did not so much constitute a sudden leap into mass consumption as make that leap self-evident. The gradual move from Christmas markets to department stores, a move that accelerated from the 1890s, triggered an increasingly vigorous debate about the failures, weaknesses, and prospects of a modernity defined by a "mass" version of bourgeois ideals. This debate takes particularly coherent form after 1900. As the toy market demonstrates, the acceleration of consumer activity opened up a number of tensions intrinsic and extrinsic to modern individualism.

Work and Play, however, is organized thematically rather than chronologically. As consumption was rooted deeply in the family lives, public culture, and economic systems of Germany, it is necessary to separate the elements and analyze them individually. This book examines why toys were purchased, the pressures shaping production, and the effect of modern retailing. After exploring the forces directly shaping consumption and production and how these influenced the shape of the market, this book considers the discursive fields that legitimized both toy consumption and critiques of toy consumption. Finally, it explores analyses of the social and economic consequences of such growing consumer industries as the toy industry.

Chapter 1 is an exploration of consumers. It does not assume that demand is a given, or that toys satisfy a natural human want. Rather, it proceeds from the assumption that consumers have specific, if not always conscious, purposes when they acquire something. As such, this chapter concerns itself with two central questions: First, why did families seek out toys to give to children? Second, what factors influenced what toys were most desirable? To answer these questions, we must understand the tensions within the middle-class ideal of domesticity.

That ideal, constructed in the late eighteenth and early nineteenth centuries, reflected both an impulse to construct subjectivities and a desire to respect and cultivate the authentic self of the child. Managing the demands to both discipline the child and allow the child his or her own identity and autonomy—the simultaneous impulse to coercion and freedom—was accomplished through family holidays, particularly Christmas. The cultural labor that Christmas was to perform influenced the types of gifts provided, to the benefit not only of toys generally but particularly of toys with strong visual appeal that also reified treasured bourgeois virtues. Taking a page from *Emile,* parents sought to both cultivate the autonomous individual in their children and direct their childrens' development through prescribed images that would ameliorate the coercive pressure of parental discipline. The specific forms toys took, however, were recapitulations of the ideals that informed parental discipline. Toys effectively naturalized the utilitarian virtues of self-assertion, self-control, and domination of nature and the environment, as well as basic gender norms. Toys thus worked both as relief from discipline and as tools of discipline. They were to recognize and cultivate a unique individuality developing according to its own nature, while also manufacturing that individuality from without. It was on this foundation that the mass market for toys was constructed.

Assessing the motivations of consumers is an inherently difficult task. Paul Betts very effectively explains: "The difficulty of ascertaining why consumers consume certain products and not others, to say nothing of how they understand and use them, is not just the problem of marketing departments. It effectively represents a sobering epistemological limit for all historians of material culture."[53] With that warning in mind, I have sought to construct a careful argument. I have elaborated an argument about the nature of the ideological construction of the German middle-class family, an argument that is thoroughly grounded in a new reading of existing scholarship. On the basis of that thesis, I turn to investigate the toys that Germans purchased. The principal evidence available is in the toys themselves as well as the commentary offered by trade journals, pedagogues, and the press. All of these contemporary accounts represent efforts to understand either what consumers do or should think. The comments of parents and children alike are rather limited in number and quality. Nonetheless, I am confident that we can make reasonable assertions about the roles played by toys in the culture as a whole. The forms that consumers chose, the analyses of observers, and the structural tensions within the ideological construction of the family and the child allow us to triangulate the structural functions of toys in nineteenth-century German society.

Chapter 2 most clearly establishes the material evidence of the increasing importance of the mass market. The toy industry demonstrates both the growth and the relativity in Germany's emerging consumer industries after 1880. The growing ability to serve a mass market created new pressures and new opportunities for toy makers. A study of the three principal toy-making regions (Nuremberg, the Thuringian uplands around Sonneberg, and the Erzgebirge) will demonstrate that how the toy makers responded to these pressures and opportunities varied substantially. Why was it that the toy industry developed vastly different systems of production in different areas? The reason for the diversity of forms is not to be found in the purported "modernity" of one part of the industry and the hopeless backwardness of the others. Rather, we must consider the complex fashions in which similar structuring incentives can have very different outcomes. All toy makers sought to respond to a rapidly growing mass market for cheap toys, a market made possible by the cultural changes observed in chapter 1. They also interacted with the cultural demands of their consumers, seeking strategically both to engage and to fashion the demand for specific forms. In that effort, toy makers imagined their consumers as isolated, individual children defined by their desires and their ability to dominate their toys.

Chapter 3 explores the evolution of retail in response to the emerging mass market. Retailers came to be the public face of German toys, thereby enveloping childrens' playthings in the apparatus of spectacle. The system of distribution for toys worked to distance producers from consumers, undermining the incentive for toy makers to establish a brand identity by communicating directly to the consumer. Instead, the cultivation of toy consumers was left to retailers. Retailers preferred to use toys as props to sell a particular experience of shopping—to sell themselves. Retailing thus influenced what types of toys were offered. But retailers also functioned as de facto mediators, framing toys in particular fashions. Toys became stock figures in the narration of the Christmas edition of urban spectacle. The result was a widespread association of toys with the urban light and spectacle of Christmas shopping. Moreover, retailers came to frame individuality in terms of desire and vision. Humans were implicitly constructed as bundles of discrete "wants" that can be activated through sight. This particular framing, both of toys and of human individualism, played an important role in the analysis of post-1900 critics. The association of toys with urban spectacle would deeply trouble critics committed to established norms of individualism.

Chapter 4 delves into the construction of toys as educational, both as a means of understanding how toy consumption became legitimate and to explore the intrusion of things into German discussions of subjectivity and modernity. Going back to the Enlightenment and Romanticism, we see that the notion that play is educational reflects emerging normative visions of the individual. For some, play was to instruct childrens' reason and prepare them for the responsibilities of adult life. For others, play developed the capacity for fantasy and creativity. These faculties were, in turn, critical tools for elaborating a healthy and vigorous subjectivity. These competing norms authorized different types of toys and different criticisms of commercial toys for failing to live up to their ideals. By exploring the question of educational toys, we also, inevitably, run up against the question of consumerism. Critiques of commercial toys revolved around the ability of the market to deliver things appropriate for the cognitive development of human beings. Was the market compatible with genuine individualism? Oddly, a society that at least appeared to be organized around "rational economic man" was seen by many to threaten the foundations of individualism.

Chapter 5 explores how some contemporary Germans assessed the social and economic implications of an emerging mass market around the turn of the twentieth century. Increasingly, consumer industries could be imagined as critical sources of national wealth and national power. They also became increasingly significant in both causing and assessing social problems. Some could imagine consumer products leading Germany out of the social crises created by industrialization: the higher returns of quality consumer goods would underwrite any number of social investments. At the same moment, some consumer industries exemplified the difficulties in both understanding and overcoming social distress. A particularly fascinating window into the relation between consumerism and social problems came in the debates over domestic industry. In these debates, we see socialists, reformers, and representatives of industry striking quite different balances between the desires of consumers, the rights of workers, and state authority. In effect, they were arguing about whether the social impact of consumer capitalism on labor might require limiting the autonomy of entrepreneurs and consumers alike, either by delegitimizing structures of labor or stigmatizing products. In the process, Germans developed and mobilized competing normative visions of modernity. The assumptions familiar to modernization theory emerge at the turn of the twentieth century in efforts to guide capitalist development toward particular goals—toward the "good society," however defined.

Taken together, the chapters in this book establish the wide impact of growing consumption on German society and culture before World War I. The transformation of structures of production, urban physiognomy, and family relations, as well as the intrusion of things and consumption into discourse, pointed to the beginnings of a consumer society. From the beginning, this society was shot through with tensions and contradictions, in both thought and practice.

1. "Underwear Was Not Christmas, but Toy Soldiers Were"

The Dynamics of Toy Demand

> And between two wars, little Johann played. Unconscious and tranquil, with his soft curling hair and voluminous pinafore frocks, he played in the garden by the fountain, or in a little gallery partitioned off for his use by a pillared railing . . . —played the plays of his four and a half years—those plays whose meaning and charm no grown person can possibly grasp: which need no more than a few pebbles, or a stick of wood with a dandelion for a helmet, since they command the pure, powerful, glowing, untaught and unintimidated fancy of those blissful years before life touches us, when neither duty nor remorse dares to lay upon us a finger's weight.[1]

Thomas Mann portrayed young Hanno (Johann) Buddenbrook as an angel at play—"unconscious and tranquil." He was kept separate from the profane world, behind partitions or in a perhaps Edenic garden. In either case, he was unconstrained in his play and in his imagination, free to pursue whatever goals his fantasy conjured. He was protected, and the adult world dared not lay a "finger's weight" on him. Mann depicted childhood as a period of autonomy, a time that was itself cordoned off from the demands of the world, a stage separate from adulthood and defined by the freedom of play, the joy of play. The boy child of Mann's portrayal was to be authorized to explore the world and, more important, himself. Mann's words all but caress young Hanno. He clearly felt a deep affinity for this vision, one that shared some commonalities with his own reminiscences of childhood.[2] In many respects, Mann's narrative is a familiar one. Play and toys are often examined from the foundations constructed by Philip Aries, exploring the creation of a "modern" childhood defined in terms similar to those used by Mann.

But consider who the young boy in Mann's narrative would become. Hanno Buddenbrook was an aesthete who spent his life seeking to retreat back into his Garden, who could not sustain himself in the world and finally dissolved his family. The play of Hanno appeared to forecast precisely this end. His "powerful, glowing, untaught and unintimidated fancy" would never be disciplined by duty. For many in Mann's turn-of-the-twentieth-century audience, Hanno's childhood no doubt appealed as a sort of archetype of innocence and authenticity, but it was also easily read as a stark warning. An unguided, untaught childhood could be intensely charming, but such rearing could undermine the type of competitive, self-controlled individual that had made the Buddenbrook family great.[3]

As a subtle contrast, in *Doctor Faustus,* Mann introduced us to Helmut Institoris and his wife, Inez, who sought to raise their daughters "perfectly." Their room was therefore well stocked with "a world of well-ordered toys, teddy-bears, lambs on wheels, jumping jacks, Käthe Kruse dolls, railway trains . . . in short, it was the very pattern of a children's paradise."[4] The girls were not to be left alone to their imaginations. Rather, they were to be guided toward proper adult roles and identities. Mann suggests in his novels that toys and play can be seen as signs of childhood innocence and as tools for the construction of a proper subjectivity. Indeed, both visions of childhood contributed to defining a field for toys and play in nineteenth-century Germany.

Toy buyers were critically influenced by the development of middle-class ideals of domesticity during the eighteenth and nineteenth centuries. The transformation of the structure and ideology of the family created fundamental ambivalences. In particular, the imperatives to allow the child to be a child and also to educate the child to be a productive citizen-*Bürger* could not be simultaneously satisfied. It was not easy to be both Hanno Buddenbrook and Lucrezia Institoris, let alone to be both Hanno and, say, John Stuart Mill.[5] The tensions within the cult of domesticity were redressed in part through festivals, particularly Christmas, which gave families a brief opportunity to live the ideal and to reconcile contradictory values: the everyday labor required to produce and reproduce *bürgerliche* norms of personal behavior could be partially laid aside, and the affectionate bonds of the family could be reemphasized. The toy as Christmas gift was an effort to make invisible emotions visible, the immaterial material. In such circumstances, the immediate joy that a toy could generate in a child made it a highly desirable gift. A child's happiness could be produced by toys with highly varied forms, because the child's enjoyment was driven by what the child did with a toy, not necessarily by what the toy looked like. Consumers were therefore also able to use toys to socialize children in middle-class ideals. Without endangering the principal value of the toy (amusement), parents sought to emphasize certain orientations on life that defined the utilitarian, *bürgerliche* worldview. They did so through the form the toy took—its surface appearance. In effect, toys offered a release from disciplinary rigors while simultaneously reinforcing the goals of that discipline.

The occasional, inevitable collisions between fundamental norms within the ideal of domesticity created an ideal "space" for consumer products. Because consumerism is, in many respects, an effort to make visible the invisible emotions and aspirations of individuals, it was well suited to manage conflicts between them. By externalizing values, consumer goods made it easier to acknowledge and move between feelings and ideals that might otherwise have remained mutely confused and self-contradictory. Consumer products could allow consumers to disentangle emotions and assign competing ideals to discrete objects, separating emotions spatially and temporally. The differentiation of values through externalization made it possible to maintain a richer and more complex emotional life. This capacity to separate and organize complex emotions allowed consumer goods, such as toys, to penetrate deeply into the social and cultural practices of the Western world. The ability of consumer goods to embed themselves in the most basic social processes, such as child rearing, was the fundamental precondition for the revolutions in industry and retail that shall preoccupy much of this book.

This chapter examines the impulses that created and sustained a mass market in toys and analyzes several case studies highlighting the values attributed to the specific forms for toys. The case studies were chosen either based on their popularity as objects of advertising (a useful stand-in for commercial success) or because of the potential cultural significance of a specific form. Thus, colonial imagery is discussed in this chapter, despite such imagery's comparatively limited sample size.

*Domesticity**

One of the fundamental bases of the transformation and modernization of European life and society was the development of middle-class domesticity. Concurrent with the rise of liberalism and the increasing spatial division of work and home, the middle classes across Europe

* Portions of this section ("Domesticity") and the next ("Christmas") were published previously in "The Structures of Toy Consumption: Bourgois Domesticity and Demand for Toys in Nineteenth-Century Germany," *Journal of Social History* (summer 2003): 857–69. They appear here with the kind permission of the editors and publishers of the *Journal of Social History*.

restructured the family and its ideological underpinnings. The decline of the home as a productive entity (*das ganze Haus*), tied with middle-class assertions of legal and political equality, undermined the old paradigm of the household. During the late eighteenth and early nineteenth centuries, the *bürgerliche* home was discursively cut off from wider society. The family was no longer the externally oriented foundation of economic well-being, social status, or political rights; it was not a *ständisch* institution. In its place rose an internally oriented, privatized social organization devoted to the fostering of healthy individual subjectivities. Despite the fact that they had lost their public role, however, families remained central to Western societies. The modern, autonomous individual was simply not conceivable without the family. Only because the family was assumed to be the source of individuality could it be endowed with such extraordinary importance.[6]

A central aspect of crafting subjectivities was child rearing. A number of historians have noted that children came to occupy different roles within society and in families around 1800.[7] A new model of parent-child relations developed, denying that parents had any personal interests to satisfy through their children. According to this model, parents were "disinterested," and parenting was a task performed entirely for reasons of love. The model overlooked all considerations of social prestige or later material well-being (there was no public provision for old age). As Rebekka Habermas explains, this "model of disinterested parenting" led to "a 'sacralization' of activities connected with bringing up children."[8] The self-sacrifice of parents established their relation with their children as something greater than a mere social connection. Parents sacrificed themselves both for their children and for their community. They were charged with "planting and cultivating the seeds of noble and sublime youth in the hearts of the sons and daughters."[9]

With the task of producing *bürgerliche* individuals in mind, many parents began to enforce a physical separation of their children from the world outside, creating, as the private sphere, a space "heterogeneous to all others and closed in upon itself."[10] The home became a separate realm wherein the modern individual was to be painstakingly constructed through constant observation and minute instruction. It is not surprising, then, that Foucault would later assert that the family was "the privileged locus of emergence for the disciplinary question of the normal and abnormal."[11] Families defined the "norm" and, through a microphysics of power, shaped individuals to approach it.

To shape the child and instill proper social values according to the model of disinterested parenting required control of the child's social environment. Consequently, middle-class parents following this model increasingly sought to limit the exposure of their children to a "chaotic" street life that might offer alternative norms of social life.[12] Cut off from other playmates, these children were thrown back on their siblings and their own resources for diversion, at least until school brought them together with other, age- and class-appropriate children. This naturally created an expanding market for toys. Thus, because *bürgerliche* parents kept their children from uncontrollable socialization with peers of multiple class backgrounds, the need to occupy them at home created a functional niche for toys. Middle-class parents found in material objects a partial replacement for a sociability that, because it took place outside the confines of the *bürgerliche* home, threatened to undermine the construction of their children's bourgeois identity.

The ideal of middle-class domesticity was far more deeply implicated in the growth of a toy market than merely in promoting a social space that toys very effectively filled. After all, children's books could have filled that social space as well. Toys were also more than "rewards," the carrots to balance the sticks in a parental training program. Playthings took on a meaning and a function far beyond that of a utilitarian counter in domestic pedagogy. They were woven into the ambivalences of what Gunilla-Frederike Budde terms the "pedagogic double ideal" of bourgeois life: children were to be allowed to be children but simultaneously were to be educated to be good middle-class citizens.[13] Those imperatives reflected the deeper tensions between the possibility of an authentic and autonomous individuality and the necessity of constructing a specific subjectivity appropriate for modern, capitalist society. The ambivalences internal to the bourgeois cult of children can be seen clearly in the efforts of historian Thomas Nipperdey to describe the place of middle-class children. He begins: "They and their individuality are objects of loving devotion and attention of the parents, the mother as well as the father . . . [They are] 'angels,' innocent, particularly close to God, reminders of the opportunities that are now closed to parents. Love and care therefore determine the relation to children—an attitude that had become possible as parents were unburdened of work and had money and time to spend." Nipperdey continues, however: "[C]hild rearing is built on authority, it is serious and severe, expressions of feeling and trust between parents and children are very limited . . . The highest goal is order."[14] Nipperdey believes that these traits in parent-child relationships were related, as they were. But he cannot accomplish—indeed, he does not really attempt—full reconciliation of parents' great affection and their inability to express it. The tenderness that middle-class parents devoted to their children was often most expressed in an authoritarian training in the values and skills deemed necessary for bourgeois life—above all, the virtues of hard work, self-discipline, and respect for authority.

Late nineteenth-century parents felt it was necessary to act as strict disciplinarians in their efforts to fashion their children into the proper sort of individuals. The memoirs describing late nineteenth-century childhood are replete with images of cold, distant parents. Parents positioned themselves as demanding, relentless authority figures. In particular, many fathers appear to have cultivated extremely restrained and sometimes even emotionally detached relationships with their children. The sexual division of labor kept fathers outside the home for much of the day and may have absorbed their attention even when they were home, while assigning the care of children to their wives. That sharp division of labor also convinced many fathers that an emotional attachment to children was a feminine quality unsuitable for men.[15] Many fathers were uncomfortable around their children; they retreated behind patriarchal authority, enforcing a strict discipline that seemed socially valuable (inculcating desirable virtues) and that kept interaction between parent and child on as unemotional a level as possible. Fathers often sought to drive and sometimes even bully their children—especially their sons—toward the ideals of hard and constant labor.

Relations between female relatives and children, particularly female children, did not reflect a domestic idyll either.[16] The social reproduction of the middle class, which was the special province of mothers, required considerable work. To balance tasks ranging from overseeing homework to imparting domestic skills and inculcating proper values and manners (all the while maintaining a suitable household), mothers often had to exert a heavy-handed pressure on their children. Beyond the practical demands of such a balancing act, the task of "modern motherhood"[17] required a close and careful control over childhood—the "silent observation" of children endorsed by Clara Zinn, for example.[18] Within the home, mothers were able to exert considerable influence over children through constant observation, selection of the physical and social environment, and direct instruction. In this way, children could be taught, in the words of child advocate Ellen Key, "to respect the real world and learn how to function under the direction of others . . . in order to become conscious that there are borders to everything."[19] Mothers were expected to inure children to authority and limits. Even the involvement of mothers in the play of children was aimed at training children.[20] Mothers were expected to watch and correct, to instruct their children on the behavioral demands of middle-class life.

It is also instructive to keep in mind that much of a child's life was work, whether that child was from the working class or the middle class. The nature of work as well as the marginal leftover time varied. Rather than requiring their children to work in the marketplace as many working-class children did, middle-class families divided their children by sex and either assigned them a great deal of household labor or demanded considerable schoolwork. Thus, it is not unusual to find in childhood memoirs a jealous recollection of the "freedom" enjoyed by children of another class; that is, working-class children envied the freedom from work and want of middle-class children, while middle-class children longed for the opportunity to play in the streets like working-class children.[21] That both groups overestimated the freedom of the other in no way detracted from the power of their projected longings. Certainly, that children across the social spectrum were kept busy cannot be allowed to obscure the fact that material deprivation and rigorous labor made working-class childhood more difficult. The essential point is that for all the stress laid on naive, joyous childhoods and loving families, children were generally expected to labor in one manner or another.

The *bürgerliche* family only loosely resembled the ideology that underpinned it.[22] The burdens of competitive labor markets, maintaining a respectable home, and raising the next generation of middle-class individuals tended to make the family a community of work and representation. The aggregation of individual tasks often limited the opportunities for the expression of affection. Many working-class families also sought to live up to the domestic ideal established by the middle classes. The difficulties encountered by *bürgerliche* families were multiplied among workers, though certainly there were loving working-class families, just as there were failed marriages in the middle class.

Parents sought to control the environment in which children grew up—observing, instructing, and disciplining their children in a refined display of a microphysics of power. The pressure of such a relationship, such an effort to construct the right sort of individuals, conflicted deeply with the notion of the individual as an autonomous self, an authentic individual who needed to develop according to his or her own personality. In effect, the effort to forcibly construct a liberal, utilitarian subjectivity conflicted with the vaguely Romantic ethos to which many subscribed. "[P]lanting and cultivating the seeds of noble and sublime youth" suggested something other than the posture of the stern disciplinarian.

The inability of the family as a disciplinary system to live up to the ideal of mutual affection did not call the domestic ideology into question. The domestic ideal was far too important—far too rooted in the values and aspirations of most Europeans—for that to happen. Domesticity and the associated cult of respectability stabilized social relations and individuals amid extraordinary change.[23] They also served as claims of moral and social superiority to the working class and aristocracy.[24] Rather than questioned or discounted, the domestic ideology was instead annually reaffirmed at Christmas. In the process, parents implicitly constructed a bastardized copy of the Romantic, expressive self.

Christmas

The history of Christmas throughout western Europe and North America in the nineteenth century was closely tied to the development of the middle-class domestic ideology. The old traditions of Christmas were everywhere reworked to transform the holiday from a public festival of social inversion to a family affair emphasizing children and an idealized vision of intimate domesticity.[25] Christmas was an opportunity to actualize the *bürgerliche* ideology, to live in the ideal. In nineteenth-century Germany, Christmas became a particularly important holiday, one that increasingly defined middle-class ideals and identity. Joe Perry claims that Christmas "articulated a model national community" based on those domestic ideals that German families found so difficult to honor during the rest of the year. Perry explains that "the modern Christmas depended on the emergence of the 'home' as bourgeois social space."[26] The various traditions that surrounded nineteenth-century Christmas emphasized the domesticity of the holiday. The decorating of the home, the family celebrations, and, of course, the gift giving made clear that this was a festival of and for the family.

The gift-giving traditions made this abundantly clear. Gifts were not merely for neighbors and the local needy but especially for family members. The ties of obligation and affection that flowed from and were represented by gifts reflected the interiorization of the bourgeois family.

The odd practice of shifting the responsibility for gifts from the actual gift giver to an anonymous, fictional figure deserves closer attention. The *Weihnachtsmann* (or *Christkind*) the German equivalent of Santa Claus who emerged in the mid-nineteenth century as an amalgam of regional gift givers,[27] served two purposes. First, he displaced the usual disciplinary figure in the household, the father. It is often argued that he was able to exert a greater disciplinary influence than the father. The imminent prospect of reward for good behavior or punishment for bad (not entirely out of the question) did exert a tremendous, if short-term, disciplining influence on children.[28] Curiously overlooked is the fact that when patriarchal authority was shifted from the father to the *Weihnachtsmann,* the father gained an opportunity to engage his children more directly without calling patriarchal authority into question. The children disciplined themselves in anticipation of the *Weihnachtsmann,* allowing the father to relax the self-imposed burden of oversight. The father had a chance to climb down from his sometimes Olympian heights. This temporary opportunity to engage children more directly also solidified patriarchal authority for the rest of the year by reemphasizing that that authority was exercised in the name of love and in the interests of the children. Another critical function of the *Weihnachtsmann* was to obscure the origins of gifts in the marketplace. The gifts were not commodities—and therefore did not have an immediate monetary value—when they were produced and distributed by the magical saint of Christmas. Parental love could bear no price tag.[29]

Christmas became an ideal holiday that separated the family from the demands of the normal social world, both in the form of labor and in the form of consumer commodities (through the intercession of the *Weihnachtsmann*). In fact, Joe Perry has depicted the emergence of middle-class Christmas in Germany as a process of "sacralization of private life."[30] This separation, in addition to the relaxation of the disciplinary demands on the part of parents, allowed a far greater level of emotional bonding than was usually the case. In this way, the domestic ideology was able to survive the gap between theory and reality during the rest of the year, ensuring the "stabilization of the patriarchally organized family ideal."[31] More precisely, Christmas redressed the balance between immediate expressions of affection and the securing of long-term socialization interests.

The ambivalence of the cultural mission of Christmas was heightened by another ironic twist in the domestication of Christmas. At the same time that Christmas was being interiorized and domesticated, it was becoming an increasingly commercial holiday. The two phenomena were not unrelated. Stephan Nissenbaum offers an explanation for the American experience that is sufficiently rooted in the structural changes of the economy and family to credibly explain the same transformation throughout the West. When the head of household offered presents largely to social inferiors who appeared at the door, it made sense to offer practical items from the home's own store. When, however, Christmas began to interiorize (when gifts began flowing not outside the home from adult to adult but, rather, inside the home from family member to family member, especially from parent to child), practical gifts from the household became quite unattractive. Something new needed to be introduced from outside the home. Such a tradition, of course, linked up nicely with the growing wealth of middle-class families and the expanding commercial marketplace.[32] The domestication of the bourgeois family was therefore deeply entangled in the commercialization of Christmas, the great sin against the family holiday that has been much lamented ever since. This linkage also brought desire into the most potent of Christian holidays and into the center of the widely recognized festival of children. The dualism of love and desire that runs through much of commercial capitalism was perhaps nowhere better demonstrated than in the structural transformation of Christmas.[33]

The cultural task of Christmas explains a great deal about the nineteenth-century toy market. Christmas dominated the market, accounting for the majority of sales. This predominance was rooted in the efforts of parents, particularly fathers, to ritually reintegrate the family as a community rooted in mutual affection. Christmas became a moment when expressions of spontaneous joy and love were accepted, even sought after. For parents, then, giving toys became a means of providing for the immediate happiness of their children.

The genuine and heartfelt joy of the middle-class Christmas was firmly tied to desire. Desire is the child of distance. Simmel observes that the "dual significance of desire—that it can arise only at a distance from objects, a distance that it attempts to overcome, and yet that it presupposes a closeness between the objects and ourselves in order that the distance should be experienced at all—has been beautifully expressed by Plato in the statement that love is an intermediate state between possession and deprivation."[34] Parents ensured that children knew Christmas was coming, that gifts of toys were in the offing. Any trip past the window of a department store could spark that curious mixture of distance and closeness that was desire. Parents were then able to abolish that distance and claim for themselves the love Plato saw in the moment between deprivation and possession.

Pleasure was to be derived from the satisfaction of some desire of the child's. Underlining the centrality of desire, rather than merely the act of gift giving, novelist Hans Fallada observed of his own Berlin childhood, "the useful was unimportant; underwear we had to have anyway; underwear was not Christmas, but toy soldiers were!"[35] The exchange of gifts was not in itself sufficient. Solidarity was not created simply through social obligations incurred in the exchange of gifts. The child's gift had to, if possible, reflect an acknowledgment and fulfillment of that child's desires. Marcel Mauss argued that a good gift "never completely detaches from those carrying out the exchange," meaning that the gift giver gave something deeply representative of himself or herself.[36] In mass-consumption societies, where the gift could have nothing to do with the giver (since its origins were in an anonymous and fleeting moment of purchase), the polarities in gift giving changed. The gift should refer not to the giver but to the recipient. It had to show an understanding of the recipient's wants and seek to satisfy them. The gift thus implicitly defined the unique individual as a specific constellation of wants. Christmas gifts assumed a construction of the individual based on authentic and unique desires. These desires and enthusiasms were individually fulfillable; otherwise, Christmas gifts had no purpose. Recognition of a child's "true" self meant identifying "true" desires and acknowledging them. This represented a sort of vulgarized vision of the "expressive self" sketched by Charles Taylor. In the place of a self that manifests its authentic essence through gesture, word, and art, parents sought to manifest the authentic essence of the child by surrounding him or her with representations of authentic desires. Only in defining a desire and satisfying it could the gift of a toy serve its purpose, to renew the emotional bonds between family members. That acknowledgment of the child's individuality also powered the toy industry's drive for novelty and variety in its products.

Over the course of the nineteenth century, children became accepted as desiring subjects during the Christmas period. The *Berliner Tageblatt,* for example, recognized that parents took elaborate measures to increase the tension and, therefore, the expectations of children. The longings of the children were deliberately increased because many adults saw the principal joy of the gift rituals of Christmas in the wanting and hoping. But the *Tageblatt* wondered whether the gifts could live up to the expectations that parents cultivated, whether the "poetry" of the holiday would ebb and ultimately fail entirely under the burden of this annual rite of disappointment.[37] Desire was partially spiritualized by parents: it was made into a constituent part of the family festival. Parents crafted desire in their children with shopping trips, Christmas stories, and, above all, the locked door that kept tree and presents from sight but not from mind.[38] In fact, the "poetry" of Christmas was in the satisfaction of the desires of others. The critical problem was not, in the view of the *Tageblatt,* desire per se but, rather, the continual failure to match expectation with reality. In another article, the *Tageblatt* worried that the Christmas wish list would stoke the flames of desire too high. The *Tageblatt* lamented that children could put anything and everything on the list, thus giving themselves grounds for disappointment later. Nonetheless, desire was accepted as a fundamental part of Christmas; the *Tageblatt* argued that the desire needed merely to be limited, corralled by financial reality.[39]

Christmas harbored an unusual relation between desire and consumption. Unlike in so many other analyses of such a relation, the impetus to consumption at Christmas was not one's own desire. "Happy faces" were linked time and again to Christmas gifts, but they were other people's faces. Desire was to be stoked in others so that it could be satisfied in a gift ritual that solidified the affective bonds of the family. The family journal *Daheim* made expectations and longing a central part of the "family festival, whose principals are the children." For *Daheim,* one of children's greatest joys was to linger in the vicinity of the locked door to the room where the Christmas tree guarded the sundry gifts: "Perhaps through the keyhole is to be spied a glimpse of all the wonderful things hidden on the other side, a branch of the tree or a colorful something that could be perceived on a doll, a rocking horse, or the fulfillment of some other wish."[40] Anticipation made the gift more than a physical thing. The gift became the fulfillment of a desire, the satisfaction of a longing crafted and intensified by the parents. The happiness of the parents was emphasized by a poem featured on the front cover of an 1899 issue of *Die Gartenlaube.* The poem, which narrates a parent's survey of the chaos of Christmas Day as the children brandish their new toys, concludes: "Dear God, how happy am I! / Even the little one under the table / sings happily on nigh / '*Weihnachtsmann, Weihnachtsmann* / O you are a very good man!' "[41]

Desire, as the *Tageblatt* had indicated, could not be allowed simply to run wild. Desire and fulfillment may have been a central dynamic of the Christmas rituals, but desire had to be kept under some control. The *Berliner Tageblatt* had worried that expectations could be whipped up to too high a pitch, bringing disillusionment and even "blaséness" (*Blasiertheit*) in its train. *Daheim* appeared to have less concern. In its 1912 poem "The Wish List," a gendered division of desire permitted a male child to demand every sort of miniature artifact of the modern world: "theater—books—airship—airplane—/ steam engine—toy car—/ maps." Altogether, young Robert had written fourteen things on his list, but he also had already written and discarded three other lists. His desires were unstable, potentially limitless. His little sister, however, knew better. She knew that their father did not have enough money for all those items, so she restricted her wish list to a few. Mausi (as she was called) requested a new doll—this being the first time in three years she had asked for a "new child." There were a few other things that she hoped for, including a sewing machine, a washboard, and roller skates. "Now," says the poem, "she has only to think for her brother."[42] Desire may have fueled Christmas joy, but it had to be held in check. Above all, the girls had to exercise that discipline. They were to limit their own wishes in number and to keep them centered on the home. In that way, desire could be harnessed without fear of its potentially destructive effects. *Daheim* also presented two models for preventing children from becoming bored or disappointed with their gifts. The female model was to limit desire, to want only a few things. The other model was rather more implicit. One can present an ever new constellation of toys to young Robert and his playmates, so that his desires can never be fully sated, leaving him always partially satisfied and pushing him toward a constant engagement with the outside world in the form of the search for ever new playthings.

Of course, *bürgerliche* parents could not easily abandon their attachment to rearing proper middle-class citizens. They may have sought to cultivate a domesticated desire for toys, but they had other values that they hoped to satisfy simultaneously. Parents sought to construct a specifically bourgeois subjectivity through objects, through the toys that they gave. Parents believed they could shape their children through play because toys were increasingly accepted as educational. This belief brought another twist in the ambivalence in bourgeois discourses about children. Children received toys as gifts in large part because parents wanted to reemphasize that they were interested in their children's happiness, both present and future. But lest they be accused of fostering dissolute values or encouraging a slackening of discipline, the toys were reinscribed as educational. The first function of the toy was still to be enjoyable. The toy was (usually) secondarily to be somehow educational. Its educational attributes were partly honest efforts to continue the educational efforts of the parents, partly reassurance for parents that they were not undoing the careful developmental program to which they adhered for the rest of the year. Toys largely existed in this uneasy discursive field defined by desire and education. They had, as much as was possible, to satisfy both. Toys were therefore both to cultivate and to condition the desires of children.

Reconciling desirability and educational benefits was not a given. Toys taken to be educational did not necessarily inspire immediate desire. They might well provide much greater benefit and even more enjoyment over the long term. The cultural function of Christmas, however, did not stress the long term. The long term was the concern of the rest of the year. Christmas was about the immediate thrill, about making a child happy on that day. The goal was to please children when Christmas Day came, so that they might say with the young Hans Fallada, "you are all so good to me, and I am usually so rude,"[43] thus renewing the (patriarchal) family foundations.

How was the family to satisfy these competing imperatives? By and large, the key was referentiality. Educational benefits were a function less of what the toy did than of what it resembled. In this way, we may understand what I believe was a fundamental divide in toys. Some toys refused to reference the human, social world, but most were relentlessly topical.

In early twentieth-century production, perhaps the largest single group of toys other than dolls were those representing animals, not the wonders of technology pushed by retailers and most big toy manufacturers. As figure 1 shows, animals were often featured in more advertisements than were technology toys, military items, or even children.[44] Animals were also popular decorations for the walls of children's rooms.[45] The affection for animals is easily taken as self-evident. Are not animals, at least some animals, universally seen as cuddly? A clue to the actual meaning behind animal tropes may be found in an article in the *Deutsche Spielwaren-Zeitung* that made suggestions about what toys were appropriate for which ages. Animals were recommended for two different age-groups: birth to one-and-a-half years of age, and one-and-a-half to four years of age.[46] Animals were intended to be played with by young children. Borrowing from Rousseau, the educational goal was often to avoid any ambitious educational goal. Animals, by refusing any reference to the social world and its conflicting values, were the ideal images for preserving innocence. Animal toys were, by virtue of their socially nonrepresentational forms, symbols of a childhood undisturbed by the demands of the adult world. Gunilla-Frederike Budde argues that animal forms represented *bürgerliche* parents' commitment to fostering imagination in children.[47] That may be partly true, but there is no inherent link between animals and fantasy. Imagination could as easily be stirred through other forms. Animals were specifically favored because they did not teach about the world that the children eventually would have to enter. Similarly, balls, which the *Deutsche Spielwaren-Zeitung* also prominently featured in its first two age-groups, refused any close reference to the modern world.

Most toys, however, were calculated to engage that world. Topicality was a remarkably effective means of bringing education and pleasure together. The pleasure was in what the game or toy did; the education was in what the toy referenced. Parents assured themselves that by purchasing toys that resembled the world in which their children would live, they were educating their children for that world. The relation to knowledge was rather like that of the newspaper. Devoid of context or explanation, portraits of discrete events and things competed for attention, with no concern for their interrelation. Knowledge was extracted from reality and distilled into independent bits of information or images, whether they be newspaper stories about strikes in South Africa or toy airplanes. The focus was on facts rather than truth.

The oversimplified relation between topicality and education hid the real education on offer. Toys were used as means of socially reproducing the *Bürgertum.* The images presented to children in their toys were

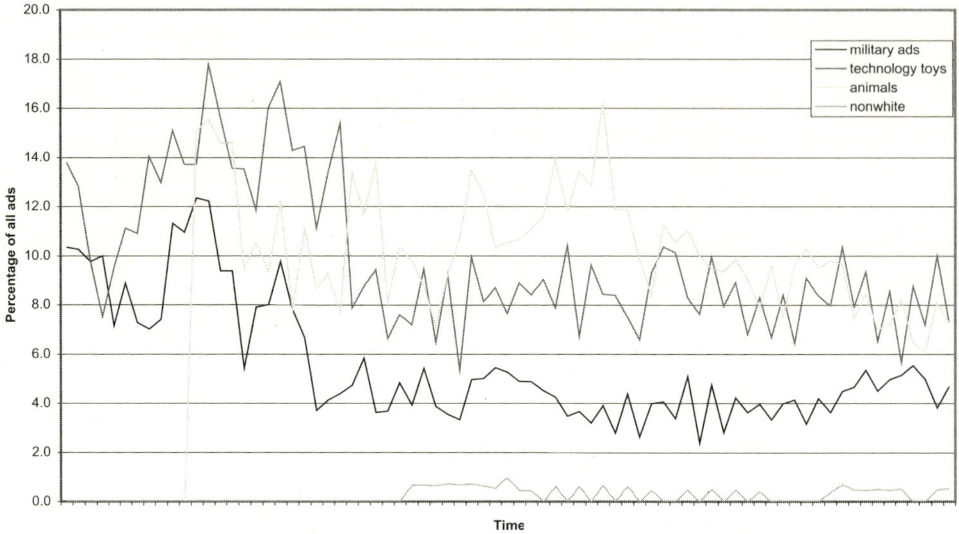

Fig. 1. Comparison of toy advertising in the *Deutsche Spielwaren-Zeitung* (Nuremberg), 1909–14.

reified middle-class ideals and values. Children were being not so much educated as conditioned. They were being trained to accept the norms of *bürgerliche* life as natural and unchallengeable. These norms influenced the specific forms that toys took, rather than determining the aggregate demand.

The equation of education and verisimilitude made all the world into possible themes for toys and eased the demands placed on toy makers. Toys did not have to provoke thought or imagination. Instead, they were called on to amuse while resembling some small portion of the world. The division of functions within the toy, between amusement and education, also had a more subtle consequence. The joy that the toy produced was often invisible. That joy was, after all, in what a child did with the toy. In playing with the toy, the child appropriated it for his own purposes, regardless of the toy's factual form. Toy soldiers could become hardy explorers or a marching band. The child's imagination was wrapped around the toy in play and thereby transformed the toy. The child might or might not have heeded the images that alleged to educate him, but those images were all that parents could see. The visual element that retailers sought to emphasize to capture the shopper's wandering eye was also precisely that by which parents measured toys. Therefore, when we assess the cultural factors that drove toy consumption, we need to examine closely the visual associations that the adult toy buyers saw. There was, thus, a dual impulse driving an increasing attention to the visual surfaces of the toy. The toy itself was an effort to externalize invisible emotions. The surfaces of the toy, meanwhile, sought to communicate specific ideas and ideals to the eyes of the child. In both cases, trends rooted deeply in the structures of Western modernity emphasized the visual engagement with toys.

Did children heed the images presented? This is an essentially unprovable proposition. The sources available, memoirs of childhood, were written decades after the fact and through the haze of adult commitments. Many of the accounts include romanticized recollections of using toys as their forms would suggest: toy trains were trains; dolls were children. Nonetheless, it also appears that children could—even if they did not always—rebel against the forms and expectations prescribed for them. Certainly, pedagogues worried about children breaking their toys. Bryan Ganaway and Miriam Formanek-Brunell have pointed to the only contemporary empirical study of play, that of Americans A. C. Ellis and G. Stanley Hall. Ellis and Hall's 1896 "Study of Dolls" demonstrated a wide preference for dolls but a nonetheless quite strong subversive streak, whether in the form of having dolls act out in socially inappropriate fashions or in the form of physical aggression against dolls.[48] This is, at best, very limited evidence, but it suggests that the autonomous imagination of children, deliberately cultivated by parents and toys, was capable of resisting the imposition of identity by parents and toys.

Of course, toys could take a wide variety of forms within the broad category of referentiality. The values that parents sought to inculcate varied between these types of toys, meriting closer examination. Parents were engaged in a project of identity construction through consumption. The freedom that mass consumption seems to offer is here circumscribed by the parent-child relationship. Identity, in this case, was something parents hoped to prescribe. From the many images offered by toys, adults chose images they thought would elaborate a stable, "normal" child, one who adhered to the dominant cultural and gender expectations of middle-class Germany. Much of the remainder of this chapter considers a number of toy themes, beginning with the military toy.

Military Toys

There is perhaps no more well-established opinion of nineteenth-century German toys than that they were militarist. Certainly a large number of toys referenced the military. Military images ranged from cavalry uniforms to tin replicas of roman legionnaires to steam-powered miniature Dreadnoughts. The images projected by laternae magicae, which were a sort of film projector, often narrated the triumph of German arms in the Franco-Prussian War.[49] The replication of military themes should not, however, simply be equated with militarism per se. Indeed, the matter begs the question of what we mean by the term *militarism.* The term has gained a number of definitions as scholars have struggled to understand the effect of military ideals on political policy.[50] As the needs of the present discussion focus more on the influence of military ideals on cultural expression, I here borrow the definition of militarism from the distinguished military historian Michael Howard: "an acceptance of the values of the military subculture as the dominant values of society: a stress on hierarchy and subordination in organization, on physical courage and self-sacrifice in personal behavior, on the need for heroic leadership in situations of extreme stress; all based on the acceptance of the inevitability of armed conflict within the states-system and the consequent need to develop the qualities necessary to conduct it."[51]

In the present discussion, I also make a further distinction between what I term *first-order militarism* and *second-order militarism.* First-order militarism refers to the immediate promotion of the military and military virtues. Art historian Dr. Paul Hildebrandt invoked first-order militarism when he argued: "War and soldier play need not lead to rawness; they mostly teach manliness and chivalrous virtues. Heroism must be shown in more than just battle; one has sometimes rich opportunities to show bravery in everyday life in defending the weak or saving a life; also, so long as world peace does not break out, the existence of the state is based on the courage, skill at arms. and soldierly virtues of its citizens."[52] In this category of militarism would be found the cavalry uniform and perhaps toy guns and such board games as Young Germany's Game of Battle, which explicitly aimed to teach battle tactics to young Germans.[53] Second-order militarism takes into account the manner in which people—in this case, Germans—see the world through the lens of the military; other values are perceived in military terms. In this category may be found Dreadnoughts, which are simultaneously military items and representatives of technological and industrial achievement. One may perceive the Dreadnought in the first place as either a war machine or an extraordinary technological triumph. This distinction between first- and second-order militarism facilitates the analysis of the multiple meanings that laid behind military toys. They were not exclusively rooted in enthusiasm for the military or the military subculture. Other values and orientations, from patriotism to technological modernism, were expressed through military themes.

In practice, the analytical distinction between first- and second-order militarism is not entirely clean-cut. Toy soldiers may have been a straightforward promotion of military virtues, or they may have been given as history lessons. History in nineteenth-century Germany was largely seen in terms of clashing nation-states, and wars were understood to be the critical instruments by which nations rose or fell.[54] Hildebrandt's previously cited confession of militarist faith implied a similar belief. Were, then, re-creations featuring Roman legionnaires massed for a crossing of the Rhine principally militarist or historical?[55] Re-creations of the 1813 Battle of Nations outside Leipzig appeared on the market in time to celebrate the centennial.[56] Was their purpose militarist or historical? How were such re-creations to be conceptually distinguished from re-creations of the court of Frederick the Great?[57] The duality of militarism and history also connected these toys to nationalism. The nation was perceived as a historically rooted cultural and/or racial community that often found its clearest demarcation in competition and conflict with other groups. Military toys could therefore have given parents the opportunity to emphasize a son's group identity, through which the individualistic child-*Bürger* was reintegrated into the community. The identification of war and history also meant normalizing conflict. Warfare appeared to be the natural and necessary condition by which history progresses.

Many parents also appear to have believed that toy soldiers were excellent tutors on current events. Every major international crisis or conflict brought forth an answering wave of tin soldiers. *Daheim* noted that already in 1863, with the Prussian campaign against Denmark, the toy industry followed military campaigns with corresponding tin combatants.[58] Likewise, *Daheim* reported that "even before the first canons of Saarbrücken roared, lead Prussian and French battles were brought onto the market by speculative producers."[59] The linkage between conflict and sales of toy soldiers was common throughout the decades before World War I. Reproductions of dramatic international conflicts—whether the Russo-Japanese War or the Italian-Ottoman War—were inevitable.[60] Even the standoff between Austria-Hungary and Russia over Bulgaria, which reached its peak in 1887–88 but never came to blows, provided material for manufacturers of tin soldiers.[61] The attraction of toy soldiers was in part their ability to represent important events around the world. Their educational claims laid in what they resembled. Their enjoyment value laid in what boys did with them. Parents hoped that their boys were learning history, politics, and geography while manipulating their tin figures. Such producers as Heinrichsen Zinnfiguren could therefore advertise their wares as "excellent educational material."[62] It was not difficult for parents to echo Paul Hildebrandt's sentiments that "there is in fact hardly a better presentation of historic or military events than the exact reproduction of soldiers, commanders, and battles, whether it is of Greeks and Trojans or Russians and Japanese."[63] Again, the emphasis was on the educational benefits provided by the forms that toys took. We should not be surprised, then, that many young boys received and played with toy soldiers.[64] They were widely perceived as educational, and their power to amuse was unquestioned. Military toys were well adapted, then, to the structural needs of Christmas.

There can be little doubt that the military and war were attractive themes beyond current events or the construction of history. The values of the military were widely embraced as normative. The military was closely associated with ethical values, such as self-sacrifice, perseverance, and personal honor. Military toys were consequently deeply gendered. The value system that underwrote both the military and military toys was ultimately intended to be exclusively male. It was to this sense that Hildebrandt appealed when he suggested that "war and soldier play . . . mostly teach manliness and chivalrous virtues." To be properly male meant to identify with war. German families often sought out military toys as a means of constructing a properly masculine identity, to fix such values as self-sacrifice, aggressiveness, and competitiveness. Thus, Schulrat Ackermann of Eisenach, for example, believed that the most important goal of play was to teach such values as "courage and determination" as well as to combat "cowardice."[65] Interestingly, war itself, rather than specifically German wars, appears to have been valued as an instrument of teaching proper male values as well as history.

It can be argued that budding consumerism extended and deepened the power of militarist norms in German society. As objects and advertising images were manipulated to take on specific meanings and to reference specific values and traditions, such cultural norms as militarism assumed a physical pervasiveness unimaginable in traditional societies. Thus, a central dynamic in consumerism, the attempt to manage and construct associations between material goods and ideal goods, can be seen to intensify the commitment of German society to military virtues. Simultaneously, however, one can perceive that the depoliticizing pressure of consumerism and the general heterogeneity of consumerist themes actually complicated the efforts of radical nationalists to enforce an exclusive, monolithic national identity.[66] Indeed, the fact that the Kopenick and Zabern affairs were used successfully in toys to satirize the army indicates that toys could also be antimilitarist. They could undercut the sanctity of the military as an institution.

There were, of course, voices decrying the emphasis on military toys. Social democracy had long condemned militarism, leading *Daheim* to complain in 1877 that a Social Democrat "would certainly rather put a guillotine on the Christmas table for his children than bestial soldiers."[67] In fact, the Social Democrats' rejection of military toys was surprisingly muted. Apparently, military toys were sufficiently well established in the culture that the official antimilitarism of the Sozialdemokratische Partei Deutschlands (SPD) rarely bestirred itself to challenge the morality of such toys. Most Christmas seasons came and went without any comment on the toys sold in the party's mouthpiece, *Vorwärts.* In fact, in December 1904, a collection was announced to provide Christmas gifts for the children of locked-out metalworkers and woodworkers, for which *Vorwärts* explicitly stated that all manner of items were suitable.[68] Nonetheless, on several occasions, articles in *Vorwärts* sharply criticized the war worship that some toys seemed to represent. For example, in 1907, *Vorwärts* saw soldier toys indoctrinating youth for fratricide.[69] A little over a week later, another article appeared asserting that "no thinking man, above all no thinking, class-conscious worker may tolerate such a 'soldier toy' under the Christmas tree or in the hands of his children."[70] The topic did not emerge again, however, until 1913, when *Vorwärts* resumed its attack, arguing that working-class boys should not be taught through toy soldiers to "worship a Moloch."[71]

The timing of these attacks was not entirely arbitrary. That such articles ran in December 1907 and December 1913 and not in other years indicates that *Vorwärts,* which was the organ of a political party, was at least partially reflecting party political feeling in its critique of military toys. The year 1907 began with an election, during which the government had orchestrated a nationalist propaganda campaign aimed primarily at the Social Democrats.[72] That campaign produced a political alliance based on a common desire to increase military spending. The passage of significant increases in military (especially naval) spending in the autumn of 1907 raised the related problem of who would pay. From bitter experience, the SPD could guess in December 1907 that if it was anyone, the workers would have to cover a large part of the expenses. German militarism was therefore very much on the mind of the SPD. In 1913, the issue was even more immediate, coming on the heels of the Zabern incident, in which a detachment of soldiers imposed de facto martial law in a small Alsatian town in response to the affronted personal honor of an overproud lieutenant.[73] The willingness of the army to disregard civil law and civilian rights inspired a political crisis and a remarkable propagandistic whirlwind in the pages of *Vorwärts.* The salvos unleashed by *Vorwärts* against toy soldiers no doubt expressed genuine feelings, but they were not central concerns. Instead, they emerged principally when the SPD had good, immediate reason to worry about the human and financial costs of militarism. By and large, the criticism of military toys was extremely muted and did little to blunt the attraction of such playthings. If anything, the critiques emphasized the staying power of military toys.

The category of "military toys" encompassed more than toy soldiers. There were board games, such as Modern Sea Warfare[74] and Sword and Shield.[75] There were also toys that represented the increasing intrusion of science and technology into the old, aristocratic preserve of war. These toys occupied an ambivalent middle ground between representations of technological and industrial modernity and representations of military might. The Dreadnought was a technological marvel. It could be admired as a stunning achievement of European science and its application in industrial processes. Only a handful of nations, after all, could build Dreadnoughts, whereas riflemen were found everywhere. The airplane possessed an even stronger dualism. Flight captured the imagination of all the West. As Peter Fritzsche writes, the "technological capacity [of aircraft] reaffirmed what so many turn-of-the-century Europeans cherished: confidence in their singular ability to remake the world."[76] The *Deutsche Spielwaren-Zeitung* reported on the enthusiasm of all France for flight, particularly heavier-than-air craft then dismissively known in Germany as *Drachen* (Dragonflies).[77] Closer to home, aerial enthusiasts abounded. The painter Günter Grassmann (born in 1900 to a prominent Munich doctor) wrote, "[T]hat as youngsters we were interested and enthusiastic about the beginning of flight [*Fliegerei*] is self-evident . . . The flight of a Zepplin to Frankfurt or Munich or even to Berlin was a national event."[78] In 1910, Grassmann would have been able to witness an air show in Munich, leading to "great demand" for toy aircraft in the local toy stores.[79] The actual aircraft were remarkable enough in themselves, representing an apparent triumph over gravity itself. From the very beginning, however, there was also a connection in the German popular imagination between flight and war.[80] The interconnection between technology and warfare that the aircraft represented certainly seemed to play to the Germans' self-perceived strengths. They also promised to make the traditional supremacy of the Royal Navy obsolete.

The multiple possible meanings that toy aircraft, like toy soldiers, possessed contributed to their popularity. They actually taught boys very little, but they referred to things about which parents believed their sons should learn. Toys helped parents shape the interests of children. They might have prompted children to ask questions. Or boys might have remained content with a facile knowledge that encompassed names and perhaps images but understood neither battles nor the causes of wars—an assemblage of trivia that amounted to little more than an uncritical conditioning to the world. Military toys offered decontextualized facts as well as reified ideals of nationalism, militarism, personal bravery, and other values. Such toys should not be taken as indicators of an exclusive enthusiasm for "aristocratic" military virtues. More significantly, German boys were surrounded by military images. They were, in effect, being conditioned to perceive war as natural and heroic. Both gender norms and history were constructed through military conflict, suggesting both the inevitability of war and its potential desirability as a test of individual manhood and as an engine of historical development.

Technological Modernity

In the German toys of the early twentieth century, technological and industrial modernity cannot be cleanly differentiated from military themes. Aircraft could be viewed as either technological masterpieces or critical war material. The numbers in figure 1 reflect that fact: aircraft and battleships appear in both categories. Nonetheless, a number of toys were more unequivocally civilian. While bearing the dual values of aircraft and Dreadnoughts in mind, it is intriguing to note that representatives of technological modernity tend to outnumber the representatives of military themes in the number of advertisements analyzed in figure 1. Similarly, the 1912 catalog of Hermann Kurtz's toy store featured pages and pages of toy trains and paraphernalia, miniature steam engines, optical toys, chemistry sets, and other primarily civilian representatives of the new industrial age, far more pages than it had of military toys.[81] It appears that the German toy market immediately before World War I tended to reflect a somewhat greater emphasis on technological and industrial modernity than militarism.[82] This is obviously a rather impressionistic survey, relying as it does on the self-presentation of the industry rather than hard sales figures. Nonetheless, given that the toy industry had no reason to be ashamed of militarism and that, over time, advertising should reflect sales, I believe the impression to be reasonably accurate. We must bear in mind, however, that these numbers are limited to a handful of years immediately before World War I. The market was certainly quite different in 1880.[83] That technology toys might have increased in popularity would certainly reflect the increasing presence of technology in everyday life. It would also, however, reflect the rapidly improving production efficiency of technology toy makers, as well as the efforts of retailers. These made technology toys far more attractive to consumers by dramatically cutting the prices of such toys, improving their "performance," and putting them constantly in the public eye.

Technological modernity was easier to represent than military virtues, because it could be expressed in either form or function. Thus, toy automobiles that came unequipped with any motor were as modern as a laterna magica, which resembled virtually nothing but, by virtue of its electrical lightbulb and the visual images it produced, also clearly participated in the world of modern science. Parents were able to associate their children with modernity, conditioning them to full participation in an increasingly industrial and technological world. This reflected not merely the needs of a modern military power but also, and more immediately, the needs of Germany's economy and the realities of everyday urban life. The game entitled The Triumph of the Twentieth Century, for example, was based on a race across Europe between an airship, an automobile, and a train.[84] The three forms of transport were cast as hypermodern (representing the "triumph" of a century only twelve years old) but also entirely civilian.

Kurt Karl Doberer, the son of an ardent Nuremberg Social Democrat, recalled: "[Q]uite early my father steered me toward technology. By the time I was five-and-a-half I possessed a small steam engine and a toy train that was drawn by a proper, alcohol-burning, steam locomotive."[85] That Doberer's father would seek to interest his son in technology through toys was the ideal of a number of enthusiasts. Paul Hildebrandt was sure that these technology toys, "in which our entire, extraordinary cultural progress is reflected," would "open to children a new, rich world." Therefore, he suggested that once a child reached seven, the parents should gradually introduce the child to the real world through modern technology toys.[86] *Der Spiel- und Holzwaren-Markt* argued that "it would be of the greatest advantage for our progress and our entire development if the joy and interest of the older children for the little models of our greatest inventions so increased that a generation would grow up that already in its childhood games had developed an enthusiasm for valuing, improving, and perfecting our technological achievements." The modern age, the author believed, brought with it increasingly bitter economic competition that required the improving technical education of Germany's youth, a task for which technology toys were uniquely qualified.[87] The *Rundschau über Spielwaren,* argued that technology toys would "not inconsequentially support the physics curriculum."[88] The emphasis placed on toys teaching science reflected closely the increasing importance that science had in determining the success of individuals in careers, as well as the success of nations both economically and militarily. Technology began to be a means of promoting two great *bürgerliche* ideals: individual success and national progress. We should not be surprised, therefore, that such toys as the famed Mecanno invented by Frank Hornsby in 1901 and Gebrüder Bing's Structator openly aimed simultaneously to entertain and to teach engineering.[89]

The duality that was explicit with Structator should be reiterated. These technology toys may have hoped to educate, but they were primarily forms of entertainment. The *Rundschau über Spielwaren* brought out this ambivalence nicely: "For boys of a certain age, windup toys naturally have no more attraction. Their hearts beat for steam and such motors . . . The truly modern youngster knows, however, only electricity."[90] The ability of a windup toy to perform its principal function, to entertain, became increasingly compromised, requiring a change. As technology evolved, entertainment values changed. The child was then identified with a particular value—modernity—on the basis of the form of energy that propelled the child's toys. F. H. Huber drew attention to the impact that changing technology in everyday life had on which toys were desirable: "The youth today want technological toys and models. They have also become more demanding in the course of the years. They grow up surrounded by the achievements of modern technology. Electricity, telegraphs, telephones, photography, 1000 hp steam engines are to the boys of today ordinary objects."[91] The value of a toy as entertainment depended in part on its ability to appear cutting-edge, suggesting that technology could satisfy the need for enjoyment and education.

Modern technology was also tied to nationalism. Mastery of technology was taken to be a sign of national virility and cultural achievement. It was also recognized as the foundation of economic and military strength. The booming electrical engineering and chemical industries in Germany established beyond any doubt the economic significance of science, even as the Dreadnought, the machine gun, and (tentatively) the aircraft proved its military importance. When parents associated their children with technology toys, therefore, they were asserting their own modernity and patriotism. Training their children to be engineers or at the very least to be interested in scientific developments served the interests of Germany. Given the rapid expansion of science-based sectors of the German economy, technology toys could be seen as launching children on secure, lucrative careers.

The economic and political freight that technology brought with it promoted a double gendering of technology toys. As long as labor was divided along gendered lines, such that ideally males left the home to pursue paid labor while females remained at home to perform unpaid labor, technology would be the privileged realm of males. Females were not encouraged to show interest in technology. If they nevertheless did show interest, it was a harmless enthusiasm, a hobby of no import because it could not lead to any long-term engagement in a profession. Males, however, could gain through technological enthusiasm. Their interests were to be promoted. Furthermore, the link between technology and nationalism brought science into the realm of politics, a realm of virile national self-assertion. There was a powerful link between nationalism and ideals of manliness.[92] When technology became increasingly linked to national potency, therefore, it became even more strongly gendered. Moreover, the mere fact that male children were increasingly urged to be interested in science made female engagement with technology suspect. This same logic led toy makers to categorize labor as "male" or "female" on the basis of the task's relation to technology and permitted toy companies to openly discriminate in pay between males and females. In production and consumption, technology had a gender.

The question remains, how could children have possibly learned about how steam engines or electrical dynamos function through playing with their toy trains? The only possible way might have been through dismantling a toy and attempting a crude reverse engineering. It is hard to imagine that the toy industry or parents had that in mind. The form of education was much more one of indoctrination, teaching children that they wanted to be engineers or simply that science was fundamental to modern life. The principle goal, which the window-dressing education facilitated, remained enjoyment. The movement that technology permitted exerted a unique fascination. Moving toys were eye-catching and enthralling in a away that board games or tin soldiers could never be; they were, in the words of the Sonneberg *Handelskammer,* "particularly suitable for entertaining children."[93] The ability to combine amusement and putative education made technology toys unusually well adapted to the demands of the toy market, replicating the advantages that they enjoyed in production and retailing.

The Non-Western World

The nationalism implicit in the German celebration of military and technology toys in the early twentieth century brings this discussion to the representation of the non-Western world in German toys. I choose the phrase "non-Western world" because formal imperialism was comparatively underrepresented in the toy world. A "soft" imperialism of knowledge, caricature, and invisibility was much more common. The world beyond the West was represented as a frontier to be conquered and a stage on which individuals could demonstrate their full abilities. These were realms where middle-class individualism could find its fullest possible expression. Those who already lived on this frontier/stage were reduced to invisible nonpersonhood.

In German toys, the two most popularly presented images of the world beyond the confines of Europe and North America were, ironically, defined by Americans. The first was the quest for the North Pole, which spanned decades and culminated in the early years of the twentieth century in a race between Americans Robert Peary and Frederick Cook. The second was Theodore Roosevelt's safari in Africa.

The drive to be the first to the North Pole produced an assortment of sensationalist accounts and images of sailors shipwrecked in Arctic deserts, menaced by ferocious polar bears. The North Pole held a remarkable fascination for Germans, resulting in two German efforts to reach the North Pole between 1868 and 1870 under the command of Karl Koldewey from Bremen, as well as an Austrian expedition in 1872–74. Even after those attempts failed, a steady flow of publications kept Arctic exploration in the public eye.[94] In addition to the wide variety of books, there were also moderately frequent articles in such publications as *Die Gartenlaube* and *Daheim*.

Why did the icy, barren North Pole exercise this fascination for Germans? In 1882, A. Woldt attempted to explain why the Arctic was important. First, he pointed to the competition to be the first nation to plant its flag on the North Pole. But, of course, competition as an end in itself was enormously relativistic: the race existed only for the race. To further justify the efforts and interest, some other goal outside the race itself had to exist. Woldt therefore continued: "[T]he central point of polar research does not lie in the particular importance of the two poles themselves, which are purely geographic points . . . [I]t lies much more in those achievements that the scientific exploration of the entire Arctic and Antarctic areas . . . will produce . . . This enormous double region amounts to almost a sixteenth of the entire globe and is continually the site of violent meteorological, magnetic, and other scientifically important processes."[95] If one distills the verbiage, one comes to the conclusion that the poles had to be explored because they were big and had interesting weather and magnetic patterns. These were worthy purposes, but they were hardly lofty calls to action.

Dr. Kurt Rudolf Kreuschner more or less admitted in a *Daheim* article that there was little cause to reach the North Pole, which, he wrote, "offers no tangible, material value." He went on to claim: "[R]ather, it has only a pure, ideal importance. Although the North Pole has not yet been reached, valuable experience with the techniques of polar travel has been collected."[96] In other words, the primary benefit of trying to get to the North Pole (at least the only benefit that Kreuschner could enumerate) was in learning how one can get to the North Pole.

The reason for popular interest in the race to the North Pole was partly the vicarious challenge of overcoming obstacles, of proving that nothing could resist the advance of the West. But it also exerted an attraction in the personal characteristics such exploration seemed to require. These characteristics were perhaps nowhere as evident as in the travelogue written by Robert Peary about his "successful" voyage to the North Pole, published in German translation by *Daheim* in sixteen parts during the winter, spring, and early summer of 1910.[97] Peary portrayed himself as a great patriot: "pride in my nationality was always strong in me, but never stronger than when I saw the Stars and Stripes at this end of the world, fluttering in the fresh air of the Pole."[98] Throughout the articles, he also portrayed himself as a courageous, determined individual, overcoming temporary discouragement and pushing on to eventual triumph.

Peary's self-portrayal brings out Kreuschner's "pure, ideal importance" of the search for the North Pole. Because the North Pole had no material benefits to offer, the sacrifices in time, money, and physical deprivation were without ulterior motive. Moreover, the way to the North Pole was enormously difficult. The dangers were highlighted by occasional shipwrecks, which were further sensationalized by the press to include terrifying bear attacks.[99] The various obstacles and dangers that had to be overcome required a full measure of many of the values that the middle class most admired in males: fortitude, courage, intelligence, and a combination of individualism and nationalism. Arctic explorers exhibited the same self-disciplined aggressiveness that brought individual success, tempered by the nationalism that reintegrated that individual into the community. Moreover, the race to the North Pole put those ideal values to the service of disinterested science, not material gain.

Is it to be wondered that Polar exploration became a popular theme for toys? The voyages were comparatively often in the news and seemed to call forth the best in the *bürgerliche* value system. There was, however, one problem. How was one to make the journey into an icy wasteland interesting? Often enough, toy makers included sensationalized elements drawn from press accounts, such as hypothetical polar bear or even Inuit attacks. One board game featured both, inviting six contestants—playing Cook, Peary, and four nameless Inuit—to conquer such impediments and arrive at the North Pole first (adding the virtue of competitiveness).[100] There were Inuit with both Cook and Peary as they sought to be first to the North Pole. But Inuit were inappropriate objects of identification. Boys were supposed to aspire to be like Cook and Peary for their achievements, not like the Inuit, though the Inuit happened to have accomplished the very same feat. Nonetheless, the Inuit maintained a certain exotic, if still anonymous, charm, allowing toy makers to capitalize by selling, for example, "Eskimo bows."[101] In any case, the *Deutsche Spielwaren-Zeitung* argued that the public love affair with the North Pole was over in 1911 and that aircraft then became the most fashionable toys.[102] Even so, in 1913, a toy came on the market based on Roald Amundsen's voyage to the South Pole.[103]

Teddy Roosevelt's safari did not have the same historical background as the discovery of the North Pole. Nevertheless, it offered a similar opportunity to fix desirable middle-class values. President Roosevelt was already well established worldwide as an icon of masculinity. His hunting trips, his famous stint as a volunteer in the Spanish-American War, and the speech he gave in Buffalo with an assassin's bullet lodged in his chest established him as a strong, courageous man. Roosevelt's persona won perhaps wider recognition than his activities as president. Roosevelt "embodied virile manhood," which combined "civilized manliness and primitive masculinity."[104] His symbolic embodiment of desirable character traits made him sufficiently famous for the German toy maker Margarete Steiff to give his name to her most famous product, the teddy bear.[105] When Roosevelt decided to go on a safari soon after leaving the White House, therefore, the trip was an international event and became a popular theme for toys.

The *Deutsche Spielwaren-Zeitung* thought immediately that Roosevelt's safari would be an excellent theme for toys. It lamented only that the moving pictures made of his journey had not appeared before the 1909 Christmas season. The visual cues that would establish a common visual idiom for toy makers and toy buyers did not arrive in proper time. The *Deutsche Spielwaren-Zeitung* had to exercise its own fantasy, imagining a fight to the death between a lion and the ex-president on the African savanna.[106] By June 1910, however, Roosevelt toys were all the rage.[107] Presumably, the moving pictures of the safari had come to the screen. It is noteworthy that although Africans appeared frequently in the films of Roosevelt's safari, they did not appeal to the toy market.

Propelled by their singular achievements and personae, as well as the developing machinery of media spectacle, Peary, Cook, and Roosevelt came to play significant roles as toy themes. As real people in the news, they served as free advertising for producers. More important, they unified the impulses behind toy buying, finding an enjoyable plaything that could be plausibly described as educational. To the usual attraction exerted by a toy, Peary, Cook, and Roosevelt added the thrill of celebrity. They also appeared to be able to teach geography and model appropriate middle-class virtues. These toys also emphasized the masculine virtues of individual strength, courage, and national self-assertion, the value structure that underwrote imperialism. They valorized the imperial project through their promotion of specific ideals of personal behavior and through writing non-Western peoples out of their own lands.

The North Pole expeditions and Roosevelt's safari were significant as well because there were few comparable phenomena for other figures or events in the non-Western world. For the most part, formal imperialism, which occupied such a large role in the imagination of Europeans, played little direct role in toys. Instead, there were a few celebrities who helped define Western individualism through their actions in the non-Western world. There, they were able to unfold their full skills and prove their individual worth against a backdrop occupied only by native "nonpeople." As Susanne Zantop observes, "only in the extra-European world could white European males define themselves as the White European Male, predestined by biology to a position of physical and cultural dominance."[108] There were a few nonwhite figures advertised in the *Deutsche Spielwaren-Zeitung,* almost entirely Chinese. Steiff made a number of non-Western dolls, but these were meant for export to the United States.[109] Particularly conspicuous was the absence of African figures. They were all but ignored. Even though Africa was at the heart of Germany's overseas empire, a review of toy advertising shows almost no African-themed toys. One horrible toy came onto the market in 1889, the heyday of German imperialist aspirations, and was called the Climbing Nigger or, alternatively, the Coconut Thief. The toy featured a caricatured African who went up a tin tree and then came down. To make the toy a bit more exotic and, frankly, more interesting, the *Wegweiser* appended a narrative describing an imagined scene involving an African scampering up the tree, limbs all atremble for fear of discovery, planning on snatching someone's coconuts.[110] Another reference appears in a 1913 article reviewing store windows. The author thought the appearance of two "elegant Negerlein" and, next, two "Young Japan" and "Young China" made for an excellent advertisement for the store—the window offering distinction by means of ethnography. There was no indication that the display items might be appropriate objects with which to play.[111]

The German toy makers' portrayal of Africans seems to have made rather unattractive toys. They were sufficiently despised from the beginning, on the basis that they offered little with which to identify. From the seventeenth century, blackness was associated with ugliness, primitiveness, even terror.[112] Before 1900, colonized imagery of black Africans was quite rare throughout German visual culture: "[S]uch themes were not widely perceived as a capable of resonating with German consumers . . . The German colonies held little charm in the wider circles of society."[113] After the Herero and Nama rebellions in 1904–7 were crushed, there was almost no chance of using African themes for toys. The initial uprising and, even more, its genocidal suppression had been widely publicized in Germany.[114] To justify the use of brutal force by the German colonial troops (the *Schutztruppen*), the African population was systematically demonized and reviled, such that they were no longer really accepted as members of the same human species.[115] They were simply not appropriate images for children. In German eyes, Africans ceased to be merely silly coconut thieves, lazy childlike beings in need of "civilizing." They were born murderers and rapists, never to be trusted or pitied.[116] Thus, while African imagery became more common (and much more racialized) in German visual culture, the associations conjured by that imagery rendered African toys highly problematic. They might be used as advertisement in posters or store windows, but they were not wonderful objects of childhood identification.

The non-Western world as portrayed in the world of toys was largely a realm for self-definition of white males. Peary, Cook, and Roosevelt all demonstrated desirable traits in faraway lands. Exoticism and celebrity added to the thrill of ordinary toys and gave them a sheen of education by introducing boys to new lands. The combination of exoticism and celebrity oriented these toys overwhelmingly at boys. The values that the heroes of the North Pole and Africa embodied were the values that bourgeois society felt important for men: courage, determination, intelligence. In addition, the educational benefits were largely believed to be in teaching geography. Geography was the province of males; even educated women rarely studied it. Girls did not need to learn about the wide world; learning about children and the home was enough.

Dolls

The best-selling type of toy in Germany in the early twentieth century was the doll.[117] There was very good reason for the doll to be so popular. As we have seen, military, technological, and imperialist themes (as well as many others) all appealed to boys, thereby splintering the "male" toy market. Girls, however, were expected to largely limit themselves to dolls and their associated accoutrements—"above all else, dolls and dollhouses are the best toys for girls."[118] The market for female-oriented toys was, consequently, much more thematically concentrated. This thematic concentration did much to prop up the Sonneberg toy industry, by creating a culturally protected demand. Thus, in the Christmas poem quoted earlier in this chapter, Robert asked for all manner of toys, especially technology toys, while young Mausi asked only for a doll and some toys for pretend housework. Dolls were believed to be the natural plaything of girls.[119] They reflected feminine nature and educated the girl to better fulfill that nature. They were, in other words, highly topical, because they represented in miniature the future experiential world of the young girl. Paul Hildebrandt spoke for many when he wrote that "where all thought and feeling of the child is directed at the doll as an object of love, the educator has an easy task."[120] The education that dolls offered was rooted in the emotions that made motherhood the exclusive destiny of women. But dolls were not desiccated educational items, as *Daheim* pointed out: "If [toy] soldiers are intended for boys, so may the scenes of daily life [translated into figurines] be thought of as intended particularly for girls. And they are the most desirable things of which one can think—they are moments stolen from a fully human life, which artists cannot better represent."[121] Dolls were presumed to be remarkably capable of unifying feminine enjoyment and education.

The power of these assumptions is perhaps best exemplified in the negative, by reactions to girls who failed to play with dolls. Margaret Bovary's piano teacher, for example, gave Margaret a doll-sized tea set for her tenth birthday, only to be scandalized when she learned that Margaret had long since given up playing with dolls.[122] An attack on the "moral sewer" among the "wellborn" in the pages of *Vorwärts* brought out the perceived unbreakable link between healthy girls and dolls.

> Fifi, the insufferable model of the Kurfürstendamm [a fashionable Berlin street] teenager, is angry that for moral reasons—ludi-

> crous!—the newest smut novel [*Schmutzroman*] that she had so desired was not under the Christmas tree. What should Fifi do with this electrically illuminated dollhouse that had cost three hundred marks? It's simply ridiculous! She's twelve years old and no longer a baby that plays with dolls. And at fifteen she will be hardened against morality [*moralisch abgebrüht sein*].[123]

That Fifi did not want to play with dolls at twelve was taken as a sign of immorality, just the same as was reading semipornographic trash. Dolls and girls belonged to one another in a way that no one plaything possessed boys. Dolls were so associated with girls, with femininity, that their rejection was not merely odd or unfortunate but could easily be immoral.

The close relationship between dolls and girls presented an additional problem. If a girl did not like dolls, there was a dearth of gender-appropriate substitutes. Whereas a boy who did not like toy soldiers had an enormous variety of substitutes, there were few alternatives to dolls. The other girl-specific toys were, like dolls, very much oriented toward the home. Indeed, many were designed specifically to be used with dolls. This added, no doubt, to the moral opprobrium attached to not playing with dolls. Since there were few appropriate alternatives to dolls, the rejection of dolls was tantamount to rejecting the female sex and its carefully crafted role in *bürgerliche* society. The toy market was then a mirror that, through the limited variety of playthings it offered to girls, faithfully reflected the comparatively circumscribed horizons permitted to women. The world of toys also helped construct those horizons. The ideological division of the lifeworld into two gendered spheres, a public one for males and a private one for females, was naturalized and promoted by the toys that parents gave to their boys and girls. Dolls were a preferred instrument for constructing gendered subjectivities. By assigning dolls to girls, parents assigned a normative feminine vision. As "doll mother" (*Puppenmutter*), the girl was to learn the emotions and skills necessary to run home and household.[124] Dolls also defined a norm for the child, a standard by which a girl's behavior might be assessed—hence the hostility encountered by Margaret Bovary. Dolls thus became a disciplinary tool to construct the modern, disciplinary mother. Girls were to be fashioned to occupy the center of a domestic sphere beset by internal inconsistencies, one requiring gifts of such things as dolls for their continuing stability. In this way, toys helped sustain the discourses about gender roles that, for example, permitted toy makers to differentiate work and pay by sex. Employers and employees assumed males should be paid more because they ought to be supporting families cared for by their stay-at-home wives, just as girls cared for their dolls while their brothers toiled at their toy trains.

Topicality, Spectacle, and Individuation

The general trend toward topicality in German toys of the early twentieth century should be clear. Toys meant for children out of the toddler stage were intended to refer to the world. In this way, they gained a measure of "educational" utility, in providing raw information in the form of accurate reproductions of real-world things or events. Through their relation to the real world, however, toys also sought to promote specific *bürgerliche* values and identities. This trend could be seen in a variety of toys. For example, Richter's Anker Steinbaukasten made a fortune by taking the old, reliable block—so beloved by Friedrich Fröbel for its nonspecificity—and making it topical. Richter's blocks were sold in sets that contained an ensemble of differing shapes so that the child could construct a specific building or type of structure. There were complete sets for building bridges, castles, even cathedrals.[125] Is it any surprise that the *Wegweiser* described these sets as "educational and entertaining" (which was, after all, "everything that one demands from a child's toy")?[126] Regardless of what the child actually built with the blocks, the sets appealed to consumers because they referenced architectural reality. One can also point to the various references to current events among toys. These ranged from references to the Captain from Köpenick, to the 1910 boxing match between Jack Johnson (the first African-American heavyweight boxing champ) and Jim Jefferies, to Lieutenant Forstner (of Zabern fame), and even to Octoberfest.[127]

Attaching emotions to visible things was never a simple or straightforward project. While topical toys may have been rooted in the ambiguities of the *bürgerliche* domestic ideology, they also participated in the increasing spectacle of German social life, with paradoxical consequences. In one respect, topicality encouraged a sort of disaggregation of experience. The emotions and values of German family life were joined in an uneasy alliance with the dynamism and visual mobility encouraged by retailers and toy makers alike. The restless reference to current events among toys, efforts to force a shifting reality into specific forms, resembled the practices of the rising tabloid press.[128]

The accelerating pace and increasing complexity of modernity overwhelmed the ability of the individual to survey and comprehend the experiential world. In the place of coherence arose a cacophony of discrete voices, ideas without reference to one another, fragments. Events, individuals, things (e.g., the Russo-Japanese War, Robert Peary, and airplanes) were taken out of the flow of reality, made distinct and, consequently, special. Once they were isolated, made special, they were easily turned into spectacles, for spectacle and fragmentation are inextricably linked. Spectacle is based on the discrete individual or event that stands outside everyday reality. Spectacle celebrates that unique, isolated phenomenon: it intensifies its particularity. The result was a steady erosion of context. In the toy world, wars did not have causes, consequences, or even casualties; they just were. The "life" of the toy came to parallel the life of the flaneur as described by Zygmunt Bauman, "[a] string of episodes without history and without consequence."[129] Toys represented reality in much the same way as did department stores' show windows: both were self-contained, ahistorical, and designed for visual consumption.

Toys, like many other consumer goods, picked up where advertising and modern retailing left off. Gradually, consumer goods began to convert themselves, their own forms, into items of visual consumption. Modernity entails the increasing dominance of vision over the other senses, for "industrial modernity transformed human perception."[130] Shoppers could be "just looking." Stores emphasized lighting, show windows, and facades. Toys emphasized the education imparted by their images, not the invisible functioning of the imagination. In this way, vision came to supersede experience. Toys and the forms that they took were caught up in a general cultural trend toward visual spectacle. Toys were meant as much (perhaps more) to be seen as to be used. The incentives that guided and structured toy production and toy retailing, as well as the particular cultural task of Christmas, all tended to privilege moving, mechanized toys. Playthings, made by large companies, ought to catch the eye and immediately seize the attention of viewers. They should also reflect some small, reified niche of the world. In this world, experience and imagination were values honored in the breach. Miniaturized simulacra were to offer children vicarious experience.

As shall be clear later in this study, visual spectacle and deceptive surfaces bereft of deeper purpose of meaning were perceived by many Germans as a problem basic to modern life, not just to toys. Toys did, however, simultaneously suggest a provisional means of overcoming a splintered reality. Whatever parents may have intended, children were able to craft new contexts—new stories—around their reified slices of life. They used their creative faculties to embed their toys in an imagined context. Toys, then, simultaneously reified a distinctly middle-class world and permitted the souls of children to animate and enforce their own order. That order, as should be clear, was one conditioned by the norms and ideals of bourgeois life. Children could create new variations on their *bürgerliche* lifeworld. The creativity and imagination of the child at play could overcome the fragmented spectacle fostered by the toy market.

Class Consumption

Thus far, this chapter has looked primarily at the manner in which the toy market reacted to certain needs in the early twentieth-century *bürgerliche* family and family ideology. Did this mean that members of the working class were left out? Ingeborg Weber-Kellermann argues, "according to cautious estimates," that in 1900 only 20–25 percent of children "were well provided [*wohlversorgt*] with commercial toys," while 75–80 percent "had to do without such things."[131] There is an ambiguity in this statement, given that children are either "well provided" with toys or had none. This is also a difficult question to assess as there are no relevant statistics and because memoirists (hardly a reliable statistical sample in any case) often mention toys only in passing, if at all. If toys go unmentioned in a memoir, however, it cannot be simply assumed that the writer had no toys. Any conclusion must therefore be tentative. Nonetheless, it appears to me that it is overly pessimistic to argue that 75–80 percent of children had to do without commercial toys in 1900. For the mid-nineteenth century, such estimates are more credible, but by 1900, toys were genuine mass-consumption goods, reaching across class lines to the bulk of the population. Members of the working class could afford some toys, and representatives of the workers assumed that they were active toy consumers.

The toy industry believed very passionately that it not only could but had to reach lower-class consumers. Toy makers sought to bring toy prices down to a level where many people could buy them, thereby increasing their sales. The business strategy of much of the industry was predicated on drastically cutting prices to expand sales. How successful were the producers at reducing costs? The Berlin store Wilhelm Stein advertised in 1899 that it had toy soldiers for twenty-three pfennig and toy trains for ninety-five pfennig. In 1900, A. Jandorf had toy soldiers between five and forty-five pfennig.[132] In 1902, Bing had a laterna magica (the Gnome) on the market for fifty pfennig. They also had a model steam engine for ninety pfennig.[133] In 1908, Lineal toy soldiers were available for forty pfennig and a windup streetcar for eighty-five pfennig; and a windup Zeppelin could be had for ninety pfennig at Hermann Tietz in Berlin.[134] In 1909, Wertheim in Berlin advertised twenty-five-centimeter-long dolls for forty pfennig, thirty-centimeter-long dolls for seventy-five pfennig, and a windup train with tracks for eighty-five pfennig.[135] The Hermann Kurtz toy store in Stuttgart had wooden blocks and complete Noah's arks, both for fifty pfennig.[136]

There were a variety toys available for under a mark. This is not to say that an extra mark was always easy to find for working-class families. For many workers at the turn of the twentieth century, however, it was possible to at least enter the marketplace for toys once a year, at Christmas. This was particularly true with the first child, as there was only one child for whom to buy and as young working-class couples were sometimes able to entrust the first child to a grandparent so that the mother could continue to work outside the home.[137] Skilled workers could probably buy toys on a more regular basis.[138] A statistical study of 522 working-class families in 1906, by Werner Conze and Ulrich Engelhardt, clearly suggests that some turn-of-the-century workers could have afforded toys priced under a mark. Conze and Engelhardt's sample averaged 21.23 marks spent annually on "amusement" (not including alcohol) and a further 67.19 marks spent annually on "miscellaneous" expenses.[139] Offering further implicit proof of my argument, *Vorwärts* repeatedly wrote as if a Christmas toy was a typical part of working-class lives. Its discussion of military toys after the 1907 election and the Zabern affair was predicated on the assumption that workers bought toys. *Vorwärts* also reported that the Berlin Christmas market was increasingly for the lower classes.[140] Likewise, *Vorwärts* announcements of collections of toys for locked-out workers[141] would have been illogical if workers were not assumed to have toys to give and if a Christmas without toys as gifts were not thought of as a form of unusual deprivation. The writers and editors of *Vorwärts* clearly considered it normal for workers to buy toys as Christmas gifts for their children. This trend not only reflected the increasing security of at least skilled workers but also a gradual, cultural embourgeoisement of the working class. They, too, had to work to overcome the fault lines between family and family ideology. Or, rather, the gap between their working-class reality and the *bürgerliche* domestic ideal had narrowed sufficiently that Christmas could, for a time, bridge it. That toys were reaching working-class consumers suggests as well that a true mass-consumption market that spanned class divides was forming. This is not to suggest that working-class toy consumption was driven by Veblenesque social competition. Rather, like *bürgerliche* parents, workers were looking for toys to perform cultural labor.

Toys were not limited to the low price range sketched previously in this discussion. In fact, in the years after 1900, the most perceptible trend in the prices of toys was for the top of the line to become still more elaborate and expensive. For example, Bing steam-powered trains ranged from 3.25 marks to 46.00 marks in 1902, from 2.15 to 117.25 marks in 1908, and from 3.60 to 192.00 marks in 1912. For electric trains, we see a similar trend, though in this case there was also an important trend downward in price for the cheapest versions, reflecting improving technology. Thus, the range was from 16.50 to 42.00 marks in 1902, from 13.00 to 90.00 marks in 1908, and from 3.80 to 115.00 marks in 1912.[142] Märklin trains showed a similar trend.[143] The expanding economy and growing wealth of the upper classes made luxury toys increasingly desirable and economically viable. Even as the forms toys took proliferated, so did their ability to represent social stratification. Therefore, the gap between upper and lower classes in the years before World War I was manifested less in who had toys and who did not than in what kind of toys a family might have—whether a few, cheap toys passed from child to child or an annually replenished stock of expensive playthings. There is therefore little reason to believe that the working class sought to "ape" those higher in the social scale, although many wealthy families apparently did seek social differentiation through toys.

Demand for toys was structured by the tensions within the ideal of domesticity. These tensions were ultimately rooted in certain incompatibilities in the middle-class vision of the individual—as inherently unique and authentic but also the product of relentless discipline and education. These ambivalent ideals were, in turn, frustrated by practice. In an effort to manage these tensions, holidays (particularly Christmas) were pressed into service. Holidays became moments in which ideology became lived reality, when external pressures on the domestic ideal could be ignored. Since toys were overwhelmingly purchased for these moments, the logic to which they responded was the holiday logic of reconciling virtues—enjoyment and education, love and obligation. To that end, the toys subordinated education to enjoyment in the interest of reaffirming the loving relationship between parent and child. Nonetheless, education and long-term obligations could not be entirely ignored by good, *bürgerliche* parents. Educational benefits were widely attributed to toys, but with little attempt to establish that they were in fact educational. That these claims required little substantiation—that parents were content to understand education as topicality—reflected the function that toys served. Education was largely a side benefit. The imperative of enjoyment often ran in the same direction as the structural trends in production and retail. Particularly attractive for many children were toys that moved under their own power. Toys able to animate themselves and move as if alive exerted a certain magic. They could thrill the (male) child immediately. That producers were making these items both increasingly affordable and increasingly "magical" merely made them more attractive. At the same time, retailers chose, for their own reasons, to feature these items in particular. Had consumers not been receptive, however, retailers' efforts would have been for naught. Though consumers helped fuel the rise of the moving technology toy, they also preserved many nonmoving, traditional toys. Board games, dolls, and tin figurines proved to be equally adept at satisfying the competing demands placed on modern toys, unifying entertainment and *bürgerliche* virtues and thereby propping up otherwise weak producers. Toy consumers structured the toy market in response to their own needs, tacitly negotiating an industrial structure with producers and retailers.

2. Making the Toys, Making the Industry

Structuring Production

In the mountains of the Erzgebirge, the toy-making process began with a man and what strongly resembled oversized wooden nickels. The man, burdened with his disks of wood, went to the lathe works. A largish building with a smallish steam engine, the lathe works was quite possibly the most important structure in the village. There, the man took the bench and lathe that he had arranged to rent for the day. Seated at his bench, next to other men with similar intent, the man shaped his wood. A hole appeared in the center of his disk. The surrounding donut of wood was then shaped so that the wood appeared to have rather unlikely waves in it. The process was then repeated and repeated.

Still burdened with his disks of wood, the man left the lathe works and returned home, to a small cottage with a kitchen, a common area, and a single bedroom, surrounded by a small garden. This home also doubled as a workshop, and there the crew was put to work. The man cut narrow sections out of his donuts, giving them a three-dimensional individuality. He then swiftly made a few additional cuts before handing the piece to his wife, who sat next to him. The woman (using the delicate skill alleged to be inherent in the hands of females) chiseled and sanded the crude piece into what was now discernibly a small wooden horse. When she was satisfied with the physical form, the woman surrendered the piece to one of her several children. That child, seated at a small table with her siblings, immediately commenced staining and painting the wooden horse. The practiced hand of the youngster worked quickly. Soon the horse was set out to dry, and she turned to the next piece and the next.[1]

In the wooded hills around Sonneberg, the process was considerably more complex. It began with the *Bossierer* (embosser or assembler) issuing a chain of orders. The papier-mâché maker received an order for bodies, arms, and legs. When he had turned his special mix into hard, light body parts, the papier-mâché maker sent them to back to the *Bossierer.* One of the small porcelain factories had meanwhile received an order for the heads. Once the heads were completed, they were sent not back to the *Bossierer* but, rather, to the eye setter, who had himself solicited the eyes from a glassblower who worked out of his cottage in a nearby village. Once in possession of both heads and eyes, the eye setter created eyes that would open or close, depending on the angle of the head relative to the earth's gravitational field. These heads were then sent back to the *Bossierer.*

The *Bossierer,* however, was not yet ready for assembly. The heads had first to be sent back out to the "barber," who placed hair (generally mohair) on the head. When the *Bossierer* received his coiffed heads from the barber, he was ready. He rapidly painted and lacquered the pieces and assembled them into a whole doll. The doll was then sent to the clothing crew, generally a group of women assembled and directed by the *Bossierer*'s wife. Soon enough, a completed doll was ready to be packaged and delivered.[2]

In the industrial city of Nuremberg, the process looked entirely different. Even between the different makers in Nuremberg, it looked very different. In one shop, the process began with the subtle hands of a sculptor, the one who created the form. The form was then used to produce a mold in brass or slate. Then, molten metal (generally a compound of metals heavy on lead) was poured into the molds, which were connected by thin channels. Once the metal cooled, the pieces were taken out and "cleaned"; that is, the stems created by the channels were taken off. The pieces were then divided up and sent out of the foundry to be painted. Painting the tiny leaden figurines, most likely soldiers from some foreign or ancient land, was delicate, time-consuming work. To keep up with the molds, a large number of women were required. These women collected the figurines and took them home, where they laboriously painted each piece, between and after the various other calls on their time. Once they finished their batch of figures, the women returned them to the foundry and collected new ones.[3]

Another shop looked very different. There, in a large building with a large steam engine and electrical lighting, troops of men and women began with offset lithography. Sheets of dull metal entered the machine and emerged brightly, if chaotically, painted. The metal then traveled from desk to desk, machine to machine. Men armed with saws, presses, punches, and lathes set to work on the metal, shaping it along the precise lines lithographed onto the metal. Meanwhile, another part of the building was doing the delicate work of constructing tiny steam engines. These masterpieces of miniaturization—complete with boiler, condenser, heating unit, and alcohol tank (the fuel)—would then be installed in the locomotive taking shape. Finally, the completed locomotive (wagons were sold separately) was packaged in-house and delivered to the distributor.[4]

Toys are not products of nature. As the preceding sketches have shown, they are fashioned by human hands. Those hands in the Erzgebirge, in Sonneberg, and in Nuremberg developed extremely heterogeneous ways of fabricating toys. This is a simple observation of considerable importance. The production of German toys was increasingly influenced by the emergence of the mass market. This chapter therefore analyzes the economic foundations and implications of mass consumption. It will explore how the needs and expectations of consumers interacted with the techniques and organization of production. The emergence of mass consumption was dependent on the construction of an industry capable of manufacturing toys extremely cheaply while continuing to generate variety in form. The German toy industry adapted to the challenge with a variety of strategies. One strategy was through mechanization. However, this was not the only strategy. This chapter will examine the multiple strategies available to toy makers in the late nineteenth and early twentieth centuries as they struggled to both construct and adapt to a mass market. The possibility of cross-class consumption, as well as the multiplicity of forms demanded by toy buyers, shaped what was possible and not possible for toy makers.

All German toy producers responded to four distinct sets of structuring incentives: technologies and structures of distribution, consumer demand, production technologies, and labor. These structuring incentives created a series of limits and opportunities that shaped the strategies that producers pursued and the forms that the industry took. They were not hard-and-fast limits on the possible but, rather, paths of greater or lesser resistance. They were also not all of equal significance, nor was the significance of each necessarily stable over time. As conditions changed in one area, the relative weight of all could shift. The emergence of metalworking machinery in Nuremberg, for example, not only increased the significance of production technologies but also had tremendous implications for labor and, eventually, the state. This chapter will first address these four sets of incentives in general terms, before turning to a closer examination of how the three industrial districts reacted to these emerging structures.

After examining the material impact of mass consumption on the toy industry, I shall turn to explore how toy makers functioned as almost cultural mediators. In their efforts to develop desirable products, toy makers were compelled to elaborate ideas about the nature and desires of their consumers. They constructed an idealized vision of their consumers. In seeking to minister to the demands of the idealized toy buyer, the toy industry intervened in German cultural life. An implicit vision of the human individual shaped their production of form and would become one of several competing visions of humanity and modernity.

The critical historical context for this discussion was the so-called Great Depression of the nineteenth century—a somewhat contradictory period. After recovering from the genuine and prolonged recession of 1873–79, the world economy entered into a period of relatively slow growth. The following decade and a half was marked by continued expansion of industrial production but also falling prices, prompting one historian to suggest alternatively calling the period the "Great Deflation."[5] This period was one of perceived crisis for the industry. As for many sectors of the economy, the toy industry struggled mightily with declining prices. Falling prices put enormous pressure on profits and were both a catalyst for and a result of increased production. In fact, the deflation was in part a function of an emerging mass market connected by railroads and sustained by transformed industries. Only with this in mind can one make sense of the various factors that shaped the toy industry. The dominant trend in the toy industry was indeed the effort to master the mass market that emerged in the 1880s and 1890s. This effort of adaptation shaped the industry and the lives of those in it. As we shall see, the specific structures of this market also shaped what was produced and at what relative prices.

Distribution

In the latter half of the nineteenth century, distribution underwent a profound transformation that is too often overlooked. It was in part technological and infrastructural, the familiar story of railroads and packet steamers. It also, however, involved exploding cities and evolving networks of merchant middlemen.

During the course of the nineteenth century, transportation costs had plummeted. The rapid expansion of canals, roads, and then railroads, steamships, and telegraphs had transformed the framework of global business. Particularly after the main rail lines were completed in Europe and North America in the 1860s and 1870s, the cost of delivering products worldwide tumbled. From 1880, moreover, shipping costs declined precipitously over the next thirty years, falling by nearly a third for transatlantic freight.[6] Declining shipping costs were an important factor enabling production for lower social circles. This also enabled the concentration of production in a relatively small area that would then service a substantial portion of the global economy. Coordinating such extended markets was only possible with the use of telegraphs.[7] The dramatic improvement in transportation allowed German toy makers to rapidly expand existing trade links with Britain and the United States, their two principal markets at least as early as the 1880s.

The influence that this infrastructure of distribution exerted on producers was increased by the parallel process of urbanization. As the economist Walter Troeltsch pointed out in 1899, urbanization concentrated consumers, particularly working-class consumers, and that concentration made it far easier for producers and distributors to reach large numbers of them. Troeltsch explains that the profitability of centrally produced mass-consumption goods became greater since less effort and money had to be expended getting products into the hands of the consumer.[8] Since the costs of distribution were dramatically reduced, it became profitable to service urban markets of consumers who were not necessarily wealthier than their isolated, rural cousins. In addition, as the sociologist Georg Simmel wrote in 1900, the move from rural, agricultural life to urban, industrial life meant an entry into an exclusively money economy. Exchanges that might have once stayed within the family or have been on a barter basis became money transactions. Consequently, compensation in the urban economy included more money, while rural workers often received a higher proportion of payment in kind. As Simmel explains, of two consumers with similar standards of living, one rural and one urban, the urban consumer likely had more money and thus could choose to buy a toy that a rural peasant might have to make.[9]

As a result of these two trends (declining transportation costs and urbanization), the number of consumers that the toy industry could reach at a manageable financial cost increased enormously. Distant

New York could become a much more important market for Nuremberg than was nearby Bamberg. The infrastructure that made mass production a reasonable business strategy was rapidly developing. This infrastructure could not help but affect how and for whom toys were made.

Equally significant for many producers was the commercial structure of distribution. The distribution system was based on a network of merchant middlemen who had developed links across much of the globe in the decades—even the century—previous. These merchants performed a variety of functions that enabled the many small toy makers of Germany to participate in a global mass market.

Distribution began when the toy producers delivered their finished products to the merchant middleman. But the activities of those merchants began much earlier. In the case of the Nuremberg toy industry, the process began as early as December, when the new models for the Christmas of the following year were unveiled by the toy makers. The merchants inspected these models and agreed on a price and delivery conditions. The merchant then arranged for customers—either retailers or other merchants—to see these models. The viewing could be done in a Nuremberg showroom or could be arranged by a traveling salesman.[10]

The locus classicus of this negotiation process, however, was the Leipzig Easter Fair (*Leipziger Ostermesse*), held every year during the second week in March. Leipzig had long been the site of relatively frequent fairs dedicated largely to East-West trade. Merchants had brought their wares directly to these periodic markets and bargain there with customers. As communications improved and the volume of trade increased, however, the fair entered into a decline. It was no longer necessary or desirable to haul one's wares to Leipzig to sell them to a merchant from Minsk or Manchester. The organizers therefore reduced the number of fairs each year to two, one in March and one in September. The reduction in the number of meetings signaled a profound change in function. The Leipzig fairs were no longer actual marketplaces. Goods were much less likely to change hands at the fair itself. The product that was traded at the fair had become information. The fair brought together buyers and sellers from around the world, briefly uniting a world market in one place. The fundamental transformation of the European economy was starkly visible in the changing Leipzig market. The volume of trade and efficiency of transportation as well as the scale of industrial production made the age-old commercial fair more than superfluous. When the format was altered to emphasize trading market information, however, the Leipzig fair became again relevant.[11] Trading had to be detached from the physical presence of the products if a mass market was to develop.

When a deal had been reached, the orders went back to the producers, then the process of production began. Deliveries to the merchant could be made on any day, but in Sonneberg at least, the usual delivery day was Saturday. Among cottage industrialists, such as those encountered at the opening of this chapter, the deliveries themselves were generally made by the children or aged members of the producers' family, so that the more able-bodied could continue production. For outlying villages, the delivery could involve up to a three-hour walk to and from the merchant's collection point. To ease the burden, the delivery was occasionally put on a crude wagon pulled by dogs.[12]

Cash was paid on delivery to the merchant. In this manner, the merchants greased the financial skids of the entire toy industry. Though the middlemen largely paid cash to producers upon receipt of the order, they themselves might not be paid for a month or sometimes three months. Thus, the merchant middlemen always covered the cost of delayed payment through the lines of credit they maintained with local banks. To offset the cost of their line of credit, they demanded a discount on cash payments. The producer therefore paid a substantial portion—perhaps even more than the time value—of the money outlaid for the toys.[13] Nonetheless, the merchants commanded much better credit than the small producers. One of the greatest liabilities experienced by cottage industrialists was their inability to access capital. The merchants provided them with indirect access to limited amounts of capital. This system required a great deal of financial liquidity on the part of merchants and banks. Expenses tended to come en masse in a season, and the payments to cover those expenses might not arrive for months. The small toy producer, needing to cover the expenses related to production, might not be able to wait months for eventual payment. To pay their own expenses, they needed that cash sooner rather than later.[14]

Changing technology restructured how and when middlemen approached toy producers. The merchants had traditionally ordered items themselves for their own inventory and had then sought to sell these products to others. Improving transportation and communication technology, however, led to a rapid decline of that practice. In the 1880s and 1890s, merchants began to issue orders to toy makers only after the merchants themselves had firm contracts in hand.[15]

This seemingly mundane change fundamentally altered the business of the merchant. Before, the *Verleger* (the local merchants who "put out" orders for production to local cottage industrialists) had performed a vital service in finding customers for producers, but they had also assumed a great deal of risk for the producers. If buyers were not found, the merchant had suffered; the producers were relieved of substantial market risk. As the *Verleger* became essentially the communicators of orders, however, their business changed subtly but enormously. They were no longer independent merchants; they no longer traded in risk. Rather, they had become service providers. Their services included such details as packaging, freight, and, in the case of exports, negotiating customs regulations with authorities.[16] The increased efficiency in communicating orders contributed to the growth of mass production. Moving away from buying on their own account meant decreasing warehousing costs. It also meant that a risk premium was no longer necessary. The middlemen did not need to charge extra to cover the possibility that some of their inventory might not be sold. Consequently, prices could come down for reasons unconnected to production.

More critically, the merchant middlemen bundled both supply and demand. Bundling made possible the decentralized networks examined later in this chapter. The merchant middlemen assembled orders from small retailers into larger groups. Once collected in this larger aggregation, they became much more attractive to producers. The costs of setting up a production line for an order of a few dozen bells or whistles outweighed any conceivable profit. Once bundled with a number of such orders, the prospect became much more attractive, since fixed costs could be shared out among a number of products. The merchants also bundled small producers together, allowing these smaller entrepreneurs to participate in the mass market. This function was particularly evident in the Sonneberg and Erzgebirge regions. The woodworkers and doll makers of these uplands could not individually produce nearly enough to satisfy a large order. A *Verleger* was able to fulfill that order by dividing that order among many producers. The same process was seen in Nuremberg as well. How was a producer with four employees to make fifty thousand tin mice on wheels, which children could push around the floor? That producer could not, but if that producer worked in conjunction with several other producers, the order could be filled.

The merchant also bundled models. A small producer might have developed six new models for a season. Most retailers wanted many more than six new types of toys. The merchant was able to present retailers with a huge variety of models and then farm the orders back to producers. In this manner, the communication process between retailer and producer was enormously simplified. Rather than having to pour through proposals from hundreds of producers, the retailer had a handful of contacts, without losing anything in the way of product variety.[17]

The merchant middlemen were pivotal in the promotion of the mass market that the railroads and cities were bringing into existence. They also protected smaller producers. This "protective" role is ironic—some would even say debatable. The middlemen were strongly criticized for their exploitative relationship with producers. For example, Karl Rosenhaupt relates that these merchants would seek out uneducated small masters and promise them an order of one thousand marks if they would deliver at a low price per unit, but only later did these craftspeople realize that the large gross did not mean that a profit margin necessarily existed.[18] An observer of the Sonneberg industry even accused the merchants of maintaining a truck system.[19]

The collapsing transportation costs associated with the railroads enabled the German toy industry to get its products to market at competitive prices across the globe. The many small producers within that industry, however, were only able to take advantage of those opportunities because they were able to use a preexisting network of merchant middlemen. These middlemen performed a variety of functions that made it possible for small producers to engage a global marketplace. The merchants bundled models, suppliers, and buyers and thereby enabled small producers to effectively service enormous markets. They also created long-term personal relationships that enabled far-flung retailers to trust that the products they received from anonymous producers in far-off Germany would be up to their standards.[20] The significance of this global network rested, in turn, on the ability of the toy industry to provide toys that consumers wanted. The ability to deliver products to markets from Austria to Australia did not matter if the toys did not sell.

Consumers

The mass market was not merely a question of geography. The market was not merely spreading across political barriers but expanding across class barriers. The most important dynamic structuring the toy industry between 1870 and 1914 was the effort to create a mass market for toys in societies still largely stricken by poverty. This effort, whether consciously formulated or not, impelled an "insanity of sinking and again sinking prices" lamented by sociologist Emmanuel Sax,[21] among other observers. Falling transportation costs could only be effectively exploited if toy prices fell as well. In this way, the industry could vastly expand sales. Producers sought to balance declining prices against increased sales, a delicate undertaking in the best of times.

"[M]ost producers strive to produce wares that are suitable for the masses, . . . the great department stores seek articles that are appropriate for the little man on the income scale. The little man whose income is under fifteen hundred marks is the one . . . who causes the trend toward cheapness."[22] So argued the *Bayerische Gewerbe-Zeitung* in 1896. Fifteen hundred marks was generous. Indeed, average wages before 1900 often remained well below one thousand marks a year.[23] Nonetheless, as the statistics cited in chapter 1 suggest, some workers at the turn of the twentieth century could have afforded toys priced under a mark: the sample averaged 21.23 marks spent annually on "amusement" (not including alcohol) and a further 67.19 marks spent annually on "miscellaneous" expenses.[24] These figures strongly suggest that by the late nineteenth century, many workers were in a position to buy toys for their children—provided that those toys were quite inexpensive. One sign of the increasing participation of workers in limited consumption was the development of low-cost retailers, such as the so-called fifty-pfennig bazaars. The Nuremberg *Handelskammer* complained in 1887:

> Another unpleasant development in the domestic market is the ever expanding establishments called bazaars. These ease the sale of cheaper and therefore often very badly constructed products. They condition the public . . . to very low prices, which considerably limits the sales of solid and lasting products. Increasingly products are forced into the price range of the bazaars at the cost of their quality, only to make room for other, still worse prod-

> ucts, to the disadvantage of producers and merchants, as well as consumers, who get certainly a cheap product, but also one that will not last long and has little taste.[25]

A parallel demand for variety and *Neuheiten* (novelties) developed among toy consumers. Variety and novelty were very much related to the mass market as well. Toy makers hoped to appeal to every conceivable taste, every possible desire, so as to maximize sales. Additionally, if parents were to be expected to buy new toys every Christmas, a wide variety of products was advisable. The industry had also to continually add models to ensure that new fashions and new desires did not escape their net. In that way, the industry also continually added to the variety of products on offer. *Billige Neuheiten* (cheap novelties) were the order of the day. Consequently, in 1882, the Nuremberg *Handelskammer* observed that both large and small producers were working very hard to create toys that were continually new and affordable. In 1883, the *Handelskammer* added: "[A] portion of our industry is dependent on the construction of the same old articles; another part is dependent on the production of annual novelties. In general the latter is more prosperous than the former."[26]

That most potential consumers could not afford expensive toys forced producers to cut costs, even as they expanded the variety of toys available. The prevailing attitude was that if the cost and novelty imperatives could only be satisfied to the detriment of quality, so be it. The Nuremberg *Handelskammer* lamented: "[P]eoples who earlier had the same needs for decades now demand novelties every year, almost every season. No wonder that through this all stability disappears and in the place of a calm, solid living grows a haste, pressure, and haggling on all sides and, in consequence of that, frequently a rapid deterioration of the products."[27] The situation in the Erzgebirge and Sonneberg was little different. For example, the Dresden *Handelskammer,* meditating on the difficulties of the Erzgebirge cottage industrialists, observed:

> [T]he stagnation of the toy industry . . . also naturally comes from the competition from other German toy-producing regions and foreigners, who, as modern times demand, come to market every year with new, attractively formed, and play appropriate [*dem Spielzweck angepaßten*] novelties . . . In this point are the local

> merchants . . . to a certain degree also responsible for the decline of the industry, insofar as they did not sufficiently promote the creation of new models.[28]

Taken together, the reports of the Nuremberg and Dresden *Handelskammer* leave little doubt that toy producers across Germany felt themselves pushed to simultaneously reduce prices and accelerate the production of new models in order to appeal to the "little man." The marketplace demanded particular wares from toy makers, wares that demanded adjustments on the part of those toy makers.

Most contemporary observers agreed that the pressure on prices and constant product innovation was the result of overproduction. They asserted that a number of anomalies in the structure of the industry had a disastrous effect on the earnings of producers. Too many people were entering the market with relatively few skills and often absolutely no sense for business. The influx of partially trained producers was encouraged by the industry's low barriers to entry, particularly the fact that at most only a few hundred marks were required in up-front capital to establish one's own business.[29] These producers were dependent on sales in a narrow and highly competitive market niche, making them desperate and exacerbating their inability to properly calculate costs. If they did not earn enough to live on from that niche of the toy market, they did not have the skills or training to make up for that shortfall by turning to making other types of toys. To this was added the narrowed marketplace as a result of protectionist trade policies. The result was a rush to accept any and all contracts without properly analyzing costs and the limitations of time.

This argument had some strong points, linking the structure of the industry and labor to the level of competition and then linking competition to prevailing price levels. It is, nonetheless, inadequate, because it treats demand as a static constant. The toy industry continued to expand in terms of both overall production volume and absolute number of production units. If, as many contemporaries suggested, tariff barriers established in the late 1870s and early 1880s had decisively increased competition among producers and thereby undermined their well-being, it would seem odd that the number and size of producers expanded. Was not their argument predicated on the assumption that protectionism was reducing sales? Production volumes could have grown through escalating levels of self-exploitation on the part of small-scale producers (the *Heimarbeiter,* discussed later in this chapter), through their working longer and driving their families harder, but why were the number of enterprises increasing? If these figures were unambiguously marching toward the dustheap of history, why did the younger generation not flee to the cities in larger numbers? The industry could support more enterprises and could keep the younger generation employed because falling prices produced growing sales among the lower classes around the world.

While competition forced prices downward, reduced prices were sustainable because the industry was also tapping into a growing consumer base, the "little man on the income scale." To fit into the limited budgets of the majority of consumers, toys had to be exceedingly inexpensive. They had to be still cheaper if many consumers were to be able to purchase multiple toys, a new toy for each child at least once a year at a time when large families were the norm. As the toy industry brought prices down (whether through mechanization, superior organization, or self-exploitation), demand grew, permitting the size and number of producers to likewise grow. In this respect, the toy market strongly resembled the harmonica market as described by Hartmut Berghoff: "The transition to mass production [in the 1880s] and the associated price reductions led in no way to the satisfaction of existing demand but, rather, to the boundless expansion of demand well beyond existing supply."[30]

The difficulties faced by the toy industry in the 1880s were largely the result of the efforts of toy producers to adapt to a mass market. They did not suffer from declining orders, the classic sign of recession and depression. In fact, a great deal of business was being done. The Nuremberg *Handelskammer* observed, "[I]t is unbelievable what masses must be produced and sold to secure the producer merely a moderate, passable life."[31] There were orders aplenty as the German toy industry adapted to the opportunities and demands of an increasingly socially diverse and global market. The problem that producers encountered was the declining prices that they received, declining prices necessary to tap a mass market. Toy makers struggled to find ways to cut costs in order to tap into ever larger numbers of consumers. How to cut costs was, however, a question fraught with uncertainty.

Production Technologies

Cutting prices made toys affordable for the "little man" and made it possible to construct a mass market. The question confronting producers was how to increase volume and cut costs without sacrificing profitability. The toy industry had little control over its material factor costs. Even the largest toy makers were too small to pressure their raw material suppliers into offering lower prices. Indeed, the prices of many raw materials were rising. If raw material costs could not be reduced, labor costs had to be. One means of cutting labor costs was to increase the productivity of labor through mechanization. One could also seek a more rational, efficient division of labor. Alternatively, one could cut the remuneration offered labor. The decisions made regarding these three strategies in large part framed the very different structures of the three industrial regions under consideration in the present discussion. The ultimate factual existence of a mass market would depend on the success of toy makers in cutting costs and prices.

Throughout the toy industry, producers were increasingly faced with a dilemma. How and to what degree should one employ machines? There were definite costs associated with mechanizing. Machines cost money, and investing in them meant investing in the uncertain hope of earning larger returns at some future point in time. The costs were measurable, while the returns were less so. As some producers were to learn, however, the costs of not mechanizing could be immeasurably greater.

The value of machines was clearly recognized by the metalworking branch of the toy industry. These industrialists praised, for example, the 1879 Exhibition of the Association of German Sheetmetal Workers (Ausstellung des Vereins deutscher Blecharbeiter) for the machinery displayed there: "[The exhibition] was of great value on account of the exhibited machines and appliances, which were widely bought and ordered. It will be possible to make many articles more attractively and faster than was the case before if the possession of these machines becomes more general. Then there will again be more activity in the entire branch."[32] The well-being of the entire branch was early seen in its mechanization. Those that failed to mechanize suffered accordingly, as the *Handelskammer* pointed out in 1879.[33]

The 1879 exhibition pointed out a critical advantage enjoyed by Nuremberg in the production of metal toys. Nuremberg was a nationally significant center of metalworking industries. This implied a dense support network and intellectual inspiration for the application of metalworking machinery to the production of toys. Sonneberg and the Erzgebirge did not have metalworking exhibitions, let alone engineers, repairmen, and salesmen. In the production of metal toys, Nuremberg therefore enjoyed a distinct advantage from its social geography, the network of human skills and interests that happened to geographically coincide with the Nuremberg toy industry.[34]

Otto Senst illustrated the meaning of mechanization with the story of one particular small-time toy maker. Senst interviewed an "industrialist" who produced small bells for use on toys made by other producers. His price was sixty pfennig for 240 bells. A competitor purchased a special machine for making small bells. The machine cost him twelve thousand marks, the market value of approximately 4.8 million bells. The machine allowed the competitor to sell 240 bells for forty-eight pfennig. The business of the first producer then declined considerably because the marketplace had been altered by the machinery of the second. Why did the first toy maker simply not follow suit? Senst does not know for certain, writing only that the first could not or would not acquire a similar appliance.[35]

While some production systems can realize considerable economies of scale by centralizing them, others would realize substantial diseconomies of scale were they to be similarly centralized.[36] The toy makers of Sonneberg and the Erzgebirge, as we shall see, employed far less machinery, in part because they did not enjoy the infrastructural advantages granted their Nuremberg counterparts. The great technological developments of the machine tool industry also disproportionately effected metalwork as opposed to leather, wood, or papier-mâché. Were the various wood-carvers of the Erzgebirge to be centralized in one factory, there would have been a substantial increase in overhead costs with no improvement in labor efficiency. As a consequence, the other toy makers had to find alternative strategies that addressed the needs of the customers, products, and technologies.

*Labor**

In the middle and late nineteenth century, the deployment of labor in the German toy industry depended enormously on the nature of the product and the level of mechanization. I will therefore spend rather more time discussing the structures of labor when I turn shortly to look specifically at the three regions under consideration in this chapter. For

*Portions of this section and the remaining sections of this chapter were published previously in "Flexible Specialization and the German Toy Industry, 1870–1914," *Social History* 29, no. 1 (February 2004): 30–40. They appear here with the kind permission of the editors and publishers of *Social History* (www.tandf.co.uk).

the moment, I would like to sketch the outlines of the cottage industrial form that many toy producers used in the mid-nineteenth century, as well as make some comments on who was working.

The majority of toy makers in the Erzgebirge and Sonneberg and some in Nuremberg remained quite small-scale producers, generally called *Heimarbeiter* by their contemporaries. Jürgen Kocka offers a useful definition of *Heimarbeit.* Although our toy makers often strayed from Kocka's definition, it is an adequate characterization to elucidate a major form of labor in the toy industry. Kocka argues that *Heimarbeiter* share the following characteristics:

(1) Clear limitations on the independence of the producers because of their dependence on the merchant-*Verleger*
   - Production is exclusively for a single, previously established buyer.
   - This buyer, and only this buyer, provides raw materials or parts.
   - The producer owns his or her own tools, but the buyer can determine the manner and order of labor.
   - Work is done in small work units, as a rule in the home or in space rented by the producer without the presence of the buyer.

(2) Production for markets outside the immediate vicinity
(3) The possibility of employing family members or nonfamily workers to work side by side with the producer/owner[37]

Kocka's definition emphasizes that although *Heimarbeiter* produced for a geographically dispersed market, they nonetheless existed in a highly circumscribed marketplace. Access to orders, material, and consumers was limited by a powerful merchant, and the labor market was shaped by dependence on the nonwage labor extracted from the producer and his family.

This cottage industrial system would develop in several directions within the industry, in response to the incentives I have already outlined. It could be used to reduce the factor cost of labor without thorough mechanization, through alternative or simultaneous specialization and superior organization and/or through cutting the remuneration of labor. The linkage between toys and cottage industry was strong in part precisely because cottage industry could evolve in several directions. It could be an ideal system for pushing costs onto the shoulders of labor while simultaneously cutting incomes. The exposure of individual craftspeople to the full power of an unregulated market permitted a sometimes terrifying level of exploitation. In another context, domestic industry easily evolved into a number of small, independent craftspeople who formed a supple, decentralized network of mutually dependent specialists. The *Heimarbeiter* were therefore at the nexus between some of the most brutal forms of capitalist exploitation and the dense networks of financially independent and economically interdependent craftspeople that characterize flexible specialization. Flexible specialization denotes decentralized webs of small- to medium-sized manufacturers that are highly competitive based on the quality and variability of their products. Their competitive advantages are rooted in the skill of the workforce, low capital overhead, project-specific subcontracting, and a variety of social and governmental institutions that socialize risk and other costs.[38] As we turn to look at the regions in more detail, therefore, the development of cottage industry will play a critical role in structuring the toy industry.

It is also important to signpost how the developing mass market for inexpensive toys determined who worked. In many parts of the industry, the price imperative strongly encouraged the use of child labor, particularly the children within the home of the *Heimarbeiter.* These family enterprises often depended on the unpaid labor that was extracted from children. Various halfhearted government initiatives to remedy this were only marginally successful. As a result, the Sonneberg region had some of the highest rates of school delinquency and childhood illness in Germany.[39]

Women, too, were impacted by the price imperative. Cultural assumptions (rather than any rational evaluation of comparative productivity) meant that women were paid considerably less than males: that is to say, the embeddedness of the economy in a cultural system conditioned and framed the calculations of "rational economic man." Women were also assigned specific types of work in accord with culturally defined notions of what forms of labor female bodies were more or less adept at performing. It was an established business practice for women to be paid less for the same labor as men. Women were presumed to be wives and mothers of male workers and therefore not to require the "family wage" a male employee deserved. Moreover, the motivation to enter the workplace was understood to be different for women than for men: men sought jobs both for self-affirmation as males and independent individuals and for a weekly income; women sought employment outside the home only to help others. For working-class families, women's service to others was rendered to one's own poverty-stricken family. These women entered the labor market exclusively for money. As females were "naturally" outside the formal labor market, their entry into that market was perceived as different, as supplementary. Because their labor was not viewed as central to supporting a family, women's wages could morally be kept well below those of men.[40] As a result, it made a great deal of economic sense to employ women in such lonely, semiskilled labor as painting lead figurines. "[M]ale labor is too expensive to make cheap things," wrote Otto Senst.[41]

Consequently, women were employed in a variety of fashions in the toy industry. The toy figures, often soldiers, pouring forth from such companies as Heinrichsen's were distributed among *Heimarbeiterinnen.* These women took the figures home to paint distinctive uniforms on them, finding time to do so at night and in the narrow interstices left by child rearing.[42] This system ensured very low costs for toy makers, based largely on the dual occupations of the female workforce as mother/homemaker and painter. Precisely because the *Heimarbeiterinnen* had two occupations, they could be paid less.

These variables clearly interacted with one another. There was not, however, a uniform outcome across the toy industry. To understand how roughly similar structuring incentives might have produced the radically dissimilar systems of production I sketched at the opening of this chapter, we need to take a much closer look at the three specific regions concerned. The region that followed most closely the usual narratives of industrialization and mass production was Nuremberg. Examining the industrialization of its toy market will allow us to explore the impact of mechanization and will also provide a narrative against which we may compare the contemporary developments in the other regions. Why did Sonneberg and the Erzgebirge differ? Were they backward and premodern? Or did they merely represent alternative forms of adapting to the multiple impulses that defined the toy market?

Nuremberg

Nuremberg was the home of the metal toy. The region's industry was very much influenced by its products, which took innumerable forms, from lead figures of Roman legionnaires to toy ships to laternae magicae. The classic Nuremberg toy was the toy train, which changed in form over time. The original toy trains were unpowered *Bodenläufer*. Soon, windup toys were introduced, followed by genuine steam engines and then electric trains. The electric trains were felt to be a great step forward, since they should have reduced the number of children burned by alcohol-fueled steam engines. The trains developed in two broad paths. One was represented by the *Storchbeine,* an effort that subordinated form to cost considerations. The form was standardized, and the number of wheels (and the consequent complexity of production) were made dependent on the needs of production. Another trend, growing stronger around the turn of the twentieth century, was that of the exact replica. Trains were painstakingly copied from existing engines, such as the Black Prince from Great Britain. Trains were especially profitable because, particularly after Märklin's introduction of standardized tracks in 1890, they were associated with accessories: wagons, train stations, bridges, signs. Toy catalogs soon filled with the accoutrements that generated increasingly complex miniature simulacra of trains and society. Nuremberg's toy industry tamed the growing power of industrial, mechanized society by using the tools of that society to represent it.

How did the Nuremberg industry respond to the bundle of structuring incentives? How did the development of a global mass market comprised mostly of impoverished consumers who largely demanded ever new toys structure the Nuremberg industry? In the middle of the nineteenth century, the Nuremberg toy industry strongly resembled that of Sonneberg and the Erzgebirge. It was dominated by small, family, cottage industrial units that worked overwhelmingly with wood. Already in 1879, however, the wood toy makers of Nuremberg lamented: "[T]he wooden toy makers cannot report any recent expansion of sales; rather, they have declined. It may be that this has its causes principally in that the metal toy industry with its machines builds its metal toys more solidly, more durably, and more cheaply. The bazaars with their low prices have also hurt this everywhere-beloved industry."[43] Because the metal toy industry had machines, it had price and quality advantages over wooden toys and therefore prospered. There were also other, very good reasons for the decline of the wooden toy industry in Nuremberg, particularly the rapidly rising price of wood around Nuremberg and the consequent comparative advantages of Thuringia, the Erzgebirge, and other wood-rich areas. Nonetheless, the metal toy trades exerted a simultaneous pull on those active in the wood trades: in Nuremberg between 1875 and 1895, the number wood toy firms declined from 69 to 60 (a decline of about 13 percent), while the number of metal toy makers more than tripled, jumping from 49 to 154.[44]

The obvious rise to dominance of metal toys in Nuremberg was rooted in the application of modern machinery to toy production. There are several ways of depicting the rise of the machine. One way is in the growing inventory of buildings and power sources. In 1876, for example, the company of Max Dannhorn built a new factory powered by three gas motors with a total of ten horsepower to mass-produce its improved musical tops and trumpets. In 1889, Dannhorn purchased a fifty-horsepower steam engine and renovated its factory to include steam heat and electrical lighting. In 1881, the firm of Jean Schoenner had a single steam engine of six horsepower. Growing demand for its models (steam engines, trains, and ships), its laternae magicae, and so on forced (or allowed) it to add a fifty-horsepower steam engine in 1887. By 1894, that firm, too, had added steam heat and electrical lighting, as well as a loud speaker. Jean Schoenner's production statistics show the effect of this expansion. It produced 495 model steam engines in 1875, 10,225 in 1885, and 575,554 in 1888.[45] Production of laternae magicae by all Nuremberg firms combined increased 23 percent in just four years, from 325,000 in 1891 to 400,000 in 1895.[46]

Around 1890, many Nuremberg firms began to use a process known as offset lithography, representing a significant step toward standardization and increased mechanization. I will here examine lithography more closely as a case study of the process of mechanization generally. Lithography entailed painting/lacquering/decorating the final product at the beginning of the process of fabrication. The design was stamped onto a flat sheet of metal and only then bent, hammered, and twisted into its final shape. This process saved enormously on the cost and time of meticulously painting each piece by hand after it had been made. Lithography thus represented a significant reduction in labor costs. It was, however, quite capital-intensive. Consequently, many smaller firms chose not to establish their own lithographic workshops, instead employing outside lithographers. The smaller toy makers thereby amalgamated lithographic capacity outside the toy companies proper.[47] Lithography had another, indirect result. Since the lines of the final product were laid down before it ever actually saw a hammer or press, the forming of the metal henceforth had to be considerably more exact and regular. The old-fashioned way of shaping sheet metal, involving hammers and wooden forms, was simply out of the question if lithography was to be used.[48] As well as replacing handwork directly, lithography encouraged the mechanization of other labor processes. Märklin, for example, which long lagged in the use of machinery, also long hand-painted its products. Not coincidentally, Märklin products cost more than some competitors. After they introduced lithography for some of their products, lithographed Märklin toys cost less than Märklin's hand-painted ones.[49] The introduction of offset lithography also underlined the self-reinforcing advantages of mechanization. It required investment in other capital-intensive machines, thereby increasing the barriers to entry into that niche of production while cutting costs and therefore improving competitiveness.

As the industry mechanized, the size of some of the producers grew enormously. Indeed, this may have been the most obvious change within the Nuremberg industry. The Nuremberg metal toy makers generally perceived considerable advantage to be gained in expansion. Larger firms had greater access to capital and were able to reduce the risks associated with concentrations of fixed capital by spreading those costs over more toys and more types of toys. The Nuremberg *Handelskammer* observed in 1889: "[O]nly individual large firms, who work with considerable capital and all the advantages that naturally result, have enjoyed increasing growth. It is not to be overlooked, however, that they thereby grow at the cost of a corresponding number of small, independent existencces, who are swallowed up more and more by the big producers."[50]

To examine this process a bit closer, first let us return to the figures mentioned earlier about the Nuremberg metal toy industry. The number of metal toy makers grew from 49 to 154 between 1875 and 1895. The average number of employees in these firms grew from 5.78 to 10.85. Not only was the number of firms growing rapidly, but they were getting larger as well.[51] We have the following breakdown for 1875:

Number of employees:	0	1	2	3	4	5	6–10	11–50
Number of firms:	4	11	7	3	7	2	5	10[52]

The total for 1875 was 49 firms, 34 of which (69 percent of the total) had five or fewer employees. Five firms (10 percent of the total) had between six and ten employees. Ten firms (slightly more than 20 percent of the total) had more than ten employees. Twenty years later, the situation was quite different. We have the following breakdown for 1895:

Number of employees:	1	2–5	6–10	11–20	21–50	51–200
Number of firms:	12	63	39	16	16	5
Total employed:	12	186	302	215	481	475[53]

By 1895, the number of firms with five or fewer employees had risen to 75, but that was only 48 percent of the total number of firms. Thirty-nine firms (25 percent of the total) now had between six and ten employees. Finally, the number of firms with more than ten employees was now 37 (24 percent of the total).

Though the absolute number of small operations had risen (in part because the barriers to entry for the smallest firms had remained low), the proportion had declined dramatically. The industry as a whole was growing faster. The principal change was the expansion of many small producers into medium producers, perhaps paralleling the experience of the second bell maker in Senst's example cited earlier in this chapter. We also can see growth in the sheer size of the largest firms. In 1895, the five largest firms alone employed better than 50 percent more workers than the entire Nuremberg metal toy industry had in 1875. Fully as telling, the Nuremberg toy industry added an annualized average of 69.4 jobs every year. This represented an average annual growth of 24.5 percent over its 1875 level. While this led to increased competition, it also indicated a remarkable vitality.

Clearly, the machine had entered the Nuremberg toy industry in force. It is equally clear that some dynamic had changed within the Nuremberg industry, triggering a heretofore unheard-of growth in the size of some toy makers. There are several ways of assessing the experience of Nuremberg's toy industry, each with substantial implications for the causes of industrialization and the structures of modern societies. One established interpretation assumes that the large, integrated unit based on mechanized production for a mass market is the embodiment of economic rationality and modernity. To synthesize several iterations, this interpretive tradition argues that the machine age creates inexorable and interlocking pressures toward the aggregation of production in large units. The introduction of railroads, steamships, and telegraphs made it possible to produce goods in one place for an exceedingly broad market, which meant that large producers could increasingly undercut smaller, local competition by means of their substantially reduced unit prices and the declining costs of transporting those units. This reduced unit price was, in turn, the result of the application of laborsaving machines to the production process. Machines vastly increased labor productivity and substantially cut unit costs—provided the volume of production was sufficiently large. Significant investments in machinery therefore necessitated production for the mass market that the new transportation systems were creating. Large, mechanized production units were necessary to overcome the first-mover advantages accrued by rivals, particularly the British. The hierarchical structure of large firms also eased the coordination of supply and demand to maximize the productivity of that machinery, ensuring the timely arrival of raw materials and the existence of buyers for the final products. That structure also protected the firm from some of the vagaries of the market, as certain transactions were brought out of the marketplace and into the company.[54] The "accepted indicators of industrial modernity" were thus capital intensity, mechanization, standardization, information control, and the division of labor.[55] As Jeffrey Fear suggests, this characterization "tend[s] to idealize American factory-based, Fordist, mass-production methods."[56]

This interpretive tradition appears to fit the experience of Nuremberg rather well. The near simultaneous development of powerful machine tools and the expansion of rail links created the preconditions for mechanized mass production. Those machines, in turn, had important consequences. Larger production units maximized the capacity of the machines, spread fixed capital costs, and eased the acquisition of additional capital. The larger firms in Nuremberg started to aggregate a large number of functions within their own walls. Lithography, for example, eliminated the need for large numbers of external painters. The larger Nuremberg firms also developed their own machine shops, packaging centers, and so on. They were increasingly centralized firms.

A revisionist account of German economic history challenges the assumption that such firms as the large Nuremberg toy makers expanded because of any immanent "logic of the machine." Gary Herrigel's insightful book on German industry, *Industrial Constructions,* argues that traditional accounts have ignored or marginalized small producers in an effort to explain the growth of large industrial conglomerates, in the mistaken belief that the large firms are the exclusive representatives of economic modernity. As a result, Herrigel claims, these analyses have missed common obstacles that large and small firms have faced, and they have therefore overlooked the real causes of their disparate strategies and sizes. Herrigel develops two ideal types to help explain his interpretation: *decentralized industrial order* and *autarkic industrial order.*

The decentralized system is effectively flexible specialization, whereas the autarkic system is essentially defined by large, integrated industrial enterprises. Herrigel's definition of the decentralized system has no explicit causal element but is closely associated with "regions that had property relations and political structures that favored the small property holder and supported simultaneous engagement in agriculture and petty industrial pursuits."[57] Herrigel includes a clearer causal statement in his definition of autarkic systems. Autarkic industrial orders "are shaped at least as much by the desire to cope with environmental uncertainty than [*sic*] by the imperatives of efficiency."[58] This means that large, integrated manufacturers developed "because of differences in regional resources, *not because* [*they were*] *involved in a fundamentally different form or strategy of production.*"[59] In this analysis, the strategies and structures of industrial producers are largely a function of a region's social structures. Where social and governmental institutions reflect the concerns and needs of small producers, decentralized industrial systems thrive, as critical services and supplies can be acquired from other small producers. Where such institutions do not favor small, independent producers, firms must themselves create services and supplies, thereby aggregating work processes within the confines of their own enterprise. In a curious fashion, Herrigel revives and reintegrates preindustrial social structures into an analysis of German industrialization.

Herrigel is quite clear that he believes that Nuremberg's large companies were the consequence of the local social and historical context. He maintains that they simply did not have the opportunity to secure components and services on the market and therefore resorted to a hierarchical control mechanism. If the social framework had encouraged small producers through partible inheritance and government support, Herrigel implies, the Nuremberg toy makers would have remained comparatively small and traded among themselves for goods and services.

Herrigel's thought-provoking model underemphasizes important considerations of consumer demand and production technology. We cannot embed these industries only in their regional societies. The frames within which businesspeople operated must be seen in the context of far wider social and cultural movements. The continuing expansion (in absolute numbers) of small toy producers in Nuremberg might be taken as a sign that Herrigel's model cannot stand on its own. The case of lithography is an illustrative example. The larger firms brought lithography equipment into the factory for internal use. There existed, however, independent lithography shops that serviced smaller toy makers, manufacturers that did not have the scale of production to justify a dedicated lithography unit. Clearly, then, the Nuremberg industry was capable of supporting independent service providers that operated on a market, rather than autarkic, basis. The larger firms, however, believed that their interests were better served by both avoiding the market price mechanism for lithography and maintaining greater direct control over the quality of the images. The introduction of lithography was significant for one more reason. Herrigel suggests that Nuremberg developed autarkic production units because of the rather sparse commercial context, the difficulty of organizing networks of independent producers. He suggests that this was not the case, however, in Württemberg. There, the rich peasant tradition and their relative political power made decentralized networks of small producers more efficient and desirable than large autarkic ones. Nonetheless, the great metal toy maker of Württemberg, Märklin, found it necessary to acquire its own lithography equipment as part of its expansion of mechanized production. Toy makers, including Märklin, turned to lithography because it promised to increase the speed of output and to reduce prices; that is, it increased efficiency. It also eliminated the need for large numbers of domestic painters, which was exactly what Württemberg's strength should have been. As we shall see, the structural commonalities across regions in the metal toy industry were in sharp contrast to the widely varying structures that emerged between metal and wood toy production.

The structure of the Nuremberg industry represented the locally most efficient means of adapting to the structuring incentives shaping the toy industry. The demands of consumers rewarded those producers who could significantly increase production while drastically reducing prices. Machines were a very attractive means of profitably responding to that dynamic. There were toy makers in Nuremberg who resisted this logic. They simply did not prosper to the same degree as those who embraced the logic of their context.[60]

The structuring incentives could not escape influencing the workforce. The larger, mechanized producers often employed large numbers of women. It was almost certainly these units that the factory inspector Anton Kopf was considering when he estimated that the workforces of toy factories were 40–100 percent female.[61] Contrary to what many contemporaries implied, there was little direct replacement of male labor with female labor. Indeed, as in the case of painting and lithography, some female labor was replaced by machines and male workers. As firms mechanized and grew in size, it became possible to reorganize the production process. A greater division of labor was introduced simultaneously with the new machinery. To save money on labor, many tasks were then allotted to females. In some respects, this constituted a replacement of skilled male labor by machines and female workers. Smaller proportions of the final product were the direct result of skilled male craftwork. Rather than a direct substitution of female labor for male labor, tasks were divided and reorganized—part taken by machines and females, part not. As Dorothea Schmidt argues, those tasks that could be associated with the reputedly subtle, skillful female hand (because women were natural seamstresses) were assigned to women. Schmidt maintains that this gendered division of labor was essentially a compromise, whether conscious or not, between entrepreneurs and male labor. As Schmidt notes, the firm could save money by using female labor, but only in tasks requiring the purely physical attribute of manual dexterity; tasks requiring mental skills remained the preserve of men.[62] Accordingly, we find many women in the toy industry involved in such tasks as lacquering, soldering, and painting. The Nuremberg toy makers restructured labor relations to better adapt to the demands of a mass market, just as they changed work processes to bring in machines to help cut costs. The response of other parts of the industry, however, was very different.

Sonneberg

Sonneberg was the land of dolls. They varied in size, hair, and apparel. In the later nineteenth century, their producers had made the switch from wax heads to porcelain ones. No longer would young girls have to take care not to leave their dolls in the sun. The dolls' faces tended to be set in expression; their clothes tended to be conservative. Though their faces betrayed little emotion, their eyes would open or close depending on the head's relative angle to the earth's gravitational field. Some could even speak haltingly.

The wooded hill lands of the Thuringian Forest around Sonneberg, extending southward toward Coburg in Bavaria, featured a thriving toy industry focused primarily on the production of these dolls. The toy industry had been brought to this region centuries before by Nuremberg merchants, who organized the impoverished local peasants as *Heimarbeiter.* The abundant supplies of wood made this an ideal site for a woodworking industry, and the wooded and craggy hills made it a less-than-ideal region for agriculture. Gradually the local producers weaned themselves of the dominance of Nuremberg merchants, replacing them with local toy merchants who cultivated an extremely broad market across Europe, extending across the Atlantic by the early nineteenth century.[63]

During the 1870s and 1880s, the Sonneberg toy industry expanded dramatically. For example, in the twenty years from the mid-1860s through the mid-1880s, toy exports to the United States grew more than 600 percent. The American consul in Sonneberg observed a marked increase in industrial and commercial activities.[64] As we have seen, the substantial expansion of trade in these years was predicated on declining prices.[65] This downward pressure on costs and prices often came at the expense of the livelihoods of the most vulnerable. As a result, the experience of many individual producers was very different than the bird's-eye perspective might suggest.

The Sonneberg industry responded to the pressures exerted by the structuring incentives (which manifested themselves in expanding sales and declining prices) in a very different manner than their colleagues in Nuremberg. Mechanization was extremely limited in the region. There was some centralized production of porcelain in a number of relatively small porcelain factories. A few small doll assembly factories developed.[66] For the most part, however, mechanization was nonexistent.

Just as mechanization remained limited, production units remained small. Emmanuel Sax's statistics from 1880 show 273 producers with between one and four employees. There were 24 producers with between five and nine employees. Only 15 producers had between ten and nineteen employees. Finally, there were 9 plants with more than twenty employees. These averaged forty-two employees per factory. Thus, according to Sax's statistics, 85 percent of all toy producers in the Sonneberg region in 1880 employed four or fewer people.[67] According to Hans Dressel, however, the number of "independent" Sonneberg toy makers of all sizes grew from 321 in 1880 to 2,395 in 1899,[68] a remarkable increase of 746 percent and an annualized average of 34 percent. The majority remained very small.

It is clear that the Sonneberg industry was growing rapidly but in a very different way than had the Nuremberg industry. The number of production units was growing much more rapidly, but these units were not growing in size. In response to the needs of the market and the nature of the product, domestic industry expanded extremely rapidly. Why did the Sonneberg industry respond in such a different way?

The pressures and incentives were generally similar but not exactly so. First, dolls were protected from competition from substitute products. Dolls and little girls were so closely identified with one another in the prevailing Western culture that replacing a doll with some other product was effectively inconceivable. A doll was widely seen as a critical tool in educating girls for their exclusive future occupation, mother.

Despite this culturally defined cushion, there was considerable pressure to produce cheap and various dolls. The Sonneberg industry responded to these priorities within the context of their already-existing cottage industrial system. Rather than developing an entirely new system as happened in Nuremberg, the Sonneberg industry gradually constructed a very different approach to production, one that leaned heavily on the skeletal structure of the *Heimarbeiter*.

As illustrated in the sketches at the opening of this chapter, the structure of production in Sonneberg was highly developed. It involved an extraordinarily dense network of specialized producers and subcontractors that were all mutually dependent. Their relations with one another were long-term, affording considerable opportunity to cultivate business relationships with those independent contractors who succeeded and also to punish those who did not make the grade. In this way, the overhead costs of the hierarchical structure pursued by Nuremberg producers were avoided. Instead, Sonneberg relied on a sort of modified market. Business links were contractual and therefore subject to elimination. They also tended to push overhead costs (in this case, primarily tools and rent) onto the shoulders of the specific production unit using the overhead. It was not, however, a pure, anonymous market. There was a sense of mutual obligation and dependence that facilitated the exchange of information between nominal competitors and cushioned the loss of direct control intrinsic to market (as opposed to hierarchical) relationships.[69]

This structure of production, one that closely resembles that of flexible specialization, was a critical source of competitive advantage for the Sonneberg industry. They did not have the advantage of readily available machinery and the infrastructure to promote and sustain mechanization. They therefore relied on an exceedingly fine and supple network of specialized craftspeople. These networks were able to rapidly and cheaply shift the specific forms of their products to suit the needs of diverse markets and shifting fashions, in effect creating efficiencies of scope. The same production infrastructure was capable of producing an extraordinary variety of products tailored to the needs of specific buyers, at low cost.

The development of the Sonneberg industry undercuts the traditional narrative of mechanization and industrialization. Confronted with a mass market, the Sonneberg toy industry did not need to develop large mechanized workshops and deploy armies of laborers and clerks. The doll makers successfully adapted to their specific context through the advantages offered by the networks of flexible specialization. As a result, doll production expanded rapidly. Given their commercial success, it is difficult to credit assertions of economic backwardness that argue that Sonneberg was "just beginning to go through the process of modernization."[70] Rather, the decentralized web of specialized producers represented an efficient response to the demands of the market.

The social and historical context in which the Sonneberg industry developed was critical. The numerous small craftspeople did not simply spring from the earth. Nor were they created by the toy merchants. The skilled craftspeople of Sonneberg were the inheritors of a centuries-old social structure based on cottage industry. Skills and expectations arose there largely as a consequence of decisions made decades and centuries earlier, first when the Nuremberg merchants organized the Thuringian farmers as woodworkers and then as the tiny principalities of Thuringia sought to stimulate local industry by encouraging the activities of local merchant-*Verleger*. As a result of this social and cultural inheritance, the Thuringian doll makers were already structured as small, independent producers—*Heimarbeiter.*[71] This points to the ambiguous relationship between cottage industry and flexible specialization in the nineteenth century. These independent craftspeople, like others in the period, managed to combine the formal independence and dense networks of flexible specialization with the economic vulnerability and exploitation associated with *Hiemarbeit.* In the case of the Thuringian doll industry, the coexistence of these characteristics made possible a remarkable expansion of production.

The social context, however, was a necessary, not a sufficient, condition. As we shall see when we turn to the Erzgebirge, the existence there of a tradition of small-scale cottage industry did not ensure the development of decentralized networks of subcontracting specialists, as happened in Sonneberg. Dolls, the chief product of the Sonneberg toy industry, were highly susceptible to disaggregation and therefore to the process of flexible specialization. Nineteenth-century dolls were quite heterogeneous. They varied in size, material, hairstyles, clothing, and so on. Critically, they had a variety of subcomponents, such as porcelain or wax heads, glass eyes, wooden appendages, textile clothes, mohair or felt hair. The multiple subcomponents and their various materials made dolls well suited for a web of decentralized specialists with diverse skill sets.

The Sonneberg industry did not, however, rely exclusively on flexibility. The system also very much thrived on the pressure that it exerted on the *Heimarbeiter.* The structure also allowed the Sonneberg industry to keep costs down by dispensing with machinery and pushing the costs of rent onto the domestic producers. Domestic production and the ability of merchant buyers to regulate access to the market also served the general need for low prices by putting constant pressure on the incomes of toy makers.[72] The price pressure made the unpaid labor of the family's children critically important. Children in this system were sources of free labor, resulting in an exceedingly widespread incidence of child labor in defiance of the weak legislation that sought to limit it.[73] The unsurprising result was undereducated, often ill children.[74] Misery was compounded as families were forced into tiny homes, averaging six people per sleeping chamber.[75] The tight conditions, coupled with frequent work with plaster of paris or fine dust, contributed to high levels of lung disease, especially tuberculosis. The proportion of fatalities resulting from tuberculosis was approximately one-third higher in the largely rural Sonneberg district than for the nation as a whole. The proportion in some parts of the district were more than three times higher than the national average. In these areas, tuberculosis would account for more than one-third of all deaths.[76]

That there were multiple craftspeople in each area of specialization also ensured competition. Critics of the Sonneberg industry (and there were many) invariably pointed to the socially disastrous impact of this competition. The sociologist Paul Ehrenberg, for example, emphatically traced the poverty of the *Heimarbeiter* of Sonneberg back to this Hobbesian competition.

> [S]o develops the most basic and damaging pressure on wages and prices through the *Hausindustriellen* themselves. Trusting in the abilities of his large family, in the speed of his work, in his skill in stealing wood, or because "quantity will do it," the *Hausindustrielle* underbids his neighbor to get an order, an order that he perhaps could never fill. He underbids also when he must be ruined even through fulfilling his orders. And because not merely one but hundreds do business in this way, the prices of all wares sink.[77]

Ehrenberg argued that competition between these desperate, yet proud, producers, far from creating a beneficial market equilibrium, undermined the well-being of all. Rather than Adam Smith's "invisible hand," we have a classic example of the "prisoner's dilemma." So long as the "players" cannot or will not trust one another, the individual pursuit of advantage leads everyone to undercut all others, leading to the disadvantage of all. Mutual cooperation would rebound to the advantage of all. Yet that cooperation is elusive as long as an individual's "cheating" on the cooperation of the group is more desirable than the rewards of working together.

As I have indicated before, this brand of analysis needs modification, as it betrays a heavy bias toward the primacy of the producer: demand is taken as a given; only supply is treated as dynamic. This is not to say that competition among producers did not lead to price cuts and a consequent strain on the living standards of producers. Rather, we must keep in mind that the negative push of competition and the positive attraction of increasing sales existed simultaneously. Together, they almost irresistibly pushed/pulled prices down. The "little man" as consumer was the beneficiary of the enormous pressure put on the well-being of the "little man" as producer.

In Sonneberg, the elimination of guild restrictions (to enable greater individual initiative and expose individual producers to greater pressure to increase production and lower prices) combined with a market demand for a large volume of low-cost toys. The result was a highly flexible and efficient network of producers and a horrifying level of self-exploitation. Cottage industrialists worked extremely long hours in unhealthy conditions. These conditions were necessitated by the volume of production and low piece rates. By one measure, the total profits from twelve dolls would purchase a half kilogram of bread.[78] The bulk of the population did not earn enough to breach the income tax floor of six hundred marks per annum. The logical complement for mass consumption in prewar Germany was thus impoverished producers. To adapt to the structuring incentives guiding the toy industry, the Sonneberg industry developed the existing cottage industrial system into a highly flexible system that retained the more oppressive, cost-cutting attributes of *Heimarbeit.* The Erzgebirge, too, adapted its original cottage industrial system, although to somewhat different effect.

The Erzgebirge

The wooden toys of the Erzgebirge were and are often seen as the epitome of Germanness. Wooden figurines and the craftspeople who fashioned them by hand are easily portrayed as remnants of an earlier, more authentic German culture. These wooden toys took many forms. The most famous was Noah's ark. Not surprisingly, the ark constituted a set of toys. Besides the wide-bodied ship, the set included pairs of animals, both familiar and exotic. The pieces were painstakingly painted.

In the Erzgebirge region of Saxony (on the border with the present-day Czech Republic), toy production was long a secondary profession, much as it had been in Sonneberg and Nuremberg. For centuries, the Erzgebirge had been an important mining region (its name means "Ore Mountains"). Starting around 1500, the local mining industry began slowly to decline. The residents of the region began turning increasingly to wood processing for supplemental income. Beginning in the eighteenth century, the wood products of the Erzgebirge began to include toys produced for Nuremberg or Sonneberg merchants. The structure of production was exclusively cottage industry.

The Erzgebirge experienced the same dynamic as the other portions of the industry: increased sales coupled with rapidly falling prices. The result bordered on the catastrophic in the Erzgebirge. Average earnings for local toy producers had plunged in the early 1880s, in some cases falling from 28.8 marks per week in 1875 to 9.6 in 1881 for a family of four workers making wooden horses. An average family of three workers making small wooden soldiers saw its weekly income fall from 15 marks per week to 1.8.[79] Even the *Handelskammer* recognized the growing misery of the working population.[80] Much as in Thuringia, the signs of impoverishment can be seen in the means of preserving life. The typical diet was totally unsatisfactory—largely potatoes, bread, coffee, and oil. Other than the father's morning wurst, meat and vegetables were very rare.[81] The homes in which *Heimarbeiter* busied themselves were generally extremely small—one floor with a surrounding garden. They had one bedroom for parents and children alike and a workroom with two to three windows and some pieces of furniture, often little more than a table, a bench, chairs, and an armoire. Much of the home and its infrastructure were in fact dedicated to the family enterprise, so living spaces doubled as work spaces, raising health concerns.[82]

The Erzgebirge toy makers focused largely on the production of small wooden figurines. They were famous for the delicate and exhaustive collection of animals that populated their Noah's arks. These wooden figures, however, were much less susceptible to disaggregation than were dolls. There were simply no subcomponents. The sweeping division of labor and networks of specialized craftspeople that one saw in Sonneberg were, consequently, impossible. The division of labor was extremely limited, primarily among family members. Again, the labor of children emerged as a critical source of income for the family. The opportunities for mechanization were likewise limited. Beyond the development of increasingly sophisticated community lathe works,[83] there was little in the work process that could be usefully mechanized. There emerged a small handful of factories, which largely produced simple wooden toys, such as building blocks or croquet sets.[84] Wooden blocks could be done entirely by lathe. As a result, besides the 607 families of cottage industrialists, there were fifty-nine enterprises employing an average of thirteen persons and four larger companies that employed an average of seventy-eight people.[85] These factories, however, were incapable of fabricating products that required greater attention to detail and variability, such as the animals aboard Noah's ark. For wooden figures, the flexibility of the human hand was necessary.

Since the wooden figurines provided little opportunity for the development of decentralized networks and since there was only slightly more opportunity to mechanize the production process, the dynamic of falling prices and increasing sales came at the direct expense of the *Heimarbeiter.* They responded through greater self-exploitation. They worked harder for less money. The specific social context of peasant industrial production could not alter the realities imposed by the globalizing mass market, their product, and the limits of existing technology. The most effective way for the families of *Heimarbeiter* to "improve" labor productivity was to reduce their own incomes. As in the Thuringian doll industry, the emergence of a liberal market serving a mass-consuming public opened the path to increases in production and declining prices, at the cost of producer poverty.

The various structuring imperatives had very different consequences in the various parts of the German toy industry. In Nuremberg, the metal toy makers benefited from the development of machine tools and infrastructure for other, much larger companies. The use of laborsaving machines defined the rapid growth of the Nuremberg toy industry. Those machines, in turn, had important consequences. Larger production units maximized the capacity of the machines, spread the fixed capital costs over more units, and eased the acquisition of additional capital. The machines of the Nuremberg toy industry also determined whose labor was deployed how. The weakness of social institutions for small producers in Nuremberg might help explain why the metal toy industry was to be found in Nuremberg, but it cannot explain why the production of metal toys was done by rapidly expanding industrial units, which were well adapted to cutting costs and were generally organized to maintain at least a moderate degree of flexibility. Producers could have remained small and relied on subcontracting to acquire particular skills or to cope with surging demand. Instead, production units grew, particularly those mass-producing simple metal playthings or the most technologically advanced toys. These products rewarded concentrations of capital to either slash unit costs or to assemble the capital for necessary equipment. The product and available technology determined how consumer demand was to be met and therefore determined the industrial structure.

By contrast, the Sonneberg and Erzgebirge branches of industry had little opportunity to mechanize. There appeared to be fewer machines to be brought into wooden toy and doll production. To meet the challenge of reducing prices while retaining product diversity, decentralized production in regional networks employing low-paid skilled labor made a great deal of competitive sense. The skilled *Heimarbeiter* were products of their historical and social context. This existing industrial structure was retained and refashioned because it was the most cost-efficient and competitive means of satisfying the demands of consumers, given the production technology. The differences between the toy industries of Sonneberg and the Erzgebirge should also be noted. The Sonneberg industry had a far wider division of labor, much more closely resembling the ideal type of flexible specialization than did the Erzgebirge industry. Both regions had traditions of decentralized cottage industry and partible inheritance. The root of the differences between these two regions was in the nature of their products. As we have seen, dolls, whose various components could be produced by different specialists, were highly suitable for subcontracting. The wooden figures of the Erzgebirge—single, solid pieces of shaped wood—were ill-suited for wide networks of specialized subcontractors. Again, the social and historical contexts of these regions help explain their competitiveness, but the fundamental logic was governed by the interaction between consumer demand and available production technology. The experience of these regions also suggests that the decentralized production systems associated with flexible specialization are not necessarily socially progressive. Indeed, liberalized markets enabled a remarkable level of self-exploitation, as *Heimarbeiter* drove themselves and their families harder to satisfy the market's demand for inexpensive toys.

The remarkable development of the toy industry, both in its overall growth and in the diversity of its production structures, was directly related to the emergence of a mass market. The rise of mass consumption, therefore, had a significant and lasting impact on the social structures and life experiences of large numbers of Germans. The emergence of a mass market in toys depended greatly on the ability of toy makers to produce and deliver toys at low cost. Toy makers, however, also had to deliver products consumers would want. They had to construct images of toy consumers before they could construct forms for their toys. It was necessary to strategically calculate the nature of demand.

Design

Reasoning from their experience and material interests, toy makers fashioned an implicit vision of human nature. Humans, they believed, were highly individualistic. People, qua consumers, were not dominated by a tyrannical majority or the fickle winds of fashion. Preferences varied widely by individual nature. Those preferences were, no doubt, influenced by fashion, gender, and national culture.[86] There remained, however, substantial individual variety. When critics suggested that toys or dolls ought to have a specific "look" or form in the service of some higher cultural vision, toy makers were quick to counter. Such reformist visions, they argued, assumed one sort of human and neglected the multiplicity of competing desires.[87] In effect, critics were accused of constructing a normative, procrustean vision that denied human diversity.

The toy makers did not merely affirm the individuality of each consumer. They also insisted that each individual had many interests and "talents." The individuality of the consumer was the conglomeration of many discrete enthusiasms; they were distinctly unmonolithic. The multiplicity of these interests meant that individuals were likely to move between separate interests. The *Rundshau über Spielwaren* reported, "The child's sensibility demands finally variety." If a child began to ignore a toy, therefore, it was not necessarily the fault of the toy. Shifting interests were intrinsic to individuality—the child found something else to amuse. He or she would soon return to the first plaything. The *Deutsche Spielwaren-Zeitung* argued that this was particularly true of "city kids," since their "lively spirits demand perpetual stimulation."[88] Indeed, the toy industry was confident that urban modernity had transformed children, making them less stolid, more sensation-seeking and demanding. The *Deutsche Spielwaren-Zeitung* maintained, "The child of our days is very different from that of grandfather's day." It argued that they required a steady diet of new images and therefore new toys, because they had been trained to absorb and master a rapidly shifting urban environment.[89] The *Deutsche Spielwaren-Zeitung* went on to claim that a "forward-moving culture" demanded such a diet.[90] The toy industry, then, viewed urban childhood in terms highly reminiscent of the urban subjectivity posited by Georg Simmel in his "The Metropolis and Mental Life" and *The Philosophy of Money*.

Toy advertising suggested that toys also deepened individuality in children. When children were shown, they were never shown interacting socially with other children. Usually, a single child was shown (see, e.g., figs. 2 and 3)—although single-child families were a decided rarity. The single child was either absorbed in play or portrayed in an attitude of triumphant domination over the toy, as in one Bing ad in which a boy stands towering astride a rushing locomotive. When multiple children were shown, generally all were absorbed in the toy. Only in the most formal sense can they be described as playing together. Rather, play and consciousness were focused on what the child saw. Play therefore both reflected and encouraged individuality.

Their assumptions about the basic nature of toy consumers meant toy makers were convinced that the market required an extraordinar-

Fig. 2. Advertising in the trade journal *Deutsche Spielwaren-Zeitung* (Nuremberg), 1912.

ily rich panoply of forms. The market appeared almost infinitely segmentable; it was kaleidoscopic, with a perpetual appetite for the new. This can be seen in the toy makers' rhetoric and in the diversity of their products—from Roman legionnaires to Chinese figures, from Catholic sacramental items[91] to reproductions of the Jeffries-Johnson boxing match,[92] from the Captain from Köpenick[93] to Oktoberfest.[94]

The apparently limitless possibilities of form were, of course, just that—apparent. For all the market's capacious appetite for form, producers nonetheless had to calculate what forms were most likely to succeed. Form was, in fact, the outcome of an arm's-length negotiation of producers and merchant middlemen.

Toy makers bore principal responsibility for toy design. The larger

Fig. 3. Richter's direct appeal in *Daheim* 49, no. 9 (30 Nov. 1912).

companies employed dedicated designers. Much as larger Nuremberg firms could maintain separate in-house lithography units, they could also afford specialized designers. These figures carefully crafted models of a large variety of toys, which were then offered to the merchant middlemen. These forms would be either put on display in modeling rooms on the premises or taken to the Leipzig Easter Fair. The inspiration for new models could be various. The introduction of new, aerodynamic locomotives—specifically the Maffei locomotives purchased by Baden—required a new, sleek, multiaxel vision of the toy train.[95] According to Margarete Steiff, a trip to the zoo inspired her nephew. Observing the play of several young bears, Richard Steiff imagined that many children had been similarly fascinated and amused. He immediately turned to design a playfully long-limbed stuffed bear.

After finding little interest in Leipzig, Steiff was on the verge of pulling the prototype when an American buying agent declared, "New York will pay any price for your delightful bear!"[96] Smaller toy makers tended to design toys themselves. The *Heimarbeiter* of Sonneberg and the Erzgebirge would spend winters crafting new objects to propose to their distributors. Given their comparatively limited experiential horizons, it is not entirely surprising that these craftspeople often tended to refine previous designs rather than offer anything radically new.[97]

Toy makers did not simply dream up forms. There was no movement or sentiment for a radical break with naturalism. Nature and the second nature of human creation were the inspiration for designers; toys were to be replicas of reality. Toy makers occasionally expressed the fear that their products might slide into caricature. Toys had to remain true to life. In part, this is a reflection of a historical understanding of what consumers wanted, but it also reflected the ease of copying the ready-made "text" offered by "reality."

The impulse to replicate a given reality can be seen in a variety of areas. The metal toy industry was very concerned to craft close replicas of the triumphs of modern technology. Toy makers labored mightily to bring cost-effective and accurate representations of locomotives, Dreadnaughts, airplanes, automobiles, steam engines, and electrical systems to young boys. Toy makers aspired to commodify the impulse to raise a generation of "builders and discoverers, of scientists, of researchers and inventors."[98] It was believed that the coming generation needed to learn technology from their toys: "Youth demands technological toys and models this moment."[99] In part, science imposed its own demand for mimesis on toys. If a steam engine was to function, it had a certain logic imposed on it. Nonetheless, toy designers often imposed a discipline on themselves, seeking to create not just toys but replicas. Toy ships received specific names to emphasize their loyalty to the original.[100] Increasingly, toy trains were not enough. The landscape and facilities that surrounded real trains had likewise to be reproduced.

The toy industry was also perpetually transforming contemporary events into toys.[101] Any and every military conflict or prospective conflict was almost instantaneously transformed into figurines. The Italian-Ottoman War,[102] the Balkan Wars, the Russo-Japanese War,[103] the Boer War, and even the periodic military standoffs that characterized the prewar years[104]—all became fodder for toy design. Similarly, events of cultural significance, such as Teddy Roosevelt's African safari[105] or Peary's expedition to the North Pole,[106] were rapidly taken up as themes. The extremely well publicized Zeppelin flights were credited with increasing sales of aerially themed toys.[107] The industry clearly believed that their consumers desired toys that referenced something identifiably real.

Toy makers did not travel about the globe observing wars, warships, or safaris. The quotations placed around the term *reality* earlier in this discussion were placed there advisedly. Toy designers produced their exact replicas of "real" objects and events based on a mediated relationship with reality. The foundation for these products were generally journalistic accounts. Oskar Stillich was amazed that one aging toy maker in the hills of Thuringia had spent his life making toy ships even though he had never left his village and never seen a navigable river, let alone the open ocean; the toy maker based his products on pictures in magazines. Ernst Rausch noted that other toy makers sought to commodify American politics based on a German edition of *Punch* or Meyer's Encyclopedia.[108] The creation of trade journals greatly facilitated this process. The *Deutsche Spielwaren-Zeitung,* for example, made a regular practice of reporting themes popular abroad (especially in Paris) and suggesting possible new ideas for toys. In addition, the only conceivable source for Nuremberg toy makers seeking to design Japanese soldiers for the Russo-Japanese War was the popular press. The close reproductions of reality that parents sought as means of educating their children were therefore actually reproductions of reproductions of isolated slices of reality. Toys were designed based on already-framed narrations of reality.

Another means of communicating designs was through the informal networks of craftspeople and merchants. This can be narrated in two quite different fashions. According to some, toy design was, in effect, a communal project. Merchants and a handful of toy makers collaborated to generate new designs. The merchants contributed their knowledge of the market, suggesting what forms or themes would be most appealing. Industrialists contributed their mastery of materials and the production process. The more successful models would then be quickly adopted by other toy makers.[109] Alternatively, the system could be plotted as something rather more sinister—little more than old-fashioned theft. From a more individualistic notion of design ownership, that the *Storchbein* train, teddy bears, and other toys were quickly adopted by rival producers appeared to be a warning sign of failure. In this analysis, that there was little effective legal protection of product design becomes extremely significant. As a consequence, successful designs were often rapidly copied by competing toy makers.[110] Indeed, distributors had a material stake in the rapid diffusion of design ideas—what modern parlance would call "theft of intellectual property." As more producers made a particular item, any particular premium paid for developing a successful form became smaller. As a result, argued one contemporary sociologist, middlemen deliberately stole and distributed designs.[111] By the beginning of the twentieth century, however, some of the largest toy makers were making annual outlays for the legal defense of patents and designs.[112] This solution, however, was apparently beyond the means of smaller producers even then. Whether design was a communal or an individual undertaking, it is clear that design ideas flowed freely through the toy-making community and that other toys were a principal inspiration for many—perhaps most—toys. At this point, the "reality" referenced by the toys is becoming quite distant from the toys themselves. Instead, "realistic" toys quoted toys that quoted toys that quoted magazines.

Toy designers had an additional concern beyond naturalism in form, and they had stakeholders to please beyond consumers. Toy designs also had to "please the eye."[113] Shoppers had to be attracted, and retailers had to be satisfied. That meant toys not only had to appeal to the mimetic longings of parents but had to be visually enticing. "Whoever wants to influence through unattractiveness will be terribly disappointed," declared the *Deutsche Spielwaren Zeitung.* "Attractiveness" was particularly important for the public face of toys, retailers. Consequently, it had to be important to toy producers. The *Deutsche Spielwaren-Zeitung* reported: "Precisely the toy retailers must strive at Christmastime . . . to direct general attention to themselves. Our toy production stands now at such a level and offers so much and so colorful that the retailer has ample opportunity to develop something impressive."[114] It was no doubt for this reason that the American consul in Sonneberg, Henry Winser, noted in 1880 an "infantile taste for bright and dazzling colors" among toy makers. Indeed, toy makers were so intent on using "brilliant hues" that they were alleged to be willing to employ paints containing arsenic, copper, mercury, and other "deleterious pigments."[115]

The German toy industry sent into the December streets of Germany wave after wave of products that represented a certain vision. Consumers, they suggested, wanted brightly colored slices of "reality." Beyond that, consumers agreed on little else. Some wanted to be masters of modern technology. Others dreamed of military conquest.

While many preferred to imagine current events, others reconstructed societies long since passed. Enthusiasms and preferences—and, with them, the demands for representation—were immensely diverse, perhaps cacophonous. To serve the mass market therefore meant imagining a fractured cultural community.

The mass market was in part called into existence by visible and measurable change. The increasing density and efficiency of transportation coupled with rapid urbanization were critical to the transformation of toy making in Germany. Equally important, however, were cultural changes in the West that brought material goods ever deeper into the daily lives and value systems of families and individuals. A fundamental cultural revolution had already begun the slow process of converting citizens into consumers. The toy industry thus was adapting to an extremely complex—indeed, highly relativistic—environment. The strategies toy makers pursued were deeply influenced by a blizzard of factors ranging from technology, traditional social and economic structures, state policy, and gradual cultural change. These elements combined in kaleidoscopic form to create differing strategies for various parts of the industry, all in an effort to mass-produce toys for a growing market of sovereign consumers.

3. "Christmas Bustle Wherever the Eye Looks"

Buying and Selling Toys

Imagine it is the late nineteenth century. Huddled in the open and aged German plaza are rows and rows of wooden stalls. Hurriedly constructed, the stalls were rented out to part-time and itinerant peddlers. Their wooden walls and roofs are largely obscured by colorful decorations and a profusion of objects for sale: winter clothing, Christmas cookies, wooden dolls, children's sabers, and so on. The breath of the salespeople comes in visible puffs as they warm their hands. Throughout the market arises a discordant melody of crude musical instruments mixed with the voices of those milling between the stalls. Over the entire scene looms the dark mass of some medieval or baroque palace, dimly perceived by the throngs below in the early gloom of a German winter's day. Despitc the cold and a darkness only partially relieved by the limited lighting, there is a remarkable, festive air about the marketplace. As the family journal *Daheim* enthused in 1887, "while trade and poetry have otherwise little in common, the magic of poetry makes itself felt at the Christmas market."[1]

Twenty years later, the scene has shifted. The wide, straight avenues are new, as are the buildings that line them. Somehow, the streets always seem to lead to a wide circle or plaza dominated by a multistory department store. Along the sidewalks stream a seemingly undifferentiated mass of people. Occasionally a small group detaches itself from the mass and hazards the risks of a street crossing. The laws regulating commerce have been relaxed in recognition of the upcoming Christmas holiday, allowing stores to open on Sunday. Entire districts of the city seem to migrate to these new streets. A closer look reveals the individuality hiding amid the mass. One man departs a small café, standing aside briefly as another man stumbles under the burden of bags and gifts he carries. The first man then slowly, carefully threads his way through the crowd, past women and children, past men of all classes speaking a veritable Babel of dialects. Inside the store windows are laid out every product imaginable. The man, having seen them all before, presses on, carefully negotiating his way forward, ignoring the windows and the calls of street hawkers. Then something—some unexpected motion—catches his eye, and he pauses to examine what is new this year. He spies a woodland village, complete with train service and figures laboring in miniature moving workshops. The man, standing next to several young boys, stares at the toy trains and moving dolls. Recovering from his momentary reverie, the man smiles and, with mock solemnity, informs the boys that even German toys work too hard to have any fun. Then he turns and plunges once more into the surging crowd, off to complete his Christmas obligations.[2]

German retailing had developed rapidly since the middle third of the nineteenth century as retail outlets expanded in number, size, and variety. The retail sector was adjusting to the demands of a growing mass market.[3] Retailing for a mass market had two consequences of fundamental importance. First, the changing context and culture of retail structured what toys would be presented to the public as desirable and how they would be received. The transformation of retail thus unavoidably entailed the transformation of toy marketing. Toys were instrumentalized by store owners, put into the service of spectacle, in the interest of more effective advertising. This inevitably influenced both producers and consumers.

Second, toys were framed as items of spectacular consumption and were so understood by the popular press and, apparently, by the urban population of Germany. The marketing of toys in the new retailing districts was one manifestation of a gradual turn toward visual spectacle and a shift toward surface realities visible in all industrial societies. In some respects, this represented a social correlate of naturalism and impressionism. Contrary to the positivist assumptions that sustained these aesthetic traditions, however, these surfaces and their images were neither stable nor representative.[4] The marketing of toys sought to turn them into signs without meaning. Divorced from their putative function as playthings, the surfaces of toys became spectacles intended to catch the eye. By rendering them bereft of real meaning, retailers transformed toys into visual images around which shoppers could construct their own narratives. Toys were, in effect, played with well before they entered the hands of any child. We can perceive, then, an emerging modernist culture precariously clinging to surfaces, spectacle, and spectatorship.

This chapter examines how the changing practices of retailing and shopping influenced both toys and German culture. Such analysis necessitates several steps. First, I shall examine how the structure of distribution left the marketing of toys to retailers. Retailers naturally sought to promote their own interests rather than those of toy producers. The nature of those interests, however, changed as the retailing industry evolved. We must therefore analyze more closely the transformation of German retailing, specifically Christmas retailing. With that in mind, I turn secondly to examine one of the classic toy-retailing venues in Germany, the Christmas market. This old-fashioned market gradually made way for new retailing districts as the geography of Germany's cities changed. The retail districts form the third topic in this chapter. These districts thrived in part on their commercial advantages (lower prices, returns, etc.). They also fostered a specific attitude toward shopping that shaped how they wished to promote toys and how toys were perceived by consumers. Since marketing was left to retailers, the developing urban culture of shopping played a disproportionate role in marketing toys. Finally in this chapter, I shall consider how Germans, particularly the tabloid press, constructed the experience of shopping as a dynamic experience defined by sights and surging crowds. This background of chaotic urban life framed the efforts of shoppers to elaborate their own narratives around items and people on display.

Distribution, Advertising, and Retailing

Toy makers almost never sold their products to the consumer. In fact, they almost never sold their products to retailers. Instead, toy makers sold to a variety of distributors. As a result, the toy industry was slow and crude in developing its marketing. Toys makers advertised lavishly in trade journals but rarely bothered to communicate with the end consumers.

As a result of the highly mediated relationship that toy producers had with toy consumers, the incentive to establish a strong brand identity was weak. Toys from various producers were often mixed together in ads, with little clue as to who made what. Individual products were quite anonymous to the consumer. Given this structure, it is not surprising that the majority of advertising by toy producers was aimed not at consumers but at retailers and merchant-middlemen. Toy advertising was thick in such trade journals as the *Deutsche Spielwaren-Zeitung,* the *Rundschau über Spielwaren,* or the *Wegweiser für die Spielwarenindustrie.* Indeed, it sometimes seemed that the *Wegweiser* was little more than a collection of advertisements. This advertising tended to be moderately sophisticated, using visual images and emphasizing the name of the producer. In the years before World War I, they even used color. Advertising in daily newspapers and magazines for the general population, however, was largely left to retailers. These stores were, naturally enough, interested in establishing their own names more than those of their toy producers. Ads for retailers therefore featured broad categories of toys, such as rocking horses or clothed dolls, but a producer's name was never mentioned (see fig. 2 in chap. 2 and fig. 4).[5] If the producers had been more closely involved in the marketing of their products, rather than leaving marketing to the merchant-middlemen, they might well have been motivated to establish a strong name identity.

An interesting exception may demonstrate the general principle. Richters Anker Steinbaukasten were artificially produced rocks, shaped to look like an enormous variety of building stones, which would fit together to form a wide array of buildings. They were a sort of nineteenth-century Lego system. Originally inspired by the cube gifts advocated by the founder of the kindergarten movement, Friedrich Fröbel, they were merely made to be more interesting than uniform wooden blocks. The patented chemical process for their production was purchased in 1880 by Friedrich Adolf Richter, the owner of a chemical and pharmaceuticals company. Richter brought to this system his business and advertising experience, establishing a thriving concern. Richter's strategy was based on the flexibility of his product. There were thousands of pieces and kits that could be ordered individually, allowing a slow accretion of pieces, kits, and possibilities. The multiplicity of kits allowed Richter to establish a booming direct-mail market.[6] Because Richters sought to deal directly with consumers, it worked to establish its name as a household word. Consequently, advertisements for Richters Steinbaukasten were frequent in the general press (see fig. 3 in chap. 2). Not coincidentally, Richters Steinbaukasten were often the only toy mentioned by name in the ads placed by major retailers.

The role of middlemen in slowing the development of brands was

Fig. 4. Retailer advertising in *Vossische Zeitung,* no. 570 (5 Dec. 1909).

significant for consumers. The task of advertising, of constructing a meaningful narrative around a toy, was left to retailers. Therefore, a rather different kind of advertising emerged. Rather than emphasize the relation between child and toy (as in Richter's ads), it emphasized large stores, bright show windows, and the fascination and desire that the toys themselves generated. Because producers would not speak for their products, retailers did. Increasingly, retailers came to speak in a language of visual spectacle. We can see the rise of visual spectacle in retailing by comparing the old Christmas markets with the emerging retailing districts of the modern city.

The Christmas Market

The oldest venue in Germany for the sale of toys was the Christmas market. Christmas markets were centuries-old annual fairs held in city centers across Germany. In Leipzig in 1785, for example, toys, cabinets, tables, chairs, beds, and various other items were offered for sale during a three-day market that was, according to one observer, so full of visitors that one had difficulty moving.[7]

The Christmas market was a recognizable folk tradition, one of the traditions of German urban life. A variant of the annual commercial fairs common to most German cities, it was also rooted in the traditions of German commercial life, a fact much emphasized by the defenders of the markets. The Christmas markets served an important role in distributing products in preparation for the festivities associated with Christmas and the New Year. The rootedness of the traditional Christmas market made it one of the most recognized images of Christmas in nineteenth-century Germany. Articles about the Nuremberg Christmas market were not uncommon in German publications, and sketches of the Berlin Christmas market were a recurring feature of the middle-class family magazine *Die Gartenlaube.* The Christmas markets also occupied the representational, political, and commercial centers of German cities. They often had residence in the vicinity of major landmarks, such as royal palaces or cathedrals.[8] The physical location was the simple outgrowth of the geographic realities of the cities. In the still relatively small German cities of the early to middle nineteenth century, the largest open spaces were those constructed to emphasize the baroque power and grandeur of the church and state.

The Christmas markets had long been quite successful commercial venues. They brought together a large number of retailers, with minimal overhead costs. It was easy and quite rational to buy there. The poverty of the tradespeople and their stalls ensured that the wares on offer tended to be cheap, in terms of both price and quality. "The Christmas market!" exclaimed the *Berliner Illustrirte Zeitung.* "Once again the old, primitive stalls are put up, in which every kind of impoverished doodad [*Kleinkram*] is piled high."[9] Of course, low price was not the only reason to favor Christmas markets as a venue. Their geographical location in the center of Germany's medieval and baroque cities lent the markets a great deal of charm. The director of the Bavarian Arts and Crafts Museum, Th. von Kramer, described the Nuremberg Christmas market as one filled with "the brisk life and activity of the looking, desiring, and buying crowd" that milled about "the stalls bathed in glowing light and with their innumerable toys, bric-a-brac, and fragrant sweets."[10] Another observer noted the "cries of large and small wandering traders, mixed with the notes from the grinding organs and harmonicas."[11] The atmosphere enveloped all of one's senses.

The toys for sale at the Christmas markets appear to have been quite simple and cheap. Such descriptions as those just cited, as well as various pictorial representations of the Christmas markets, suggest that only the most basic toys were to be found there. Toys had to be able to withstand inclement weather. There was also little space to demonstrate the possibilities of mechanized toys. In addition, the traditional roots of the Christmas market may have encouraged an emphasis on more traditional toys. In any case, the more sophisticated products of the toy industry were not to be found in the Christmas market.

Thus, Christmas markets, combining low prices and aestheticized experience, were not really ideal commercial sites. The markets were increasingly sidelined as the nineteenth century drew to a close. The process was most dramatic in Berlin, where Christmas markets were eventually physically banned from the center of the city, forced into the working-class districts surrounding the commercial and political heart of the Reichshauptstadt (imperial capital).[12] The gradual decline of the Christmas market was a much commented on development, one with a number of contributing factors. Contemporaries tended to assume that the Christmas market was simply another inevitable victim of the forward march of capitalism, the "spirit of the times."[13] Just as the small handworker had no chance against the factory, the Christmas market had no chance against the department store. History was on the march and was not to be impeded by a handful of tradespeople's stalls.

Just as the development of the toy factory did not suddenly sweep away all toy producers before it, the department store did not by any means eliminate all small-time retailers. Indeed, some small shops prospered because of their proximity to department stores, profiting from the ability of those stores to attract customers from across the city.[14] Nonetheless, enormous pressure could be and was placed on the economic independence of the stall operators at the market. The Christmas markets were vulnerable at several points. First and foremost, they were outside. The *Berliner Lokal-Anzeiger* did not idly refer to the "old, worthy, uncomfortable Christmas market."[15] It could be quite cold, the growth of electric lighting passed outdoor facilities by, and the quality of goods was limited by the possibility of damage from weather or loss from theft. Certainly the more expensive electric-powered toys coming to market in the early twentieth century were not going to be available at Christmas markets. Furthermore, the tradespeople of the Christmas markets had little or no contact with producers. This, combined with their very low sales volumes, meant that they were in no position to either eliminate middlemen or pressure producers for lower unit prices.

The Christmas markets had another, rather more insidious weak point. They were set up on public (i.e., state-owned) property. In fact, the state paid to set up the structures, remove snow, provide police protection, and perform a variety of other services. The state then attempted to recoup these expenses through fees charged to exhibit and sell.[16] This dependence on the state entailed a threefold problem. First, as was the case in Munich, if the market did not at least break even (i.e., if the city did not regain the money it spent on the market), there could develop pressure from within the state to eliminate the market. Even if this were not the case, the temptation to seek a quick fix in Munich by simply moving the market to another location proved irresistible. As the exhibitors argued, this almost certainly limited the number of people who came to the market, for its exact location seemed uncertain to prospective consumers.[17]

Second, the market was vulnerable to political pressure from neighbors who did not enjoy the noise, light, and strangers it generated. In Munich, efforts to extend the duration of the Christmas market (thereby increasing revenue for tradespeople and fees for the city) were delayed for years by the fierce resistance of its neighbors. Similarly, the SPD daily, *Vorwärts,* argued that the most famous neighbor of the Schloßplatz, the kaiser, had the Berlin Christmas market removed from the vicinity because it was a nuisance.[18] In fact, the Berlin police president fought for years in the 1880s and 1890s to remove the Berlin Christmas market from the city center, arguing that the products were too cheap and the people too loud and ill-disciplined to be permitted in the representational heart of the unified *Reich.*[19]

Finally, the market became vulnerable to pressure exerted on the government by its competitors. The Berlin Christmas market, for example, had been removed from the Breitestrasse on Museuminsel in the 1880s as a result of the efforts of some local tradespeople, especially Rudolph Hertzog.[20] People who were against extending or even continuing the Munich Christmas market maintained that it only hurt established local retailers.[21] The number of small retailers expanded enormously during the late nineteenth century, as the economy and society struggled to adjust to a mass market.[22] Many of these retailers sold toys as a sideline. Specialty toy stores also emerged, such as Bernhard Keilach in Berlin, Hermann Kurtz in Stuttgart, and Joseph Obletter in Munich. These year-round establishments had higher overheads and therefore something to fear in the price competition of the Christmas markets. They thus had motive to attempt to persuade the government to alter the retailing market to their own advantage. These tradespeople preferred to manipulate the state to establish a preferred or even mandatory form for retail commerce in the city centers. They argued that the temporary, potentially transgressive stalls of the Christmas markets ought to be removed from the representational spaces, in favor of the large, stable merchants and their stores. In fact, the Berlin police preferred the large stores in part because the Christmas markets were difficult to police and discipline.[23]

Given the dependence of Christmas markets on state authorities, it is perhaps not surprising that they found themselves scuttling from place to place. Indeed, what may be most surprising is that the Berlin market persisted until 1890 to occupy the open areas before the (now-vanished) Hohenzollern palace, land with a unique ability to represent the power of the German monarchy. The removal of the markets from central locations had important consequences. The markets lost one of their central draws: the aesthetic ambience created by the baroque city centers. They also became increasingly bound by geography and class. *Vorwärts* noted that once the markets were removed from the city centers, their "audience" was "no longer collected from all classes as it once had been." *Vorwärts* explained, "Each social circle has its own quarter, and the Christmas market is now intended especially for the lower classes."[24] Since the principle customers were now the working class, the items sold had to be particularly cheap, putting pressure on the traders themselves.

Nonetheless, the traders in the Christmas market doggedly defied predictions of their imminent demise. A *Vorwärts* study found that the number of traders in the Berlin Christmas market had, with some volatility, actually increased from 3,142 in 1890 to 3,640 in 1904 (of course, the population of Berlin was growing at a considerably faster pace). In addition, a number of tradespeople gave up on the formal Christmas markets and began instead to wander through the new retailing districts of Berlin, pursuing the consumers who no longer came to them at the Christmas market.[25] This trend suggests an expanding market for Christmas gifts among the lower classes. Despite the rise of vigorous competition from established retailers and department stores and despite the gradual disappearance of well-to-do customers, the class-segregated Christmas markets actually grew. These Christmas markets served as critical outlets, supporting small toy producers in a sort of impoverished community of misery. The markets were no longer the central retailing venue for toys or Christmas presents more generally.

Markets for a Mass Market

The Christmas markets were ceding ground, literally and figuratively, to new retailing districts. To fully understand the emerging dynamics of urban retailing, one must keep in mind that these were growing cities. Many of what became the great shopping districts of pre–World War I Germany, such as Leipzigerstrasse and the area around the Gedächtniskirche in Berlin as well as the Frankfurt Zeil and the western part of Munich's Altstadt, were not principally retailing areas in the 1880s. Indeed, there was little of anything where Leipzigerstrasse approached Potsdamerplatz.[26] Modern retailing thrived on space—room for display and circulation. This often meant annexing new ground and creating new centers for Germany's cities. The changing culture of retailing—pioneered, but in no way monopolized, by department stores found in these new districts—would come to structure what and how toys were presented to the public.

Department stores derived their initial—perhaps primary—competitive advantage from their efforts to maximize the turnover of stock. Profit margins on individual items were drastically cut, nonnegotiable prices for cash only sales were set, and direct contact with producers was established (thereby cutting out a minimum of one wholesaler). Low prices were obviously an enormous incentive to buy. They were central to the construction of a mass market. Other innovations also served to encourage people to visit the store and to buy. Unlike traditional retailers, department stores did not have an unwritten compact that to enter the store implied a commitment to purchase. When prices had to be negotiated, or haggled over, the tradespeople felt it only appropriate that they be guaranteed that after all that effort, a sale was certain. The department stores also agreed to accept returns if the product turned out to be undesirable for some reason. Buyers therefore did not feel that they had to be ultraconservative. Mistakes could be corrected later.[27]

In this way, department stores transformed the relationship between buyer and seller. When buyers were committed to a purchase as soon as they entered a store, when they were forced to haggle over prices, and when all sales were final, the consumer was locked into an overt conflict with the retailer. The sale was a battle for individual advantage, a struggle over maximizing individual utility. One fought to protect one's own rationally defined interests. When one visited a department store, the conflict between buyer and seller was obscured. Because conflicts in interest were less visible, opportunities to enjoy and aesthetically appreciate the experience were significantly increased.

The second characteristic of these department stores was the attention paid to aesthetics. The way toward an improved aesthetics of shopping had been cleared by the reduced prices and camouflaged conflict of interests already mentioned. The consumer could use his or, more likely, her fantasy to imagine owning various commodities, to enjoy the shock of the new and unexpected without overt suspicion of the retailer. The way was open for individuals to enter a store with no intent to buy. The shopper came to look. The eye dwelt on the surface, and shoppers and stores conspired to keep initial impressions at a level of immediacy conducive to aesthetic enjoyment and imaginative engagement. The primacy of the visual and of the surface allowed shoppers to transform themselves into "passionate spectators"[28] of retail's spectacle. The construction of retail as an aesthetic experience gradually made the consumption of visual spectacle an equal partner to the prosaic act of provisioning a household. The opportunity to choose not to choose, to remain a spectator, allowed shoppers to imaginatively try many possibilities, thereby strengthening the individuals identity as "one who chooses."

To encourage aestheticized, impressionistic shopping, elaborate measures were taken to make the physical structures resemble palaces. In effect, retailers moved merchandise from the exterior of real palaces (Christmas markets) to the interior of ersatz palaces (department stores). Large, multistoried, glass-roofed foyers called "halls of light" were built to provide a cheap source of illumination. Such halls also provided a central organizing and aesthetic motif for the store. With the development of electrical lighting, however, such halls were no longer, strictly speaking, necessary. The cost of the electricity might well have been recouped through the additional merchandise that could have been put on the floor and sold. Nonetheless, the "halls of light" were integral to every major German department store before World War I because they had a critical aesthetic-commercial purpose: the intimation of space, luxury, and openness.[29] The aesthetic purpose was to assure shoppers that nothing was hidden from them. More important, the aesthetics asserted that this rich world of commodities was available to all. The wasteful use of space reinforced the perception of wealth and luxury created by the sheer multiplicity of products within the store, a sense of status and ease alien to all but a tiny minority in their lives outside the department store.

Aesthetic promises continued well beyond the "halls of light." A number of other architectural devices were employed to reinforce the central messages that department stores hoped to communicate to their customers. The earlier department stores used ever expanding show windows. The culmination of this trend was the Hermann Tietz store built on Leipzigerstrasse in 1900; it celebrated both commodities and visibility with an almost entirely glass facade.[30] As department stores began to attract customers from further up the social ladder, the luxurious accents multiplied. The Düsseldorf store of Leonhard Tietz constructed in 1908, for example, featured Sienese marble in its central "hall of light" and the occasional use of mahogany paneling.[31] In fact, in its use of materials, this store strongly resembled King Ludwig II of Bavaria's unfinished palace on Herrnchiemsee. The Wertheim store on Leipzigerstrasse featured a wide, bright, central "hall of light" with a marble statue called *Labor* and had two lavishly decorated rooms intended exclusively to allow customers to withdraw from the hubbub for a few moments of quiet repose.[32] Then there was the lighting. The Leonhard Tietz store in Düsseldorf employed 450 arc lights and 6,500 lamps for "general lighting"; outside, 200 lamps illuminated the building and another 72 arc lights were assigned to the show windows. There were also two hundred outlets scattered around the store for local "effect lighting."[33] Such lighting guaranteed a brilliant, glittering presentation of the merchandise and, more important, of the store itself.

This emphasis on visual presentation was critical because it was, in effect, the only advertising the majority of toys ever received. Given the structural disincentives for producers to create strong brand names or even to approach the consumer, retailers assumed the critical role of "speaking for" the product. This speech overwhelmingly took the form of visual spectacle. Increasingly, stores sought to foster an approach to shopping that emphasized the visual experience, a process that came to encompass both the store and the merchandise.

The attention paid to the glittering surfaces had a twofold, mutually reinforcing effect. First, it encouraged the shopper to approach the store and its merchandise in an aesthetic, spectating frame of mind, rather than a rational, calculating one—Romantically rather than utilitarianly. The focus was to be shifted as much as possible from the relation between the price tag and the pocketbook to the contemplation of surfaces. Second, by focusing on the surfaces, the aestheticization of shopping helped stoke consumer desire. Stores sought to construct a distance between objects and shoppers through the aestheticization of experience. That distance permitted shoppers to ape the flaneur, to become "passionate spectators" of retail spectacle. Distance, as Georg Simmel noted, is critical to desire.[34] Distance was the challenge to be overcome, the obstacle to possession that made possession valuable. Stores created distance so that shoppers could readily abolish it. They could walk into what resembled a palace, but unlike when visiting a real palace, they could walk out with the furnishings. In speaking the language of aesthetics and spectacle, stores spoke the language of desire.

I will return to desire but must here note one important consequence of this language of desire. The toy departments of the new department stores sought to address parents and children exclusively on the grounds of desire. One Munich department store, for example, explained that their "toy department, which assembles all the longings of the child's soul, all the desires of youth, has the third floor to itself."[35] Likewise, a Hamburg department store bragged that it had the "wonderful things that . . . form the longing of the hearts, and frequently the objects of dreams, of the children."[36] The stores sought to wrap toys in the aura of wonder and desire, not merely to sell more toys, but also to contribute to the sales strategy of the store as a whole. Naturally, the toys that they sold had to strive to fulfill the promises made by the store promoters. Toys, like the retailing system in which they were embedded, had to be spectacular.

In sum, over and above low prices, the department stores surrounded their merchandise with a sensual richness with which the Christmas market could not hope to compete. Department stores were even heated. Thus, Gustav Stresemann could write in 1900, "When one hears in a family, 'we are going to Wertheim,' it does not mean in the first place, we need something particularly critical for our home. Rather, one speaks almost of a day trip, which one makes to some beautiful local place."[37] The attraction that this intimate attention to luxurious detail exerted on large numbers of individuals created another enormous draw: the crowds. Department stores became an exquisitely decorated venue for people watching and the discrete fantasies that it engendered. They offered the world of commodities and the world of society. Was it any surprise, then, that both H. Tietz and Wertheim battled over the rights to use a globe as their exclusive symbol?[38]

The development of these new shopping norms recast the experiences associated with entire districts: the regions were themselves consumable. Everyday people from all walks of life came to enjoy the "experience" of Leipzigerstrasse or the Zeil. They consumed the surface spectacle as well as the physical products offered for sale. This dual activity constitutes "impressionist shopping." One was certainly not limited to department stores in ferreting out this "experience." One could sit at a café, order a beer at one of Aschinger's chain of pubs, or just wander the street, enjoying the sights and sounds or even the unpredictable eruptions endemic to an urban populace going many directions simultaneously. Then one could plunge into a store and go shopping. Even many of the smaller specialty shops adapted to the retailing environment promoted by the department stores. One prominent toy store in Berlin, Bernhard Keilach, began advertising promiscuously in newspapers ranging from the archconservative *Kreuzzeitung* to the socialist *Vorwärts.* It even ran advertisements about its nineteen show windows (see fig. 4 earlier in this chapter).[39] Keilach apparently believed that if you have plenty to display, people will come and will buy. Many specialty stores established fixed prices, offered catalogs, or even joined a buying cooperative to squeeze producers and traders into reducing their prices.[40] The competitive pressure from department stores forced other retailers to improve their own rational and aesthetic performance.

Christmas Shopping, Christmas Spectacle

The visual pleasure of "just looking" was a central part of the spirit of modern Christmas, the most important sales season for toys. Certainly, spectacle was in no way new to Christmas. Christmas shopping had long been associated with the consumption of visual images. The 1785 Leipziger Christmas market was reportedly very full with people "admiring the beautiful things" but "buy[ing] nothing."[41] The portrayals of the Berlin Christmas market in *Die Gartenlaube* in the 1890s emphasized the shopper as visual consumer. In one 1891 sketch (see fig. 5), a small crowd of onlookers stands transfixed, silently enjoying the mere sight of a hodgepodge collection of toys. A slightly hesitant desire is clearly evident in the faces of two young girls, as they chew absentmindedly on a finger while they stare fixedly at the merchandise. Meanwhile, two young boys are apparently gently wrestling for a better position from which to see.

There can be little doubt, however, that the new shopping districts excelled at Christmas spectacle. The opportunity to see was in large part the attraction of shopping. During Christmas, the visual stimulation normal to the new retail districts was multiplied. Christmas spectacle became a central motif for both retailers and, just as important, the popular press. Both collaborated to emphasize an experience of Christmas shopping predicated on the energy of crowds and the visual spectacle of urban retail.[42]

The construction of the shopping experience as an aesthetic pleasure was central to much of the feuilleton reporting on Christmas shopping. Peter Fritzsche argues, "Newspapers rewrote the city as a perpetually replenished sensation and, accordingly, addressed readers as compulsive spectators."[43] Even the socialists at *Vorwärts,* though committed to somewhat dry, rational arguments about socioeconomic change, could not avoid narrating the sensual attractions of Christmas in the city: "Christmas bustle wherever the eye looks! It gleams and shines and entices and dazzles from the shining show windows. There is a coming and going, an astonishment and testing; there gleam the eyes longingly and the transient come unwilling and through their lips comes a bewildered, happy astoundedness: see there, how delightful!"[44] Alfred Kerr wrote in the *Breslauer Zeitung* in 1899: "[O]nce a year I will not exchange with any other place, however joyful it may be, living in Berlin. That is at Christmas . . . Here is everything that belongs to it [Christmas]: namely, on the one hand, big city luxury; on the other, the festive Christmas atmosphere of an enormous working population . . . Christmas is a sweet family affair here and at the same time a business event."[45]

The *Berliner Lokal-Anzeiger* observed that during the Christmas season, people thronged to the department stores, "which attract everything to themselves like magnets."[46] According to the *Berliner Tageblatt,* entire sections of Berlin seemed to empty on the Sundays

Fig. 5. "Before the Toy Booth in the Christmas Market," *Die Gartenlaube* 38, no. 49 (1891): 110.

before Christmas. They had all gone shopping.[47] Indeed, as the press reported, the major cities drew visitors/shoppers from the surrounding countryside, who rode the commuter trains added especially for the Christmas season to go shopping in the bustling new shopping areas of the metropolis.[48] In this fashion, the press emphasized the inclusiveness of Christmas shopping, the universal attraction exerted by the spectacle of the new districts. No one, they suggested, was immune to the allure of Christmas shopping.

Christmas shopping was a multifaceted attraction in the view of the popular press: "Despite the extreme cold, the principle commercial streets were flooded by a multitude looking to buy . . . And those who did not want to attack their savings quite yet wandered around on the clear winter day and watched. So the street scene offered a colorful many-sidedness . . . In the afternoon and evening hours, the cafés in the Friedrichstadt were naturally the common rendezvous points for gift-laden pedestrians."[49] People would combine their purchasing with socializing and leisure. The mere opportunity to wander down streets lined with exquisitely decorated show windows was considered entertainment as well. The windows could even be a pretext for a family outing, as Stresemann had suggested. The venerable *Vossische Zeitung* concurred: "[T]he smallest sons and daughters were taken along for the great trek through the commercial streets of Berlin because of the beautiful show windows that present everything a child's heart demands in overwhelming abundance. And they were thrilled by all the wonders that were presented to them in the radiant light."[50] The *Münchner Neueste Nachrichten* reported, "[I]n no other activity can one make the principle 'Combine the pleasurable with the useful' so valid as in Christmas shopping."[51]

For the press, then, Christmas shopping was far more than buying. The specific geographic focus of most descriptions of Christmas shopping bears this out. Rather than emphasize the interior of stores, most journalists narrated Christmas as a story of the street. The streets were portrayed as an integral part of an elusive citywide "Christmas spirit." When the newspapers reported on the great Christmas shopping days, the three Sundays before Christmas,[52] they focused on the street scenes. They were as likely to report on a café as a department store, because the "story" was the overall "experience." That experience was a jumbled collision of department stores, show windows, cafés, specialty stores, streetcars, and people—huge crowds of people. When the *Berliner Tageblatt* sought to prove that Berliners were deeply emotional, it looked at the streets during a Berlin Christmas. The *Tageblatt* found Berlin's Christmas in gift-laden shoppers, in show windows, with street-corner toy peddlers, and on streetcars.[53] The construction of Christmas as a sort of street carnival led the press to emphasize the energies exerted at cross-purposes, the fugitive and the ephemeral that emerged and disappeared in the crowds of Leipzigerstrasse and elsewhere across Germany.

The melding of Christmas shopping and spectacle had important consequences. The readers of the popular press were confronted with a narrative configuration of their own experience that built on the sales strategies of the new retailing districts. According to both shop owners and journalists, consumers impressionistically consumed the spectacle of lights and crowds, the external glitz of the new retailing districts. For this reason, retailers carefully decorated and illuminated their premises: "The desire to buy is much more tied to the externally offered than the internally necessary. And our current day man in the field knows that."[54] For this reason, even *Vorwärts* (as cited earlier in this chapter) emphasized big city "bustle" and its relation to "the eye."

Merchandise, of course, was not immune to the consequences of the reconfiguration of the consumer into a desiring spectator and potential buyer. The object of retailing was to make shopping a spectacle, thus attracting people as "passionate spectators" and then transforming them into a buyer. This imposed a certain logic vis-à-vis the products stores hoped to sell, a structure that simultaneously encouraged and took advantage of shopping practices that incorporated *flanerie.* The products must be presented as desirable, not necessarily as useful. Some products are, naturally enough, more suited to spectacular presentation than others. Toys were one such product. The Christmas season abounded with toy exhibitions and presentations. The department stores in particular seemed to treasure toy displays. The show windows featuring scenes animated by toys were very popular: "Certain exhibitions become increasingly the rallying point of big and small people. The toy industry has allied itself with the panorama and uses it as a prop for fabulous alpine landscapes in which humans and animals prance on the mountainsides, waterfalls roar into valleys, thunderstorms threaten, alpine trains laboriously climb upwards and through long tunnels, triumphantly arriving at their destination. That is wonderful to watch."[55]

Of course, these were not just any toys. Mechanical, metal toys were best of all. They had the capacity to mesmerize through motion. The alpine landscape was populated by mechanical trains as well as moving people and animals. When the *Deutsche Spielwaren-Zeitung* reviewed toy show windows, it only noted toys in motion. Movement captured the eyes of shoppers and captivated their attention. The imperatives of sensational shopping militated in favor of that which astonished passersby. Mechanical toys did more than just add to the luster of the new retailing districts. They also broke up the seemless surface of the stores and store windows, the "straight-linedness" (*Geradelinigkeit*) of the avenues that conspired to push the crowds along.[56] Moving toys, being spectacles that developed through time, encouraged shoppers to pause, to eddy in the street. The movement shifted attention from the surfaces of stores and crowds of people to a specific product. The mechanical toy thus served a purpose beyond earning a profit. It defeated the "straight-linedness" of the city. Retailers did not use mechanical toys to advertise toys but, rather, to advertise themselves. Moving toys were able to accomplish the ideal of German advertising at the turn of the twentieth century. They were eye-catching and stood out from the crowd of competing images, even while remaining tastefully in the realm of the familiar.[57] The onlooker was enticed without being alienated. That the toys in the store window were children's playthings was, ultimately, unimportant and meaningless.

According to the tabloids, even the wandering toy hawkers on the street corners, refugees from the Christmas markets, prized mechanical toys above all. "The street corners stand . . . under the sign of the mechanical toy," asserted the *Berliner Tageblatt* in 1902. Three years later, it declared that "the kings of the street are the peddlers with the mechanical toys." The *Berliner Tageblatt* observed that the mechanical peddlers "with their cars, poodles, boxers, trains, june bugs, etc. were greedily surrounded by children."[58] In 1892, *Die Gartenlaube* depicted just such a scene, in which a toy peddler demonstrates his small, white, metal mouse on a street corner, surrounded mostly by children but also by adults, all of whom are fascinated by the mouse's antics.[59]

These street-corner toy peddlers point out the unique relation between toys and Christmas sensationalism. Toys, perhaps more than any other major product, were dependent on Christmas sales. This dependence meant that the majority of toys were sold under the sign of Christmas and Christmas shopping. These events were taken out of the everyday and assigned great cultural importance, endowing them with an aura that affected everything it touched. As toys appeared in particular abundance at Christmastime, they became a sort of sign for Christmas. The street-corner hawkers did not peddle toys in August. Furthermore, toys could be designed specifically to attract attention, to be spectacles in themselves. They were, therefore, more vulnerable to spectacularization than many other products. The retailing of toys was thus deeply affected by the changing retailing techniques. By contrast, other products and other retailers may have been less affected by spectacularization because many small shop owners resisted the growth of transclass, homogenizing, Fordist consumption.[60]

Retailers and reporters sought to turn mechanical toys into spectacles, to present them as images for visual consumption. Inevitably, this encouraged shoppers to assume a somewhat aesthetic attitude toward toys. The press argued that shoppers took advantage of the distancing effect of the aesthetic mode of perception to mentally play with the toys that retailers presented them. Toys were endowed with identities that drew on political or cultural events. The mouse depicted in the *Gartenlaube* sketch, for example, was called an *Altersversorgungsmaus,* a reference to recent social legislation.[61] Colorfully dressed dolls might be named "the beautiful Madame Boulanger" to general merriment.[62] Or one could mention the variety of toys growing out of the incident of the Captain from Köpenick.[63] Shoppers took the surfaces of toys and referred them to current events in a manner entirely removed from the alleged purpose of the toy. They set spectacles against one another, manipulating them to generate incongruity. The intellectuality of this manner of "playing" with toys seemed particularly suited for the urban mentality posited by Georg Simmel.

> [M]etropolitan life . . . underlies a heightened awareness and a predominance of intelligence in metropolitan man. The reaction to metropolitan phenomena is shifted to that organ which is least sensitive and quite remote from the depth of the personality. Intellectuality is thus seen to preserve subjective life against the overwhelming power of metropolitan life, and intellectuality branches out in many directions and is integrated with numerous discrete phenomena.[64]

Up-to-date, even faddish jokes made in the course of Christmas shopping or incorporated directly into childrens' playthings are examples of intellectuality "branching out." Shoppers strolling through the throngs of other Christmas shoppers enjoyed the opportunity to apply their intellect to the arbitrary events, sights, and objects they encountered. Through this intellectuality, they learned how they could enjoy the novelty and excitement of the constantly changing surfaces—the ever new sights that modern retailing provided—without fear of being overwhelmed by the demands of the city. Intellectuality provided an emotional distance that permitted engagement with diversity, a distanced interaction similar to that of the flaneur. Much as the creation of meaning for the observed minutiae of city life lay at the heart of *flanerie,* so consumers imposed "stories"—or meanings—on the commodified toys of the marketplace. Vignettes taken from the pages of the popular press were turned into makeshift contexts that fleetingly reintegrated anonymous toys into the cultural world of consumers. Surfaces and images were consumed without reference to the underlying object. Shoppers joked about Madame Boulanger in relation to a toy because of surface resemblances. That the toy was a doll to be played with was irrelevant. Therefore, the toy became significant as long as shoppers sustained the narrative or joke. The foundation for these narratives was the popular press. Just as the press supplied images for toy makers, the press elaborated the stories around Boulanger and the Captain from Köpenick. Shoppers were not creating their own ideas or constructing authentic identities through these jokes. Drawing on a ready-made pool of imagery provided by the daily press, shoppers amused themselves by relating the unrelated.

In fact, retailers sought to encourage this fleeting reappropriation by placing their toys in imaginative scenes, such as the alpine panorama previously described. In this way, shoppers were presented not with the mute, alienated things that producers and distributers provided to stores but, rather, with toys incorporated into familiar scenes and stories. The sensual atmosphere of impressionist shopping cultivated by modern retailing encouraged an immediacy of observation that permitted and even enabled this assertion of imaginative sovereignty over commodities. The presentation of toys and stores as surfaces suited to visual consumption cultivated a habit of playful speculation on the part of the shopper about the possible meanings or stories that could adhere to otherwise blank objects. Shoppers thus created meaning out of visual stimuli, recapitulating in debased form the role of the flaneur.

Given the paradigmatic significance the flaneur has enjoyed since the work of Walter Benjamin, it is worthwhile exploring this connection further. Mary Gluck argues in her outstanding study of modernism in nineteenth-century Paris: "In the *flaneur*'s perceptive vision, what appeared incoherent and meaningless gained focus and visibility. He brought alive and invested with significance the fleeting, everyday occurrences of the city."[65] Through his vision, the flaneur was able to stabilize and assign meaning to the unstable and illegible experience of modern public life. Gluck distinguishes between two types of significance and therefore two types of flaneur: the popular and the avant-garde. Whereas the "popular *flaneur*" used his "gift of imagination . . . to penetrate beneath the surface of appearance of things and to discover their hidden essence,"[66] the "avant-garde *flaneur*" saw that "modernity had ceased to exist as a social text, that waited to be deciphered . . . and became an aesthetic construct, that needed to be freshly created through the . . . imaginative act."[67] The impressionist shoppers who populated the pages of Berlin's tabloids had learned to remain on the surface of urban spectacle, to delight in the surface and use the "imaginative act" for private amusement. They shared an attitude, if not an ambition, with the avant-garde flaneur. Rather than seeking to tease out some hidden truth that inhered in toys or other consumer products, they simply narrated their own.

The shopper and the avant-garde flaneur shared a common aestheticizing approach to the visual contents of the city. The level of truth they sought to construct, however, varied enormously. The flaneur followed Baudelaire and sought to fashion an ever new modernity through the heroic faculties of their own imagination. They sought to divine the transcendent in the ephemeral. Shoppers, by contrast, sought to manufacture associative links between isolated phenomena, links that bespoke of little more than superficial likeness.

As a sort of side effect to the aestheticization of shopping, children were increasingly defined by retailers in terms of desires. Constituting the child as filled with desire was perceived as a highly ambivalent enterprise. On the one hand, a child's longing for a toy was relatively innocent, even charmingly naive. One could certainly argue that children's desires were safe as long as they were directed at objects properly defined as childish. One sketch by *Die Gartenlaube* depicted a toddler striving to reach a toy presented by a family member (see fig. 6). That portrayal of infant desire was in no way condemnatory. The child's obvious longing was directed in a safe direction and could be easily seen as sweet and innocent.

A child's desire for toys was acceptable and even lovable as long as it was disciplined and limited by adults, particularly parents. A problem then emerged: what happens if adults do not properly limit the appetites of their children? One critic of the toy industry wrote: "How is it possible that such pompous toys find praise and are bought? If the youth [*junge Welt*] can stare at the glittering, colorfully painted, extremely tastefully assembled toys in the show windows of the department stores, then naturally there emerges the desire to own such things. The overly tender mother can not deny her sweeties a wish, and the good uncle and the loving aunt cannot stop the flattery of the nieces and nephews, and so the decorative, costly toys are bought."[68] Suddenly the child became sovereign. The *Berliner Tageblatt* referred to children at Christmastime as "despots" who "tyrannize" their parents.[69] This was obviously hyperbole, but it alluded to a problem many felt was real. When the individual was no longer capable of dominating the urges that retailers cultivated, danger intruded in the form of overturned social hierarchies.

Fig. 6. "At the Christmas Market for the First Time," *Die Gartenlaube* 43, no. 49 (1895): 813.

Retailers consciously sought to cultivate desires in children. They approached children as desiring creatures and portrayed them as such. The toys they showcased, which they thought most salable, were therefore toys designed to be visually stimulating—toys that would appeal to the distant, distracted passerby. These were especially the mechanical toys.

In this respect, trends internal to the retail sector worked to favor certain types of toys. For their own reasons, leading retailers strongly preferred specific types of toys. The toy industry's trends favoring metal, mechanical toys were thus powerfully reinforced from without. Mechanization and spectacular retailing worked hand in hand to promote a particular branch of the toy industry.

One need only take a second look at the development of the toy industry itself with the developments in retailing in mind to see the industry's modernization in a different light. The rise of large makers of mechanical toys owes something to the efforts of retailers to attract people as *Schaulustige* (people looking to look) and then to transform them into paying customers. Mechanization of production processes and the development of interdependent production networks must cede some explanatory space to the appetite of retailers and consumers for spectacle.

The changing practices in the retailing sector emerged out of many of the same forces that were reordering production: improving productivity, rising wage demands by labor, and so on. From the perspective of retailers, these factors allowed a considerable increase in sales volume. But first, a new approach to retailing was required. This entailed a sort of rationalization and "modernization" of retailing. Within the retailing sector, however, rationalization often brought with it an expectation that the consumer would abandon reason. It became rational to encourage the customer to become not irrational but, rather, a-rational, aesthetic. The consumer should evaluate a product not on the basis of its usefulness but, rather, on the basis of its momentary attractiveness. The rationalization of the retailing and toy industry owed some of its dynamism to the assumption that consumers could be approached as beings guided more by aesthetics than by reason.

The retailing market also shaped consumer preferences, presenting a vision of modernity to German parents and children. In show windows, toy retailers constructed a toy world that reflected the world outside those windows. Speed and movement predominated on both sides of the glass. The fascination with movement demonstrated by retailers was rooted in the dynamics inherent to the refashioned norms of sales. An unintended by-product of the retailing revolution was an increasing intellectual reappropriation of alienated products, such as commercial toys, as shoppers constructed stories around the commodities presented for their visual stimulation. This fundamentally creative act anticipated the imaginative appropriation of toys made by the eventual toy consumers, children. The anarchic, hyperindividualized play of imagination around toys, on the parts of both shoppers and children, provided the central joy of toys, as well as one of the most important sources of criticism of "modern" toys.

4. Toys Are Good to Think
Education, Play, and Consumption

By the end of the nineteenth century, toy makers and toy consumers alike assumed that toys were, somehow, educational. Parents clung to this belief, which ensured that they were assisting their children, not corrupting them. Toy makers were quite content to reinforce that notion. To believe that play and toys may educate requires a certain vision of cognitive development and, by extension, of human individuality. If we are to believe that play can shape the mind or communicate important information, we must believe that interaction with the world constitutes learning. Differing constructions of human "nature" have yielded different defenses of the educational value of play and things, with implications for what purposes toys had and which toys were desirable. Broadly speaking, two approaches dominated nineteenth-century perceptions of play and education, each approach rooted in philosophical systems of the eighteenth century. The first was an outgrowth of the empirical psychology of John Locke and the Enlightenment. This tradition emphasized the communication of information, whether in the form of facts or activities. The second approach was rooted in Romanticism and emphasized the cultivation of imagination and fantasy as a necessary element in the construction of a healthy subjectivity. By considering the elaboration of ideas about the role of play in cognitive development, we are inevitably engaging the efforts of German middle-class society to construct certain types of individuals. If toys were to be educational, they had to educate toward a particular goal.

Examining the ideas of play and education has a threefold purpose. First, the assertion that play and toys were educationally valuable emerged as a critical legitimizer of toy consumption. As we saw earlier, parents were quite keen to believe they could educate while amusing. Second, in defining material objects as tools for the development of autonomous individuals, writers necessarily entered into a discussion of consumption. Analyses of the educational value of toys had to engage the possibilities inherent in the construction of subjectivities through things. The interaction between individuals and their environment could not, in the late nineteenth century, avoid the increasingly commercial provenance of that environment. In debating the pedagogical value of toys, therefore, Germans were at the very least implicitly debating the role of commercial objects in the elaboration of identity and self. By 1900, they often were explicitly discussing the role of commerce in self-formation. In that fashion, the basic philosophic discourse in Western society about the nature of human subjectivity inevitably became implicated in both constructing and critiquing consumption. Third, and for that very reason, critiques of the educational potential of commercial toys were simultaneously critiques of modernity. To engage the failures of things to properly construct individual subjectivities was to engage the possibilities of modernity and its failures.

These were not the concerns of obdurate conservatives, yearning after a medieval idyll. In many respects, toy critics were cultural modernists. They believed they could revive and sustain the most basic normative aspiration of modern society, the autonomous individual. Their concerns about toys grew out of more general cultural movements, such as the *Kunsterziehungsbewegung* (art education movement) and the *Kunstgewerbereformbewegung* (Arts and Crafts reform movement). One can even find the echoes of a Nietzschean self-construction. These movements developed the discursive language that informed the critiques of modern toys. Toys became a means for these writers to explore how individuals interacted with their material environment in a society moving toward mass consumption. Toy critics joined theorists of art education, such as Konrad Lange, and sociologists, such as Georg Simmel, to argue that human beings should not passively observe their world. One had to actively organize it, they argued; one had to make one's environment a reflection of one's own self. Otherwise, individuals would find themselves excluded from their own world, impoverished amid their wealth.

The Roots of Educational Play

An investigation of the educational capacity of toys should begin with a brief discussion of empirical, or sensationalist, psychology. The toy industry and some pedagogues in the late nineteenth and early twentieth centuries would take positions rather similar to those of the sensationalists, and other theorists were, in part, reacting to the eighteenth-century orthodoxy of sensationalist psychology. Since later disputes would resemble that of the Enlightenment sensationalists and their German critics, an understanding of how and why play came to be accepted as educational is indispensable.

The notion that human cognition was the sum of its sensory inputs became the basic psychological doctrine of English and French psychology during the eighteenth century.[1] It was argued that the notions and structures of the mind—the tools we use to know the world—are given to us through our senses, that we passively receive them after birth as we adjust ourselves to the environment into which we are born. According to this doctrine, ideas and even reason are not inherent attributes but, rather, are learned through observation; we are, as Locke famously asserted, "blank slates."

The development of sensationalist psychology firmly associated the cultivation of human thought and reason with objects outside the human mind. The child's interaction with the world, while playing, could therefore be associated with the development of cognition, a critical innovation. Perhaps it is not surprising, therefore, that Locke actually suggested toy blocks with letters on their sides as an elementary tool for teaching reading. The persistent observation of the world was then a useful tool for learning the most basic tools of life. Rousseau clearly reflects this view in *Emile,* suggesting that outside play would imperceptibly teach Emile to reason properly.

From Locke's sensationalist psychology and the wider Enlightenment developed a related German pedagogical theory, philanthropism. The *Philanthropen* hoped to give people useful skills for the developing capitalist economy and, in so doing, to simultaneously help society and individuals. Some *Philanthropen* also hoped that they could shape productive workers and citizens through play. They were concerned that children be habituated to useful values and trained in desirable skills, and they maintained that information could be presented to the senses through play. Rather than emphasizing the teaching of facts, such as with Locke's alphabet blocks, the *Philanthropen* hoped to teach values and activities, through modeling.[2] This hope anticipated the belief of many late nineteenth-century academic pedagogues. The argument was that play educated through mimesis, on the assumption that our subjectivities are principally receptive organisms, reliant above all on vision.

An alternative basis for the educational benefits of play was developed by the German Romantics. The rebels of the Sturm und Drang and Romantic movements reacted violently against the utilitarian orthodoxy of sensational psychology and the *Philanthropen.* Given its emphasis on the senses, sensationalist psychology implied that humans were passive learners, that sensory images impressed themselves on the consciousness of individuals and thereby changed those individuals. This implication of dependence on the senses brought up a variety of urgent philosophical questions. What impelled people to learn? How could humans be creative? If human consciousness was an amalgamation of accumulated sensory inputs, how could humans ever be more than their environment?

The Romantics clung to a vision of humanity that emphasized the moral and cognitive freedom of the individual, which Kant had so forcefully defended. According to the Romantics, humans retained an inalienable freedom to choose their actions and shape their world, and from this fundamental urge to connect emerged the creative faculty that undergirded artistic productivity. What then developed, particularly among the writers of the Sturm und Drang and Romantic movements, was what philosopher Charles Taylor has termed an "expressive self." Human beings were portrayed as unique individuals, each with an inner access to truth and morality. The true self was within, free of external restraint or pressure. As Taylor explains, this authentic self had to be "made manifest" (expressed and constructed) through action in and on the world, primarily through acts of creativity. Without the act of expression, the individual could not know himself or herself, nor could the individual know the voice of nature, truth, and morality. Consequently, self-expression and creativity were fundamental to both morality and autonomy.[3]

The sources of human creativity fascinated the proponents of both the Sturm und Drang and Romantic movements. Both saw creativity as central to full humanity: through creation, one molded the external world to define oneself and master reality. Enlightenment sensationalist psychology, however, seemed to leave little room for human creativity. It is not surprising, therefore, that it was on this front that many chose to attack Enlightenment values.

To flesh out this tradition, I will briefly consider the works of Friedrich Schiller and Jean Paul Richter. Both were widely admired authors and poets, but they also took time from their artistic production to develop nuanced and influential works on education. In his youth, Schiller had written an almost paradigmatic work of Romanticism and Sturm und Drang, *The Robbers.* I will here focus, however, on his later essay about aesthetics, *On the Aesthetic Education of Man.* In that essay, Schiller retained a number of basic points of view characteristic of Romanticism but attempted to find a certain harmoniousness that would allow a stable relationship with established society.

Friedrich Schiller plays a somewhat anomalous but critical role in the present analysis. As we shall see, Schiller's discussion of what he terms "play" was focused more on adults than on children. Thus, while his principles hold for children, they were not conceived with children in mind. Schiller developed a thesis that made play not merely useful but a moral good. He thereby established the theoretical foundation that would allow writers a century later to link commercial toys to a wider critique of consumer capitalism.

Schiller's principal argument in *Aesthetic Education* was that modern individuals suffered from a highly fragmented self, which undermined the possibility of real morality and real happiness. Schiller further argued that before political freedom in any meaningful sense could be achieved, humankind had to arrive at a higher moral plane. Political liberty required prior self-restraint. To understand why this was so, we must first consider the point at which humans had arrived in their development. Schiller defined modern humans as the imperfect union between two principles, one rational and the other sensual. This was the fundamental divide within the human breast. The rational impulse sought after the timeless and immutable in life, while the sensual impulse hoped to disappear into the chaotic flow of the transitory. The one was incompatible with life, the other with any higher purpose. Schiller believed that individuals had to achieve a harmonious union between these two principles (although their very definitions were antithetical to one another) to find the balance necessary for political freedom.

How were these opposed principles to be yoked into an effective, cooperative relationship? According to Schiller, the aesthetic brings the two principles together into a well-rounded whole. He termed this aesthetic principle the "play drive." Schiller gave an enormously wide definition of play. In essence, he saw play as an absorption in the moment, such that time moved because the individual was active, but such that the connection to external time was eliminated. Time existed but did not exist. This remarkable achievement was only possible because the individual was applying rational, timeless forms to the fleeting contents presented to his or her attention. The rational and the sensual principles were brought into an alliance in the service of aesthetics. Only when these two principles were roughly balanced could humankind maintain a link to life while overcoming the momentary, dangerous impulses that are so characteristic of life. As one historian of German aesthetics put it, "in play, man expresses his complete nature, no longer divided into sensuality and morality."[4] Otherwise, individuals degenerated into either bloodless abstracters trapped among the social forms they had created or sensual beasts incapable of pausing to consider interests beyond their own or the consequences of their actions. In the eyes of Schiller, therefore, play was a means of attaining a higher morality, an ability to integrate and moderate the disparate sides of human nature to bring out the ideal man within. This "ideal man," briefly discussed in the fourth letter of *Aesthetic Education,* was inherent in every individual. The "great task" of human existence was to harmonize the real, empirical individual with this "ideal."[5] The form-giving impulses inherent in play first teach the individual to imaginatively conceive of a higher good (related to Kant's moral categorical imperative) and then allow the individual to impose that vision on the shifting contents of reality. Only through play and creativity was the "ideal man" who combines moral duty and sensual pleasure possible. In this manner, creativity became either a critical assistant to realizing the imperatives of morality or a means of subsuming morality into a still higher, aesthetic good. In either case, play and creativity were valorized as means of realizing the ideal. In this way, Schiller was among the first to thematize the "widely shared sense that the creative imagination is an indispensable locus of moral sources."[6]

Schiller asserted a necessary link between the construction of the self and form-giving action in the physical world. If we extend these principles to toys, several conclusions are inescapable. First, for the child to become so absorbed in a toy that the child is active yet disconnected from external time, the toy ought to require some manner of action from the child. Mere watching is insufficient. Second, if the child is to apply the formal drive, the toy should be somehow incomplete; it should offer the child the opportunity to refashion it.

The Romantic poet Jean Paul Richter brought the idea of an active and coherent personality into an explicit discussion of education and toys in his popular *Levana, oder Erziehungslehre.* How might play contribute to the developing child? Jean Paul was not immediately clear. He began with a definition: "Play is, in the first place, the working off at once of the overflow of both mental and physical powers . . . Play is the first poetry of the human being." This definition led him to conclude, "[P]lay forms all the powers, without imparting an overwhelming influence to any one."[7] That was a rather vague and unhelpful definition, although it does recall Schiller's emphasis on a balanced personality. If we look further, however, we will see that Jean Paul was clearly drawing on the notions of Fichte and Herder (Jean Paul had been a friend and protégé of Herder's) to fashion a theory of play.

> During the first months of existence the child knows nothing of creative play or efforts, only of the passive reception of impressions. During that period of the most rapid physical growth, and inpouring of the world of sense, the overwhelmed soul does not direct itself towards those active games in which afterwards its superabundant powers find relief. It can only look, listen, catch, touch: so laden, its little hands and arms quite full, it can do and attempt little with them.
>
> It is only at a later period, when, by means of the five acts of the five senses, the knowledge of the outer world is attained, and one word after another gradually liberates the mind, that greater freedom produces active play, and that fancy begins to move, whose unfledged wings language first plumes. Only by words does the child obtain an inner world opposed to the outer, by which he can set the external universe in motion.[8]

The mixing of Herder's equation of language and thought with Fichte's definition of the self through the opposition between the internal ego and the external nonego is unmistakable.[9] Play was the expression of the self-consciousness of the child; it was coextensive with activity and therefore was closely associated with thought and language.

Jean Paul warned, "[G]ive no plaything whose end is to be looked at; but let every one be such as to lead to work."[10] A great deal was wrapped up in Jean Paul's statement. It was in part a reflection of the Romantic movement's distrust of any overreliance on vision.[11] Jean Paul therefore explicitly links the acquisition of knowledge of the world to the "five acts of the five senses." There was a particular concern, however, about sight and play.

The Romantics, Jean Paul included, saw imagination and fantasy as a cognitive process that created new forms and images within the mind and soul of the individual. Images crafted by fantasy were not provided by external sensory inputs. Fantasy was therefore a sign and guarantor of individual freedom and independence, since the self could generate its own images and therefore its own ideas. If the mind was dependent on the outside world for its images and ideas, how could the individual ever truly assert his or her independence, ever be more than a mechanistic processor of images entirely dependent on the surrounding world for even its most intimate ideas? This was a direct contrast and challenge to the cognitive orthodoxy of the radical Enlightenment as well as sensationalist psychology.[12] While explicitly dismissing the privileging of vision, however, Jean Paul and the Romantics were not entirely able to ignore the power of the simple assumptions that led Voltaire, for example, to define an idea as "an image that paints itself on my brain" and to claim, "The most abstract ideas are the consequences of the objects I've perceived."[13] As a result, Jean Paul simultaneously downplayed and feared the power of sight. There was considerable anxiety that an overreliance on vision could exert a substantial and deleterious influence on the individual. In the view of Jean Paul and others, a one-sided reliance on sight could come to displace the internal images generated by fantasy and imagination. An improper education could make Voltaire right and could thereby eliminate the possibility for genuine creativity and autonomy. Thus, parents were warned to "give no plaything whose end is to be looked at."

The central requirement for educational play was that the child do something to and with the toy; one ought never sit passively. Jean Paul wrote, "[T]he child plays with things, consequently with himself."[14] Jean Paul was not limiting himself to physical play. Indeed, while physical play was important for developing the body, he granted pride of place to the role of the mind in play: "In beasts the body alone plays, in children the mind."[15] The play of the mind was ultimately imaginative, fantastic. The playthings of children should therefore be as abstract—as nonspecific—as possible. For that reason, Jean Paul warned that "colors . . . weaken the creative faculty." More to the point, he argued, "so much more readily does fancy invest an invisible Adam's rib with human limbs and fashionable costume, than a doll which only differs in size from a lady, and which, on its side, appears to the imagination at the next tea-party so perfect that it can be improved in nothing."[16] According to Jean Paul, the imaginative faculty, the most active mental operation available and necessary to self-definition, was to be encouraged through imaginative play. Indeed, Jean Paul suggested that the finest "toy" around was one with almost no form whatsoever, sand.[17] In his estimation, imagination and experience were explicitly and strongly privileged over vision.

Jean Paul also considered the gender differences that both demonstrate themselves in play and stem from it. In so doing, Jean Paul illustrated the remarkable ability of gender discourses to take on different forms with very different implications and remain unquestioned. We have already seen that Jean Paul assumed a hostile attitude toward dolls. Dolls were associated with unimaginative, mentally inactive play; they were too perfect and therefore required little cognitive effort on the part of the child. Jean Paul held the doll up to ridicule and suggested that it was better to entirely fabricate an imagined woman than to carry around a too-perfect prop. Who, precisely, was the child he had in mind when making this statement? Surely it was a girl who had the choice between the doll and the imagined "Adam's rib." Girls, too, were thus admitted to Jean Paul's club of imagining, thinking beings. He explicitly recommended sand (that perfect toy) for both sexes. Indeed, for Jean Paul, the sovereign power of creativity in the formation of an individual suffered no infringements or limitations as long as the focus was on creativity and children generally.

But when, in a later chapter of *Levana,* Jean Paul returned to discuss specifically the education of girls (a discussion that was in itself a significant development), his discourse changed. This change was most clearly expressed when Jean Paul asserted: "Men love *things* best; for instance, truths, possessions, countries: women love *persons* best . . . Even when a child, a woman loves a mock-human-being, a doll, and works for it; a boy gets hold of a wooden horse and a troop of tin soldiers, and works *with* them."[18] This statement did several things. First, females became defined by the fact that they played with dolls; it was inherent in their nature qua females. The former suggestion that girls could benefit from more imaginative playthings and the explicit condemnation of dolls disappeared. Furthermore, there was a critical change in preposition between the two sexes. Girls worked "for" their toys, boys worked "with" theirs. Boys were thereby defined as more independent. There was also an implication of greater creativity and thought in the play of boys, since their play was not constrained by the limitations of their plaything. The possibilities of human creativity offered by one part of Jean Paul's text were later divided into gendered categories that were then linked to the social roles that boys and girls would assume later in life. In effect, in one section of his book, girls were enlisted in the project of exalting the imagination, while in another chapter, they were shunted aside into a secondary category defined by their reproductive functions. This was a pattern that would repeat itself throughout the century. Girls were included in the general project of education through play, but that education was often anticipated as a narrow conditioning for motherly duties. The allegedly universal concern for fostering the vigorous mind and creative personality that underpinned the conceptualization of educational play was allowed to silently pass by girls.

The *Philanthropen* and the Romantics believed that play was a useful means of constructing a specific and desirable individual. The project for both was to elaborate a proper individual and, from that foundation, to construct a fit society. Nonetheless, despite the common aspiration to construct a healthy society on the basis of healthy individuals, there were clearly differences. The *Philanthropen* quite emphatically hoped to fashion hardworking, socially docile subjectivities. Their utilitarian aspirations were designed for a capitalist economy and society, a self that had become accustomed to self-control and self-manipulation, in part through the agency of play. The Romantics, by contrast, emphasized the cultivation of quite different individuals for quite different ends. They sought to construct a whole, healthy subjectivity—one that integrated the multiple facets of human life and expressed an authentic self. The doctrinal positions of the Romantics and the *Philanthropen* reflected different assumptions about human nature and purpose, despite their common commitment to individualism.

Friedrich Fröbel

Against this intellectual background of the theory of the expressive, creative personality and the privileges granted children, we can situate the founder of the kindergarten movement, Friedrich Fröbel (1782–1852). Fröbel was a doubly important figure to the present analysis. He dedicated a great deal of thought and ink to the role of self-activity and play in the development of children. In particular, Fröbel put toys in the center of his program. "Things" were absolutely critical to proper development, he argued. After Fröbel, toys were rarely far from discussions of educational play. He was also important for the movement he spawned. Far more than any writer considered thus far in this discussion, Fröbel was able to disseminate quite widely the notion that toys have an important role in human development. He did this through his own schools, through the training of Kindergarten teachers, through his writings, and, most important, through the recruitment of lieutenants who passionately spread Fröbel's message. These followers, particularly Bertha von Marenholtz-Bülow, continued to write and speak on Fröbel's theories long after he himself had passed away.[19] Moreover, Fröbel's advocacy of women's rights tied his doctrine to early German feminism and thereby won supporters who might otherwise have passed by his writings.[20] Consequently, although Fröbel did not enjoy the same professional approbation as other pedagogues, his message was far more widely spread.

Friedrich Fröbel was a rather intriguing figure, one who drew on a wide variety of intellectual sources. The breadth of his sources may explain some of the reluctance of the academic pedagogues to embrace Fröbel.[21] The influences of Comenius, Rousseau, Pestalozzi, Fichte, Schelling, Jean Paul, and Hegel were relatively benign. Those of the seventeenth-century Silesian mystic Jacob Boehme, Neoplatonism, and a form of microcosm-macrocosm analogy reminiscent of Paracelsus were rather more suspect.[22] Fröbel, in other words, had a genius for heterodoxy.

The roots of Fröbel's pedagogical theory of play lay in his Romantic, expressive notions of human individuality. He maintained that each human had an irreducibly individual character or personality, an "ideal man," and that the goal of education in the broadest sense was to encourage the full development of this personality. "The purpose of education," he wrote, "is the representation of a true-to-its-calling [*berufstreuen*], pure, undamaged, and therefore holy life."[23]

This statement warrants closer examination. The adjective *berufstreun* requires a bit of explanation. *Beruf* is often translated into English as "vocation." Fröbel, however, was not talking in terms of vocational education. For his purposes, *Beruf* is literally a calling, the divinely predetermined task or works of the individual. Once it is understood that Fröbel is referring to God's purpose for the individual, the language about a "pure, undamaged, and therefore holy life" makes a great deal more sense. If the individual leads his or her life according to the purposes envisioned by God, that life must be pure—indeed, holy. Only if the individual resists those purposes, for whatever reason, may a "damaged" life develop.

Even more important in Fröbel's statement is the noun "representation." For Fröbel, the nature of the individual, his or her "calling," was hidden deep within the personality. Much as nature was a cipher to

Fröbel, so was the individual's "identity."[24] The task of education was, consequently, to help the child recognize himself or herself. To this end, Fröbel emphasized self-activity, self-education. From the very moment of birth, activity, or movement, was "the beginning of the child's becoming self-aware [*des Selbstbewustwerdens*]." The play of the child had a "high seriousness and deep purpose."[25] Through the child's own activity, particularly through his or her play, the child represented to himself or herself his or her own nature: "[T]he impulse to activity . . . corresponds fully to her [human] nature, which is to have the power to perceive, to comprehend, to obtain self-knowledge, to become more and more conscious of her own personality."[26] Within each individual, then, Fröbel saw an "ideal man" that was predetermined and immutable. But that ideal did not necessarily fully emerge. It had to be gradually freed, realized through the free representation of the self in play. In this respect, Fröbel's doctrine exemplifies the role of creative expression as both articulation and construction of the self.[27]

Fröbel argued that play simultaneously exercised the "organs by which [the child] can make the external internal" as well as the limbs by which the child "can represent her internal nature outwardly." He resolved this duality, in almost Schilleresque fashion, by emphasizing the power of the individual as a "perceptive and uniting spirit."[28] The individual spirit was both the synthesis and the agent of the urge to shape the external world according to the desires of the internal personality and the ability of external stimuli to shape the individual.

Fröbel crafted very specific toys that were, he argued, perfectly designed to encourage the child to recognize the structure of the universe and his or her role in it. These toys, all age-specific, began with a ball, moved on to rectangular blocks, and progressed from there.[29] These shapes were to represent the basic structures of the universe. They were therefore highly abstract. The child was forced to employ his or her imagination powerfully to create games from these toys, much like Jean Paul's children would have to use their imaginations to play with sand. Given the "high seriousness and deep purpose" inherent in play, how could it be otherwise? The demands placed on the imagination would then give the child the opportunity to represent—almost allude—to his or her own ideal self. Throughout Fröbel's work, there is a persistent commitment to a Romantic, expressive self. The individual was not constructed by external forces, but it was, in a sense, mutable. Humans each had a unique, mysterious essence that had to be represented to the child. Fröbel institutionalized the role of play and toys in cultivating the expressive self. Toys, in Fröbel's system, became central to the proper elaboration of individuality.

Play in the Pedagogical Community

As a necessary effect of the expanding educational system throughout the German lands, the second half of the nineteenth century saw a growing community of dedicated pedagogues. Social and state demand for professional teachers led to academic training programs and thence to a field of scholars devoted to the study of education and human development. The new discipline of education explored in scientific fashion the whole of pedagogy, including the role of play and toys in early childhood. Within this professionalizing community, we find roughly the same dichotomy as existed in the eighteenth century. There remained an influential school of thought that validated play and toys as a means to communicate information, generally either proper habits or desirable occupations.[30] This utilitarian school focused on the preparation of children for the capitalist economy. The second school was a rather pale reflection of the Romantic line of argument, advocating a cultivation of creativity that was detached from the wider claims made by their predecessors.[31]

Such writers as Eduard Ackermann (the director of the Karolinenschule and the Lehrerinnenseminar in Eisenach) or even the social reformer Paul Natorp were very concerned to tame play. These individuals did not deny that play had educational benefits. Indeed, Ackermann wrote explicitly, "[W]hoever views the play of children only as entertainment misunderstands its meaning as a not unimportant means of education." Nonetheless, Ackermann viewed play as a means of inculcating the values of patience, perseverance, self-sacrifice, respect for rules, and such.[32] Play was thereby disciplined even as it disciplined the child. The imaginative element was downplayed, and cooperative, social values were praised in its place. The potentially unruly aspects of play, the anarchistic exercise of individual fantasy, were sidelined. Paul Natorp went even further in disciplining play. Significantly, Natorp's pedagogy was based in large part on the assumption that modern society suffered from an overindividualization based in liberal ideology. The task of pedagogy, in Natorp's view, was to root the individual more firmly in the community. Natorp's attitude toward play reflects this ideological position. Play was a manifestation of imagination, but, Natorp reassured his readers, "the gradual crossover of play to purposeful, more and more consciously goal-oriented work offers a wholesome counterweight against the danger of a one-sided overflow of fantasy."[33]

Both these writers represented a tradition that saw fantasy as overly individual, potentially subversive. The individual caught up in his or her fantasy became detached from society and reality. In fact, fantasy and play could undermine the possibility of a productive life. The Leipzig gymnasium teacher Gustav Siegert argued: "[W]eak and nervous children like to play when they should be working . . . Deficient strength of will, spiritual incapacity, inability to rule the body or control the fantasy are all the principle signs of *Spielerei.*"[34] *Spielerei* can be translated as "horsing around," but clearly much more was meant here. Siegert had medicalized and stigmatized children who enjoyed play too much. It is instructive that what made *Spielerei* dangerous was the ability of fantasy to overrule the will. The child threatened to become socially valueless because the link between fantasy and play encouraged the child to cease setting goals. Play and fantasy tended to be without any immediate goal; indeed, many critics defined play as activity without any immediate purpose. If the child became overly inured to such purposelessness, the consequences could be grave indeed, argued Siegert and others. Precisely what made play deeply moral for Schiller made play deeply suspect for Siegert. Siegert's investigation of pathological play clearly laid out what Ackermann and Natorp merely implied. Play and fantasy were useful but also potentially dangerous. They had to be kept within bounds lest they overwhelm the individual to his or her detriment and to that of society. For these writers, play was a threat to the development of individual autonomy, rather than (as it had been for Romantics) a critical tool for its creation.

More moderate were those who saw play as a means of preparing children for adult life through imitation of adults. The most important figure in this tradition was most certainly Karl Groos. Groos was a professor of philosophy at the University of Basel.[35] In his landmark studies of the play of animals and the play of humans, Groos challenged such theories of play as Herbert Spencer's, which posited it as merely the discharge of excess energy. Groos elaborated an evolutionary theory of play, arguing that the more advanced the species, the less it depended on instinct. To make up for what instinct did not provide, higher animals learned to play. Through play, animals and humans learned the skills and adaptability that would allow them to survive as adults.[36] For humans, there were two broad manners of play, the dividing and the uniting—or, more scientifically expressed, the analytical and the synthetic. The analytical trend sought to understand how things worked, what happened when two things/people/forces were set against one another. This could lead quickly to the disassembly of toys or to competitive games.[37] The synthetic tendency led to imitation, "the mediator between instinct and reason." Imitation in play effectively transmitted skills and cultural values, more quickly and surely than any compulsory lessons. The young boy learned to be a blacksmith by setting up a pretend smithy in imitation of his father, while his sister learned to be a mother by caring for her doll.[38] Groos thereby related play simultaneously to the impulses of the human subconscious and the skills necessary for adulthood.

Groos was in no way alone in believing that imitation was a critical element of play. Julius Schaller wrote in 1861: "[T]he child imitates all the forms of activity that impress it, which appear to him strange or valuable. The differences between the sexes makes itself felt very early. The boy imitates riding, traveling; the girl imitates the handling and guarding of children. Different individualities are impressed by different things. What thrills one child leaves the other cold."[39] A. Döring, director of a Berlin gymnasium and privatdozent at Berlin University, concurred: "Children play school; boys play soldier or robber; girls care for dolls like children, play house, cook, visit, and whatnot. So they learn playfully the skills for the future career. And generally the total immersion in play, playing with heart and soul, which can in a certain sense be called the child's vocation, is the preschool for future vocational excellency. Who has played well will be an efficient person."[40]

Play as imitation was clearly viewed as a means of transmitting cultural ideals to following generations. These ideals reveal fascinating biases. Before turning to the clear gender issues, let us first note that in the systems of Schaller and Döring, no one played banker, clerk, or miner. The careers they envisioned for boys were remarkably old-fashioned. The conservative bias is inescapable. These educators were clearly unprepared to modernize the implications of their own educational theory. Modern occupations apparently lacked some quality that would make them paradigmatic for children. Boys presumably needed to be educated to be physically vigorous, active beings, so that later they might be mentally active. What seems to unify the categories Schaller and Döring provided—and what separated them from modern careers—was the level of physical activity involved.

The role of gender in play as imitation is most striking of all. That girls would grow up to be wives and mothers was presumed to be a fact rooted in nature. But the choice of play was based on individual preference and environment. One cannot imitate what one does not see. Why, then, were there no boys imitating their mothers? Sex remained an ineradicable difference, a cleft so deep that the rules that these authors presumed to be universal could not overcome it. The assumption of sexual difference preceded the assumption of universal rules of cognitive development, meaning that where those two beliefs came into conflict, the latter retreated. Schaller explicitly cited individual variation in imitative play but could not bring himself to allow individualism to bridge the chasm between the sexes. Instead, children were expected to "naturally" choose to imitate and learn from the proper gender role models, in a sort of genetically predetermined selection of cultural traits.[41]

Other pedagogues cited creativity as a crucial educational benefit of play. As we have seen, fantasy and creativity have long been implicitly or explicitly seen as positive benefits of play. Artists and the Romantics were particularly interested in placing creativity at the center of human identity. Many pedagogues in the last decades of the long nineteenth century echoed that view. Tied up intimately with that critique was also the issue of the role of the aesthetic in the human personality and education.

When a child played, the critical characteristic and attraction of that play was freedom of imagination and activity—that is, creativity. For many followers of Fröbel, this characteristic flowed directly from the notion that play represented the child's inner nature to the child. Within the academic pedagogical community, creativity was a rather vaguely defined goal. Unlike the Romantics and other writers outside the narrow circle of educators, academics did not always see creativity as a value unto itself. It was, rather, a tool, a means of personal development. Characteristic was the formulation of this position by Max Enderlin. Enderlin tied play very closely to freedom; it was then through that freedom that the child developed and made physical and spiritual "progress."[42] Bertha von Marenholtz-Bülow, Fröbel's most prominent lieutenant, went so far as to identify the "highest task" of humans as the "transformation of the products of nature into products of culture," adding that "[t]his form-giving drive is in every sense the drive to culture."[43] The "highest task" of humanity was then linked to play (the earliest expression of the "form-giving drive") and therefore to human culture.

There were naturally writers who crossed the abstract categories laid out here. Max Reischle, a professor at Göttingen, argued that play developed the physical abilities of the body and inculcated courage, decisiveness, and perseverance. But he also maintained that play trained the senses and therefore the imaginative faculties, as well as the capacity for reason. Finally, he thought that imitative play also prepared children for practical life.[44] The preceding categories do, however, sketch out the discursive field of play within the community of educational specialists. Very striking in the discussion of these educators is the degree to which they had stepped back from the claims of their forerunners. Georg Simmel noted: "[T]he eighteenth century pedagogical ideal was focused upon the formation of man, that is upon a personal internal value, which was replaced during the nineteenth century, however, by the concept of 'education' in the sense of a body of objective knowledge and behavior patterns."[45] Perhaps because they were not engaged in a philosophic investigation of self-consciousness and the problem of reason, these academic pedagogues did not claim a special place for play in forming an aesthetically based morality or in grounding reason. Instead, the academic pedagogues focused primarily on training individuals for the liberal social and cultural order, seeking individuals capable of radical self-control through instrumental reason and a disengaged subjectivity capable of manipulating itself. The pedagogues focused on training autonomous and rational individuals for an industrial economy that was, as we shall see, slowly sapping the social and cultural foundations for such an ideally autonomous and rational individual.

Educational Play and the Toy Industry

In light of the relative consensus within the academic community that play was educational, it is not surprising that the toy industry, too, argued that their products were educational (i.e., productive). It is instructive, however, to see how the discourse changed when it left the confines of academic discussion and entered the marketplace. I will here first examine the internal discussion that the toy industry had with itself about the educational benefits of toys, before briefly turning to the external discussion the industry had with—or directed at—consumers.

The toy industry began promoting the notion of the educational benefits of toys as early as 1889, when the *Wegweiser* proclaimed, "Toys should not merely entertain the child, they are fated to be tools of education."[46] The internal discussion took off, however, after 1909, with the establishment of the *Deutsche Spielwaren-Zeitung* and the *Rundschau über Spielwaren.* These journals assured their readers, all involved in the toy industry, that their products were socially valuable. "The toy industry is just as irreplaceable to our culture as food and drink, and in any case it is more interwoven into our lives than many other branches of industry," argued the *Rundschau.*[47] "The idea that perhaps nothing is so appropriate as toys for exercising educational influence is becoming popular in ever wider circles of society," bragged the *Deutsche Spielwaren-Zeitung.*[48] All three journals proclaimed the gospel of educational play. Toys were not merely enjoyable; they were valuable.

Finding assertions of the educational benefits of toys in these magazines is not difficult. Determining what they believed constituted those educational benefits is rather more challenging. One of the most coherent efforts to express a theory of play appeared in 1909 in an article entitled "On the Cognitive Value of Toys."

> The educational value of toys is too seldom praised. Their importance lay in the information that the child draws from the observation and use of toys. It is not presented to him through school lessons in dry and immediate forms but rather by way of entertainment and enjoyment . . . The toy will sharpen the observational skills of the child and make it familiar with natural and mechanical processes . . . We cannot, therefore, too vigorously urge parents and educators to direct their attention to the importance of toys as educational tools and, when choosing a toy, to proceed from the observation that toys are the teachers of children as well as their comrade and friend.[49]

The educational emphasis was placed on observation and the possibility that children would be more likely to retain knowledge if they enjoyed the learning process. What was learned was, above all, information, facts. The toy became an alternate schoolhouse rather than a unique means of developing the self. Thus, the *Deutsche Spielwaren-Zeitung* could see the large dioramas erected by the Hermann Tietz department store on Leipzigerstrasse in Berlin in honor of the two-hundredth birthday of Frederick the Great as proof of the educational benefits of toys.[50] Similarly, the board game based on the race between Cook and Peary to be the first to reach the North Pole was alleged to "expand geographic knowledge."[51] Knowledge was not the product of active engagement with the world. It was, rather, a reward for passive observation. The North Pole game, which did require activity, did not require activity to master the purported educational benefits. The geographic information was presented as a background to be observed. The child was at no point asked to brave the Arctic elements or construct imaginary miniature icebergs. The educational value of commercial toys was the same as the value of Locke's alphabet blocks. Toys taught by being presented to the eyes of the child.

The theory of education advanced by the toy industry ultimately reflected and reinforced the advantages that spectacular, mechanical toys enjoyed in modern retailing. The emphasis placed on observation and capturing attention in toy retailing found a clear echo in the passive learning advocated by the toy industry. Passive observation was privileged in both advertising and education. In such cases as Tietz's dioramas, the distinction between observation and education ceased to be of significance. *Deutsche Spielwaren-Zeitung* remarked: "Fantasy is losing ground. But at the same moment the educational power of the toy grows . . . It is no longer the fairy tale or adventure story that awakens these ideas [of Arctic adventures]: reality, the present, has conquered the child's soul."[52]

There were points of overlap between the discourses of the academics and the toy industry. Such commonalties were primarily with regard to the importance of imitation. There was a wide consensus, for example, that dolls could productively teach girls to be mothers.[53] There was less agreement about what boys should observe and imitate. The toy industry was far more interested in having boys play with toys that mimicked the world of technology and industry. Note, for example, that according to the article "On the Cognitive Value of Toys " (cited earlier), toys were expected to instruct children in "natural and *mechanical* processes" (my italics). In a review of a metal engineering set, the Structator, the *Deutsche Spielwaren-Zeitung* observed: "[T]he ideal goal of the producer is to unify the toy and the teaching tool . . . The Structator . . . represents one of the finest means of simultaneously amusing and teaching the child."[54] The small journal *Der Spiel- und*

Holzwaren-Markt recommended model steam engines for youth: "For our progress and our general development, it would be an enormous advantage if the enthusiasm and the interest of the older children in small models of our greatest discoveries grew. Then a generation would grow up that would have already developed an enthusiasm for the reevaluation, improvement, and perfection of our technological achievements."[55] Technical toys were to educate boys to be the proud inheritors and masters of a brave, new, industrial world. The hesitancy of such educators as Schaller and Döring to embrace the new was clearly not an issue for toy makers, who were no doubt influenced both by their own experience and the higher profit margins enjoyed by many mechanical toys. The toy industry thus promoted the values and experiences that defined and sustained their own world, their own success. The industry's emphasis was not on the self as expressed through action but, rather, on the self as manipulated by a disengaged reason, according to the imperatives of a liberal socioeconomic system that privileged material success and the scientific control of nature.

When the toy industry approached consumers, the message about the educational benefits of toys became even more simplified. One advertisement for a toy store simply featured a silhouetted cavalryman with a banner that proclaimed, "Toys are Educational Tools."[56] Advertisements for Heinrichsen tin soldiers praised them as being "excellent teaching materials."[57] Richter's Anker Steinbaukasten was advertised as "a truly solid and educationally rich Christmas gift for children of all ages."[58] As befits the advertising format, these claims of educational benefits were made without proof or theoretical elaboration. That no substantiation was required allowed toy makers and retailers to make a simple, if intellectually dishonest, equation: if some toys are educational, all toys are educational.

Pedagogical Critiques of Toys

The professional educators of the late nineteenth and early twentieth centuries were in no way convinced that all toys were educational. The pedagogues were painfully aware of the spectacle surrounding the department stores. They were also deeply suspicious of the conversion of toys as tools into toys as consumables. The growing commercialization of toys—that is, their emergence as objects of mass consumption in the late nineteenth century—seemed to introduce principles into toy making that were alien to proper education. Toys could be educational, or they could be sensationalistic.

Max Enderlin's critique was scalding.

> Above all, the colorful, inartistic trash [and] the insubstantial, unsolid doodads that lend their signature to the show windows of our department stores at Christmastime are not merely entirely valueless for the development of the child; they are often well-nigh damaging. They destroy the healthy sense for the useful and solid, transmit to the child totally false ideas of the form and quality of things . . . After only a short while—indeed, after only a few hours—these toys lay in ruins, joy transformed into disappointment.
>
> Unfortunately, the toy market has been overwhelmed by such trash, which has led to the almost total disappearance of the good and truly valuable.[59]

Enderlin was not alone in his opinion. Max Reischle asked: "What should a child do with a toy that is so artistically and solidly assembled, furnished with such fine mechanics and so carefully thought out, that one can do nothing with it? . . . That is, a toy with which you cannot play, rather that at most can be looked at—or destroyed?"[60]

These two critiques, so different in their appreciation of the workmanship of commercialized toys, shared several assumptions. Their primary assumption was that toy industry was not providing educationally appropriate toys but was instead providing toys designed to be looked at. The end result of such ill-conceived toys, they argued, was generally the destruction of that toy. Indeed, the pedagogical community was mildly obsessed with the notion of children destroying their toys. Many interpreted such behavior as a manifestation of hostility toward misguided toys. In other words, critics maintained that the toy market, though overflowing with toys, was delivering products to children that were at best valueless wastes of money, while at worst, the market was rewarding toy producers for damaging the youth of Germany. On the level of delivering culturally desirable products, they argued, the market was simply failing. Consequently, it was better to make your own toys than to venture into the marketplace for one of those "elegant, bought things."[61] The liberal market based on the autonomy of individuals, they implied, failed to provide the materials necessary to construct the individuals necessary for its self-perpetuation. To these academics, consumerism illogically appeared to undermine the cultural prerequisites for endless production.

*Another Critique of Toys**

Outside the specialist community of academic pedagogues, there developed another critique of the toy industry. This critique emerged from a movement best described by the term *bourgeois reform movement,* a very broad term that nonetheless properly encompasses the variety of this movement. The critique that I shall here examine emerged from a complex of concerns held by the middle class—particularly the classically educated *Bildungsbürgertum*—about the consequences of modern industrial society. In this respect, the critique of toys reflected an ambivalence on the part of many members of German middle-class society regarding the society they helped create. Their ambivalence was in part aimed at other members of the middle class, the caricatured, crass new rich. It was, then, an effort to reclaim the ideals of German neohumanism from the teeth of an allegedly heartless materialism. The movement was more expansively seen as an effort to elaborate a vision of a new, better Germany, a Germany based on a revived culture with reinvigorated individuals.

The toy critics I shall examine here were animated by concerns similar to those that made Nietzsche into a cult hero in the same period. The desire for cultural renewal and for authentic individuality unfettered by social constraint informed both Nietzsche's reception and the arguments of these critics. The enthusiasm that Nietzsche engendered may be taken as a cultural register that suggests broader concerns.[62] Many people were concerned that Germany would be unworthy of its heritage if it found wealth at the cost of genuine, whole humanity, losing the rich creativity that had inspired generations of artists and philosophers in exchange for a cold, lonely cage of refined social relations and heedless individualism. In response, what Kevin Repp terms the "Generation of 1890" developed a broad reform movement based in civil society and oriented toward direct action to transform German culture and society—what Repp refers to as "anti-politics."[63] In many

*Portions of this section and the next sections of this chapter were published previously in "Romanticism, Spectacle, and a Critique of Wilhelmine Consumer Capitalism," *Central European History,* spring 2005, 250–68. They appear here with the kind permission of the editors and publishers of *Central European History.*

respects, these critics combined a Nietzschean concern for the proper construction of the self with Schiller's anxiety about the fragmentation of the modern self.[64] As one part of their response, they followed Schiller in defining play and imagination as the concerns of both children and society.

The leading edge of these critiques was to be found in a handful of cultural journals. Prominent among them were Ferdinand Avenarius's *Der Kunstwart* and Alexander Koch's stable of magazines: *Innen-Dekoration, Deutsche Kunst und Dekoration,* and *Kind und Kunst.* In addition, I will here consider such publications as *Dekorative Kunst* and other observers of the applied arts movement in Germany. After examining the criticisms elaborated in these periodicals, I will turn my attention to the echoes found in the more mainstream press.

On a number of occasions, Ferdinand Avenarius personally penned bitter attacks on the German toy industry. Avenarius was the founder and editor of perhaps the leading cultural journal in Wilhelmine Germany, *Der Kunstwart.* He also was the founder of the Dürerbund, a nationwide organization to preserve German culture and physical spaces from the encroachments of commercial life. Avenarius was consequently a significant figure in the cultural life of German society,[65] and he found German toys highly objectionable. In 1902, he declared the "fashionable toy" to be the "worst enemy" of "fantasy, the daughter of heaven." He then went into more detail.

> The automaton with clockwork in its belly, the dollhouse with all its furniture copied in painful detail, the toy train that runs figure eights on its tracks . . . they suck the blood out of the minds of children. It is a crime that the old, crudely cut wooden toys in the Christmas markets are ever rarer. Praise God that there are still enough useful things to make the speculative products dispensable. That with toys the true value usually stands in inverse ratio to its dazzle makes the struggle harder for weak minds.[66]

Avenarius associated the old, valuable toys with the declining Christmas markets, while he argued that the new toys relied on the dazzle of the new retailing. In his view, stores and their wares were not easily separated. Unfortunately, Avenarius lamented, consumers with "weak minds" were unable to differentiate between true value and dazzle.

This was by no means an isolated assault. The following March, Avenarius complained: "[F]ashionable toys . . . do not excite fantasy but, rather, limit it, and they wean [the child] from work because they are far too finished . . . [T]hey are not artistic, only artificial."[67] In 1905, he led a December issue of *Der Kunstwart* with a five-page essay entitled simply "Toys."[68] Additional articles appeared in following years,[69] but "Toys" deserves closer attention.

Avenarius opened "Toys" with a description of a visit to an alpine village in Oberbayern.[70] There, he watched children play, creating their own games and their own toys from whatever was around them. They had to transform the ordinary objects of a small village into toys through the power of their own imagination. They were occasionally given "new, fine toys," but after a short time, they always abandoned these manufactured toys and returned to their invented ones. Nonetheless, visitors from the cities always brought new toys: the toy train moving in figure eights or the "living doll" that "travels under its own power, talks while going, sleeps and lives," and "is wonderfully dressed and has excellent mechanics." Avenarius was clearly opposing modern, commercialized toys to invented toys. Commercialized toys were independent of the viewer, coming to life and acting in utter indifference to the child. The invented toy could only be animated by the imaginative activity of the child. It was entirely dependent on the viewer and demanded a naive identification between child and toy to exist as a toy at all.

These village children prompted Avenarius to ask why we play.

> The young girl knows that her doll is not her daughter, the little boy that his tin soldier is not real, even if she cares for it with such sweetness and if he feels fully as proud as any field commander. With this wonderful double consciousness, however, is guaranteed independence and freedom . . .
>
> Certainly this expansion of self beyond one's own narrow circle does not always and without fail end well. God preserve us from an education that did not give truly serious learning as a counterweight to play . . . There is play enough that leaves to fantasy the role of the servant, who opens the doors for more important people—games with which skill, observation, decisiveness, courage, and other good characteristics are exercised on the theater first constructed by fantasy. The harmonious man cultivates these as well but does not neglect the others.[71]

Avenarius maintains that fantasy and play are the gatekeepers for a variety of desirable characteristics and that they have a critical role in the development of the ego itself. He admits that these are not new ideas: "All this is not in the least new. Astounding is only that, despite how old it [the ideas about play and fantasy] is, toys like the 'living doll' are still possible and not even only in 'rich' and 'distinguished' circles but even in such that were otherwise 'educated.'" Avenarius explains what he perceives to be wrong with these toys: "What should a child do with the thing that already does what the child herself had to contribute in order to enjoy expanding her emotions and develop her powers herself through play? . . . Not 'excellent mechanics' but the soul of the child animates a doll." How is it possible that society could come to such a point that children were being stunted, rather than developed, through their play? Avenarius concludes: "Every toy catalog shows and every toy retailer confirms that the most beloved 'novelties of the branch' every year are fantasy-killers. Adults buy what pleases them for a moment or what makes a 'big impression' on the child for a likewise fleeting moment."[72]

In a later article in *Der Kunstwart,* Joseph Augustus Lux took up the problem of modern toys. Lux saw in the material world of the child a reflection of the times.

> We live in an age of technology, so may the future engineers nurture their talents on models in the playroom. That is the opinion of many parents, who want to form specialists before the human is formed. The toys are chosen by the big people instead of the little . . . These poor children of the rich! They are placed in a child's world that is finished and built up and leaves nothing to be perfected. Now play! For the child, play is necessary work in which it develops and uses its powers. In this finished world, its work begins with destruction. Destroy, in order to build anew.[73]

Lux echoed many of the themes developed by Avenarius. He regarded toys that were self-contained, that operated under their own power, as dangerous, because they left fantasy no purpose and imagination no purchase. He argued that the responsibility for this situation laid not with the children or even with the industry, which was ultimately only secondarily at fault. According to Lux, parents, trapped in a utilitarian, materialistic society, were wounding their own children. Certainly, they did not intend to hurt their children. One can infer that the parents Lux criticized gave technology toys to their children in hopes of helping them. Nonetheless, the culture had so warped expectations that parents sought to raise "specialists before the human is formed."[74] Children were being conditioned for the capitalist market rather than allowed to develop their own authentic individuality. Parents were seduced by toys that fascinated them for a few moments in a store's show window. As Avenarius wrote, adults wanted to see "the greatest possible effect" when their gift was opened, so they bought toys that promised the most immediate impact, disregarding all long-term value.[75] In this formulation, precisely because adults loved children, they were hurting them. Furthermore, precisely those who had money, even those who had education, were most at fault. Those who could afford to train their children to be engineers and had the intellectual or cultural resources to aspire to an engineer's education were the ones doing the most damage. The "fashionable toy" as sketched in the pages of *Der Kunstwart* was a devastating indictment of the middle class itself for losing its own humanity in the name of technological and material progress. Progress might be desirable, but critics asked whether it was so at any cost?

Avenarius and, to a lesser extent Lux, seemed to reprise the role of the Romantic writers of a previous century. They claimed to see in the products of the toy industry an implicit return to the sensational psychology of Locke and Condillac. Just as Schiller and others found Locke's description of human thought and being unconvincing and distasteful, Avenarius attacked modern toys in the name of a more active, free personality. *Der Kunstwart* revived Jean Paul's admonition (cited earlier) to "give no plaything whose end is to be looked at." The critique of toys could also be easily expanded into a critique of modern retailing and the emerging urban culture of spectacle. Modern individuals were becoming increasingly passive in their play and in their shopping. They were presented with a flashy, finished world and had to do nothing more than watch.

Moreover, the products offered by industry were shaped and designed for commerce, to seize immediate attention, to make "the greatest possible effect." The external commercial pressures that literally gave toys their form could not be further from the Schillerian ideals of beauty and the role of play. The simple, natural plaything responded to the inner necessity of both object and child far better than did any commercial toy.

The *Kunstwart* critique of toys was replayed in a number of other cultural journals, if not always with the same vigor or vitriol. Alexander Koch's publications, for example, took up the cause of bringing more "artistic" toys to children, toys that demanded more imaginative labor. Koch was a highly successful cultural entrepreneur. He began his publishing empire with a small journal that sought to teach taste to carpet buyers and carpet makers. He soon found an astonishingly profitable market niche in educating the senses for everyday life. In particular, Koch took up the cause of creating a market for contemporary styles; he was hostile to the historicism that had dominated nineteenth-century home decoration. Koch established more magazines: *Innen-Dekoration* in 1890, *Deutsche Kunst und Dekoration* in 1891, and *Kind und Kunst* in 1904. Koch's readership was most definitely well-to-do. A one-year subscription to *Deutsche Kunst und Dekoration* cost twenty marks in 1897 and thirty marks by 1912. By way of comparison, such journals of high culture as *Jugend* (the journal for which Jugendstil was named) and *Ver Sacrum* were less expensive, but *Pan* was more costly. *Kind und Kunst* was twelve marks a year in its first year. Under the terms of the 1911 labor contract, an unskilled male laborer in the Nuremberg toy industry would have had to work ninety hours to afford a subscription to *Deutsche Kunst und Dekoration;* a skilled craftsman would have had to work sixty hours. We can assume, therefore, that Koch's periodicals were intended for individuals of means and education, those with the resources and inclination to spend a substantial sum on maintaining currency on matters of taste.[76]

Deutsche Kunst und Dekoration and *Kind und Kunst* did not have the same polemical edge as *Der Kunstwart.* More often than not, their criticisms of modern industrial products were implied in what and how they chose to praise. I will return shortly to the objects of their praise, after first examining some of the clear criticisms that were offered. *Deutsche Kunst und Dekoration,* for example, attacked the "silly flashiness and tasteless [*geschmackswidrig*] doodads" that one found in the rooms of German children, and it expressed the hope that new toys might replace the "insane poison" of commercial toys.[77]

Stronger broadsides were in the offing from Koch's empire. In December 1904, Hans Boesch wrote an article entitled "The Doll as Toy for the Child" for Koch's newest undertaking, *Kind und Kunst,* a journal intended to tap into the growing interest in the aesthetic education of children. After rehearsing some of the history of dolls, Boesch elaborated a familiar, if more restrained, critique of dolls.

> As a mother loves a sick child more deeply, so may the child be more fond of a primitive doll. Her fantasy is excited most power-

> fully; she sees in it, despite everything, her sweet, sweet child. The little girls were surely also delighted when they received the formal dolls with moving limbs, as they grew real hair, which [the girls] could comb and braid, as the dolls opened and closed their eyes, as they said mama and papa, as they moved by means of clockwork and mechanisms. But with that, it is quite enough, since what remains left for the child's fantasy with such dolls? It is to be feared that the doll makers are not yet done perfecting dolls . . . and that the child will have an artificial object instead of a toy, which at the beginning will stir their greed and participation but will soon leave them cold . . . The child will possess an alleged toy that, appropriate to the age of the automobile, offers not the least inspiration, does not stir the imagination, gives the mind absolutely no nourishment, but, rather, will produce only blasé children.[78]

Boesch raised again the issue of "perfection," of toys (in this case, dolls) that leave nothing for the child to do except watch. He contended that though they might please the child for a moment, the interest could not last—that humans, particularly children, had to be able to actively engage the world, to wrap their fantasy around something and make it their own. In Boesch's estimation, these new toys were too independent; they refused to be incorporated into the child's imaginative world. He argued that simple, crude toys that children make themselves were far better than the wonders of modern technology offered by the toy industry.

The journal *Dekorative Kunst* concurred. An article appearing in 1905 made much the same argument, in much the same language, as *Der Kunstwart* and *Kind und Kunst.*

> [T]he organic, the influence of form . . . releases far more and far livelier images in the child than flat aping [of the natural world], which after first blush leaves nothing but blasé boredom . . . [A]n inspiration works productively by simultaneously convincing and alluring, simultaneously giving and inspiring to give; thereby the imagination becomes lively. And because everything is not there and finished and instead room is left open, it [fantasy] weaves and works in unconscious joyful play. How dead it [fantasy] remains, however, when through mechanical, detailed copying, all purposes and all possibilities are already fulfilled to the outermost

> limit and nothing remains left for the child's soul to do. Such a thing exhausts itself.[79]

Here again we see the accusation that what is finished, that which shows no rough edges or imperfections, is the enemy of imagination.

Among the previously cited criticisms, we can notice an interesting assumption. The imagination does not need the raw material of naturalistic images, these critiques imply. The imagination needs only rough shapes to inspire it into activity. Once active, the less material there is available, the better. Much as with Jean Paul, these critics were suspicious of any overreliance on sight as a substitute for the work of the imagination. The various critics, however, went beyond Jean Paul in their analysis of toys and sight. They argued that toy makers were profiting from the weaknesses of modern parents qua consumers. These parents, they all agreed, purchased the momentarily attractive rather than the lastingly valuable. Parents saw something that purported to be a toy and fell under the spell of its movement and the "dazzle" offered by the retailer. The parents were captured by the allure of visual spectacle, and the children were sure to suffer for the "shortsightedness" of their guardians.

To the analysis of vision, imagination, and play offered by Jean Paul and others, the critics therefore added an additional level that indicted the power of modern retail and modern consumer capitalism to overwhelm "weak minds" (to quote Avenarius, cited earlier) by manipulating sight. The failure of such "weak minds" made the proper cultivation of a child's imagination all the more important. Following Schiller, these writers believed that a well-developed and independent mind, predicated on the creative faculties stimulated by play and aesthetics, was perhaps the best means of resisting the shallow attractions of modern consumerism and the lure of mass society. The construction of a mass market, which has been the central element of this work, was seen as a fundamental challenge by such writers as Avenarius and Lux, one that threatened to undermine treasured and established norms that defined both the good life and true humanity.

The New Toy Makers

The various critiques I have thus far addressed were not merely sterile complaints. They addressed themselves to consumers but also to a new sort of toy maker. These new toy producers appeared dramatically in

1903 with the Dresdner Werkstätte für Handwerkskunst. The Dresdner Werkstätte was an effort by prominent artists to bring aesthetic sensibilities to household goods in the interest of both art and commerce.[80] Among the products that these artists designed and produced were toys. Such artists as Richard Riemerschmid, Frank Wedekind, Franz von Lenbach, and Friedrich August von Kaulbach, to name a few, contributed toy designs to the effort.[81] From these designs emerged a new category, artistic toys (*künstlerisches Spielzeug*), sometimes known simply as Dresdner toys (see fig. 7).

The forms these toys took could probably be inferred from the criticisms previously elaborated. They tended to be somewhat crudely shaped; they were colorful, based on traditional themes, and made of wood. A review by *Kind und Kunst* noted: "[T]he trusted, old objects of childish play have [been] given new forms. Simplicity of lines, powerful coloring and solidity, these bases of modern arts and crafts are also to be observed here." The journal observed that as opposed to the usual strong naturalism of the toy industry, the Dresdner toys were "strictly stylized." The turn away from naturalism was praised by *Kind und Kunst,* because, it was argued, children see differently than adults; the sight of children was "summarizing," able only to observe the rough outlines of reality. The argument was that only later, after much visual experience, would children be able to establish the individuality of the various objects that they see. Therefore, concluded *Kind und Kunst,* it was pointless as well as damaging to give children careful copies of nature to play with, a fact the Dresdner toy designers understood.[82] The *Neue Deutsche Rundschau* found the Dresdner toys "delightfully stylized."[83] *Deutsche Kunst und Dekoration* described them as "divine," exclaiming: "One sees . . . with what joy our young artists have labored on these, with how much pleasure they have stepped back into the fantasy of children . . . The toys themselves will arouse the approval of our readers and require no recommendation to find a ecstatic welcome in the children's schools, not the least because they are also right cheap."[84] *Der Kunstwart* greeted the appearance of the Dresdner toys warmly, wishing them "success and successors."[85]

The call for the union of art and toys did not stop with the Dresdner Werkstätte für Handwerkskunst. The same spirit made the *erzgebirgisch* family Kleinhempel into minor stars of the toy world. Their wooden figurine toys were featured in a variety of articles. *Kind und Kunst* exclaimed: "After such artificial toys, . . . it must suffice for friends of children and afficionado's of joy to see that recently a num-

Fig. 7. Dresdner toys. "Ausstellung der 'Vereinigung für Angewandte Kunst,' München 1905," *Dekorative Kunst* 9 (Oct. 1905): 45.

ber of artists have not disdained to reinvigorate the ancient toy industry of the Saxon Erzgebirge through their designs. To them belong the Kleinhempel siblings in Dresden, who are themselves members of an Erzgebirge family . . . Must not the simplicity of form and the humorous execution speak to the child's heart?"[86] In 1904, *Dekorative Kunst* dedicated a long, richly illustrated article to the wooden toys of the Kleinhempels.[87] The Kleinhempels were also prominent among the many toy makers lauded in a 1905 *Dekorative Kunst* article on artistic toys.[88] Another toy designer who would find considerable enthusiasm was Professor Conrad Sutter. Sutter's toy animals emphasized three-dimensionality. Their simplified forms were intended to be roughly true to nature from every angle, a sort of summarizing realism.[89]

Joseph Augustus Lux observed in *Der Kunstwart* that with regard to toys, "one had to observe the world through the eyes of a child, naive, unconditioned, let us say artistically." The mountain villages had been delivering such products cheaply for centuries. But now, Lux noted, artists, "gifted with similar naive sensibilities as any toy maker in a mountain village, have created new, happily painted, primitive toys, which are to be made by hands trained in centuries-old traditions of toy makers and are now known as 'Dresdner toys.'"[90] These various toys all shared a carefully crafted, stylized primitivism. Primitivism, by virtue of its roughness and incompleteness, demanded more imagination of the child. One may also ask if the toy critics, by favoring primitivism over perfection, were not tacitly conceding the inadequacy of Western technology for satisfying emotional needs inherent in human beings.

Later, the *Rundschau des modernen Kunstgewerbes* summarized succinctly the ideology of the artistic toys and the task for toys generally: "The central issue for toys is: Leave aside everything unnecessary and bring back everything necessary enlarged. The fantasy of the child provides for everything else."[91] According to the *Rundschau des modernen Kunstgewerbes,* the task of the toy industry was to take up the challenge of the Dresdner toys and turn its products into agents of positive social change. In 1912, Wilhelm Krieg rehashed the rhetoric about the inadequacy of finished toys. Krieg then pointed out that those who designed toys were not parents, pedagogues, or child psychologists but, rather, producers and merchants who were guided only by profit and who designed products not with the child but, rather, with the sale in mind. Rather than the developmental interests of child development guiding the toy industry, Krieg saw everything as driven by the hopes of seducing the consumer. It was critical, Krieg argued, that the toy industry cease to produce expensive, useless toys and devote itself to inexpensive, educationally valuable toys.[92] Another author pointed out the difficulty of successfully satisfying all desirable purposes for toys at a reasonable cost. This author argued that a principal impediment to the "rational" development of toys, however, was also to be found in the retailers and their demand for novelties, a demand that led producers to mistake changes that would "turn heads" for improvements.[93] Again commercial toys were inextricably linked to the demands of impressionistic shopping.

Krieg returned to the topic of toys in 1914, to argue that the toy industry produced too many "expensive and complex toys that can only be seen as objects to create sensations or fame" and that "therefore the child can enjoy them for only a short time."[94] It is interesting that the cost-cutting incentives of mechanized production were never mentioned. Nor were labor relations. To the extent that the toy industry could be faulted, it was, according to the critics, because the toy producers disregarded all educational concerns (a point the industry disputed) in order to seduce through transitory flashiness. In fact, critics explicitly praised the most socially retrograde portion of the toy industry, the Erzgebirge wooden toy makers, because they were not dazzling consumers. This point was well illustrated by a *Daheim* article that commented that after the dreadful stories about the misery of the Erzgebirge *Heimarbeiter* at the 1906 *Heimarbeitausstellung,* one could almost dislike Erzgebirge toys, but fortunately they were too delightful to ignore.[95]

The same critique that launched the Dresdner toys also initiated a doll reform movement. Both *Dekorative Kunst* and *Deutsche Kunst und Dekoration* agreed that credit for bringing the reform movement to dolls belonged to Marion Kaulitz, an artist active in Munich and Gmund, a rather tony artists' retreat on the Tegernsee south of Munich. Kaulitz had shaken the doll world with her entries at a 1908 Munich exhibition of handcrafted articles. *Deutsche Kunst und Dekoration* explained:

> Until only a few years ago, a deadening ideal of beauty dominated that special world of dolls. The most impartial [*sachlichste*] and least dispensable toy was artistically and practically devalued in the name of a misguided urge to decorate. [They possessed] ridiculous costumes, expressionless cute faces, and caricatured overall form . . . An extraordinary chasm lies between those dolled-up, fur-clad little ladies that one until now believed appropriate to the sweet care of the child and the dolls here [Kaulitz's] . . . Every head has character, but each is so stylized that undesirable realistic influences are ruled out.[96]

Dekorative Kunst described Kaulitz's dolls as "individual beings" that "nevertheless . . . have a certain note of the typical." The journal continued, "The physiognomy avoids the flashy, cute; they have character."[97] Kaulitz found her greatest success at the 1911 International Doll Exhibition at Frankfurt am Main, where she won the prize for most original artist's doll. She also won first prize at a doll exhibition in Breslau and honorable mention at Chemnitz, where her dolls were not even exhibited.[98] For many observers, the development of a doll reform movement was an extension of the toy reform movement. The language about rejection of overperfection, of humanizing the products, is clear. The writers appear to have considered it unnecessary to discuss their larger concerns, perhaps because the logic should be already known, or perhaps because dolls, the plaything of young girls, were not as critical to the development of richly creative individuals.

The critique sketched by these cultural elites should now be clear. The focus on momentary dazzle by both parents and producers was a critical flaw with modern toys. Both tended to emphasize visual impressions that thrilled the viewer for an instant. Rich designs and technical perfection were emphasized. But such qualities, the critics argued, were in no way appropriate for children. Children needed to exercise their fantasy; they had to dominate their toys imaginatively. The toy industry did not provide for imagination. Their products aimed to seize the ephemeral attention of the shopper, not to occupy the mind of a child. The cultural critics parted company somewhat from the pedagogues at this point. Both had seen commercial toys as overly perfect. The cultural critics, however, placed the issue of creativity at the very center of their analysis and created a much broader critique. They believed that capitalist society had detached itself from the ideals of a whole and harmonious individuality, the ideals that had underpinned the old theories of play as education. The appeal to individual desires and individual impulses had become a threat to a normative vision of individuality. By reviving those values, the cultural critics of toys were taking aim at the society in which they lived. They maintained that the products of their contemporary capitalism stole fantasy from individuals, that toy makers created their own fantasy world rather than allowing consumers to exercise it themselves. Given that creativity was thought to be closely associated with individuality itself, the critics concluded that the crowding out of imagination was dangerous—far more dangerous than the academic theorists of education would admit. Toy reformers, heeding the arguments of the critics, designed artfully primitive toys and dolls. These playthings were consciously designed to be sufficiently crude that the child would be forced to exercise his or her imagination, to fill in what the toy maker left out. The critics maintained that humans required such imaginative exercise and that the impulse toward ever greater technological perfection threatened it. The requirements and bounties of technology thus had to be balanced by concern for preserving the human and cultural interests of individuals and society. It was the task of artists, the critics and reformers suggested, to preserve the critical human element amid the triumphs of industrial technology. The artist had to offer a cultural modernism to balance the weight of technological modernism.

A Public Debate

There were many criticisms of the German toy industry offered by members of a privileged, educated elite. But did that matter? Was the general public even aware that there existed observers deeply discontented by the toys that were bought and sold in Germany's department stores and toy shops? That is a difficult question to assess. As a surrogate for that question, I will consider the opportunity for Germans to know of this critique by examining the press outside the narrow cultural journals.

In the 1880s, the family journal *Daheim* had a number of articles about toys. For the most part, these articles praised the technological progress of toys and the joy that they could bring: "[P]lay should be, above all, recreation for the child, not a lecture in another form . . . That goes above all for the big cities with their already unnatural environment for children."[99] Dr. Friedrich Schäller argued in *Daheim* that play could provide images for the brain, the raw material of cognition, but that was about all.[100] Nonetheless, there were some who expected toys to do more than amuse. Hans von Spielberg managed to be on both sides. He lamented: "O weh—the poor children! They should learn even at play." But at the same time, he indicted the toy industry for overly finished toys that did not inspire the child's imagination to independent activity.[101] Another author thought tin soldiers were excellent tools for teaching history.[102]

Starting in the 1890s, periodicals began to run more articles accepting the notion that play might be an important constituent part of cognitive development. An 1892 article saw a danger that modern toys might lead to blasé children if the children were too young when they received them, but it argued that older children must be familiarized with the achievements of modern technology.[103] An 1897 review of Karl Groos's book *Der Spiele der Tiere* called play a "natural precondition of physical and mental development."[104] In 1898, another author tied playing with dolls very firmly to becoming a good mother: "Buy dolls, mother, but not [ones that imitate] the elegant salon women . . . no, the sweet, loving thing that can be washed, clothed, and cared for to the heart's content."[105] The *Berliner Lokal-Anzeiger* claimed that "simple toys are the most interesting" but then went on to praise technology toys "reflecting all the changes of culture" and representing the "duties" of a "youth from the century of technology."[106] In 1903, the liberal *Berliner Tageblatt* associated toys exclusively with enjoyment and maintained that enjoyment came particularly from the fact that the toys moved.[107] By 1906, the *Tageblatt* saw a great deal of educational benefit in toys. The *Tageblatt*'s notion of education did not, however, coincide with that of the cultural critics. The *Tageblatt* saw the task of toys as bringing children up to date with events and technology. Accordingly, it argued that toy makers should produce tin soldiers from the most recent wars and copies of the most recent inventions.[108]

Thus far, the daily press's impression of the educational value of toys and play seemed rather limited. If toys came to their attention at all, it was as likely as not to be as a source of enjoyment. If toys could serve as anything more than that, it was often merely as the source of visual images or discrete facts. The press's ideas tended to parallel the sensationalist psychological assumptions of the toy industry. The exception was the doll. The press's assumption was that the doll was able to train a young girl to be a mother. Other than that, the discourses of toys and education were very different between the cultural elites and the mainstream press.

A new doubt, however, slowly began to infiltrate the mainstream press. In 1909, the *Berliner Tageblatt* recalled *Der Kunstwart* when it observed:

> The age of technology has also colored the toy and makes it ever more complex. Parents buy [toys] because they promise their children a special education and mental excitement.
>
> It is questionable, however, whether these mechanical toys, which move themselves in prescribed ways, truly satisfy the child's interest, a question whose answer is in no way immaterial. In play the child tries and develops his abilities, and there are enough pedagogues who ascribe to the play of children a significant influence over the formation of the human being.

The *Tageblatt* maintained that toys should incite the child to free self-activity and that "[t]he mechanical toy is not able to give the child precisely this incitement." Because the child was not properly engaged, the child instead engaged his or her analytical drive, as explained by Karl Groos, and dismantled the mechanical toy to see how it worked. The *Tageblatt* argued that parents should not punish children for breaking an expensive mechanical toy; if it was anyone's fault, it was the parent's, for not providing toys appropriate to the child's soul.[109] Two days earlier, the *Vossische Zeitung* had counseled parents to avoid mechanical toys and instead recommended the Dresdner toys and the wooden figures of Professor Conrad Sutter.[110]

In 1911, the rather petit bourgeois and conservative *Berliner Lokal-Anzeiger* asked itself what toys should be given to children. It noted that there were two great opposing "army camps." The one wanted as naturalistic a toy as possible. The other wanted a highly stylized toy that would retain only the necessary characteristics. The latter, observed the *Lokal-Anzeiger,* had achieved a remarkable success in exciting the child's imagination and also reviving the old traditional forms of German toys. The other camp, however, saw the task of the toy to provide the maximum number of accurate images that could fuel the mind and imagination later. The *Lokal-Anzeiger* associated these with Professor Sutter and called them "Hessian toys" (Sutter was from Wiesbaden). The problem with both camps, in the view of the *Lokal-Anzeiger* author, was that they overemphasized the admittedly important question of child development. The *Lokal-Anzeiger* argued that the toy is to be enjoyed and, therefore, that the consumer should seek something appropriate for the individual child, something that will inspire smiles and laughter, with some consideration given to the attractiveness of the toy, but without any strict adherence to the programmatic considerations of the two camps.[111] Meanwhile, *Vorwärts* argued that children could neither learn from nor enjoy self-powered toys: "The child first finds joy in the mechanically powered toy locomotive when the spring drive is broken." According to this view, the joy and the learning were in the doing. The learning, as defined by *Vorwärts,* had little, however, to do with imagination. Educational play was a process of "assembling sensory experiences" that were then developed into abstractions.[112]

Daheim took an interest in the doll reformers in particular. It reminded its readers that play was not mere "fooling around" but, rather, had a "high pedagogical value." Accordingly, the journal argued, "the doll should be a true and proper playmate." The artistic doll had a particular task before it: "[T]hat is to form for our children a likable, beautiful, tasteful, harmonic doll-child that they may love consciously from the heart. That can only happen if one gives the new dolls the highest artistic liveliness and the most childish beauty." *Daheim* praised in particular the simplicity and naturalness of the dolls.[113] Later, *Daheim* returned to the topic of the new dolls: "The child does not want to be satisfied with looking. It wants to be able to love its doll from the heart, and none of the earlier types of dolls could withstand this drive of the child while giving sustenance to its fantasy."[114] The new dolls were setting out to resolve that dilemma.

The wider press began, for the most part, to pick up on the cultural critique of toys several years after it appeared in the cultural journals. With a few exceptions, the press had considered toys to be of limited educational value at best. Often enough, that educational value was seen as a communication of facts, much as the toy industry had portrayed it. In the last years before World War I, however, the toy critique escaped the narrow social bounds of the cultural journals. Toys became somewhat problematic even for representatives of the cultural mainstream.

Dolls occupied a particular place for the everyday press. Dolls were assigned a more definite educational mission than other toys. Even writers who felt that toys were of little pedagogical value could accept that dolls educated future mothers and housewives. The *Daheim*'s reviews of the reform dolls also suggested that the new dolls needed to do more than inspire imagination—that dolls should foster emotional states, should cultivate the values of unconditional love and empathy that a mother "must" possess. In some respects, the critique of dolls in the mass-circulation press could be more demanding than that in the cultural periodicals. *Daheim*'s critique of dolls no doubt reflected a conservative anxiety to reemphasize the centrality of motherhood to feminine identity. A 1913 article in *Deutsche Kunst und Dekoration* suggested another reason why a reform might be more urgent for dolls than for toys generally. "A proper education in taste means much more" for girls than for boys, it argued, explaining that a "backward taste is much less a hindrance later in life for boys than for girls, because for them matters of taste and character are not as innerly connected as with females." Unfortunately, continued the article, many girls "breathe in a good bit of false culture" through their own fashionable clothes and those of their dolls.[115] If women were to have good taste and therefore good character, girls needed more appropriate clothes and dolls. The suggestion that female character was more closely associated with taste than was the case with males is fascinating. The article refused to discuss why that might be true. One is left to assume that the sexual division of labor meant that males could demonstrate character through their actions, while women had to rely on the barely legible signs of taste. Hence, proper dolls could be critical in maintaining widely accepted definitions of gender roles and in training girls to reveal their character in the best possible manner. A writer in the *Rundschau des modernen Kunstgewerbes* seemed to second this notion, arguing that dolls had the "special purpose" of awakening in girls both the sense for beauty and that for good clothing.[116] Given that the definitions of gender roles and of burdens placed on feminine taste were much more broadly agreed on in society than the definitions of human individuality offered by the toy critics, it is not surprising that dolls became more remarked on in the mainstream press.

Roots of a Critique

I return now to examine the cultural critique more closely. The cultural critique of toys drew on notions of human individuality and the centrality of creativity that were over a century old. Nonetheless, it was a movement that cannot be explained exclusively by reference to inherited discourses. Such discourses played a role, but the principal impetus came from contemporary society, from issues that the critics themselves saw and lived. The critiques were responses to existing social and cultural issues. That the press first began to include cultural critiques of toys after 1909 may have reflected the growing prominence of the broader cultural criticisms. Germans were increasingly interested in protecting the norms of middle-class society from the disruptive impact of consumer and technological society.[117]

The cultural critique of toys had two immediate forebearers: the *Kunsterziehungsbewegung* (art education movement) and the *Kunstgewerbereformbewegung* (Arts and Crafts reform movement). These two branches of the bourgeois reform movement provided the ideological framework and analytical tools that the toy critics turned on the toy industry. As we explore these two traditions, the debt that the cultural critique of toys owed to these two movements should become clear.

The *Kunsterziehungsbewegung* emerged in the 1890s as a movement to improve the aesthetic capabilities of Germany's youth. It reached its peak in energy and enthusiasm in the early 1900s with three nationwide

Kunsterziehungstage (conventions), in 1901, 1903, and 1905. The movement included such prominent figures as Alfred Lichtwark and drew on the cultural criticism of Wagner, Nietzsche, Lagarde, and Langbehn. The movement drew on a long intellectual tradition to claim that art was uniquely suited to the construction of whole personalities. Art was, by virtue of its freedom from immediate, quotidian interests, able to draw the individual out of the everyday and permit the individual to fully develop all of his or her abilities and express his or her true nature.[118] Lichtwark closely associated the *Kunsterziehungsbewegung* with efforts to foster a moral renewal in Germany.[119]

One of the foremost theorists of the movement was Professor Konrad Lange. Lange was a professor of aesthetics at the University of Königsberg when his "programmatic" book *The Artistic Education of German Youth* was published in 1893. He argued that an early exposure and instruction in aesthetics was critical to a child's well-being. According to his view, human beings develop certain formal concepts from the infinite sensory impressions we receive, and these impressions are constantly interacting with the ideas that we have already formed. From this, Lange concluded that children had to learn early to properly organize their perceptions aesthetically and to avoid being overwhelmed by the variety of sensory inputs.[120] In Lange's formulation, play taught children to perceive and organize nature and helped create the formal concepts that will guide the individual through life. The playing child was simultaneously artist and audience, both creating and enjoying the production. Indeed, Lange held that a toy that was not taken up and transformed by the child remained as useless and inert as a stone before the sculptor set the chisel to work.[121] For this reason, he argued, toys ought not be slavish copies of nature. Lange thought that because children needed to be able to envelop their toys in their imagination, "impressionistic" toys were preferable. In fact, Lange condemned the realist trend in toys as "one of the many symptoms of a decrepit, unproductive, fantasy-less culture."[122] Lange contended that an individual was ready to appreciate and create art only after a childhood of productive, imaginative play. Her further asserted that the result of a proper aesthetic education would be a society prepared to enter a new cultural epoch.

Lange built on *Artistic Education,* establishing himself as perhaps Germany's leading expert and theorist of art education. He penned the article "Aesthetic Education" for the *Enzyklopädisches Handbuch der Pädagogik* in 1903 (by which time he had moved to the University of

Tübingen). In that article, he more vigorously articulated an overarching purpose for aesthetic education: "For human beings, aesthetic education has the value of an expansion, a perfection of his/her pure human essence. A person who has no aesthetic education leads an incomplete existence; it is not a full and harmonically developed existence." Building on Schiller's definition of play, Lange then tied play firmly to art, since both were apparently purposeless but "served for the perfection of the human essence."[123] The following year, when Alexander Koch was seeking to establish the credentials of his new publishing venture *Kind und Kunst,* he asked Lange to contribute an article (Koch also published endorsements from Ferdinand Avenarius, Karl Groos, and Max Liebermann, Germany's leading impressionist artist). In his contribution, Lange emphasized that "the feeling of creative activity, of spiritual freedom" was the goal of art and play, activities that were "basically identical." Art and play, he argued, were critical to human individuals if they were to "assert their personality in the outside world."[124]

The ties between Lange's call for artistic education and the cultural critique of toys should be clear. In fact, to draw too clear a line of demarcation between the two would be misleading. Lange made a criticism of some commercialized toys as a part of the larger project of aesthetic education. The purposes of that education also shared common assumptions with those motivating the toy critique. The goal of education as a directed development of the human being was to create whole individuals. Interestingly, Lange eventually tied creativity and "spiritual freedom" to individuals' ability to "assert their personality in the outside world." In this, he was clearly harkening back to the neohumanist/Romantic conceptions of human beings from a hundred years earlier. According to these conceptions, the human individual had to be able to organize the flood of impressions he or she received from the external world. Only then was an effective interaction with the world possible. Thus, aesthetics was fundamental to human life.

The other major movement was the *Kunstgewerbereformbewegung.* This movement was a truly vast alliance of often highly diverse groups and interests. The object of their reform efforts was itself somewhat ambiguous. Strictly speaking, *Kunstgewerbe* referred to objets d'art of little or no practical use. To this was opposed *Kunsthandwerk,* by which was meant beautiful items of everyday use, such as an artistically designed and executed chair or lantern. Nonetheless, both categories tended to be subsumed under the term *Kunstgewerbe.* By eliding the two terms, a single category was created that could comprise anything from statuettes to factory buildings, including toys.

The breadth of the category meant that the *Kunstgewerbereformbewegung* attracted enormously diverse interests. Traditional master craftspeople were involved, as were designers and architects (e.g., Richard Riemerschmid), cultural mavens (e.g., Avenarius), sociologists (e.g., Werner Sombart), and even politicians (e.g., Friedrich Naumann). In fact, the German Werkbund—diverse organization that it was—was merely one (substantial) branch of the movement.

Efforts to transform and revivify German product design emerged in several corners of Germany in the 1890s, an outgrowth of either traditional aesthetic concerns or economic development strategies. Munich, Darmstadt, Stuttgart, and Dresden all saw the emergence of small cadres of artists and architects, some with official patronage, some without.[125] By the middle years of the first decade of the twentieth century, concern for the fate of German *Kunstgewerbe* began to spread across wider circles of the middle class. The problem was moving beyond the economic fate of the handworkers to encompass the problem of international competition and the maintenance of an authentically German culture. The crux of the matter was form. The form that a consumer good took was presumed to have great impact on consumer and producer alike. The question of form therefore brought together a number of concerns.

One central issue of form was the rapid changes in outward form that modern capitalism demanded of consumer goods for reasons of fashion or novelty. The reign of fashion and novelties meant that producers were responding to stimuli from outside the "logic" of their product. Furthermore, fashion could not be an organic development, because it referenced the perpetually present and always transitory. Fashion was always modern, because it had no past. Finally, fashion placed the emphasis of production on the exterior of the product. The purposes of that product, whether it would last, whether the exterior accurately reflected its actual value—these concerns all faded into the background of the fashionable product. Fashion was pure sensationalism, a visual assertion of modernity. The fashionable product was in no way an expression of the producer; it was instead an alienated object produced exclusively for cash. With fashion, the producer lost any claim to self-expression. Since fashion was not oriented toward the self-expression of the producer or the demands of utility, it was easily depicted as arbitrary and incoherent.[126] Similarly, toy novelties were often portrayed as mindless, pointless alterations of form done exclusively to give the consumer the illusion of something "new."

The problem with fashion was that it was fundamentally impersonal. It referred entirely to the relations between people, not to people themselves. Fashion could never be an expression of self (how could selves be both so uniform and so transitory as fashion?). It was at best an expression of authentic individual desire—desire for money, for higher social status. At worst, it highlighted an inability to properly define oneself in public, an utter domination of the individual spirit by others. By its very instability, fashion suggested to critics an uncertainty and slavishness in modern life. Individuals were left overwhelmed by the constant churning of "proper" forms, unable to build an established form or learn to define their own individuality. Indeed, fashion frowned on individuality in taste. Fashion imposed taste from without. The greatest problem with fashion was, ultimately, less what it was than what it was not: it was not an expression of self or of genuine individual freedom. In this respect, fashion operated rather similarly to the spectacles used by retailers and producers to tempt consumers. Fashion, like spectacle, sought to impose desires on consumers. Recall Avenarius's argument (cited earlier in this chapter) "[T]hat with toys the true value usually stands in inverse ratio to its dazzle makes the struggle harder for weak minds." Both spectacle and fashion, in this analysis, were efforts to draw an individual to a form without providing the individual an opportunity for self-expression through form. In both cases, consumerism appeared in no way to be increasing individual freedom. Quite to the contrary, the individual gradually lost the ability to define himself or herself or to impose his or her will on the external world. The purely formal increase in the number of options available came at the expense of "positive" freedom.

Consider Georg Simmel's argument on styles (as opposed to fashion) in his 1908 essay "The Problem of Style." Simmel published this essay in *Dekorative Kunst,* a journal closely associated with the *Kunstgewerbebewegung.* Frederic Schwartz describes the essay as Simmel's response to the foundation of the Werkbund and as the elaboration of what became the Werkbund's essential mission.[127] In it, Simmel remarked that the aura of a material environment varied enormously based on whether the aesthetic "law" to which it adhered was established by producers or by the consumer.

> The apartment as it is furnished by the individual according to his taste and needs can have a swelling color from that which is personal, inalienable in the particularity of the individual, which would be unbearable if each concrete item in it had that same individuality. This may seem at first glance paradoxical. But if we accept that it is valid, then it would explain why the room that is decorated rigorously in a single historical style has something essentially unpleasant, estranged, and cold, while those that are composed from individual pieces of differing, but no less rigorous, styles according to an individual taste, which of course must be very strong and unified, can strike one as extremely livable and warm. An environment of things that are entirely of one historical style creates a closed unity that excludes the individual living in it. There are no holes into which she could pour her personal life, so different from that past style . . . This strangely becomes entirely different as soon as the individual imposes her own style on the multiply styled objects in the environs. Then they receive a new center.[128]

Simmel argued that styles became warm and human when they expressed the well-formed taste of an individual. When the style was a uniform continuity dictated by others, with no "holes," it was cold, inhuman, and alienated from the owner. Did the consumer then master the products, or did the products master the consumer? This argument amounted to a reformulation of Schiller's vision of aesthetic education for an age of consumerism and material abundance, in which the lifestyle became a work of art.[129] In this reformulation, the aesthetic sensitivities of modern consumers must be developed so that they might playfully impose their own personalities on the material world that surrounded them. Through an educated aesthetic taste, the individual could harmonize the timeless self with the frantically changing forms developed by modern capitalism. The home was animated by the forms given it by the homeowner, just as the toy came to life in the imagination of the child. The purpose was still to find a balance between the individual and existing society, but the emphasis had changed from taming politics to taming consumerism.

Simmel attributed the unaesthetic reliance on unified, historical styles to a "subjectivity and individuality" that "had escalated up to the breaking point."[130] Those styles provided, in his view, a de-emphasis or lightening of the burden on an overindividuated personality.

Simmel's modern, urban subjects were constantly on the verge of submerging under the tidal wave of sensory inputs, from surging crowds to flashing signs—the assault of the consumerist spectacle. They were overextended and nervous, requiring some means of distancing themselves from the demands placed on them. Historical styles represented a flight from individuality rather than any statement of it.[131] Thus, the consumption of certain items ironically becomes a means of managing the psychological strains engendered by the desperate efforts to make every store and object desirable. Much as with Avenarius, modern commercial life is portrayed as impinging on the cognitive ability of the individual to assert and express intellectual and emotional autonomy. The result of this inability to assert autonomy was a hyperindividualism, an individualism rooted in alienation and isolation rather than in an understanding and fulfillment of the needs of the subject.

The question of historical styles needs to be examined more closely. In his fullest and most mature treatment of the impact of modern commerce on the urban subject, *The Philosophy of Money,* Simmel makes few claims about specific types of consumer goods. He is largely interested in generic desire and, more important, the relativizing influence of money on culture. He does make, however, a handful of very suggestive comments. In the midst of his speculative comments on the origins of conscious subjectivity and its relation to desire, Simmel clearly draws on Schiller's aesthetics to define aesthetic experience. It is, he suggests, the union of subject and object, such that the subject is no longer conscious of the division between them. This is significant for us insofar as he then suggests that this sort of aesthetic experience was only possible if one defined specific objects that one desired. Simple longing for an experience or sensation meant that the object that satisfied that longing was a matter of indifference. The subject could not define itself against the object, because the object was insignificant, thus "the Ego cannot develop."[132] That object was defined by its utility. When an individual desires a specific object, however, such that no other object will serve, the individual's perception of the object has changed: "[I]t has now become an object of contemplation from which we derive pleasure by confronting it with reserve and remoteness."[133] This formulation is more significant than it might seem at first glance. It suggests that a cultivated, aesthetic sensibility is a necessary predicate to proper consumption. When we couple it with Simmel's discussion of the blasé attitude, which he associated with "the modern preference for 'stimulation' as such in impressions, relations and information—without thinking it important to find out why these stimulate us,"[134] we have important clues as to why historical styles were dangerous. They offered "sensations," the thrill of associating oneself with certain objects, traditions, and historical individuals, but without any real attachment to those periods or knowledge of the original styles, let alone the underlying products. The historically styled room therefore offered no opportunity for the ego to develop. The modern individual, however, did not mind, because modernity was too psychologically taxing.

One result was that the individual was increasingly estranged from the products of the collective society. This was particularly true of the material goods of everyday life. Those objects were no longer dependent on their owners.

> We experience their independence as an antagonistic force only when we are at their service. Just as freedom is not something negative but rather is the positive extension of the self into the objects that yield to it, so, conversely, our freedom is crippled if we deal with objects that our ego cannot assimilate. The sense of being oppressed by the externalities of modern life is not only the consequence but also the cause of the fact that they confront us as autonomous objects. What is distressing is that we are basically indifferent to those numerous objects that swarm around us.[135]

The problem that Simmel detected was clear: the modern individual was overburdened and alienated from much of his or her environment. The individual was no longer able to dominate his or her physical surroundings. Rather, objects were closed off, inaccessible to the individual. At least one means of overcoming this deep alienation of the urban subject was suggested later in Simmel's essay "The Problem of Style" (cited earlier). He observed that objects only take on a more personal, warm aspect when the individual can impose his or her personality on them. Given that the division of labor in modern industrial capitalism prevented expression of self through crafting objects, authentic self-expression remained possible only through the aesthetics of consumption. It was therefore of great importance that individuals learn to dominate and assimilate objects. This is, Simmel suggests, the basis of positive freedom.

The concerns of the toy critics and Konrad Lange can also be seen through this lens. The problem was how to train children to impose aesthetic systems on the chaos of forms thrown up by modern capitalism, both in the products and in the advertising and retailing used to sell them. Spectacle and fashion had to be redeemed through individual creativity and imagination. Only in this way could individuals, to quote Lange, "assert their personality in the outside world." Indeed, that the toy critics never considered the problem of age-specificity in toys would seem to indicate that they had more on their mind than specifically the relation between child and toy. The problem with toys, education, fashion, and styles for these writers was in the relationship between object and subject in general. The object resisted appropriation by the subject. Several years after the publication of *The Philosophy of Money,* Avenarius (cited earlier in this chapter) wrote, "Not 'excellent mechanics' but the soul of the child animates a doll." The subject could only live a fulfilled, happy life if its physical environment was composed of things that it could and had made its own, that reflected its own unique individuality. Then the individual had a home. If, however, those objects were their own masters (with their purported owners reduced to simple observers), the individual was everywhere a visitor. The individual betrayed no signs to himself or herself or to others that might suggest precisely who the individual was—what his or her values, ideals, and enthusiasms might be.

The toy critics and art education reformers were not cultural pessimists hailing the slow collapse of Western culture. They prophesied a genuine opportunity for cultural renewal. They argued that moderns were still able to enter direct relationships with objects; they were still able to assimilate objects and forms into their ego and thereby dominate them. The objects had to be themselves properly designed; they had to make themselves available for appropriation. A toy that moved on its own, creating its own fantasy world, resisted, through its action, the child's efforts to impose his or her own imaginative world on the toy. If the child became accustomed to such a relationship to commodities, what hope was there for the adult? If the child learned to impose his or her own vision on the toy, manipulated the toy (in Jean Paul Richter's language, played with it rather than worked for it), the adult stood in a better position to impose his or her own personality on his or her material world, rather than vice versa. Surely, this was a recipe for overcoming modern, bourgeois alienation.

Before turning to the response of the market to these ideas, I would like to pause to consider how extraordinary this historical moment was. Georg Simmel, Ferdinand Avenarius, and others recognized a remarkable, insidious challenge in the growing culture of consumption. In some important respects, this challenge was far more radical to these writers and their milieu than was the much more obvious and politically significant "social question." The maldistribution of wealth and opportunity created substantial political instability and undermined the utopian contents of early liberalism. Nonetheless, the normative moral qualities that both legitimated and sustained the liberal order in politics, economics, and culture could be rescued. The autonomous, rational self remained. It was necessary to construct highly dubious hierarchies of human value to protect the putatively universal moral qualities, impugning the humanity of women, workers, and other races in a bid to demonstrate that the rational individual was a suitable and operative foundation of a stable and moral society. The existence and health of the classical modern self was not, however, seriously called into question by the social question. The commercialized urban spaces created by modern industrial capitalism and particularly the attractions of consumption challenged autonomous subjectivity more directly. This challenge was sometimes addressed as one of morality and displaced onto women. In the waning years of a long peace, however, the new culture of urban spectacle and consumption seemed to leap the barriers erected by morality. To some, this emerging culture appeared to affect the process of cognition and the construction of the self. Both the emergence of modern retailing and the products offered for sale seemed to privilege vision to the detriment of experience and imagination. The consequence, critics feared, was an increasing passivity and dependence that imperiled the most basic ideals of middle-class society. The emphasis on the mimetic surfaces of toys and on visual spectacle, they argued, blocked the full flowering of individual creativity and therefore of autonomy.

In this historical moment, an increasingly individualistic society, predicated on "rational economic man" and the sovereign consumer, was portrayed as an existential threat to the possibility of a normative individual subjectivity. To the aforementioned observers, modernity threatened to undo itself. Nonetheless, as Jürgen Habermas has pointed out, "Kant and Hegel, Schiller and Goethe were contemporaries" for these critics. Habermas observes, "The fundamental concepts of Kantian-Schillerian aesthetics—freedom and necessity, spirit and nature, form and substance—are the ones Simmel used."[136] Simmel and others, therefore, were employing the still living armory of classicism and Romanticism to analyze the challenge of consumerism, as well as to construct remedies. Their analyses started with the expressive self and sought ways to preserve that self from the onslaught of images and commerce. An overabundance of images and objects appeared ready to endanger that armory. The rational processes and calculations of individual advantage that drove producers, retailers, and consumers was fostering a fundamental cultural transformation. Within the womb of modernity was developing an entirely new culture. These critics sensed this change and, with the discursive tools at their disposal, sought a diagnosis and a program of recovery predicated on rescuing the Romantic ideal of a deep, autonomous and whole individual. Because of the continuing power of this engagement, the concern about spectacle and commerce was not principally about the possibility of illusory images. These critics did not worry about the instability of what confronted the human eye or about the fact that images were little more than illusions, as did many contemporary critics in France.[137] Rather, they were feared that the superabundance of and an overreliance on images threatened to undermine the carefully defined freedom central to the "expressive self," that the self threatened to retreat into a dazed and passive shell (of which Simmel's blasé personality was but one example) that was no longer capable of active engagement or assimilation of the outside world.

In addition, because they began from this century-old foundation, the toy critics could not fully embrace an alternative culture based on the surface play of the consumer, on imposing narratives on the fleeting visual images provided by urban commerce and thereby constructing and defining one's self through surface images. They believed that the healthy individual had to impose a personality on and through durable and stable objects, and they therefore could not imagine the "postmodern" answer: playing with shifting, fugitive images. Hence, they were hostile to fashion. The contrast between these critics and contemporary consumers is apparent when one compares the shoppers who were visually consuming the surfaces of toys, playing with and admiring the images presented to them in complete disregard for the underlying objects (toys), with the formulations of Jean Paul, Thomas Mann, and Ferdinand Avenarius, who praised toys that all but dispensed with surfaces, preferring sand and sticks, which the individual could annex to his or her own imagination.

The Market Responds

The cultural critique, we have seen, found an echo in the popular press and drew on wider ideas discussed in German society, particularly in middle-class society. But did it have any actual impact on the toy market? The toy industry, the target of so much scorn, doubted that its critics would have any substantial success. In 1910, the *Deutsche Spielwaren-Zeitung* repeatedly argued that while the Munich artists' dolls, featuring Marion Kaulitz's productions, met with striking interest at the Leipziger Easter Fair, they would find little in the way of sales.[138] The *Rundschau über Spielwaren* argued that the toy critics were being unrealistic: there were too many poor people who could not afford any artistic toy.[139] The *Deutsche Spielwaren-Zeitung* also attacked toy reformers for being hopelessly out of touch with financial realities: "The German people are not so wealthy and their buying power is not so enormous that producers may produce only expensive goods."[140] Moreover, it was argued that in their enthusiasm for educating children with their artistic toys, the toy critics had entirely ruled out delightful toys that children, despite all the theories of the critics, truly enjoyed.[141] The representatives of the toy industry portrayed toy critics as starry-eyed aesthetes and regarded all artistic efforts as exceedingly expensive. In fact, *Daheim* joined their criticism of doll reformers, alleging that the artistic dolls were in fact better suited to adults than to children.[142]

Was the industry right? Was there any hope for creating a real market for artistic toys? There are good reasons to think so. First, let us turn to wood toys. Most of the toys designed by artists—whether the *Dresdner Werkstätte,* the Kleinhempels, or Professor Sutter—were made of wood. Interestingly enough, the wood toy industry began to experience an upturn from around 1905. In 1912, Gustav Rudi observed in *Rundschau über Spielwaren:* "[S]everal years ago a new direction and spirit came to the fabrication of wooden toys. The primitive, often slapped together wood toys of earlier times, which were so flimsy and ugly, made way for artistic characters . . . About seven years ago, the production of wooden toys began to transform."[143] This was not merely the *Rundschau*'s enthusiastic propaganda in support of a down-and-out part of the industry. In 1908, the Nuremberg *Handelskammer* reported a sharp increase in business for wooden toys. After the international financial crisis of 1908–9, the wooden toy industry of Nuremberg was again reporting extremely strong sales. The *Handel-*

skammer reported that the cause of the upswing in demand for wooden toys was that "the dominant taste had decisively improved."[144] The Sonneberg *Handelskammer* also noted the increasing sales of wooden toys, particularly those that were "artistically designed."[145] Likewise, the *Deutsche Spielwaren-Zeitung* reported "enormous demand in *erzgebirgische* wood toys."[146] Another source reported that while sales in 1911 were not all that had been hoped for, "at least the improved taste remained."[147] Causality may be difficult to establish, but there was at the very least a serendipitous improvement in demand for "artistically designed" wooden toys only a few years after the emergence of the Dresdner Werkstätte.

Meanwhile, the predominant taste in dolls also began to evolve. Inspired by the 1908 Munich doll exhibition, the great coming-out party for Marion Kaulitz,[148] Sonneberg firms, led by Krämmer and Reinhardt, began trying new forms for dolls. Krämmer and Reinhardt remained extremely uncertain about the marketability of the new "realistic" baby heads. The clothing and haircuts of the new models had also been designed to be as realistic as possible. The producers did everything they could to make these new dolls lifelike (just as had the Munich doll reformers) while also permitting the dolls to be mass-produced. To the relief of Krämmer and Reinhardt, the dolls were an enormous success when they came to market in 1909, known to all the world as "character dolls."[149] The Sonneberg *Handelskammer* had doubted whether these character dolls would succeed, because they seemed to stray too far from the established models. To succeed, they would have to change the prevailing market taste, and in the opinion of the *Handelskammer,* they were not up to such a task.[150] In 1910, the *Handelskammer* overlooked this prophecy when it admitted that character dolls were experiencing extraordinary market success. The next year, the *Handelskammer* noted that character dolls were selling particularly strongly in Germany.[151] The Munich *Handelskammer* concurred, complaining that deliveries of character dolls in 1910 were well behind demand.[152] Again, causality may not be easy to prove, but dolls modeled on those of the reformers began very quickly to sell extremely well. The *Deutsche Spielwaren-Zeitung* observed, "[T]he drive toward artistic individuality is also influencing the toy industry and has created, to name just one example, the character and artistic dolls."[153] It seems likely, then, that the toy critics had touched a nerve in the culture. Artistic toys appealed to a public that shared some of the concerns and aspirations articulated by Avenarius and others. The interventions of members of the cultural elite had a quantifiable result in the form of increased sales.

The most interesting example of the impact of the toy critique on the marketplace was in the rise of Käthe Kruse. Kruse was born in Breslau and had an impoverished childhood. While still a teenager, she moved on her own to Berlin to become an actor. While pursuing her acting career, she had ample opportunity to familiarize herself with the intellectual currents of her time, particularly as she enjoyed spending time at the famed Café des Westens, the center of Berlin's intellectual life.[154] There she met Max Kruse, a reasonably successful sculptor, who later became her husband. At the Café des Westens and through her husband, she also associated with Max Reinhardt (Germany's leading stage director) and many other leading cultural figures. After marrying Max, Kruse and her children retreated to a small mountain village in Switzerland. When she appealed to Max, who had remained in Berlin, to send them some new dolls, Max refused, lamenting that the dolls available in Berlin were all horrible. "How can one fulfill motherly feelings with a hard, cold, stiff thing?" he wrote,[155] encouraging Kruse to make her own. So Kruse did (see fig. 8). It took a number of years for Kruse to produce the dolls she wanted. It seems that the nose in particular gave her trouble. But she continued working to find a form that would delight her children, dolls that they could believe were "real, living children."[156] When she was finished and showed her dolls at a 1910 exhibition organized by the Tietz department store on Leipzigerstrasse in Berlin, she became an overnight sensation.

An early reviewer, Anna Plotow, exclaimed, "Artists and laity stand admiringly before these dolls."[157] *Deutsche Kunst und Dekoration* wrote enthusiastically: "An artist is the mother who crafted them [the dolls] with humor, with fantasy, and warm understanding for the minds of children . . . They have no hint of caricature, which so easily subverts artists even in the land of dolls, such as Marion Kaulitz or the Steiff family. Here everything is lovely, droll children . . . They are not designed for the glass cabinet or the doll exhibition; one can and must play with them."[158] Kruse herself described her dolls as "the union of primitivism and naturalism."[159]

By her own testimony, Kruse was particularly amused by the commercial doll producers' reaction to her production. They were, she relates, shocked and dismayed at her dolls without wigs of real hair and without moving limbs or eyes, proclaiming them hardly dolls at all. Nonetheless, Kruse found a doll maker interested in licensing her

Fig. 8. Käthe Kruse dolls. "Kruse-Puppen," *Deutsche Kunst und Dekoration* 29 (1911): 277.

dolls for mass production.[160] Unfortunately, the mass-produced versions were, in Kruse's words, "in no way beautiful." She lamented, "Everything was so exactly and carefully worked, like I never would have created."[161] The company appears to have also received complaints from buyers that the Kruse dolls did not move. Kruse therefore took over production in early autumn 1911. Only a few days later came a telegram from the United States ordering 150 Käthe Kruse dolls to be in Bremen by 8 November. Soon after that, five hundred more dolls were ordered by the same firm. Käthe Kruse, entrepreneur, was up and running.[162] Soon, her advertisements were running in the *Deutsche Spielwaren-Zeitung,* and her dolls were being glowingly reviewed by *Daheim.*[163]

The language that Kruse used to describe her dolls, admittedly many years after the fact, demonstrated a strong affinity to the ideas of the toy reformers. She intended her dolls to cultivate direct, emotional relations with children. They were a direct response to the "hard, cold" dolls of the commercial producers, and those producers were, she believed, incapable of either understanding or producing the proper form. She wanted her dolls to be "primitive" and "naturalistic"; the union of those two characteristics enabled Kruse's dolls to find a market that eluded Marion Kaulitz, whose dolls were touched by "caricature," the opposite of "primitive." Kruse's dolls were opposed to the moving, active dolls of the Sonneberg companies. Her "primitivism" allowed her dolls to be "naturalistic" without hair or moving body parts. She even insisted on handcraftsmanship in production,[164] thereby tapping suspicion of modern capitalist production. The dolls instrumentalized an educated discourse on the ills of modern society and gave concrete form to the reform agenda. That agenda argued that capitalist society alienated individuals with a surfeit of remote, inaccessible objects that refused the appropriating glance of the subject, reducing the consumer to a passive observer. They offered a few moments of fascination, enough to seize the attention of the flaneur, rather than any healthy relation between subject and object. Reformers believed that the proper forms/dolls could, however, break down the distance between object and subject, allowing the consumer to emotionally and creatively connect with the object and thereby to assimilate it into the subject's ego. Kruse's rhetoric was the reformers rhetoric. Therefore, the cultural reformers fully embraced her product, making it a lasting standard for dolls. Kruse dolls became signposts for caring, sensitive parents who sought to raise well-cultivated children.

Of course, as they were lovingly made by hand, they were also quite expensive, just as the toy industry had suggested. Kruse told *Daheim:* "[A]sk the reader not to wonder so much at the price. If the price were lower, then demand would be monstrous and the dolls could not each remain, as they are now, my particular charge. Should these, too, become an industrial product? No, no one wants that, least of all me."[165] The price made Kruse dolls exclusive indicators of both cultural and financial capital. The consumer had to be relatively aware of new demands placed on dolls and toys to be willing to pay the substantial price for a Kruse doll, and they also had to have the resources to be able to pay that price. The embodiment of the bourgeois toy reform movement was transformed into a status symbol by a conscious manipulation of the price mechanism of the capitalist marketplace. A sociocultural reform movement aimed at improving all society then became a nearly inaccessible sign of distinction. It was no accident that in *Doctor Faustus,* Thomas Mann assigned Käthe Kruse dolls to the children of the socially ambitious professor of aesthetics, Institoris. The Kruse dolls communicated Institoris's sense of his own cultural sophistication and material well-being. He recognized the value of cultivating the imaginations of his children, and he could afford the most sophisticated, primitivist doll available. Fully as interesting, this status symbol was a consumption item intended to teach taste (an emotional delicacy) to young girls while also conditioning them to their future roles as mothers, not the "unnatural" roles of businesswomen or artist assumed by their creator. Finances, cultural politics, and gender roles combined to define a specific sociocultural position, a market niche that Käthe Kruse filled marvelously. On the basis of this strong cultural position and healthy profit margins, Kruse was set to be one of the few toy makers of her era to survive to the present day.[166]

By the end of the nineteenth century, toys had long been theorized as agents of individual development. The guided interaction between subject and object was seen as an important tool in constructing a normative self, whether the norm was utilitarian-liberal or Romantic-expressive. These norms were basic to the project of modernity, legitimizing—indeed, demanding—the emergence of a liberal economic and political order as well as an increasingly modernist cultural order organized around consumption. By the end of the nineteenth century, however, the social order constructed in the image of individualism was increasingly seen as a threat to those normative visions of individualism. The defenders of both utilitarian and Romantic individualism were deeply troubled by the emergence of capitalism as a cultural force—that is, by consumerism. Not only did the products thrown forth by consumer capitalism not fulfill the functions assigned them by the classical theorists of modern subjectivity, but they actively obstructed the articulation of a healthy self. Between the idealized self-description of German modernity and the social expressions of those ideals, there existed a space that permitted and likely required the elaboration of critiques of modernity.

In the years before World War I, ideas about the importance of play were reworked to stand as an indictment of modern capitalism. Urban life, the harried rush through crowded streets, created structural incentives for the toy industry to offer products that drew attention to themselves through movement and spectacle. Parents and friends, seeing these toys as delightful examples of modernity, lovingly purchased them as gifts. But they deceived themselves, argued a powerful group of writers, editors, and intellectuals, who maintained that the dazzle that attracted parents was produced by making toys self-sufficient objects of visual consumption. According to this formulation, the commercial toy, like Simmel's historically styled apartment, "excludes the individual." Critics increasingly saw the modern individual as a lonely, alienated being, one who could no longer define himself or herself and his or her environment through a creative imposition of an individualized order on chaos. Instead, too many individuals withdrew behind the emotional walls of the blasé personality. Children were no longer educated to be creative, even though the demands on the imaginative faculties of modern adults were growing. These critics argued that humans needed more fantasy, not less. Only then could children grow up to actively assimilate the things of their environment, to turn cold objects into a warm home. Only thus could the century-old ideal of the expressive self survive the fragmenting pressures of modern consumption and its associated spectacle. Unfortunately, argued many critics, the objects best suited to train children to be creative were themselves wrapped up in the same structural, fantasy-denying logic that made toys critical in the first place. Unfortunately, most parents had very different goals for their toys and ideas about what constituted education. The toy critics set out to change that.

The critics behind the toy reform movement encouraged new designs, new toys that partook of parallel discourses (e.g., those of the *Kunsterziehungsbewegung* and the *Kunstgewerbereformbewegung*), easing the task of reaching new audiences. Their ideas were general concerns transposed onto toys. Their critique of toys was therefore readily understandable to anyone familiar with the general ideas. They won over a portion of society. A market emerged for toys that corresponded to their prescriptions, suggesting that perhaps their larger concerns about technological capitalism were shared more broadly. Nonetheless, the better part of the toy market remained much as it had been. This bifurcation of the market made the reformed toys into status symbols, reified signs of cultural sophistication and financial well-being. The marketplace created a space for the toy reformers to realize their program, at the cost of transforming cultural reform into fashion.

5. "Keep in Mind What Those Cheap Prices Mean"

Consumer Industries and the Social Question

The emerging web of mass consumption and mass production created new constellations of economic possibilities and social organization. The transformation of the toy industry in the last decades of the nineteenth century showed clearly how the push and pull of a new marketplace had kaleidoscopic effects on the organization of production and the distribution of wealth. Shaping the economic and social challenges posed by expanding production became a growing theme of argument in the new century. Just as the developing culture of consumption had generated considerable criticism, argument, and tension, the increasing significance of the mass market opened the doors to substantial debates about the social role of the mass production of consumer goods.

I begin this chapter with one contemporary analysis of the connections between the domestic economy and international influence, particularly the interaction between the export of consumer products and national power. It is not my intention to privilege this analysis as somehow authoritative or normative. Rather, it will be used to explore how Germans could tie together many of the questions I shall examine here. This discussion of the place of consumer goods in Germany's future will open up a variety of perspectives: the nature of national power; the connection between social reform and consumption; the possibilities for promoting light industries, such as the toy industry; and the connections between industrialization, product design, and labor. In this line of argument, consumer goods could be seen as a positive social good. Other lines would neatly invert these claims of social utility. Once I have shown how one analyst tied these topics together, I shall unpack them once again. I shall examine how the toy industry and others offered competing understandings of the significance of trade and tax policy and of mechanization and social policy at the dawn of mass consumption. In disputing the relation and significance of these factors, a variety of normative visions of modernity were elaborated, which only served to emphasize the disagreements about the proper nature of the modern. These debates become clearer when we turn to consider the expanding role of *Hausindustrie* in the production of consumer goods, like toys.

Friedrich Naumann, Aesthetics and Economic Power

One of the most vigorous advocates of improved consumer goods was Friedrich Naumann. Naumann, an evangelical pastor, had given up his missionary work in Frankfurt am Main to pursue politics. By the early 1900s, with the aid of his newspaper *Die Hilfe,* his own voluminous writings, and his numerous prominent friends, Naumann had established himself as the leading New Liberal politician in Germany. He was also a pivotal figure in the "bourgeois reform movement," because his wide interests led him to consider topics ranging from international politics to industrial policy to aesthetics.[1] Naumann was, then, well placed to relate the philosophic and aesthetic concerns of such individuals as Simmel or Avenarius to the problems of social reform and the uses of national power. His was one of the "compelling—if also competing—visions of a twentieth century German national culture and global economy"[2] that emerged in this critical historical moment. His work is thus a useful tool for exploring the interconnections between, on the one hand, the cultural and aesthetic concerns examined earlier in this book and, on the other, economics and politics. He was also a thoughtful and forceful advocate of the interests of light industry, so Naumann's ideas also serve as a launching pad from which to consider the narrative the metal toy industry constructed to explain their challenges and their successes. Through such consideration, we can explore some of the optimistic hopes inspired by the emergence of modern consumer industries and the possibilities that seemed to hide in the combination of aesthetics and technology.

As Naumann's faithful lieutenant Theodor Heuß argued, Naumann was becoming increasingly concerned by 1900 about how Germany's rapidly growing population was to be supported in the future.[3] The answer Naumann developed was, in somewhat simplified terms, international trade and better products. His controversial commitment to the expansion of the navy and imperialism were portrayed as necessary supports for the central imperative: expansion of German commerce.[4] It is important to emphasize that while expanding trade was critical, Naumann did not propose to trust in lower tariffs and the free market. Naumann believed that the way forward for Germany entailed a conscious effort to reform German industrial products, coupled with imperialism. Trade and improved consumer goods were, in Naumann's mind, linked. He was convinced that the key to Germany's future well-being was in concentrating on higher value-added products, leaving lower-value products to other countries. Thus, he explained, "our grain lies on La Plata, our sheep graze in Australia, and our iron is mined in Sweden."[5] Germany could not, in Naumann's mind, remain competitive and powerful as a producer of raw materials. Agriculture and mineral extraction were to be allowed to migrate abroad: Germany's grain would come from Argentina, not Pomerania (or, significantly, from the United States or Russia); Germany's iron would come from Sweden, not Lorraine. Germany's future lay not with those protected by Bülow's tariffs but with those hurt by them. Instead, Germany had to focus on producing consumer goods of high quality, meaning both durable and attractive.[6] Naumann's commitment to the Werkbund has to be seen in this light. Both emphasized that the elaboration of proper commercial form was central to Germany's future.[7] Naumann argued, "[A] people that wants to earn billions for its labor must learn to see aesthetics in economic terms."[8]

That simple observation had enormous implications. Not only did product design become a national concern, but it transformed the question of labor policy. A beautiful, profitable design meant nothing if it could not be converted into material reality. The hand had to be as skilled as the mind. With the argument that "cheap labor is bad labor"[9] (neatly inverting the liberal interpretation of wages), the improvement of form became a central issue for workers' compensation. Rather than wages following the value or quality of labor, Naumann appeared to hope that they could drive the value or quality of labor. Naumann reasoned that wages ought to rise, for bad labor cannot be expected to fashion quality products.

Form also became an issue of national security. How else was the government to cover the costs of mushrooming defense spending if not by taxing industry? Naumann maintained: "Our production must double our income; that means it must be the most technically and aesthetically advanced production in the world. Only on this basis shall we remain a great power."[10] In this way, high-quality, aesthetically pleasing consumer products were assigned enormous importance in the world views of Naumann and his collaborators. Such aesthetic consumer products, they argued, would create two virtuous cycles. Improving wages would promote improved labor, which would enable high-quality products that had margins sufficient to pay higher wages. This would, moreover, integrate the working class into German society, closing a dangerous and yawning societal divide. Aesthetic consumer goods would also secure the financial basis for imperial and naval expansion, which were in turn the critical shields of expanding commerce. The key was in the higher prices and margins that quality goods could secure, from which could be extracted higher wages, better social programs, and a powerful navy. How one begins these virtuous cycles, however, was left rather unclear.

The arguments advanced by Naumann and his associates were predicated on the belief that German consumer goods were not, at present, of terribly high quality. There seemed to be a general consensus that during the course of the nineteenth century, the quality of German products declined. The reports of the *Handelskammer* repeatedly lamented the pressure of competition that forced down the level of quality. The *Wegweiser* likewise argued that price competition was preventing quality work.[11] Theodor Heuß and Werner Sombart agreed that during the nineteenth century, quality declined precipitously across the spectrum of German consumer goods industries.[12] The cause of this slide into cheap, shoddy production was variously ascribed to machines, overproduction, competition, and the greed, vanity, and stupidity of consumers.

Naumann did not believe that low quality was the unavoidable market response to a complex mosaic of factors. The fundamental optimism of the reform milieu led him and his allies to argue that they could reverse the causal chain. In that way, the multiple factors undercutting quality production, once inverted, would be transformed into opportunities to exert a beneficial influence across a wide variety of areas of German life. Besides increasing national power and overcoming endemic poverty, for example, Hermann Muthesius, a leading figure in the Werkbund, suggested in a February 1907 speech that improved quality could reconcile hostile classes. He argued that quality consumer products—in this case, a genuine aesthetic style that reflected the purpose and origins of a product rather than the social pretensions of the consumer—would reduce the vanity and parvenu ostentation of German society and thereby reduce the visual display of class differences.[13] Quality consumer goods, sacrificed in the first generation of industrialization, therefore appeared to offer a solution to many of the problems created by that first generation. In fact, aesthetic, quality consumer goods were assigned an almost utopian power to cleanse Germany of social ills.

Machines were one of a multiplicity of factors adduced to undermine the quality of German products. Examining this perception of machines leads us directly to perhaps the center of Naumann's argument and, indeed, the argument of the entire Werkbund. The German Werkbund famously broke with the Art and Crafts tradition of John Ruskin and William Morris. The Werkbund acknowledged the permanence of mechanization but sought to guide the course of industrial production into a new, more culturally desirable path. Nonetheless, the Werkbund saw machines as a critical factor in destroying quality.[14] The double life of machines as both destroyers and re-creators of quality, aesthetic wares is perhaps best explained by the widely respected professor of architecture Theodor Fischer, first president of the Werkbund. In an address to the German Werkbund in Munich in July 1908, Fischer made it abundantly clear that shoddy production norms stemmed from "modern forms of production." He ascribed this unfortunate influence not to machines in themselves but, rather, to their place in organizing production. Because labor was organized around machines and because production centered around whatever machines could do most effectively, the proper relationship was inverted. Production superseded and determined the product, rather than the product determining how it should be produced. Fischer framed the matter simply by asking, "[W]hich is the means and which is the end?"[15] The problem, then, is how to use the machine properly, how to subordinate machines to the needs of society and culture rather than vice versa. The argument that machines have been misused (placed in the service of production rather than products) plays into the economic ideas presented by Naumann.

The suggestion that machines have been allowed to organize production indicates that industry had sought to win its profits by concentrating on reducing the costs of production rather than improving quality and therefore raising the price of the product. The corollary—pressuring the wages of workers to further reduce costs—more or less suggests itself. Thus, the subordination of production to machines could also be represented as the source of the social question, that is, of the misery and poverty of workers. Fischer, Naumann, and the Werkbund hoped to convince industry to seek profits instead by harnessing the power of machines to form high-quality products. In this way, industry would no longer be obsessed with slashing costs. Rather, it would seek, through properly employed machines subordinated to skilled, well-compensated labor, to profit through selling higher-quality products at a premium. The connections between quality consumer products and the general level of wages were then considerable.

The arguments advanced by Naumann were shared by many. Peter Jessen, the director of the Royal Arts and Crafts Museum in Berlin, for example, argued in an essay published by the German Werkbund that "a great industrial nation cannot survive over the long term by undercutting others; it must beat them through the quality of its labor."[16] Hermann Muthesius and Ernst Jäckh argued for a reform of the applied arts for similar reasons, although they did not emphasize to the same degree the potential for social amelioration.[17] Not surprisingly, one could also find the argument in the pages of *Die Hilfe.*[18]

Naumann and his associates in the Werkbund turned several older arguments on their heads. In their view, the sources of national power were not to be found in agriculture[19] or the mighty ironworks of Krupp, Thyssen, and the other iron masters; power was mercantile. As cited in this book's introduction, the Sonneberg *Handelskammer* suggested, with regard to the San Francisco World's Fair, that a "place in the sun" was to be secured by more than Dreadnaughts: wealth and commerce were the real foundations of power. Wealth purchased the Dreadnaughts and national solidarity that would sustain Germany's rise to supremacy. This is, in its own way, a highly mercantilistic notion. It also, however, differed substantially from the mercantilistic bases of official German trade policy. Chancellor Bülow and others had sought to use government action to shore up domestic support, by demonstrating the efficacy of the state in serving the interests of certain interest groups, particularly agriculture and heavy industry. Bülow's government believed in part that the interests of the state and the nation were best served by ensuring the continuing vitality of these social and economic interests, as they provided many of the human and material resources that made Germany a great power. Naumann, by contrast, argued that if Germany's strength was to continue to grow, the foundations of national strength had to expand. National wealth would have to increase exponentially. This was only possible if Germany dedicated itself to selling enormous quantities of higher value-added products. In this way, substantial returns would be realized that could be used both to secure the loyalty of the working class and to support an expanding military and colonial establishment. Such high value-added production was, in turn, only possible with a highly trained, motivated, and well-paid workforce. In effect, Naumann was developing a new vision of society, one that linked aesthetics, consumers, wealth, national unity, and imperialism. In this constellation, the link between aesthetics and consumers created the foundation on which everything else stood.

Imperialism, Government Finance, and Social Conflict

Without addressing his aspirations directly, toy makers stood in ambivalent relation to the analyses that informed Naumann's vision of high-quality commerce allied to social reform at home and imperial expansion abroad. To understand why the metal toy industry narrativized its successes and failures in the fashion it did, we must contrast their experience with the diagnosis offered by Naumann. He had argued that an expansive foreign policy was a necessary means of protecting and advancing the commercial and therefore the social and national interests of Germany. That policy, however, triggered the fatal tightening of alliances (in the words of Henry Kissinger, the "political doomsday machine") that would lead to World War I and the absorption of consumer industries into the national war effort.

Even before the opening of hostilities, the naval and imperial policies supported by Naumann came to exercise an unhealthy influence on the toy industry. Rather than a shield for commerce, the navy came to resemble more a sword of Damocles over light industry. Despite the increased levies on imports of agricultural and industrial raw materials, the burden of the escalating arms races spurred by Germany's international ambitions continued to threaten the well-being of government finances. As a result, another round of taxes became necessary.

The story of the tax law of 1909 is extremely complicated and need not be retold in its entirety here. In short form, the government had to raise additional income, largely to pay for its escalating naval construction program. Before 1909, the *Reich* had been forced to rely heavily on debt financing of its international ambitions. The annual forays of the German government into the world financial markets were politically embarrassing and financially unsustainable. New taxes were necessary. But then came the eternal questions: whom to tax, what to tax, and how much to tax.

When the dust settled, Chancellor von Bülow had resigned, the coalition that had supported him had collapsed in acrimony, and a coalition of conservatives, Catholics, and Poles had passed a tax bill that featured no meaningful inheritance tax, the only constitutional means of taxing accumulated wealth. The burden of the new taxes was placed overwhelmingly on the urban population. The bill included a number of taxes on financial transactions meant to raise money from industry and finance. It also featured a variety of increases in consumption taxes, particularly on tobacco, coffee, tea, alcohol ("spirits"), and beer.[20] The Nuremberg Chamber of Commerce characterized these tax increases as a "very painful increase in prices" and greeted them "with great bitterness."[21] Much like the agricultural tariffs in the 1902 trade law, these consumption taxes disproportionately affected low-income families. Rather than imperial expansion engendering greater national unity, it exacerbated social conflict.

The Nuremberg *Handelskammer* worried greatly about the impact of these policies, referring repeatedly to the increased cost of living ("Verteuerung der Lebenshaltung"). When one adds to these new consumption taxes the old agricultural tariffs and the effects of a bad harvest, workers, including those in the toy factories of Nuremberg and Württemberg, had considerable cause to demand higher wages and to be willing to fight for them. These levies disproportionately affected the lower classes within Germany, hitting light industry indirectly but, nonetheless, quite hard. The most determined and successful wage movements within the industry, those of 1904 and 1911, both correlate closely with government-induced spikes in living expenses. In 1905, after the signature of the 1904 labor contract in the toy industry and as the trade treaties based on the 1902 tariff law were ratified, the *Handelskammer* drew a straight line between increased labor costs and the "painful rise in the price of meat and other food items."[22] The logic was crystal clear. Rather than allow their living standards to fall because of the trade treaties, workers and their unions took action to ensure higher wages.

The 1911 strike, the largest in the toy industry before World War I, deserves closer examination. Negotiations lasted throughout July. The workers, represented by the Deutsche Metallarbeiterverband, argued that the employers had de facto backed out of parts of earlier agreements; they pointed to some female workers who were still making sixteen or seventeen pfennig an hour.[23] The industry argued that the wage demands of the workers were in no way modest, and it characterized the raises offered in 1905 and 1906 as "large." Fulfilling the demands of the workers was described as "simply impossible," as it would lead to the "ruin" of the industry, particularly since business was slowing in 1911. Furthermore, raw material prices were again rising more rapidly than toy prices (see fig. 9), raising concern among toy producers about how they were to continue bringing toys cheaply and profitably to market. The *Deutsche Spielwaren-Zeitung* reported: "The demands of the workers, particularly for the young and female workers, are so high that it is impossible for the producers to agree to meet them even halfway, since a corresponding hike in the sale prices in most cases . . . was simply no longer possible. The sale prices of most articles are now so close to the highest possible price that even the smallest price increase makes the article unsalable."[24]

Negotiations broke down over the length of the workweek and wages for new hires. A limited strike ensued as workers at twelve firms walked off the job on 24 July. When still no progress was made, the industry locked out 60 percent of the remaining workers in the metal toy industry. The union immediately called a strike for the remaining 40 percent. Thirty-five firms were shut down and, according to the factory inspectors, 2,739 workers idled. The industry alleged that more than three thousand workers were affected. It assured itself that it had made a number of large wage concessions and that "it is better to close the factories than to continue production under such difficult conditions [as would be imposed by the demands of the unions]." On 18 August, an arbitration committee was established to bring the strike to an end. The arbitrators retained the fifty-six-hour workweek and codified mutual concessions on wages. On 28 August, work resumed.[25] That same summer, the great metal toy maker of Württemberg, Märklin, also experienced a strike, one that lasted nine weeks. Eventually Märklin agreed to a raise of three pfennig an hour, a 9.5-hour workday, and 20 percent additional pay for overtime, rising to 25 percent after 1 January 1912.[26]

The timing of these multiple strikes could not have been entirely accidental. The negotiations were harder and the conflict was longer and larger in 1911 than in either 1904 or 1906. In 1906, the union had backed down rather than risk a lockout. In 1911, they were again threatened with a lockout. This time, however, the union chose to escalate the conflict rather than settle.

Food prices had been particularly high in 1911. The Nuremberg *Handelskammer* itself noted the "extraordinarily painful" rise in food

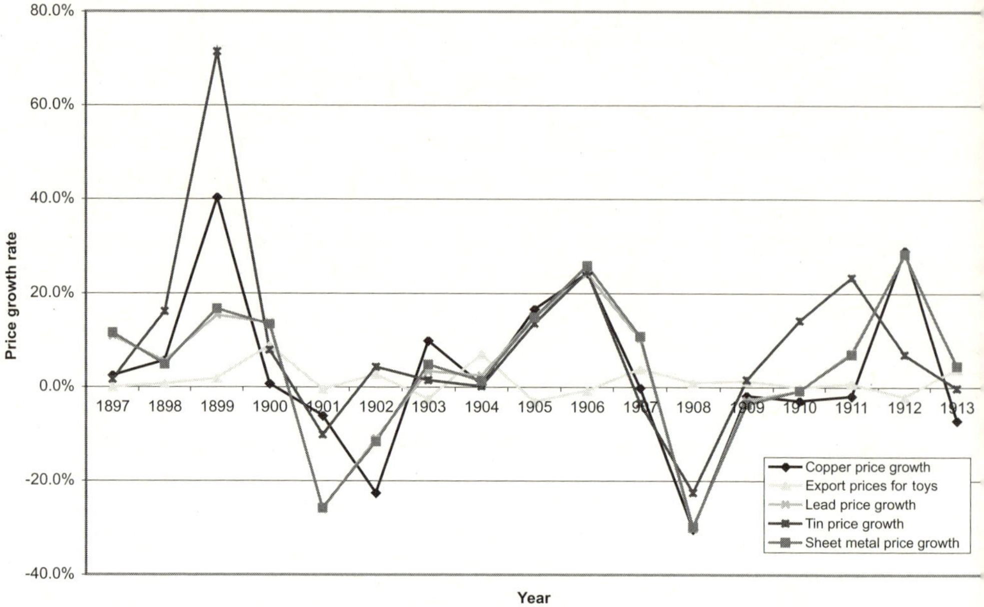

Fig. 9. Export prices of toys relative to input prices. (Data from *Monatliche Nachweise über den auswärtigen Handel des deutsche Zollgebietes* [Berlin], 1892–1914.)

prices.[27] The broad consumption taxes introduced a year earlier, coupled with the earlier tariffs on foodstuffs, had done much to stoke the anger and demands of labor. There was, therefore, a direct connection between financing Germany's confrontational foreign policy and the structural increase in the industry's cost structure.

As a consequence of this labor militancy, wages in the metal toy industry grew. The leading journal of the toy industry calculated that wages in the Nuremberg toy industry rose 40 percent between 1902 and 1912.[28] Much of the Nuremberg toy industry was profitable enough to concede rising wages but too weak to risk the sort of prolonged battles seen, for example, in the coal industry. The union's 1911 wage demands were not met in full, and they did not get the reduction in hours they had sought. The calculations for annual income made on the basis of their demands can therefore serve as a rough guide to the finances of toy workers (because they worked more hours at a slightly lower hourly rate). Male wages between 900 and 1,400 marks per annum would put the metal toy industry among the top half of industries.[29] Female workers would earn between 550 and 800 marks annually. If one compares what a married couple could make in the Nuremberg toy industry with what a family of Erzgebirge *Heimarbeiter* could expect, often not even 600 marks, the difference was enormous.

The toy industry therefore saw at best a limited sign of a virtuous cycle ignited by imperialism. The efforts to construct a naval fleet, leaving aside the dangerous escalation in tensions with Great Britain that came in its train, meant increasing social tension and a rising cost structure for industry, as both labor and raw materials became dearer. According to Naumann, this should have been offset by the ability of high-quality producers to extract higher prices from global consumers. Overall, however, toy prices tended to stay relatively flat (see fig. 9). The relative inelasticity of toy prices made it extremely difficult for companies to pass along increases in input costs. Higher margins were not simply conjured into existence.

Mass Production, Factor Costs, and Mechanization

The metal toy makers of Nuremberg saw the imperial and fiscal policies of the government as problems rather than boons. Nonetheless, despite rising taxes, growing labor strife, and labor costs, many firms were able to grow and prosper. They could afford to raise wages and support a slowly expanding welfare state. In explaining this success, the metal toy makers implicitly constructed a narrative that explicated economic development and the contributions of consumer products to national prosperity and social well-being.

The large toy makers prospered extraordinarily. For example, the three toy makers that went public—Gebrüder Bing, Max Dannhorn, and Bayerische Celluloid—all registered very respectable profits (see fig. 10). While the profits garnered by Dannhorn and Bayerische Celluloid did not grow as evenly as those of Bing, they generally remained above one hundred thousand marks in annual gross. Profits in 1910 for Bing, Bayerische Celluloid, and Dannhorn had grown 95 percent, 136 percent, and 296 percent, respectively, over profits claimed in 1900 (Bing's profits started from a considerably higher point in 1900, then being more than six times greater than Bayerische Celluloid and around twelve times those of Dannhorn). Between 1897 and 1913, Bing and Bayerische Celluloid never distributed dividends of less than 10 percent. Perhaps more telling is analysis of the companies' earnings per

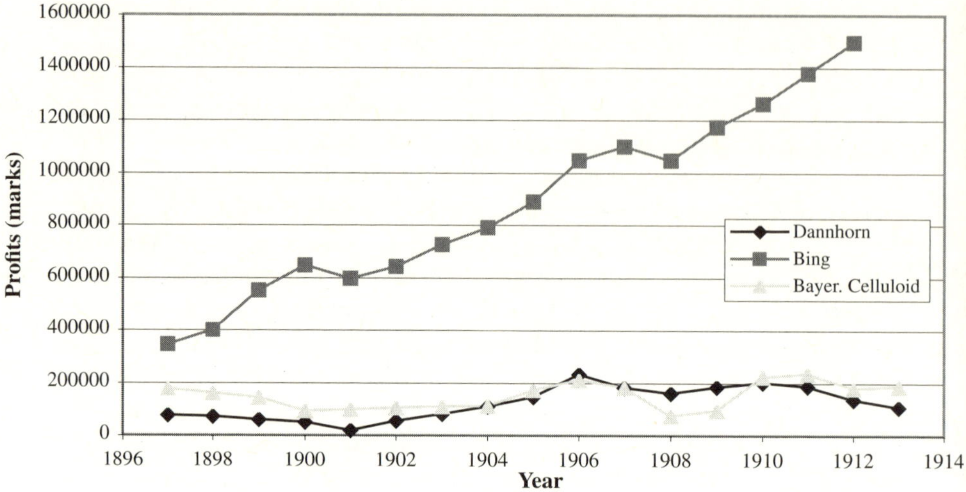

Fig. 10. Comparative profits of three toy makers. (Data from *Handbuch der deutschen Aktien-Gesellschaften* [Berlin and Leipzig], 1896–1914.)

share (see fig. 11). Earnings per share relates profits to the size of the firm, thereby giving an idea of the firm's efficiency at generating profits. If one excludes the crisis year of 1908 and the year following (the first half of which suffered from the hangover of the 1908 crash), earnings per share remained above 100 marks per share for all three firms. By and large, all three registered earnings of between 150 and 250 marks per share. For purposes of comparison, the mammoth shipping company Norddeutsche Lloyd had earnings per share of 21.2 in 1904 and 48.3 in 1907. A more ordinary firm, the Leipziger Gummi-Waaren Fabrik, a maker of rubber goods, had earnings of 88.2 and 69.5 marks per share, respectively. Though analysis of the toy makers' price-earnings ratios defies expectations (see fig. 12),[30] the toy makers were by any measure highly profitable enterprises.

While one might suggest that Bing was a uniquely successful company, there seems little reason to assume that Dannhorn and Bayerische Celluloid were wildly more successful than their large rivals who had chosen to remain private corporations. Otherwise, firms as successful as Märklin, Steiff, George Carette, Ernst Planck, and Georg Schoenner (the last three all had seats on the board of directors of the Verband bayerischer Metallindustrieller [Association of Bavarian

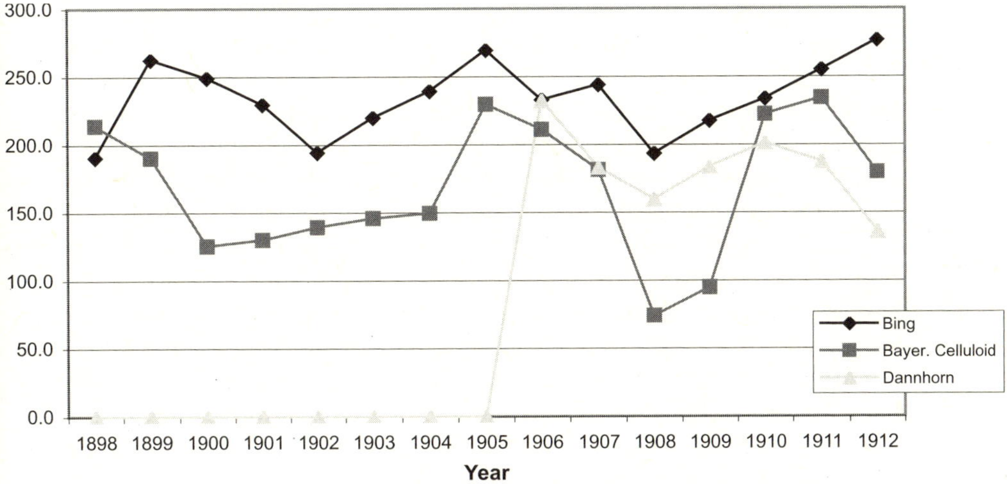

Fig. 11. Earnings per share for three toy makers. (Data from *Handbuch der deutschen Aktien-Gesellschaften* [Berlin and Leipzig], 1898–1912.)

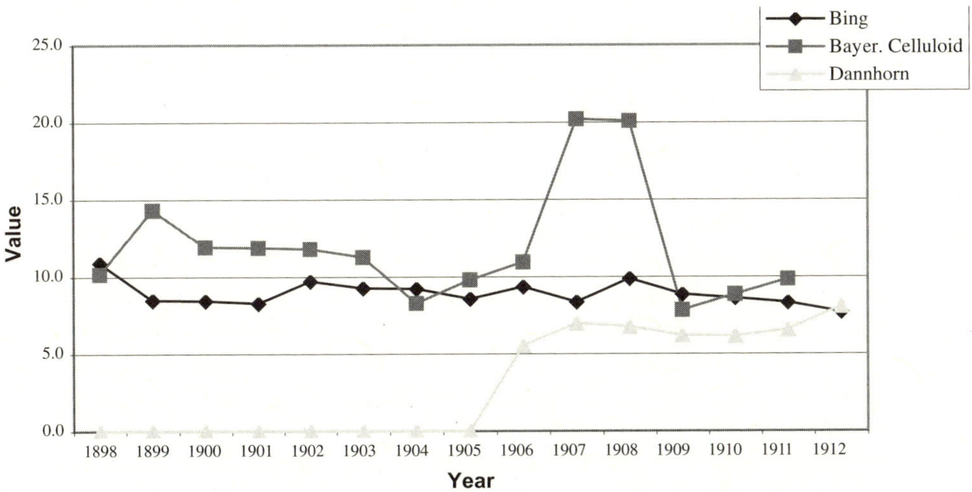

Fig. 12. Price-earnings ratio for three toy makers. (Data from *Handbuch der deutschen Aktien-Gesellschaften* [Berlin and Leipzig], 1898–1912.)

Metal Industrialists])[31] would surely have gone public to secure the benefits reaped by Dannhorn and Bayerische Celluloid.

The larger firms, public and private, believed that they were able to successfully overcome rising wages and raw material costs primarily because they were able to assemble the considerable capital resources necessary to mechanize. Bing reported, "A balance [against rising labor and raw material prices] could only be created if the technical production equipment were used in greater scale, which explains the rapid increase in mechanical equipment."[32] Mechanization had earlier helped metal toy makers contend with the price demands of poverty-stricken consumers. Now it allowed them to escape the dilemma posed by input costs that grew faster than prices for the final product. Wide-scale use of machines allowed companies to vastly improve labor productivity so that the additional financial costs could be reconciled with profitability. As one scion of the industry put it, the largest toy makers in Nuremberg ultimately owed their success to "the most thorough division of labor" as well as their efforts "to produce themselves as many of the necessary part as possible, most even to the point of semi-finished materials."[33] It is not surprising, then, that the *Rundschau uber Spielwaren* would assert that the rising costs "can only be kept in balance through technical achievement."[34] It was, of course, precisely this approach to machines—the emphasis on machines as cost cutters—that Professor Fischer and the Werkbund hoped to escape.

The introduction of ever more machinery was coupled in the toy industry with increased flexibility. The stereotyped Ford model of specialized machinery tied to standardized products did not hold in the German toy industry. Specialized machines could be used to produce large numbers of individual parts that would then be applied to a variety of quite different end products. A kettle for a model steam engine and a steam locomotive, for example, were not necessarily different. In this way, these highly capitalized companies were also flexible mass producers.[35] Bayerische Celluloid, for example, credited an increase in profitability to an increase in the variety and sophistication of their products, which in turn was rooted in a prior expansion of buildings and equipment.[36] The consumers demand for varied products was thus very effectively and profitably met by highly capitalized toy makers.

In Nuremberg, therefore, the drive to mechanize ran full steam ahead as the metal toy makers spent more and more on machines. Table 1 provides an approximate idea of the quantities that the three toy joint-stock companies invested annually in machines. To make this table more understandable, one should keep in mind that the value of machinery depreciated at an annual rate of 10 percent[37]—that is, the accountants believed a machine used up 10 percent of its total value each year until, after ten years, it had exhausted all value. I suspect, however, that many machines remained in operation long after the ten-year milestone. Nonetheless, according to the accounting rules, if the value of a firm's stock of machinery then declined by 10 percent, we can assume that essentially no new machinery was added. If the value declined more than that, it is possible that some machinery was sold, either because a product line was closed or because the firm required a short-term infusion of cash. It is also possible that a fire or industrial mishap destroyed some portion of the machine stock. When the value of the stock remained the same, the firm purchased just enough new machinery to replace that which was, according to the accountants, too old to be useful. Finally, an increase in value over the previous year meant that the company was expanding its machine "portfolio."

The expansion betokened by the new buildings and outlays for new machines is reflected in the employee numbers as well. In 1895, the Nuremberg toy industry, when viewed through the prism of employment, looked as follows:

Number of employees:	1	2–5	6–10	11–20	21–50	51–200
Number of firms:	12	63	39	16	16	5
Total employed:	12	186	302	215	481	475[38]

There was a total of 1,671 workers in 141 firms. The employment figures emphasize the dramatic growth of the industry as a whole, but particularly among the largest companies. The 1907 industrial census broke the industry down as follows:

Number of employees:	2–5	6–10	11–20	21–50	51–200	201–500	500+
Number of firms:	83	36	31	31	17	5	1
Total employed:	253	294	490	919	1,358	1,350	695[39]

There was a total of 5,359 employees at 204 firms. Most of that growth occurred among the largest toy makers—those with fifty-one or more employees. Whereas there were five companies with more than fifty employees in 1895, there were twenty-three such firms twelve years later. Six of these were substantially larger than anything seen in 1895.

The Nuremberg toy industry was clearly growing. The cause of this growth in size was the desire to improve labor efficiency through mechanization. For the metal toy makers, particularly the larger firms, the rising cost structure acted as a positive incentive to mechanize and improve labor productivity. Thus, we see that even with the increasing use of labor-saving machinery in Nuremberg, employment in the Nuremberg toy industry grew 221 percent in the twelve years between 1895 and 1907 (an annualized average in excess of 18 percent), as compared to 46 percent in the Erzgebirge.

The employment figures suggest that the large toy makers were growing faster than smaller ones. Many of the smaller toy firms remained small precisely because there was no advantage in growing. The makers of toy trumpets, swords, kaleidoscopes, and such relatively simple toys still used substantial manual labor in shaping and soldering. One sympathetic observer of the industry asserted flatly, "The machines to replace this manual labor had not yet been discovered."[40] As a result, large factories could produce such items no more cheaply than small shops. This was also largely true of tin figures.[41]

The relative difficulty of the smaller toy makers to increase labor productivity through mechanization created a number of problems. Most immediately, it made these producers much more sensitive to the

TABLE 1. Value of Machine Stock (in marks)

Year	Gebrüder Bing	change prev. year (%)	Max Dannhorn	change prev. year (%)	Bayer. Celluloid	change prev. year (%)
1897	202,967		81,216		82,156	
1898	263,816	23.1	87,261	6.9	99,373	17.3
1899	387,764	32.0	101,399	13.9	118,144	15.9
1900	562,419	31.1	114,550	11.5	123,317	4.2
1901	616,218	8.7	99,594	–15.0	122,269	–0.9
1902	655,044	5.9	84,970	–17.2	99,053	–23.4
1903	719,193	8.9	97,425	12.8	99,659	0.6
1904	839,418	14.3	87,655	–11.1	105,010	5.1
1905	863,558	2.8	84,029	–4.3	115,298	8.9
1906	966,321	10.6	84,052	0.0	119,699	3.7
1907	1,029,162	6.1	77,558	–8.4	120,674	0.8
1908	1,153,652	10.8	69,802	–11.1	150,113	19.6
1909	1,120,739	–2.9	62,822	–11.1	209,231	28.3
1910	939,384	–19.3	58,211	–7.9	218,431	4.2
1911	784,515	–19.7	54,288	–7.2	290,417	24.8
1912	866,938	9.5	54,016	–0.5	305,435	4.9
1913	762,231	–13.7	54,437	0.8	311,587	2.0

Source: Data from *Handbuch der deutschen Aktien-Gesellschaften.*

rising costs. The tin figure industry, which sometimes reported to the *Handelskammer* separately and therefore gives us a more detailed depiction of smaller toy makers, complained repeatedly about the high cost of labor and shortage of skilled workers.[42] Bing, by contrast, rarely complained about labor costs and offered its *Arbeiterstamm* (the loyal core of long-term skilled workers) a variety of benefits, including rent subsidies, rebates on health insurance premiums, and, after ten years of continuous employment, a modest savings account (one hundred marks for males, fifty for females).[43] In this way, Bing sought to keep its skilled labor disciplined and off of the labor market. In good times, the smaller toy makers had much more difficulty finding the labor they wanted at what they believed to be reasonable prices. In periods of recession, the makers of tin figures admitted to surviving only through "the most extremely reduced wages and undesirable labor conditions."[44] Given the difficulty in limiting costs, the tin figure industry was fortunate that demand was buoyed by endemic international tension.[45]

Small and middling toy makers also found that they were unable to pass along rising costs to consumers. Their relatively limited level of mechanization meant comparatively low barriers to entry and a high level of competition. Furthermore, their small size precluded large-scale production. As a result, smaller producers did not have the resources and market share to force through price increases.[46] The difficulty of pushing through price increases played an important part in spurring efforts to organize toy makers.[47] The recently formed Verband deutscher Zinnfiguren-Fabrikanten (Association of German Tin Figure Producers), for example, led an effort to cooperate to impose a 5 percent price increase.[48] By contrast, larger firms, such as Bing, found that their international customers had "understanding" for the necessary price increases.[49] The substantially larger volume of production, coupled with comparatively high barriers to entry, made it possible for larger companies to successfully impose conditions, an important factor that only very fragile associations of smaller producers could match.

Those barriers to entry also reserved a highly profitable niche of toys for the larger companies. The machines of Bing, Carrette, Dannhorn, and others were critical for the construction of technology toys that used the wonders of nineteenth-century and early twentieth-century science and industry to fascinate and educate young boys. As I discussed in chapter 1, many parents were willing to spend more on toys that would inure their boys to the dawning age of technology. Electric toy trains and steam-powered battleships could be sold for more in a less competitive market, ensuring higher returns for the largest toy makers.[50]

Suggesting another means by which the concentration of capital could have advantages regardless of product quality, Bing began constructing an in-house sales and distribution system, while it continued to work through established merchant houses. As early as 1899, Bing employed twelve traveling salesmen to canvass the European continent.[51] In 1906, Bing maintained sales offices in "Berlin, Hamburg, London, Paris, etc." at a cost of 146,814 marks. In 1910, Bing operated offices in Leipzig, Berlin, Hamburg, London, Paris, Brussels, Barcelona, Zurich, Amsterdam, and Milan, all at a cost of 360,088 marks annually. By 1913, Bing had added offices in New York City (1911), Munich (1912), Düsseldorf, Vienna, and Sydney (1913). This extensive network cost Bing 383,405 marks in 1913.[52] The opening of an office in New York drew particular notice, as it was the first producer sales office outside Europe. Both the *Deutsche Spielwaren-Zeitung* and the *Rundschau über Spielwaren* ran articles mentioning this new producer outpost. As the *Rundschau* pointed out, however, most producers, even large ones, could not follow Bing's example: only a "world firm," such as Bing, with its "large capital resources and skilled personnel," could be so ambitious as to seek to trade directly with the United States, the largest customer of the German toy industry.[53] The largest toy maker was seeking to switch more of its business relations from a market-based system to one based on hierarchy and direct control. This would enable Bing to turn distribution into its own profit center, as well as providing better market information, since the company was in more direct contact with retailers.

The metal toy industry suggested that the accumulation of capital was an extremely valuable tool in creating employment and raising incomes. The accumulation of labor-saving machines enabled the larger toy makers to simultaneously absorb higher costs and post substantial profits. They were able to do this because the products they offered were susceptible to mechanization. As a result, mechanization substantially reduced production costs and permitted a substantial expansion of the types and forms of toys offered for sale. The largest companies could then offer low-priced toys for lower-income consumers, higher-margin toys to well-heeled parents, and a vast array of surfaces to appeal to the multitude of desires that were assumed to define genuine individuality. The partial mechanization of smaller toy makers left them vulnerable to the wage demands of workers (demands influenced by the profitability of the larger firms) and to escalating raw material prices. Machines were then depicted not as keys to aesthetic production but as tools for overcoming escalating factor costs in the race to provide low-cost and varied products to consumers.

Social Reform: Regulating Domestic Industry

According to Naumann and his supporters, increasing quality and margins were tightly, reciprocally associated with social reform. The right sort of labor would produce the right sort of products, which would pay for that right sort of labor. A particularly interesting fault line in this analysis lay in domestic industry and opens up broad questions about relations between state policy, structures of production, and consumption. For many, domestic industry represented a decidedly less attractive vision of how mass consumption could influence social organization. The growth of *Hausindustrie* to serve expanding markets for consumer goods brought into question a simple confidence in the social benefits of mass consumption.

In the late nineteenth century, *Heimarbeit* was widely seen as an anachronism in the age of mechanized factories. History has tagged the lonely *Heimarbeiter* for destruction. Nonetheless, as we saw with the toy industry, the late nineteenth century saw a considerable increase in *Heimarbeiter* engaged in all manner of consumer production,[54] even as these products were increasingly available in the stores and streets of Germany. The extremely close connection between domestic industry and consumer items meant that the growth and expansion of one was closely correlated with the growth of the other. This unexpected development left Germans in a conceptual and policy impasse. The troubled discussion of domestic production revealed an increasing consciousness of the role of consumption in the German economy and unease about the possible ramifications. The discursive field surrounding cottage industry reflected one effort to define legitimate norms of production and describe legitimate products of consumption. Debates over *Heimarbeit* therefore sketch a complex field in which alternative normative visions of modernity were elaborated. To explicate these visions, I here consider three broad fields of analysis of cottage industry: Marxist, middle-class reformist, and that defined by the toy industry.

SOCIALISM AND DOMESTIC INDUSTRY

The foundation stone for socialist—indeed, for many bourgeois—analyses of cottage industry was that presented by Karl Marx in *Capital.* Within Marx's understanding of *Heimarbeit* was a strong evolutionary dichotomy between mechanized factories and cottage production. Production in the home was an antiquated holdover from an earlier era. Domestic industry had to gradually give way to the factory. Given this dichotomy, it is worthwhile to consider briefly Marx's analysis of mechanization.

Despite all their historical progressivity, Marx portrayed machines in capitalist societies as agents of extraordinary misery. While Marx acknowledged the enormous expansions of output and labor productivity, these were not, in his view, the most significant outcome of industrialization. Marx argued that surplus value—the source of profits and therefore the lifeblood of capitalism—"arises from variable capital alone"; that is, profits could be squeezed only from labor, not from machines. This could only be a disastrous development in Marx's view, since industrialization "converts what was formerly variable capital . . . into machinery which, being constant capital, does not produce surplus value."[55] As a result, mechanization led inevitably to a more intensive exploitation of those workers not displaced by machines. Capitalists were thoughtlessly driven to increase the length and intensity of the workday and turn to female and child labor to derive their accustomed surplus from fewer workers. In the orthodox Marxist perspective, then, machines could not be reconceived as the foundations of aesthetic production, nor could they yield the increment of wealth that would enable social reform. As long as machines were employed in a capitalist social context, they had to be agents of exploitation.

At first glance, Marx's analysis of the social consequences of mechanization could suggest that domestic industry might escape the misery of factory labor. Mechanization meant that a smaller number of workers had to be exploited more thoroughly to maintain surplus value. One might extend the logic and expect domestic industry (Marx sometimes referred to it as "modern manufacture") to escape the intensified expropriation experienced in factories. Quite to the contrary, Marx argued: "[E]xploitation is more shameless in the so-called domestic industry . . . Economy in the means of production, first systematically carried out in the factory system, . . . now shows its antagonistic and murderous side more and more in a given branch of industry, the less the social productive power of labour and the technical basis for combination of processes are developed in that branch." Marx maintained that *Heimarbeit* was more "shameless" and "murderous" precisely because "the substitution of machines for muscular power, and the light character of the labour, is almost entirely absent from manufacture," while *Heimarbeiter* still had to compete against modern industry and "the masses made 'redundant' by modern industry and agriculture."[56] Marx argued that the emiseration of the *Heimarbeiter* continued until capital met "at last with natural obstacles that cannot be overstepped." Once incomes were reduced to an irreducible minimum, he concluded, domestic manufacture would loose its economic foundation. Marx lamented, "So soon as this point is at last reached—and it took many years—the hour has struck for the introduction of machinery, and for the thenceforth rapid conversion of the scattered domestic industries and also of manufactures into factory industries."[57] In essence, cottage industry can sustain itself in a modern industrial economy only through escalating exploitation, as the individual labor power exerted for a product comes to equate the socially necessary labor, thereby endangering the existence of surplus value. The conversion of this extreme form of exploitation to the "ordinary" expropriation experienced in the factories could not come fast enough. Fortunately, suggested Marx, this process could be artificially accelerated through legislation,[58] as legal regulation of hours and hygiene meant that the "obstacles that cannot be overstepped" were raised slightly higher.

This analysis plays an important role in the socialist understanding of domestic industry. The analytical framework and rhetorical flourishes factored into the socialist arguments after 1900. Turn-of-the-century socialists were deeply concerned about *Heimarbeit.* Socialist congresses discussed the issue, and the Reichstag party faction introduced legislation. The free labor unions organized a 1906 exhibition in Berlin that highlighted the misery associated with common consumer items, including toys. I will here examine the socialist analysis of cottage industry through an intensive examination of the 1904 General *Heimarbeiter* Protection Congress, called by the socialist labor unions and attended by a cross section of labor activists, socialist politicians, and middle-class reformers. The purpose of the congress was to devise a common platform to assist a class widely perceived as "the poorest of the poor."

Most analyses of *Heimarbeit* retained the contrast with factory work as a central element. Modern cottage industry was often defined by its variance from the standard of factory labor. In an extensive review of the literature, sociologist Robert Liefmann lamented the continual reliance on what he termed a purely superficial distinction between centralized factories and decentralized *Heimarbeit.*[59] Nonetheless, the persistent view that *Heimarbeit* retained important ties to the factories is important, particularly in the socialist analyses. That distinction defined the socialist understanding of the origins of modern *Heimarbeit* and their preferences for its future. Already in 1902, the socialist trade unions had called for the banning of *Heimarbeit.*[60]

Perhaps more telling was Klara Zetkin's discussion. Building on an orthodox reading of Marx, she told the congress: "[T]he idea of bringing factories to rural areas through a progressive transportation policy has emerged publicly . . . It is quite worthy, but incorrect."[61] Zetkin allows for the attractiveness of switching cottage industry to factory industry, the essential goal of the plan to push railroads into regions with cottage industrial networks. For skilled workers, she implies, factory work is indeed far better. The concentration of workers at machines may be desirable. The problem was not the organization of work as much as the organization of society. Zetkin observed: "First and foremost, the capitalist factory is not progressive, rather greedy of profits. It is ready at any moment to sacrifice the greatest technical improvement of the greatest social backwardness to the love of profits."[62] Capitalism made *Heimarbeit* into a rival of factories; wherever possible, capitalists, in their bid to maximize exploitation, would limit and abandon the possibilities opened up by machines and factories. While Naumann and others might assert the advantages offered by mechanization in itself, Zetkin was certain that the "capitalist factory" was "not progressive."

Zetkin's indictment of the social system as a whole usefully suggests the socialist analysis of the origin of *Heimarbeit:* exploitation. The specific causes and form of that exploitation might vary, but the causal significance of exploitation did not. Many turn-of-the-century socialists argued that employers sought to evade government regulations regarding hours, hygiene, and social insurance requirements, by shifting production out of factories into private homes, thus seeking shelter from the bourgeois state by invoking the bourgeois distinction between public and private. At the General *Heimarbeiter* Protection Congress, a representative of the tobacco workers added the argument that employers in his industry also sought to evade government taxation by "putting out" labor.[63] The work process moved from property owned or leased by the employer to that of the employee, thus shifting legal responsibility without changing the underlying economic relationship of dependence. From this dynamic, socialists argued, flowed a number of baleful consequences. Separating *Heimarbeiter* from and setting them against one another—in what congress attendee Luise Zeitz called "the struggle of all against all"[64]—left them economically defenseless. Employers were able to push incomes relentlessly down to the threshold of subsistence—just as Marx had described. The predictable result was miserable lodgings and diet, culminating too often in disease. As Zeitz explained in a vaguely eugenicist turn, this led necessarily to the "degeneration" of "national labor power and the national defense."[65] We can see this logic clearly two years later in a discussion in *Vorwärts* of the toy industry specifically: "Exploitation of children from the earliest youth, undernourishment and overwork, in general result in degeneration, which is visible in the high mortality rates."[66]

The line of analysis pursued by socialists assumed a basic conflict between factory work and *Heimarbeit.* Fated by history for extermination, the system of "putting out" labor persisted largely as a means for capitalists to circumvent social protections in their perpetual quest for profits. Consequently, argued congress attendee Lily Braun in an interesting departure from Marx, "*Heimarbeit* encumbers workers in factories and workshops in their struggle to improve their position, because many employers seek to evade the demands of worker protection and insurance laws through greater use of *Heimarbeit;* workers in *Heimarbeit* are . . . the most dangerous competitors of factory and workshop workers."[67] Rather than *Heimarbeiter* existing on the rapidly narrowing margins of economic life, as Marx suggested, Braun and her colleagues portrayed cottage industry as an expanding effort to circumvent and even undermine progressive labor protections. The unexpected growth of domestic production was not and could not be conceptually tied to increasing consumerism. To suggest that increasing consumerism was restructuring relations of production would imply sources of economic behavior outside the expropriation of wealth by the bourgeoisie. Turn-of-the-century socialists, therefore, emphasized the chicanery of employers as the causal impulse behind the expansion of cottage industry.

Socialists agreed that "self-help" and charity were insufficient: "The

Reich, the state, must intervene."[68] Nonetheless, reflecting the larger socialist split between reformers and radicals,[69] there was a certain uncomfortable schizophrenia in socialist prescriptions for *Heimarbeit.* There was a very clear reformist agenda. The ameliorative program advocated at the congress sought to bring cottage industry into the framework of factory protections and social legislation—indeed, to go beyond this by introducing minimum wages and including the homes of cottage industrialists in the hygienic and protective codes applied to factories, complete with residential inspections.[70] This reform program sought to attend to the individual symptoms of *Heimarbeiter* misery by making the labor process visible to state regulation. When one reform-minded bourgeois sociologist at the congress argued that the socialist movement ought to feel some trepidation at extending government police supervision into working-class homes, his concerns were immediately dismissed as "Manchesterism." His opponents argued that state action was necessary to protect *Heimarbeiter* and to curb the exploitative impulses of capitalists.[71]

The alternative to an ameliorative project was outright elimination—banning *Heimarbeit* as a structure of production. This had the advantage of logical consistency. If *Heimarbeiter* were backward, exploited, and a threat to the well-being of the industrial proletariat, why preserve *Heimarbeit*? As the congress representative of the metalworkers put it, "*Heimarbeit* hurts industrial workers, and therefore industrial workers have every reason to fight *Heimarbeit.* Thus, we can say aloud that the only means of eliminating the damage of *Heimarbeit* is the elimination of *Heimarbeit.*"[72] Some supporters of an outright ban believed that reform would "lead to nothing."[73] Several speakers at the congress supported the reform efforts merely because they thought illegality was an impossible political goal; these speakers also sometimes expressed the hope that "reform" would itself destroy *Heimindustrie.*[74]

Both of these paths would substantially increase the supervisory and disciplinary powers of the state. Agents of the state would necessarily acquire the right to penetrate private homes to ascertain the presence and extent of economic activity. Indeed, the 1911 law that would result from the political activities of the socialists and middle-class social reformers largely defined *Heimarbeit* in terms of overlapping living and working spaces.[75] The proposal to eliminate *Heimarbeit* would, in effect, define legitimate and illegitimate economic spaces as well as acceptable and unacceptable structures of production. Such a law would recognize accredited factories, offices, and retail establishments, thereby codifying an acceptable and unacceptable vision of modernity—sacrificing a measure of freedom in favor of security, to use a typology drawn from Zygmunt Bauman.[76]

At first blush, the socialists appeared to invite male supervision of female labor in order to protect male labor. Given that *Hausindustrie* had a complicated gendering, however, it resisted such narrow gender readings. Some types of *Heimarbeit,* such as the toy-painting industry in Nuremberg and the sewing industry in the big cities, employed females only. Other types, such as toy making in Thuringia and the Erzgebirge, employed the whole family, with the father acting as the representative and public face. The gendering of cottage industry as a whole was not, therefore, straightforward. The dichotomy was not simply male-dominated factory work versus female-dominated *Heimarbeit.* Perhaps for this reason, the analytical paradigm of the socialists emphasized capitalism and class over gender. Women as a particularly exploited group appeared comparatively rarely in the congress proceedings. For example, in the five theses that Lily Braun of the League of Progressive Women's Associations offered the congress, she singled out women only twice, both times as details offered in support of general, nongender points.[77] Rather than portrayed as direct threats to male skill and labor, women were usually mobilized in the company of children, as symbols of innocence abused by a heartless and predatory system.[78] The clearest gender analysis at the congress came from Klara Zetkin, who argued in essence that the old, patriarchal economy was being destroyed by "triumphant capitalism," forcing families in the middle and peasant classes to mobilize women as *Heimarbeiterinnen* for additional income to maintain their accustomed, class-based consumption patterns.[79]

Interestingly, some socialists appear to have sought a coalition between middle-class consumers and working-class *Heimarbeiter.* The vehicle for this alliance was public health. The congress featured prominently the problem of disease in *Hausindustrie.* The working draft of the congress resolution featured health prominently, and one of the two opening orations—a speech made by a middle-class physician, Dr. Sommerfeld of Berlin—was specifically on the question of public health. Dr. Sommerfeld appealed to his standing as a man of science and not of party. The title of his presentation was "The Health Dangers of *Hausindustrie* for the Consuming Public."[80] Concern for the well-being of the *Heimarbeiter* was linked to concern for the health of consumers. The discussion tended to center around the proposal to label products as fabricated by *Heimarbeiter.* Supporters argued that this would serve two important functions: first, labeling would protect consumers from diseases communicated from workers via their products; second, it would empower consumers to act as a disciplining force to ensure that cottage industrialists were well treated. "The great mass of the public must be brought into the fight against *Hausindustrie,*"[81] argued Kaming in presenting the working draft of the resolution at the opening of the congress. Lily Braun, however, questioned the drive to label products of *Heimarbeit.* She asserted that this would further reduce incomes. She also warned that it would create a clearer class differential among consumers, as some became all the more dependent on "these cheapest and worst products of *Heimarbeit.*"[82]

Consumers appeared in the socialist accounts of domestic industry, but only in episodic fashion, with little coherent analysis and even less agreement on the wisdom of mobilizing Germans as consumers. Interestingly for the purposes of the present discussion, perhaps the congress's clearest socialist analysis of the role of consumption in *Heimarbeit* came from the Reichstag representative from Sonneberg, Reisshaus. First, Reisshaus sketched the misery of *Heimarbeit* in his district, which he labeled the "El Dorado of cottage industrial exploitation." Focusing on child labor and life expectancy, he maintained that the cause of these catastrophic conditions was the cooperation of local merchants and British and American wholesale buyers. This cooperation concentrated economic power, he argued, and left the *Heimarbeiter* helpless. "Keep in mind what those cheap prices mean," he warned. Reisshaus also expressed the fear that introducing labeling of *Heimindustrie* products at the same moment as protective legislation would mean that conditions would not improve before consumers began to act on the information newly available to them, thereby punishing *Heimarbeiter* harshly for their previous exploitation. "We do not want legislation to protect consumers but rather to protect workers," he argued.[83] Reisshaus thus called into question the possibility of common interests joining workers and consumers.

Socialists generally offered a critique of cottage industry rooted in, on the one hand, a notion of progressive historical development that led to a thoroughly mechanized society with no place for *Heimarbeit* and, on the other hand, an analysis of capitalism rooted in the labor theory of value, which asserted that objects acquired value from the labor performed on them. Consequently, profits were realized by expropriating the workers of the value they added; that is, capitalism is inherently exploitative. These ideas were firmly rooted in both Marxism and the experience of the early industrial revolution and reflected a clear vision of what modern society was and what it should be. The combination of these assumptions made the total elimination of *Heimarbeit* an appealing goal for many, even for those who supported protective legislation. Elimination of *Heimarbeit* would remove what was perceived as one of the worst evils of the capitalist system, while pushing society toward the normative factory system of production. Possible avenues of investigation through gender or consumption were raised on occasion but rarely pursued in any depth. These avenues were treated, rather, almost as props, useful tools with which to elaborate and emphasize the misery and injustice of *Heimarbeit* and thereby to speed the day of its extinction. There was at best an intermittent acknowledgment that the expansion of consumption might require rethinking the dynamics of industrial society.

REFORM AND DOMESTIC INDUSTRY

In 1899, the prestigious Verein für Sozialpolitik published the results of its extensive and formal investigation of *Hausindustrie* throughout Germany and Austria. The Verein für Sozialpolitik wanted to examine the reasons for the expansion of cottage industry and consider its multiplicity of forms. It also believed that greater understanding of the nature and structure of cottage industry was necessary if Germans were to be able to properly consider including *Heimarbeiter* in the legal protections offered factory workers.[84] The result of this interest in cottage industry was a wide variety of close studies of individual branches of *Hausindustrie.* The products manufactured in domestic industry make clear the close connections between this form of labor and growing consumption: they include the Nuremberg tin figure painters and Sonneberg toy makers, as well as clock makers, seamstresses, weavers, and many others.

Far from serving as the definitive and final statement of reformist interest in *Heimarbeit,* the study by the Verein für Sozialpolitik appears to have initiated a steady expansion of middle-class interest in the question of cottage industry in a modern, industrialized society. The positions and assumptions that structured reformist opinion were quite heterogeneous. By the early twentieth century, factories and machines were widely accepted, even if their specific role was open to debate. The point of consensus among reformers lay more in their acceptance of mechanization than in their analyses of *Heimarbeit.* The place of decentralized networks of producers laboring for a mass market did not have an immediate place in the visions of the future elaborated by the Werkbund and others.

The middle-class reformers tended to emphasize the complexity of *Heimarbeit.* The Verein für Sozialpolitik made this complexity the second reason for investigating the topic. Robert Liefmann likewise indicated that the dense interconnectedness of the networks of producers drew him to the topic.[85] The complexity of structure is brought out by individual investigations by the Verein für Sozialpolitik as well as by other studies, such as Willy Bierer's examination of the Sonneberg doll industry[86] and Käthe Graebel's study of urban *Heimarbeit.*[87] In this line of analysis, the dichotomy between factory work and *Heimarbeit* becomes blurred. In most cases, the dichotomy does not disappear; but in almost all cases, it becomes much more difficult to pin down. Liefmann, for example, makes a very substantial effort to break down the clear distinction between employers and *Heimarbeiter.* He wants to make particularly clear that in many cases, *Heimarbeiter* were acting as both employer and employee, as *Zwischenmeister.* Graebel emphasized that not all *Heimarbeiter* had the same expectations and demands for their economic activity—many sought some sort of paid activity that could be negotiated with other demands in their lives, whether physical limitations or the demands of family life. The exploitative foundations of cottage industry were thus reaffirmed but simultaneously complicated. In the place of the socialist narrative of an almost Hobbesian world prompted by the avarice of employers, many reformers suggested that *Heimarbeiter* actively participated in exploitative relations, whether of themselves or others.

As a result of this investment in complexity, the middle-class reformers tended to tread rather more carefully around the regulation of *Heimarbeit.* Alfred Weber told the 1904 General *Heimarbeiter* Protection Congress that an outright ban was undesirable and that many of the protective laws would not work if simply extended to *Heimarbeiter.* He also warned that increased state supervision was dangerous particularly for the socialist movement, that placing police in every home was not practical or desirable.[88] Likewise, Dr. Wilbrandt of the Bund deutscher Bodenreformer emphasized an indirect route to encourage a gradual switch from cottage to factory industry for most, though not all, *Heimarbeiter.* Rather than police inspections, hygiene laws, and social insurance, he emphasized market access (trains) and minimum wages as means to change the market calculations of entrepreneurs.[89] Edgar Jaffe thought the difficulty in defining *Heimarbeit* undermined legislative reform efforts.[90] The liberal *Münchner Neueste Nachrichten* feared that the reform efforts of the socialists would "drive the *Heimarbeiter* directly into the factory"[91] (which was indeed the socialist hope).

There were members of the social reform movement that dissented from this indirection and gradualism. The editor of *Soziale Praxis,* Ernst Francke, called for greater state oversight. He argued that child labor laws had already demonstrated that the family home may be penetrated by the state when family life is mingled with economic life.[92] Alice Salomon of the League of German Women's Associations (Bund deutscher Frauenvereine) also represents an important exception.

Salomon and the league were keenly interested in what was sometimes called the "new *Heimarbeit*"—urban domestic industry, particularly female seamstresses working in the clothing industry. At the congress, Salomon insisted on the necessity of home inspections to enforce hygienic laws for the protection of "the larger part of working women." She argued that any higher expenses that the introduction of sanitation laws might introduce should be made up by collective bargaining or a minimum wage and that, in any case, the costs of compliance should not be born by the *Heimarbeiter.* Salomon also put gender firmly in the center of her analysis. While acknowledging the economic factors that led many working-class women into *Heimarbeit,* Salomon pointed to the nature of a patriarchal society for driving middle-class women into cottage industry, thereby creating additional competition. Salomon argued that *bürgerliche* women who sought some extra income were often prevented by their male kin from working outside the home.[93] Dr. Elizabeth Heiner likewise emphasized the link between expanding *Heimarbeit* and the exploitation of women, arguing that the competitiveness of *Heimarbeit* rested on "an endless reserve army of women and children."[94]

Other representatives of the middle-class reformist milieu would likewise pay attention to the role of women in *Heimarbeit,* but they drew rather less-radical conclusions. Käthe Graebel, for example, argued that some level of cottage industry was perhaps desirable. Mothers and adolescent girls in particular found it practically or morally preferable to work from the home rather than seeking work in a factory. The freedom from time-discipline was particularly valuable, according to Graebel.[95] Paul Ehrenberg echoed Salomon's emphasis on class expectations as an influence in leading middle-class women into *Heimarbeit.*[96] The suggestion that perhaps *Heimarbeiterinnen* might prefer their type of work paralleled the observation many middle-class sociologists made in observing the toy industry in the Erzgebirge and Thuringia—the *Heimarbeiter* did not want to become factory workers, preferring to remain *Heimarbeiter* for noneconomic reasons, specifically the aura of independent craftspeople as opposed to dependent factory hands.[97]

Noneconomic factors could explain why labor was available, but not necessarily why *Heimarbeit* was expanding. If growing domestic production was not the result of entrepreneurial chicanery, how was it to be explained? Many reformers drew connections between domestic industry and specific types or styles of consumption. Several observers noted that *Heimarbeit* was particularly suited to certain types of products, specifically those that needed to be inexpensive and sensitive to changing fashions and forms.[98] Analyses of the consumption of the products of *Heimarbeit* often questioned the type of consumers who would buy such trash—most egregiously when Graebel suggested the only future market for *Hausindustrie* was "with Kaffirs and Hereros" and "not however with the great *Kulturnationen.*"[99] In this case, Graebel was merely expressing the common assumption that low levels of technology and wages meant low quality and low margins. Similarly, Friedrich Naumann argued in an article about *Hausindustrie:*

> Industries that can exist only with the starvation of its workers are not justified given the present position of the German economy. They must be forced to raise their level of quality in order to provide a worthy existence. Presently, however, there is a disastrous cycle of minimal values: low-cost labor produces, for an impossible wage, things with which nothing can be earned. The entrepreneur says, "I cannot pay more because these are mass products, which otherwise will be made in foreign lands." To a certain extent, he is right, since only bad wages can be paid from bad products. The question is whether we cannot entirely eliminate the cheap mass trash, from which no healthy workers can live. World demand for better products is rising everywhere, and we should leave the worst work to peoples whose human capacities [*Menschenqualität*] are not sufficient for greater achievement.[100]

There was a causal link between *Heimarbeiter,* their misery, and consumers. Naumann leaves a little unclear which was the cause of the misery—the structure of production or the demand of consumers. In any case, both Graebel and Naumann would have preferred to have left the production and consumption of "mass trash" to those they deemed racially inferior. In effect, both writers longed to export the socially undesirable aspects of consumerism to imperially dependent populations, a "colonial fantasy" in which colonial power purifies German society.[101]

The link between *Heimarbeit* and "mass trash" was observed by many. Oskar Stillich, for example, made quite clear the connection between impoverished toy consumers and the "expansion of *Hausindustrie* and of the emiseration of its workers."[102] The emergence of mass consumption was then linked to the expansion of *Heimarbeit.* This link between consumption and *Heimarbeit* prompted Dr. L. von Weise to lament, in the pages of *Soziale Fortschritt,* "how close the pleasure of one is connected to the pain of the other, and how, in all our culture of luxury and in the multitude of things, there remains a bit of barbarism and brutal, thoughtless selfishness."[103] For many reformers, the appetite of consumers for "mass trash" had dire social consequences. Rather than rooting *Heimarbeit* in relations of production, some middle-class reformers saw it as the unfortunate outcome of particular patterns of consumption. In one fashion or another, *Heimarbeiter* were condemned to low wages as long as people were unwilling to pass up cheap products. The question for some then became how the consumer was to be disciplined in the name of social progress. Alice Salomon, for example, argued for educating consumers to their social mission.[104]

The heterogeneity of structures that social reformers detected in *Heimarbeit* made it a useful system of production for a mass market. The low prices and responsiveness to fashion made it economically viable and doubly suspicious. *Heimarbeit* combined social misery and shoddy, tasteless products. That same heterogeneity led many reformers to see *Heimarbeit* as a particularly difficult nut for social policy to crack. It was perhaps a limit case for policy. Vigorous action by the state threatened to vastly expand state power, with apparently limited prospects for success. Since *Heimarbeit* was defined in law by the mingling of living and economic spaces, the regulation of the economic sphere brought the state into the vast realm of the intimate sphere, in the hopes that consumption could be controlled from the production side.

TOY MAKERS AND DOMESTIC INDUSTRY

The toy industry saw the issue of *Heimarbeit* quite differently. The toy industry spoke and behaved as if *Heimarbeit* were part of its inheritance, legitimized by time and tradition. When the toy industry discussed domestic industry, it was in part to explicate, in part to defend. The industry's analysis was therefore occasionally defensive. For example, the industry and their representatives almost always sought to undermine the portrayal of *Heimarbeiter* as poverty-stricken "slaves" ruined by the exploitation of the heartless capitalists.[105] The earliest and most uncompromising version was offered by one of the principal figures in the midcentury liberalization of the Sonneberg economy, Adolf Fleischmann. Fleischmann argued simply and vigorously that any signs of misery or poverty were individual cases and were rooted in the failures of those individuals, that the moral failures were not those of the system but, rather, those of the occasional *Heimarbeiter.*[106] Most defenses were rather more diplomatically phrased. The *Handelskammer* and others often agreed that social conditions were not always wonderful. Nonetheless, they argued, it remained possible to make a decent living—even "move up"—with hard work and intelligence.[107] For its part, the *Handelskammer* of Middle Franconia (including Nuremberg) investigated conditions in cottage industry in the region. While conditions might be terrible elsewhere, the *Handelskammer* concluded that wages in Franconia were approximately the same in domestic industry and factories and that the differences in income resulted from the cheaper nature of cottage industrial products and the limited hours worked by *Heimarbeiter.*[108] Linked to this argument was the assertion that *Heimarbeiter* were sometimes commercially naive and/or aesthetically challenged.[109] The result was bad business decisions and sometimes sloppy products, leading to poverty. The solution to such problems was generally seen as improved education by special trade schools. The problem was not social and economic organization but, rather, individual skill. The proposed solution to social problems in *Hausindustrie* was therefore collective efforts to improve individual abilities rather than the limitation of economic structures. Consequently, the Dresden *Handleskammer,* representative of the Erzgebirge toy industry, embraced the Saxon government's efforts to build a network of trade schools for toy making.[110]

The toy industry also sought to challenge critics on the relationship between factories and *Heimarbeit.* The notion that factory workers and *Heimarbeiter* were competing in any consequential fashion appeared absurd to toy makers. *Hausindustrie* was incapable of competing directly against factories. As a consequence, cottage industry was either destroyed or forced to take up products that factories could not produce.[111] A sociologist closely linked to the Erzgebirge toy industry explained: "Factories produce . . . better as well as cheaper . . . The rise of the factory has not destroyed *Hausindustrie,* as one had feared, but rather directed it in different directions . . . A greater part of *Hausindustrie,* however, was not influenced at all by the rise of factories, since they delivered products . . . that were not appropriate for factories."[112] In this way, the industry sought to problematize one of the central tenets of the socialist position. It argued that the incidence of *Heimarbeit* was determined not by any reaction to social insurance and factory legislation but, rather, by the nature of the products. Cottage industry made what factories could not. The toy makers thereby cast *Heimarbeit* as a complement to the factory rather than as a competitor. In addition, the Nuremberg makers of lead figures pointed out that one of the reasons they used *Heimarbeiterinnen* was the relative shortage of female workers for the factories.[113] In their mind, female labor was more easily mobilized in the home than it could be in the factory.

The industry also tended to emphasize—considerably more forcefully than the middle-class reformers—the complexity of the production process. The industry was not shy about the implications for any effort to regulate the industry. The toy industry emphasized over and over the multiplicity of forms (a writer close to the Sonneberg *Handelskammer* suggested that there were twenty thousand to thirty thousand different articles produced in Sonneberg),[114] the complexity of the networks, and the difficulty of establishing wages when raw materials and other costs had to be deducted.[115] The industry believed that the sheer number and fugitive quality of forms made it impossible to determine prices by anything other than immediate negotiation (i.e., the market). Moreover, the uncertainty of wages, the vague costs incurred by *Heimarbeiter,* and the difficulty of determining who was an employer and who was an employee and for what portion of a given product combined to make it impossible to ascertain wage percentages.[116] Rather than analyzing the desired structures of modern society, the toy makers argued that the ambiguities of *Hausindustrie* rendered state action at best "a two-edged sword,"[117] at worst impossible. There simply was not the transparency and predictability that would make possible classification and then rational state action.

Finally, the toy industry pointed to the nature of their market, which demanded ever changing forms and cheapness: "[P]articularly for them [cheap mass products] there is now as always a strong demand, above all in the lower classes of the people. Even in bad times, the German worker buys his children toys, cheap certainly and not terribly solid."[118] The toy industry felt that its products targeted German workers, not Graebel's "Kaffirs and Hereros." The nature of demand, based on the desires of consumers, meant that unregulated *Heimarbeit* remained critical, argued toy makers. Factories could not produce everything, and regulation was likely to undermine the flexibility of market relations that made the toy industry (e.g., Sonneberg doll production) highly sensitive to changing consumer demand. As a result, the tin figure makers argued that the elimination of cottage industry would lead to the absolute destruction of their industry.[119]

The toy industry made a fascinating rhetorical move, pushing sovereignty onto consumers. Toy makers thereby emphasized the dynamic and amorphous quality of capitalist society. Modern consumers preferred variety and fashion in their products, often for low prices. Satisfying that demand, toy makers argued, structured the industry: the capacity to generate new systems of production for each order was seen as the key to success for many toy producers. Shifting forms necessitated shifting structures, which made the rigidities of state regulation counterproductive. That apparently self-abnegating gesture, however, also pushed responsibility onto the diffuse body of consumers, away from industry. Toy makers claimed for themselves a freedom to respond to "necessity" without reference to social morality or public concerns.

The last twenty years of imperial Germany saw increasing conflict between a welter of social and economic groups. The toy industry, a highly successful branch of light industry, could not escape those conflicts. These were not merely contests for the relative advantages that could be wrung from state preferences, strong though that element was. Ideological constructions that legitimated and sustained those material interests emerged. This chapter examined one such ideology, the arguments elaborated by Friedrich Naumann, who is a valuable heuristic tool not only for his links to writers examined in chapter 4 but also because his analysis would have put export-oriented light industry at the center of state policy. He argued that consumer industries had a great deal to offer to Germany—indeed, that they were the key to a wealthy, powerful, and united Germany. His analysis has considerable attraction, since it purports to explain how capitalist development can overcome the problems that it has created. It is also remarkable for the fact that it places the manufacture of consumer goods in the center of both economic development and national power. Toys were, from the perspective offered by Naumann's logic, not simply diversions for children; they were one highly important profit center that generated the growth and profits necessary to sustain German strength and improve German life.

That vision of an authorized consumerism as the salve to the wounds of industrialization assumed a teleology of industrial development. Industrialization had a proper path and destination. Parts of the toy industry indicated, albeit with some points of conflict, the possibilities of that vision. Mechanization would serve as a useful foundation for creating the value-added products to support higher wages and better social provision. Whether it would do that while simultaneously underwriting Naumann's imperial aspirations was open to question.

The portions of the toy industry that did not mechanize—that sought to grapple with the demands of the marketplace through organization, flexibility, and low wages—conflicted with the confident teleology sketched by Naumann, Marx, and many others. In the light of this conflict, the expansion of consumption appeared to be a genuine social problem. In this case, attending to the shifting and ephemeral demands of a consumer society suggested a system of production that defeated organized labor and impoverished the craftspeople. The ties between poverty and consumption in domestic industry complicated the narrative of modernization sketched by Naumann and his associates. Consumption thus came to play central roles in both an optimistic vision of social progress and a pessimistic indictment of exploitation and disastrously uneven development.

Conclusion

The mid-nineteenth-century liberal historian Friedrich Dahlmann famously described the Prussian state as "the magic spear which heals as well as wounds."[1] The overweening bureaucratic state created by the Prussian monarchy did much for the liberal cause. It rationalized governance, aided economic growth, and educated children. Some of the basic goals of the Enlightenment program to which Dahlmann subscribed were made real by the authoritarian Prussian state. The Prussian state also censored, harassed, and generally bullied liberals, such as Dahlmann, in the name of preserving the authority of a reactionary monarch and nobility. The state was, for Dahlmann, simultaneously an agent of progress and a profound obstacle to freedom.

In a similar, perhaps more elusive fashion, Germans in the succeeding *Kaiserreich* came to see the emergence of consumerism as a sort of "magic spear." Consumerism underwrote the rapid expansion of industries, such as the toy industry, and the rising wages of the Nuremberg toy makers. Growing cross-class consumerism also lay at the foundation of the expanding network of impoverished *Heimarbeiter.* Consumer objects could aid in the elaboration and construction of desirable subjectivities. Consumer objects encouraged superficiality and put selfish desire at the center of human emotional life. Consumerism created a certain excitement and joy, a perhaps fleeting sense of freedom and sovereignty in the marketplace. Consumerism was blamed for causing nervous exhaustion and blaséness. Consumerism consistently managed to vex German society, posing in the same moment as a blessing and a curse.

Toys show us this quite clearly. Toys played a multivalent role in the German home. They served as a relief from the disciplinary pressures exerted by parents and as an acknowledgment of an authentic individuality in the child. They were signs of the freedom and innocence of the child. Nonetheless, the toy's mission only took on meaning in relation to the work and relentless oversight of the daily life of the child. Moreover, the forms that toys took served to naturalize and therefore advance the goals of parental discipline, casting some doubt on the assertions that toys encouraged the child's freedom and authentic individuality.

Falling costs of transportation and production, coupled with innovations in the organization of distribution and production, permitted toy makers to tap the consumer potential in the tensions within the modern home. Toy production grew extremely rapidly from the 1870s. In places, this was coupled with rising wages. In places, it was coupled with disease and malnourishment. The economic consequences of mass consumption therefore varied according to the nature of the product and the possibilities of mechanization.

The frictions of an emerging consumer society were felt by Germans. The potential upset of the ideal foundations of society was acknowledged and discussed. It is not surprising, then, that Germans sought to address the problems arising from the production and consumption of things. For the sake of individual freedom, dignity, and security, things had to change. Form had to improve, structures of production and business strategies had to evolve. The resulting reform efforts, however, were motivated by different problems and aimed at different ideals. As a result, different reform efforts set off in different directions. They aimed at a better Germany with better Germans, the natures of both of which were defined in quite different fashions. The ambitions of Simmel or Avenarius, on one side, and Naumann, on the other, represent one register of this conflict. The fate of the 1914 Werkbund Exhibition in Cologne might represent another.

In certain respects, this self-contradictory, self-obstructing vision of consumerism's impact suggests a kinship with Detlev Peukert's Janus-faced modernity. Peukert elaborated a four-point definition of modernity drawn from Weber, which paralleled those elaborated by the structuralists in Bielefeld. Modernity was identified with a capitalist market, a bureaucratic state structure, scientific control of nature, and rationalized and self-disciplined lifestyles.[2] What Peukert did with this rationalist vision of modernity differed dramatically from the Bielefelders. Rather than using Weber's sociology to map and thereby stabilize modernity, Peukert emphasized the epistemological doubts expressed most forcefully in Weber's "Science as a Vocation." In Peukert's formulation, Weber emerged as a *Zeitkritiker,* one who shares with Nietzsche a common suspicion of the moral and epistemological foundations of contemporary society and knowledge. Peukert maintained that with no possible clear foundation for knowledge, Weber was grimly determined to fashion a science and an identity suited for a "time alienated from God and bereft of prophets."[3] Peukert seemed to suggest that this represents a paradigmatic dilemma. Modernity offered no firm base to individuals or society; the four points defining modernity rested on nothing. In Peukert's analysis, the efforts to construct sound moorings through science and the modern, disciplinary state unexpectedly became the engines of fascist tyranny and mass murder. Rather than being a normative vision, then, modernity emerged as a problem in the same moment as a solution.

The present study similarly emphasizes the strains within modernity. There is, however, more to modernity than Weber's iron cage. When we shift our attention slightly to encompass both capitalist structures of production and the cultures of consumption, modernity becomes more complex. The rationalist model that Peukert proffers leaves little ground for the fugitive, ephemeral experience of modernity emphasized by Baudelaire or Simmel. Mary Gluck characterizes this "alternate version of the modern" as one "associated with the elusive and dynamic experiences of urban life and consumer culture, . . . capable of giving expression to the novel realms of consciousness, subjective experience, and aesthetic creativity opened up by modern life itself."[4] As Gluck implies, this is a modernity that forswears an integrating narrative of development. The "alternate" modernity emphasizes in its place the remarkable experience of modern life, particularly modern urban life. Modernity is depicted as disjointed and seemingly illogical, united primarily by the subjectivity of the individual. Indeed, Gluck cites Baudelaire to suggest that modernity is defined by the absence of a collective sense of mission that would order and orient experience. This idea is in contrast to the classical notion of culture as a meaningful description of collective life. Purpose has instead been privatized. In Baudelaire's formulation, the proper themes and heroism of the contemporary age were to be found only in the lives and ambitions of "private subjects."[5] The emphasis on experience in aesthetic modernity rescues the fullness of individual lives and the possibility of finding meaning in the apparent meaninglessness of modern life. The aesthetic modernity of Baudelaire emphasizes the dynamism and multiplicity of modern life—the outcome of an individualized society where millions of private passions and ambitions inevitably both collide and disperse. Rather than explore the possible "laws of motion" guiding this unstable whole or the efforts to control and guide it,

Baudelaire's modernism investigates experience and the construction of meaning from the shifting and arbitrary contents of life.

Work and Play seeks to reconcile these visions of the modern through an emphasis on individualism in modernity. I claim individualism not as an exclusive foundation of modernity but, rather, as a common one. Individualism was the ideological and social heart of capitalism and consumerism. The multiplicity of individual identities and purposes underlay the ephemeral and illegible quality of the modern experience. The competing definitions of the "authentic" individual competed and obstructed one another. By framing the history of toys and the history of consumption in this manner, I hope to highlight the conflicted, fractured nature of the emerging German modern. Other approaches have and will be taken to interrogate that modernity. The approach taken here does not resolve all problems, even issues that emerge as important exogenous factors in this study. To take just one example, the variable mastery of nature (i.e., levels of technology) plays an important role in constructing a global market and in determining how different toy makers responded. Nonetheless, the concentration on the individual brings into focus innumerable points of friction and outright contradiction in the modern consumer society that Germans were slowly, painstakingly, and ambivalently constructing.

Notes

Introduction

1. Ernst Jäckh, "Deutschland in San Francisco," *Der Kunstwart* 27, no. 2 (Oct. 1913): 168.

2. See discussion of Jäckh and the ambitions of Naumann and Muthesius for the Werkbund in John V. Maciuika, *Before the Bauhaus: Architecture, Politics and the German State, 1890–1920* (Cambridge, 2005), 252–56, 274–79.

3. See Frederic J. Schwartz, *The Werkbund: Design Theory and Mass Culture before the First World War* (New Haven, CT, 1996).

4. Between 1905 and 1910, Japanese toy exports by value rose by almost 150 percent. By 1915, they had risen by another 200 percent. See Ernst Planck, "Die Nürnberger-Fürther Metallspielwaren-Industrie mit besonderer Berücksichtigung der Optischen Metallspielwaren-Industrie" (PhD diss., Friedrich-Alexander-Universität, Erlangen, 1922), 39–40, StadtAN Av 6381.4.

5. Bericht der Handels- und Gewerbekammer zu Sonneber für 1913 (Sonneberg, 1913), 33–40.

6. The position of the foreign ministry was directly challenged in "Die deutsche Regierung und die Weltausstellung in San Franzisko," *Deutsche Spielwaren-Zeitung,* no. 26 (15 Dec. 1913): 3–7.

7. See "Schluß der Generaldebatte im Reichstag," *Münchner Neueste Nachrichten* 66, no. 636 (13 Dec. 1913): 1. For a more general discussion of German finances, see Peter-Christian Witt, *Die Finanzpolitik des deutschen Reiches von 1903 bis 1913: Eine Studie zum Innenpolitik des Wilhelmischen Deutschland* (Lübeck and Hamburg, 1970).

8. "Die deutsche Spielwarn-Industrie und die Weltaustellung von San Franzisko 1915," *Rundschau über Spielwaren* 5, no. 145 (10 Sept. 1913): 2289 (emphasis in original).

9. Gustav Rudi, "Die deutsche Spielwaren-Industrie und die Weltaustellung in San Franzisko 1915," *Rundschau über Spielwaren* 5, no. 146 (20 Sept. 1913): 2304.

10. "Die Spielwaren-Industrie Deutschlands und die Weltausstellung von San Franzisko," *Rundschau über Spielwaren* 5, no. 149 (20 Oct. 1913): 2351.

11. See Hartmut Kaelble, *Industrielle Interessenpolitik in der Wilhelminischen Gesellschaft: Centralverband Deutscher Industrieller, 1895–1914* (Berlin, 1967).

12. "Die Debatte über San Franzisko," *Deutsche Spielwaren-Zeitung,* no. 1 (1

Jan. 1914): 13. The leader of the National Liberal Party in the Reichstag, Ernst Bassermann, had collected around three hundred supporters in the Reichstag for a bill authorizing money for an official exhibition in San Francisco. When confronted with credible evidence that there was too little time left to properly organize an exhibition and that it would cost more than expected, the bill was allowed to die. See "Allgemeine Etatsdebatte im Reichstag," *Münchner Neueste Nachrichten* 66, no. 630 (10 Dec. 1913): 1–3; "Schluß der Generaldebatte im Reichstag," *Münchner Neueste Nachrichten* 66, no. 636 (13 Dec. 1913): 1.

13. "Zum Jahreswechsel!" *Deutsche Spielwaren-Zeitung* (1 Jan. 1911): 3.

14. Konrad H. Jarausch and Michael Geyer, *Shattered Past: Reconstructing German Histories* (Princeton, 2003), 273.

15. Victoria De Grazia, "Changing Consumption Regimes in Europe, 1930–1970: Comparative Perspectives on the Distribution Problem," in *Getting and Spending: European and American Consumer Societies in the Twentieth Century,* ed. Susan Strasser, Charles McGovern, and Matthias Judt (New York, 1998).

16. Alon Confino and Rudy Koshar, "Regimes of Consumer Culture: New Narratives in Twentieth-Century German History," *German History* 19, no. 2 (2001): 136.

17. Peter Gay, *Weimar Culture: The Outsider as Insider* (New York, 2001). Thomas Rohkrämer makes a very similar point regarding critiques of technology and "technology society," in *Eine Andere Moderne? Zivilisationskritik, Natur und Technik in Deutschland, 1880–1933* (Paderborn, 1999), 25.

18. See Schwartz, *Werkbund,* 164–212. See also the advertising trade journal *Seidel's Reklame* (1913–14) and the 1913 yearbook published by the Werkbund, *Die Kunst in Industrie und Handel* (Jena, 1913), 113–22 and attached advertisements after 122.

19. David M. Ciarlo, "Consuming Race, Envisioning Empire: Colonialism and German Mass Culture, 1887–1914" (PhD diss., University of Wisconsin—Madison, 2003), 97.

20. Karl Rosenhaupt, *Die Nürnberger-Fürther Metallspielwarenindustrie in geschichtlicher und sozialpolitischer Beleuchtung* (Stuttgart, 1907), 60; Georg Estelmann, "Die Nürnberger Spielwaren-Herstellung von den Aeltesten Zeiten bis zur Gegenwart" (PhD diss., Universität Frankfurt am Main, 1923), 117, StadtAN Av 6463.4.

21. Calculated from *Monatliche Nachwiese über den auswartigen Handel des deutschen Zollgebiets* (Berlin, 1892–1914).

22. Hans Dressel, *Die Entwicklung von Handel und Industrie in Sonneberg* (Gotha, 1908), 98.

23. Confino and Koshar, "Regimes of Consumer Culture," 135–61; Hartmut Berghoff, ed., *Konsumpolitik:Die Regulierung des privaten Verbrauchs im 20. Jahrhundert* (Göttingen, 1999); Jarausch and Geyer, *Shattered Past;* Paul Betts and Greg Eghigian, *Pain and Prosperity; Reconsidering Twentieth-Century Germany* (Stanford, CA, 2003); Paul Betts, *The Authority of Everyday Objects: A Cultural History of West German Industrial Design* (Berkeley, 2004). See also, on the use of consumer products, Detlev Peukert, *Inside Nazi Germany: Conformity,*

Opposition, and Racism in Everyday Life (New Haven, CT, 1987); Detlev Peukert, *The Weimar Republic: The Crisis of Classical Modernity* (New York, 1989); Andrew Stuart Bergerson, *Ordinary Germans in Extraordinary Times: The Nazi Revolution in Hildesheim* (Bloomington, 2004).

24. Schwartz, *Werkbund;* Maciuika, *Before the Bauhaus;* Ciarlo, "Consuming Race, Envisioning Empire"; Bryan Frederick Ganaway, "Toys, Consumption, and Middle-Class Childhood in Imperial Germany, 1871–1918" (PhD diss., University of Illinois at Urbana-Champaign, 2003). Such works as Lynn Abrams's *Workers' Culture in Imperial Germany: Leisure and Recreation in Rhineland and Westphalia* (New York, 1992) and Peter Fritzsche's *Reading Berlin, 1900* (Cambridge, MA, 1996) also explore the emergence of a society deeply influenced by consumption patterns.

25. Kenneth D. Brown, *The British Toy Business: A History since 1700* (London, 1996).

26. Gary Cross, *Kids' Stuff: Toys and the Changing World of American Childhood* (Cambridge, MA, 1997).

27. Ben Fine, "From Political Economy to Consumption," in *Acknowledging Consumption: A Review of New Studies* (London, 1995), 135.

28. Fine, "From Political Economy to Consumption," 142–43; Ben Fine and Ellen Leopold, *The World of Consumption* (London and New York, 1993).

29. See, for example, Niel McKendrick, John Brewer, and J. H. Plumb, *Birth of a Consumer Society: The Commercialization of Eighteenth-Century England* (Bloomington, 1982); Peter Stearns, *Consumerism in World History: The Global Transformation of Desire* (New York, 2001); Colin Campbell, *The Romantic Ethic and the Spirit of Modern Consumerism* (Oxford, 1987); Daniel Roche, *A History of Everyday Things: The Birth of Consumption in France, 1600–1800* (Cambridge, 2000). Rosalind H. Williams (*Dream Worlds: Mass Consumption in Late Nineteenth-Century France* [Berkeley, 1982]) suggests a distinct "courtly" consumer regime that manifested a constellation of values and gestures in specific material objects dominated in eighteenth-century France and Europe. She argues that in the nineteenth century, this sense of luxury was "democratized." This model accords with that presented by Leora Auslander in *Taste and Power: Furnishing Modern France* (Berkeley, 1996).

30. Daniel Bell, *The Cultural Contradictions of Capitalism* (New York, 1976).

31. Frederic Jameson, "Postmodernism and Consumer Society," in *The Cultural Turn: Selected Writings on the Postmodern, 1983–1998* (London, 1998). See also Perry Anderson, *The Origins of Postmodernity* (London, 1998).

32. Don Slater, *Consumer Culture and Modernity* (London, 1997), 23.

33. See Steven Shapin, *Leviathan and the Air-Pump: Hobbes, Boyle, and the Experimental Life* (Princeton, 1989); Jürgen Habermas, *The Structural Transformation of the Public Sphere* (Cambridge, MA, 1989); Roger Chartier, *The Cultural Origins of the French Revolution* (Durham, NC, and London, 1991); Max Weber, *The Protestant Ethic and the Spirit of Capitalism* (London and New York, 1997). Examples may be extended enormously.

34. Charles Taylor, *Modern Social Imaginaries* (Durham, NC, 2004).

35. Taylor, *Social Imaginaries,* 69–82.

36. This is also suggested, in slightly different form, by Bruno LaTour, in *We Have Never Been Modern* (Cambridge, MA, 1993).

37. Anthony Giddens, *Modernity and Self-Identity: Self and Society in the Late Modern Age* (Stanford, CA, 1991), 81.

38. Giddens, *Modernity and Self-Identity,* 5, 80–88. See also discussion in Slater, *Consumer Culture and Modernity,* 64–68.

39. See Daniel Miller, *Material Culture and Mass Consumption* (Oxford, 1987).

40. Giddens, *Modernity and Self-Identity,* 83.

41. This point is made by a variety of writers from multiple perspectives. See, for example, Jean Baudrillard, *For a Critique of the Political Economy of the Sign* (St. Louis, 1981); Gary Cross, *Time and Money: The Making of Consumer Culture* (London, 1993).

42. See, for an excellent treatment, Vanessa Schwartz, *Spectacular Realities: Early Mass Culture in Fin de Siècle Paris* (Berkeley, 1998); Schwartz treats the academic discourse around spectacle and mass culture on pages 1–12.

43. Honoré Balzac, quoted in Mary Gluck, *Popular Bohemia: Modernism and Urban Culture in Nineteenth-Century Paris* (Cambridge, MA, 2005), 91.

44. Fritzsche, *Reading Berlin,* 4.

45. See "Schaufenster-Revue über Spielwaren," *Deutsche Spielwaren-Zeitung,* no. 25 (1 Dec. 1913): 9.

46. Georg Simmel, "The Metropolis and Mental Life," in *Classic Essays on the Culture of Cities* (New York, 1969), 60.

47. Michel Foucault, "Two Lectures," in *Culture/Power/History* (Princeton, NJ, 1994), 214.

48. See Charles Taylor, *Sources of the Self: The Making of the Modern Identity* (Cambridge, MA, 1989), 368–90; Frederick C. Beiser, *The Romantic Imperative: The Concept of Early German Romanticism* (Cambridge, MA, 2003), 88–105.

49. See Max Weber, *The Protestant Ethic and the Spirit of Capitalism* (New York, 1930); Bell, *Cultural Contradictions.*

50. Karl Marx, *Capital,* vol. 1, in *Collected Works,* vol. 35 (New York, 1996); Karl Polanyi, *The Great Transformation: The Political and Economic Origins of Our Time* (Boston, 2001).

51. Quoted in Matthew Jeffries, *Imperial Culture in Germany, 1871–1918* (New York, 2003), 191.

52. Williams, *Dream Worlds,* 7.

53. Paul Betts, *The Authority of Everyday Objects: A Cultural History of West German Industrial Design* (Berkeley, 2004), 19.

Chapter 1

1. Thomas Mann, *Buddenbrooks* (New York, 1961), 342–43.

2. See Mann's letter discussing his onetime "secret identity" (a "Prince by the name of Karl"), quoted in the introduction to Paul Hildebrandt's *Das Spielzeug im Leben des Kindes: Reichillustriertes Haus- und Familienbuch* (Berlin, 1904). Mann

put a very similar imaginary play into *Felix Krull* (Thomas Mann, *Bekenntnisse des Hochstaplers Felix Krull* [Frankfurt am Main, 1998], 13–14).

3. Many conservative readers took the novel as a celebration of bourgeois virtues, such as duty and hard work, and as a warning against frivolous waste. See Hugh Ridley, *The Problematic Bourgeois: Twentieth-Century Criticism on Thomas Mann's "Buddenbrooks" and "The Magic Mountain"* (Columbia, SC, 1994).

4. Thomas Mann, *Doctor Faustus: The Life of the German Composer Adrian Leverkühn* (New York, 1975), 329.

5. Compare John Stuart Mill, *Autobiography* (New York, 1989), 25–48.

6. For the development of the German *bürgerliche* family ideology, see Gunilla-Frederike Budde, *Auf dem Weg ins Bürgerleben: Kindheit und Erziehung in deutschen und englischen Bürgerfamilien, 1840–1914* (Göttingen, 1994); Heidi Rosenbaum, *Formen der Familie: Untersuchungen zum Zusammenhang von Familienverhältnissen, Sozialstruktur und sozialem Wandel in der deutschen Gesellschaft des 19. Jahrhunderts* (Frankfurt am Main, 1982); Ingeborg Weber-Kellermann, *Die deutsche Familie: Versuch einer Sozialgeschichte* (Frankfurt am Main, 1974); Marion Kaplan, *The Making of the Jewish Middle Class* (New York, 1991); Karin Hausen, "Family and Role Division: The Polarisation of Sexual Stereotypes in the Nineteenth Century; An Aspect of the Dissociation of Work and Family Life," in *The German Family: Essays on the Social History of the Family in Nineteenth- and Twentieth-Century Germany,* ed. Richard Evans and W. R. Lee (Totowa, NJ, 1981); Nicholas Stargardt, "German Childhoods: The Making of a Historiography," *German History* 16, no. 1 (1998): 1–15; Thomas Nipperdey, *Deutsche Geschichte, 1800–1866* (Munich, 1983), 114–30.

7. See, for example, Rosenbaum, *Formen der Familie,* 279–83; Edward Shorter, *The Making of the Modern Family* (New York, 1975), 227–30.

8. Rebekka Habermas, "Parent-Child Relationships in the Nineteenth Century," *German History* 16, no. 1 (1998): 52.

9. Immanuel Niethammer, *Der Streit des Philantropismus und Humanismus in der Theorie des Erziehungs-Unterrichts unserer Zeit* (Jena, 1808), quoted in Habermas, "Parent-Child Relationships," 53.

10. Michel Foucault, *Discipline and Punish: The Birth of the Prison* (New York, 1977), 141.

11. Foucault, *Discipline,* 216. In exploring the impact of middle-class domesticity, I shall be working with a framework drawn in some respects from Foucault. I do not mean to suggest, as does Foucault, that the disciplines represent a totalizing system of control. In fact, my argument here depends critically on the limits of discipline.

12. See Margarete Flecken, *Arbeiterkinder im 19. Jahrhundert: Eine sozialgeschichtliche Untersuchung ihrer Lebenswelt* (Weinheim and Basel, 1981), 157; Ingeborg Weber-Kellermann, *Die Kinderstube* (Frankfurt am Main, 1991), 15–36; Ganaway, "Toys, Consumption, and Middle-Class Childhood." For the family as the generative source of the *Bürger,* see Budde, *Auf dem Weg,* 12; Kaplan, *Jewish Middle Class,* 4–5, 120. For a fascinating account of how the American middle class began to see the streets as a moral danger and to enforce a physical

separation between their own children and those from lower social classes, see Stephen Nissenbaum, *The Battle for Christmas* (New York, 1997), 90–131.

13. Budde, *Auf dem Weg,* 78.

14. Nipperdey, *Deutsche Geschichte, 1866–1918,* 1:55–56.

15. See Rosenbaum, *Formen der Familie,* 359; Budde, *Auf dem Weg,* 85.

16. See Rosenbaum, *Formen der Familie,* 359; Kaplan, *Jewish Middle Class.*

17. For a fascinating and suggestive account of the perceived social significance of "modern motherhood," see Timothy Mitchell, *Colonising Egypt* (Berkeley, 1988), 111–13. British colonial officials and Westernized Egyptians clearly saw mothers, acting as disciplinary agents in Foucault's sense, as central to the construction of healthy, vigorous, and productive individuals.

18. Clara Zinn, *Kinderspiel und Spielzeug* (Leipzig and Berlin, 1910), 2.

19. Ellen Key, *The Century of the Child* (New York, 1909), 129.

20. See Ganaway, "Toys, Consumption, and Middle-Class Childhood," 52–58.

21. See Mary Jo Maynes, *Taking the Hard Road: The Life Course in French and German Workers' Autobiographies in the Era of Industrialization* (Chapel Hill, 1995), 65–66.

22. For alternative approaches to the gap between domestic ideals and domestic realities, see Roddy Reid, *Families in Jeopardy: Regulating the Social Body in France, 1750–1910* (Stanford, CA, 1993); Sharon Marcus, *Apartment Stories: City and Home in Nineteenth-Century Paris and London* (Berkeley, 1999).

23. See George Mosse, *Nationalism and Sexuality: Respectability and Abnormal Sexuality in Modern Europe* (New York, 1985); Peter Gay, *Education of the Senses* (New York, 1984).

24. See Budde, *Auf dem Weg,* 12.

25. For changing Christmas traditions in nineteenth-century Germany, see Ingeborg Weber-Kellermann, *Das Weihnachtsfest: Eine Kultur- und Sozialgeschichte der Weihnachtszeit* (Lucerne, 1978); Joseph B. Perry, "The Private Life of the Nation: Christmas and the Invention of Modern Germany" (PhD diss., University of Illinois at Urbana-Champaign, 2001); Weber-Kellermann, *Die deutsche Familie,* 112–13; Dietmar Sauermann, ed., *Weihnachten in Westfalen um 1900: Berichte aus dem Archiv für westfälische Volkskunde* (Münster, 1976); Angela Meinel, *Kinderleben und Kinderkultur in Sachsen: Versuch eines Uberblicks* (Dresden, 1998), 87; Barbara Beuys, *Familienleben in Deutschland: Neuer Bilder aus der deutschen Vergangenheit* (Reinbeck bei Hamburg, 1980), 443–44; Budde, *Auf dem Weg,* 85. On the transformation of Christmas in the United States, see Nissenbaum, *The Battle for Christmas.* On Christmas in the United States and Great Britain, see J. M. Golby and A. W. Purdue, *The Making of Modern Christmas* (Athens, 1986); Daniel Miller, "A Theory of Christmas," in *Unwrapping Christmas,* ed. Daniel Miller (Oxford, 1993); James G. Carrier, "The Rituals of Christmas Giving," in D. Miller, *Unwrapping Christmas.*

26. Perry, "Private Life of the Nation," 8, 26; for fuller discussion, see 6–12, 20–91.

27. See Perry, "Private Life of the Nation," 35–39.

28. See Weber-Kellermann, *Die deutsche Familie,* 112–13; Budde, *Auf dem Weg,* 86.

29. See Weber-Kellermann, *Die deutsche Familie,* 113; D. Miller, "A Theory of Christmas," 19–20; Carrier, "Rituals of Christmas Giving," 55–56; Nissenbaum, *The Battle for Christmas,* 132, 172–75.

30. Perry, "Private Life of the Nation," 43–54.

31. Weber-Kellermann, *Weihnachtsfest,* 122.

32. See Nissenbaum, *The Battle for Christmas,* 132–33.

33. The relation between consumerism and love is best explored in Daniel Miller's *A Theory of Shopping* (Ithaca, NY, 1998). The link between consumption and desire has been one of the most common tropes and theses of Western literature and scholarship for centuries. See, for example, Williams, *Dream Worlds;* C. Campbell, *Romantic Ethic.* Classic formulations from the time period investigated in this project include Emile Zola's *The Ladies Paradise* (Berkeley, 1882; reprint, 1992) and Werner Sombart's *Luxury and Capitalism,* trans. W. R. Dittmar (Ann Arbor, 1913; reprint, 1967).

34. Georg Simmel, *The Philosophy of Money,* trans. Tom Bottomore and David Frisby, 2nd ed. (London and New York, 1990), 76.

35. Hans Fallada, *Damals bei uns Daheim: Erlebtes, Erfahrenes und Erfundenes* (Stuttgart, 1958), 165.

36. Marcel Mauss, *The Gift,* quoted in Carrier, "Rituals of Christmas Giving," 56. Carrier acutely analyzes the problem of giving impersonal commodities as gifts.

37. "Der Tag der Erwartung," *Berliner Tageblatt* 29, no. 651 (23 Dec. 1900): 1. Beilage, 1.

38. For a useful discussion of the elaborate rituals parents used to construct and abolish distance in Christmas celebrations, see Perry, "Private Life of the Nation," 30, 35, 45–46. See also Weber-Kellermann, *Weihnachtsfest,* 118–27.

39. "In der Bescheerungsfrage," *Berliner Tageblatt* 29, no. 638 (16 Dec. 1900): 1. Beilage, 1.

40. "Weihnachtsfreuden," *Daheim* 25, no. 12 (22 Dec. 1889): 1. Beilage, 1. With its typical petty jingoism, *Daheim* managed to cast doubt on the familial and religious devotion of all other Europeans, while insisting that only Germany celebrated Christmas properly.

41. Paul Härtel, "Am heiligen Abend," *Die Gartenlaube* 46, no. 49 (1899): 821.

42. Raimond, "Der Wunschzettel," *Daheim* 49, no. 11 (14 Dec. 1912): 29.

43. Fallada, *Damals,* 164.

44. The analysis offered in figure 1 is based on the rich advertising in the *Deutsche Spielwaren-Zeitung.* It looks at three of the five years in which the periodical ran before the beginning of World War I. As the leading professional journal of the toy industry, it reflects the marketplace rather well, though it in all likelihood does have a slight bias toward the products of Nuremburg. Included among the total number of ads are advertisements for services (especially legal services), ads looking for specialized help or jobs, and many ads that give no hint of the

product the advertising company offered. The percentages for the various toy categories should consequently be viewed with the proviso in mind that they are low because the total number is inflated by other types of ads. They are, therefore, best used as means of comparison between categories of toys.

45. See Budde, *Auf dem Weg,* 78.

46. "Welches Spielzeug wähle ich?" *Deutsche Spielwaren-Zeitung,* no. 11 (15 Mar. 1912): 11.

47. Budde, *Auf dem Weg,* 78.

48. A. C. Ellis and G. Stanley Hall, "A Study of Dolls," *Pedagogical Seminary,* Dec. 1896, cited in Ganaway, "Toys, Consumption, and Middle-Class Childhood," 225–26, and in Miriam Formanek-Brunell, *Made to Play House: Dolls and the Commercialization of American Girlhood, 1830–1930* (New Haven, 1993).

49. See Ganaway, "Toys, Consumption, and Middle-Class Childhood," 76–78 (and, more generally, 254–78).

50. For a guide to these debates, see Volker R. Berghahn, *Militarism: The History of an International Debate, 1861–1979* (New York, 1982).

51. Michael Howard, *War in European History,* 109, quoted in Geoff Eley, *From Unification to Nazism: Reinterpreting the German Past* (Boston, 1986), 108.

52. Hildebrandt, *Spielzeug,* 265.

53. See "Jungdeutschlands Schlachtenspiel," *Deutsche Spielwaren-Zeitung,* no. 18 (20 Aug. 1912): 19–21.

54. On the German view of history, see Georg Iggers, *The German Conception of History: The National Tradition of Historical Thought from Herder to the Present* (Middletown, CT, 1968), 14–15, 88–89; Nipperdey, *Deutsche Geschichte, 1866–1918,* 1:636. David Blackbourn (*The Long Nineteenth Century: A History of Germany, 1780–1918* [New York and Oxford, 1998], 306) argues that imperial Germany was particularly obsessed with history.

55. The choice of Roman legions as an example here refers to the Christmas gifts that Hans Fallada received one year: German tribesmen, Roman legionnaires, and an Anker bridge-building set. "Finally," exclaimed Fallada (*Damals,* 164), "I will be able to let Caeser build his bridge over the Rhine."

56. See "Neuheiten die zur Messe gebrachet werden," *Deutsche Spielwaren-Zeitung,* no. 6 (1 Mar. 1913): 11.

57. See "Das Spielzeug als Erzieher," *Deutsche Spielwaren-Zeitung,* no. 22 (15 Nov. 1911): 659.

58. "Des Weihnachtmanns hauptsächlichste Werkstätten," *Daheim* 2, no. 12 (Dec. 1865): 179. That there was no reference to Austrian soldiers, even though it was a joint Austrian-Prussian campaign, might reflect bias in toy making on the part of Protestant Nurembergers.

59. "Der Nürnberger Zinnsoldat," *Daheim* 27, no. 12 (20 Dec. 1890): 185.

60. See *Handleskammer Mittelfranken, 1904,* 217; *Handelskammer Mittelfranken, 1911,* 153; "Was die deutsche Spielwaren-Industrie nicht versäumen sollte," *Deutsche Spielwaren-Zeitung,* no. 1 (2 Jan. 1911): 11; "Die aktuelle Spielwarenindustrie," *Deutsche Spielwaren-Zeitung,* no. 22 (15 Nov. 1911): 697.

61. See "Der Nürnberger Zinnsoldat," *Daheim* 27, no. 12 (20 Dec. 1890): 185.

62. *Daheim* 44, no. 10 (7 Dec. 1907): 47.

63. Hildebrandt, *Spielzeug,* 285.

64. See, for example, Friedrich Ahlers-Hestermann, *Pause vor dem dritten Akt* (Hamburg, 1975), 10; Johann Baptist Gradl, "Als Kreuzberg noch kaiserlich war," in *Kindheit im Kaiserreich: Errinerungen an vergangene Zeiten,* ed. Rudolf Pörtner (Dusseldorf, 1998), 214; Ernst von Hippel, *Meine Kindheit im kaiserlichen Deutschland* (Meisenheim am Glan, 1975), 78; Fallada, *Damals,* 164–65; Julius Posener, *Fast so alt wie das Jahrhundert* (Berlin, 1990), 73; Hans Wendt, "Als Hindenburg zum Ersatzkaiser avancierte," in Pörtner, *Kindheit im Kaiserreich,* 176.

65. E. Ackermann, "Spiel und Arbeit," in *Encyklopedisches Handbuch fur Pädagogik,* vol. 8 (Langensalza, 1910), 720.

66. See Fritzsche, *Reading Berlin,* 132–34.

67. "Die Spielsachen unter dem Weihnachtbaum," *Daheim* 14, no. 12 (22 Dec. 1877): 197.

68. "Eine Weihnachtsbescherung," *Vorwärts* 21, no. 288 (8 Dec. 1904): 2. Beilage, 1.

69. "Weihnachtszauber," *Vorwärts* 24, no. 291 (13 Dec. 1907): 3. Beilage, 1.

70. "Der Säbel in der Hände der Kinder!" *Vorwärts* 24, no. 299 (22 Dec. 1907): 6. Beilage, 2. Note that in this argument, the guardian of worker morality, who must reject militarist toys, was portrayed as male. Also, that workers participated in the toy market was portrayed as self-evident.

71. "Weihnachtssoldaten," *Vorwärts* 30, no. 329 (14 Dec. 1913): 2. Beilage, 1.

72. For an extensive treatment of the so-called Hottentot election, see George Dunlop Crothers, *The German Elections of 1907* (New York, 1941).

73. See David Schoenbaum, *Zabern 1913: Consensus Politics in Imperial Germany* (London, 1982).

74. See the 1912 catalog of the Hermann Kurtz toy store in Stuttgart: Hermann Kurtz, *Spielwaren und Puppen, 1912* (reprint, Stuttgart, 1983), 75.

75. See *Daheim* 45, no. 11 (12 Dec. 1908): 46.

76. Peter Fritzsche, *A Nation of Fliers: German Aviation and the Popular Imagination* (Cambridge, MA, 1992), 1.

77. "Französische Spielzeug-Neuheiten," *Deutsche Spielwaren-Zeitung,* no. 1 (2 Jan. 1912): 9.

78. Günther Grassmann, "Man liebte russische Literatur und fürchtete die 'russische Dampfwalze,'" in Pörtner, *Kindheit im Kaiserreich,* 142.

79. *Handelskammer München, 1910,* 158, 400.

80. Fritzsche, *Nation of Fliers,* 2–5, 35–43.

81. Kurtz, *Spielwaren und Puppen, 1912.*

82. The works of other historians allow a crude and tentative comparison in the popularity of military toys. According to Kenneth Brown ("Modelling for War? Toy Soldiers in Late Victorian and Edwardian Britain" *Journal of Social History* 24 [1990–91]: 237–55), toy soldiers were quite popular in Great Britain, particularly among the elite, while Gary Cross (*Kids' Stuff,* 66) argues that before World War I, Americans purchased few military toys. If that is so, we may perhaps hypothesize that toys reflecting military values were more popular among Euro-

peans because of the antagonisms built into their state system, while the United States, which at that time remained largely unentangled in that system, remained mostly aloof from the military enthusiasms of the Old World.

83. An analysis of the December 1886 ads in the *Münchner Neueste Nachrichten,* for example, shows five explicit ads for military toys (representing 4.5 percent of total toy ads) and none for modern, technology toys. The vast majority (82 percent) of the toy ads were for retail outlets, and these usually did not mention any specific merchandise.

84. Kurtz, *Spielwaren und Puppen, 1912,* 75–78.

85. Kurt Karl Doberer, "Der Pfennig war das Mark der Währung," in Pörtner, *Kindheit im Kaiserreich,* 224. Doberer's father had been a cashier until he was fired. He then got a job as an SPD party functionary.

86. Hildebrandt, *Spielzeug,* 124–25.

87. "Modelldampfmaschinen und Betriebsmodelle als Spielzeug," *Der Spiel- und Holzwaren-Markt* 7, no. 9 (1 May 1911): 1.

88. "Zur Entwicklung der Spielwaren-Industrie," *Rundschau über Spielwaren* 1, no. 1 (1 Sept. 1909): 4.

89. See Asgar Henze, "Eisenzeit: Geschichte und Technik der Metallbaukästen," in *Eisenzeit, Geschichte des Metallbaukastens* (Nuremberg, 1995), 39–40; "Neuheiten," *Deutsche Spielwaren-Zeitung,* no. 7 (20 Mar. 1914): 9–11. Hornsby invented his toy Mechanics Made Easy in 1901. He changed its name to Mecanno in 1907, after which the toy immediately became very popular. In 1914, he entered into a joint partnership with Märklin, the Deutsche Mecanno Gesellschaft, which was promptly seized by the German government in World War I. In 1913, Richter, the maker of the famous Anker Steinbaukasten, came out with their version of the toy, the Imperator (see Henze, "Eisenzeit," 49).

90. "Elektrische Motoren für Knaben," *Rundschau über Spielwaren* 4, no. 112 (10 Oct. 1912): 1634.

91. F. H. Huber, "Nürnbergs Spielwaren-Industrie," in *Bayerns Industrie und Handel,* ed. Adam Guttman (Nuremburg, 1906), 112. This statement begs the question of how many young boys of the time had any direct experience with one-thousand-horsepower steam engines.

92. See Mosse, *Nationalism and Sexuality.*

93. *Handelskammer Sonneberg, 1905,* 94. The way this statement is structured makes the toy the active agent and the child a passive spectator.

94. I here supply a partial list of German books on the exploration of the Arctic between 1870 and 1914: *Die zweite deutsche Nordpolar-Expedition* (Brunswick, 1870); Karl Koldewey, *Die erste Deutsche Nordpolar-Expedition im Jahre 1868* (Gotha, 1871); Gustav Karl Laube, *Reise der Hansa in's nördliche Eismeer: Reisebriefe und Erinnerungblätter* (Prague, 1871); Karl Koldewey, *Die Zweite deutsche Nordpolfahrt 1869–1870: Vorträge und Mittheilungen* (Berlin, 1871); Karl Koldewey, *Die zweite Deutsche Nordpolfahrt in den Jahren 1869 und 1870, unter Führung des Kapitän Karl Koldewey* (Leipzig, 1873); F. J. Singer, *Unsere Nordpolfahrer: ein Wort an das Volk zur Feier der Rettung und Heimkehr der Helden des Tages* (Vienna, 1874); Martin Theodor von Heuglin, *Reisen nach dem Nordpolarmeer in*

den Jahren 1870 und 1871 (Brunswick, 1974); Otto Finsch, *Die Zweite deutsche Nordpolarfahrt in den Jahren 1869 und 1870, unter Führung des Kapitän Koldewey* (Leipzig, 1875); Julius Payer, *Die österrichisch-ungarische Nordpol-Expedition in den Jahren 1872–1874: nebst einer Skizze der zweiten deutschen Nordpol-Expedition 1869–1870 und der Polar-Expedition von 1871* (Vienna, 1876); H. Albrecht, *Die Eroberung des Nordpols* (Leipzig and Berlin, 1879); Richard Andree, *Die Kampf um den Nordpol: Geschichte der Nordpolfahrten* (Bielefeld, 1872/?/1880/1883/1889); August Burger, *Die Wege zum Nordpol* (Tauberbischofsheim, 1894); Max Wilhelm Meyer, *Der Kampf um den Nordpol: Scenisch ausgestatteter Vortrag gehalten im wissenschaftlichen Theater der Urania zu Berlin* (Berlin, 1897; reprinted in 1905 by Hermann Schmidt); Franz Helbing, *Die Eroberung des Nordpols: Schilderung der Fahrten und Entdeckungsreisen* (Berlin, 1898); Fritz Regel, *Die Nordpolarforschung* (Berlin, 1899); Ferdinand Lupsa, *Die Nordpolsphinx, oder Frage der moderner Nordpolar-Forschung* (Laibach, 1903); Hermann Cardauns, *Der Kampf um den Nordpol* (Kempten, 1910); Karl Koldewey, *Nordpolfahrten* (Berlin, 1910).

95. A. Woldt, "Die neue Aera der Polarforschung," *Die Gartenlaube* 29, no. 9 (1882): 146–47.

96. Curt Rudolf Kreuschner, "Der Kampf um den Nordpol," *Daheim* 43, no. 1 (6 Oct. 1906): 14.

97. The "success" of the voyage remains in question because of a still lingering controversy about whether Peary reached the North Pole.

98. Robert Peary, "Die Entdeckung des Nordpols," *Daheim* 46, no. 23 (5 Mar. 1910): 11.

99. See illustrations in A. Woldt, "Die neue Aera der Polarforschung," *Die Gartenlaube* 29, no. 9 (1882): 146–47.

100. See "Ein deutsches Nordpolentdeckungsspiel," *Deutsche Spielwaren-Zeitung,* no. 10 (15 Dec. 1909): 151; "Spielwaren," *Vossische Zeitung,* no. 565 (2 Dec. 1909): 6. Beilage, 4.

101. Kurtz, *Spielwaren und Puppen, 1912,* 51.

102. "Französische Spielzeug-Neuheiten," *Deutsche Spielwaren-Zeitung,* no. 1 (2 Jan. 1912): 9.

103. See "Neuheiten die zur Messe gebracht werden," *Deutsche Spielwaren-Zeitung,* no. 6 (1 Mar. 1913): 11.

104. Gail Bederman, *Manliness and Civilization: A Cultural History of Gender and Race in the United States, 1880–1917* (Chicago, 1997), 44. Bederman distinguishes the self-control displayed in "civilized" manliness from the physical domination associated with "primitive" masculinity.

105. See Sabine Völker-Kraemer, *Wie ich zur Teddymutter wurde: Das Leben der Margarete Steiff nach ihren eigenen Aufzeichnungen* (Stuttgart, 1996), 92–101; Norbert Mendel, "Die Gechichte der Puppe und des Puppenspiels," in *Geschichte der Kinderspiels: Ein Puzzelspiel zur Bundesdeutschen Zeitgeschichte,* ed. Robert Deutsch and Bernhard Hertlin (Heidelberg, 1980), 85–104.

106. "Englische Bazar-Neuheiten," *Deutsche Spielwaren-Zeitung,* no. 9 (1 Dec. 1909): 137–39.

107. See "Neue Vorbilder für Luxus Spielwaren," *Deutsche Spielwaren-*

Zeitung, no. 12 (15 June 1910): 279; "Roosevelts Spielzeug und Spielzeug-Luftschiffe populär in Paris," *Deutsche Spielwaren-Zeitung,* no. 12 (15 June 1910): 287.

108. Susanne Zantop, *Colonial Fantasies: Conquest, Family, and Nation in Precolonial Germany, 1770–1870* (Durham, NC, 1997), 5.

109. See "Neue Spielwaren," *Deutsche Spielwaren-Zeitung,* no. 6 (20 Mar. 1910): 137.

110. "Klettender Negger," *Wegweiser für die Spielwarenindustrie und verwandte Branche* 4, no. 59 (10 Sept. 1889): 662. Apparently, the precondition of the German annexation of the African land and tree was not considered theft.

111. "Schaufenster-Revue über Spielwaren," *Deutsche Spielwaren-Zeitung,* no. 25 (1 Dec. 1913): 9.

112. See Zantop, *Colonial Fantasies,* 11; Sander Gilman, "The Figure of the Black in German Aesthetic Theory," *Eighteenth-Century Studies,* summer 1975, 373–91.

113. Ciarlo, "Consuming Race, Envisioning Empire," 185.

114. See Ciarlo, "Consuming Race, Envisioning Empire," 295–301.

115. See John K. Noyes, "National Identity, Nomadism, and Narration in Gustav Frenssen's *Peter Moor's Journey to Southwest Africa,*" and Helmut Walser Smith, "The Talk of Genocide, the Rhetoric of Miscegenation: Notes on Debates in the German Reichstag concerning Southwest Africa, 1904–1914," in *The Imperialist Imagination: German Colonialism and Its Legacy,* ed. Sara Friedrichsmeyer, Sara Lennox, and Susanne Zantop (Ann Arbor, 1998); Amadou Booker Sadji, *Das Bild des Negro-Afrikaners in der Deutschen Kolonialliteratur (1884–1945): Ein Beitrag zur literarischen Imagologie Schwarzarfrikas* (Berlin, 1985), 176–208; Joachim Warmbold, *Germania in Africa: Germany's Colonial Literature* (New York, 1989), 67–87. For an overview of German colonialism, see Woodruff D. Smith, "Colonialism and Colonial Empire," in *Imperial Germany: A Historiographical Companion,* ed. Roger Chickering (Westport, CT, 1996), 430–53. Given the discussion of technological modernity earlier in the present chapter, it is enlightening to note that one of the "proofs" offered for the inhumanity of Africans was their technological backwardness—that is, the absence of sewage systems, running water, and so on.

116. See Marieluise Christadler, "Zwischen Gartenlaube und Genozid: Kolonialistiche Jugendbücher im Kaiserreich," in *Die Menschen sind arm weil sie arm sind: Die Dritte Welt im Spiegel von Kinder und Jugendbüchern* (Frankfurt am Main, 1978).

117. Approximately one-third of total toy sales were registered by dolls. See Alfred Leopold, "Alte und Neue Puppe," *Leipziger Illustrirte Zeitung,* 29 Dec. 1910, 1249.

118. Zinn, *Kinderspiel und Spielzeug,* 22.

119. For competing visions of what sort of motherhood girls were to be trained for, see Ganaway, "Toys, Consumption, and Middle-Class Childhood," 200–253.

120. Hildebrandt, *Spielzeug,* 325.

121. "Der Nürnberger Zinnsoldat," *Daheim* 27, no. 12 (20 Dec. 1890): 186. See

also Rene Schickele, "Puppen," *Neue Deutsche Rundschau* 20, no. 1 (1909): 157; see, more generally, Budde, *Auf dem Weg,* 223–24.

122. Margaret Boveri, *Verzweigungen* (Munich, 1978), 28.

123. "Weihnachtsgeschenke," *Vorwärts* 27, no. 298 (21 Dec. 1910): 3. Beilage, 1.

124. See Ganaway, "Toys, Consumption, and Middle-Class Childhood," 49–63.

125. See Peter Zwijnenberg, *De Geschiedenis van Richter's Anker-Steenbouwdozen* (Alphen aan den Rijn, 1982), 3–4; Annette Noschke and Günter Knerr, *Bauklötze Staunen: Zweihundert Jahre Geschichte der Baukästen* (Munich, 1986), 51–53.

126. "Der Anker-Steinbaukasten," *Wegweiser für die Spielwarenindustrie und verwandte Branche* 9, no. 183 (5 Nov. 1894): 2642.

127. See *Münchner Neueste Nachrichten,* (1 Dec. 1906): 6; "Deutsche Spielwaren," *Deutsche Spielwaren-Zeitung,* no. 19 (1 Oct. 1910): 463; "Vom Berliner Puppenmarkt," *Vossische Zeitung,* no. 645 (20 Dec. 1913): 1. Beilage, 1; "Vorbildliche Typen für Spielwaren bei der Jahrhundertfeier des Münchner Oktoberfest," *Deutsche Spielwaren-Zeitung,* no. 21 (1 Nov. 1910): 515.

128. For an excellent treatment of the German tabloid press, see Fritzsche, *Reading Berlin.*

129. Zygmunt Bauman, "Desert Spectacular," in *The Flanuer* (New York, 1994), 140.

130. Janet Ward, *Weimar Surfaces: Urban Visual Culture in 1920s Germany* (Berkeley, 2001), 191; see, more generally, 1–43, 191–240. See also V. Schwartz, *Spectacular Realities.* On the power of smell, see Alan Corbain, *The Foul and the Fragrant: Odor and the French Social Imagination* (Cambridge, MA, 1986).

131. Weber-Kellermann, *Die deutsche Familie,* 151.

132. See *Berliner Lokal-Anzeiger,* 3 Dec. 1899; *Berliner Lokal-Anzeiger,* 2 Dec. 1900.

133. See Claude Jeanmaire, *Bing, die Modellbahnen unserer Grossväter* (Villigen, 1972). Unfortunately, many of the annual catalogs in Jeanmaire's collection do not include prices.

134. See *Berliner Lokal-Anzeiger* 26, no. 611 (1 Dec. 1908).

135. See *Berliner Lokal-Anzeiger* 27, no. 779 (1 Dec. 1909).

136. See Kurtz, *Spielwaren und Puppen, 1912,* 38, 57.

137. See Nipperdey, *Deutsche Geschichte, 1866–1918,* 1:67.

138. Inge Litschke's analysis of one Ruhr mining community (*Im Schatten der Fördertürme: Kindheit und Jugend im Revier; Die Bergarbeiterkolonie Lohberg 1900 bis 1980* [Mercator-Verlag, 1993], 48–49) concludes that approximately 22 percent of miners earned enough so that, by my analysis, they could have regularly purchased inexpensive toys as Christmas gifts, while another 44 percent would have been able to occasionally buy toys with careful budgeting, particularly if they had a small family.

139. Cited in Volker R. Berghahn, *Imperial Germany, 1871–1914: Economy, Society, Culture, and Politics* (Providence, RI, 1994), 326.

140. "Vom Weihnachtsmarkt," *Vorwärts* 15, no. 296 (18 Dec. 1898): 1. Beilage, 1; "Der Ebrliner Weihnachtsmarkt," *Vorwärts* 22, no. 291 (13 Dec. 1905): 4. Beilage, 1.

141. "Eine Weihnachtsbecherung," *Vorwärts* 21, no. 288 (8 Dec. 1904): 2. Beilage, 1.

142. Jeanmaire, *Bing.*

143. See Otto Höllerer, *Märklin: Handbuch für Ausstattungsstücke zu den großen spurweiten, 1895–1939* (Munich, 1999).

Chapter 2

1. See Gertrud Meyer, *Die Spielwarenindustrie im sächsischen Erzgebirge* (Leipzig, 1911), 37, 48, 60; Bernhard Westenberger, *Die Holzspielwarenindustrie im sächsischen Erzgebirge unter besonderer Berücksichtigung der Hausindustrie* (Leipzig, 1911), 141; "Die Spielwaren unter dem Weihnactsbaum," *Daheim* 14, no. 12 (2 Dec. 1877): 195.

2. See Willy Bierer, *Die Hausindustrielle Kinderarbeit im Kreise Sonneberg: Ein Beitrag zur Kritik des Kinderschutzgesetzes* (Tübingen, 1913), 36.

3. See Wilhelm Uhlfelder, *Die Zinnmalerinnen in Nürnberg und Fürth: Eine wirtschaftliche Studie über Heimarbeit* (Leipzig, 1899), 12.

4. See Otto Senst, *Die Metallspielwarenindustrie und der Spielwarenhandel von Nürnberg und Fürth* (Erlangen, 1901); Hans Lotter, *Gross-Industrie und Gross-Handel von Nürnberg-Fürth und Umgebung* (Nuremberg, 1894); Marion Faber, "Von Dockenmachern und Wildrufdrehern," in *SCHUCO, Bing & Co.: Berühmtes Blechspielzeug aus Nürnberg,* ed. Jürgen Franzke (Nuremberg, 1993), 66; Charlotte Parry-Crooke, *Märklin, 1895–1914* (London, 1983), 17, 19; L. C. Beck, "Die Fabrikindustrie Nürnbergs," in *Festschrift zur 40. Haupt-versammlung des Vereins Deutscher Ingenieure in Nürnberg vom 11.–15. Juni 1899* (Nuremberg, 1899).

5. Hans-Ulrich Wehler, *Deutsche Gesellschaftsgeschichte, Dritter Band, 1849–1914* (Munich, 1995), 548–51, 570–74. See also Knut Borchardt, *Die Industrielle Revolution in Deutschland* (Munich, 1972), 69–71; David S. Landes, *The Unbound Prometheus; Technological Change and Industrial Development in Western Europe from 1750 to the Present* (Cambridge, 1969), 231–44; Eric Hobsbawm, *The Age of Empire, 1875–1914* (New York, 1987), 35–53.

6. See S. B. Saul, *The Myth of the Great Depression, 1873–1896* (London, 1969).

7. Alfred Chandler lays considerable emphasis on the completion of the rail networks in the 1870s for the development of modern industrial production and associated corporate production units. See Alfred D. Chandler Jr., *Scale and Scope: The Dynamics of Industrial Production* (Cambridge, MA, 1990); *The Visible Hand: The Managerial Revolution in American Business* (Cambridge, MA, 1977).

8. Walter Troeltsch, *Über die neuesten Veränderungen im deutschen Wirtschaftsleben* (Stuttgart, 1899), 63.

9. Simmel, *Philosophy of Money.*

10. See Rosenhaupt, *Metallspielwarenindustrie,* 94.

11. See "Meßnachklänge," *Deutsche Spielwaren-Zeitung,* no. 7 (1 Apr. 1911): 219.

12. See Oskar Stillich, *Die Spielwaren-Hausindustrie des Meiningen Oberlandes* (Jena, 1899), 80–81.

13. See Rosenhaupt, *Metalspielwarenindustrie,* 94–95.

14. See Westenberger, *Holzspielwarenindustrie,* 102; Ernst Rausch, *Die Sonneberger Spielwaren-Industrie und die verwandten Industrieen der Griffel- und Glasfabrikation unter besonderer Berücksichtigung der Verhältnisse in der Hausindustrie* (Berlin, 1901), 40; Adolf Fleischmann, *Die Arbeiter-Agitatoren des Katheder-Sozialismus und die Sonneberger Spielwaren-Industrie und ihr Handel* (Berlin, 1884), 20.

15. See *Handelskammer Mittelfranken, 1887,* 136; *Handelkammer Dresden, 1892,* 182.

16. The United States, in particular, had a reputation for difficult and underhanded customs agents.

17. See Senst, *Metallspielwarenindustrie Nürnberg,* 73.

18. Rosenhaupt, *Metallspielwarenindustrie,* 98–99.

19. Bierer, *Hausindustrielle Kinderarbeit,* 130–31. A truck system is one in which laborers are paid in cash but forced to use that cash to buy products from the employer, invariably at inflated prices.

20. For a persuasive account of how important this distrust of strangers in commerce was in limiting and structuring the American market, see Naomi Lamoreaux, Daniel Raff, and Peter Temin, "Beyond Markets and Hierarchies: Toward a New Synthesis of American Business History," *American History Review* 108, no. 2 (April 2003): 404–33.

21. Emmanuel Sax, *Die Hausindustrie in Thüringen,* vol. 1, *Das Meiningen Oberland* (Jena, 1885), 37.

22. "Der Zug nach Billigkeit," *Bayerische Gewerbe-Zeitung* 9, no. 9 (1896): 210.

23. Of the twenty-five nonagricultural sectors sampled by the economist Ashok Desai in *Real Wages in Germany, 1871–1913* (Oxford, 1968), only five had average annual earnings above one thousand marks in 1900. In 1890, there were only two sectors with average annual wages above nine hundred marks.

24. Cited in Berghahn, *Imperial Germany,* 326. Granted, these numbers are for 1906, but given the slow progress that the working class made in the decades before 1906, they are nonetheless germane.

25. *Handelskammer Mittelfranken, 1887,* 136–37.

26. *Handelskammer Mittelfranken, 1883,* 120–21. See also *Handelskammer Mittelfranken, 1882,* 162–63.

27. *Handelskammer Mittelfranken, 1888,* 94.

28. *Handelskammer Dresden, 1877–1880,* 279.

29. See Rosenhaupt, *Metallspielwarenindustrie,* 69.

30. Hartmut Berghoff, *Zwischen Kleinstadt und Weltmarkt: Hohner und die Harmonika 1857–1961; Unternehmensgeschichte als Gesellschaftgeschichte* (Paderborn, Munich, and Vienna, 1997), 80–81. According to Berghoff (83), Hohner was wholesaling harmonicas for between thirty pfennig and 4.50 marks in 1886. David Landes (*Unbound Prometheus,* 242–44) also suggests that a mass market was developing in the Western world in the last decades of the nineteenth century.

31. *Handelskammer Mittelfrankens, 1888,* 94.

32. *Handelskammer Mittelfranken, 1879,* 105.

33. *Handelskammer Mittelfranken, 1879,* 128–29.

34. For an exploration of the intangible advantages offered by such social networks, see Michael Porter, *The Competitive Advantage of Nations* (New York, 1990).

35. Senst, *Metallspielwarenindustrie Nürnberg,* 57–58.

36. See Chandler, *Scale and Scope,* 27.

37. Jürgen Kocka, *Arbeitsverhältnisse und Arbeiterexistenzen: Grundlagen der Klassenbildung im19. Jahrhundert* (Bonn, 1996), 224, 227–28.

38. For discussions of the structure and advantages of flexible specialization, see Michael J. Piore and Charles F. Sabel, *The Second Industrial Divide: Possibilities for Prosperity* (New York, 1984); Charles F. Sabel and Jonathan Zeitlin, eds., *World of Possibilities: Flexibility and Mass Production in Western Industrialization* (Cambridge, 1997); Gary Herrigel, "Large Firms, Small Firms, and the Governance of Flexible Specialization: The Case of Baden Württemberg and Socialized Risk," in *Country Competitiveness: Technology and the Organization of Work,* ed. Bruce Kogut (New York, 1993); Gary Herrigel, "Industry as a Form of Order: A Comparison of the Historical Development of the Machine Tool Industries in the United States and Germany," in *Governing Capitalist Economies: Performance and Control of Economic Sectors* (New York, 1994); Gary Herrigel, *Industrial Constructions: The Sources of German Industrial Power* (New York, 1996); Phillip Scranton, *Endless Novelty: Specialty Production and American Industrialization, 1865–1925* (Princeton, NJ, 1998); Nancy L. Green, *Ready-to-Wear and Ready-to-Work: A Century of Industry and Immigrants in Paris and New York* (Durham, NC, 1997).

39. See Bierer, *Hausindustrielle Kindarbeit,* 21–22, 76–77; Bruno Schönlank, "Die Hausindustrie im Kreise Sonneberg," in *Sozialpolitische Zeit- und Streitfragen,* vol. 8 (Munich, 1884), 12.

40. See Kathleen Canning, *Languages of Labor and Gender: Female Factory Work in Germany, 1850–1914* (Ithaca, NY, 1996); Julie Matthaei, *An Economic History of Women in America: Women's Work, the Sexual Division of Labor, and the Development of Capitalism* (New York, 1982).

41. Senst, *Metallspielwarenindustrie Nürnberg,* 36.

42. See Uhlfelder, *Zinnmalerinnen,* 162–71.

43. *Handelskammer Mittelfranken, 1879,* 121.

44. Rosenhaupt, *Metalspielwarenindustrie,* 44–45.

45. See Lotter, *Gross-Industrie und Gross-Handel,* 134, 146–47, 135–36.

46. Planck, "Nürnberg-Fürth Metallspielwaren-Industrie," 161.

47. See Faber, "Von Dockenmachern und Wildrufdrehern," 66.

48. See Parry-Crooke, *Märklin,* 17, 19.

49. See Hermann Kurtz, *Spielwaren und Puppen, 1913* (Stuttgart, 1913), 4.

50. *Handelskammer Mittelfranken, 1889,* 137–38.

51. See Rosenhaupt, *Metallspielwarenindustrie,* 49.

52. Rosenhaupt, *Metallspielwarenindustrie,* 58.

53. Rosenhaupt, *Metallspielwarenindustrie,* 60.

54. See, for example, Chandler, *The Visible Hand;* Chandler, *Scale and Scope;* Landes, *Unbound Prometheus;* Alexander Gerschenkron, *Economic Backwardness in Historical Perspective* (Cambridge, MA, 1962).

55. Bernd Dornseifer and Jurgen Kocka, "The Impact of the Preindustrial Heritage: Reconsiderations of the German Pattern of Corporate Development in the Late 19th and Early 20th Centuries," *Industrial and Corporate Change* 2, no. 2 (1993): 233–48.

56. Jeffrey R. Fear, *Organizing Control: August Thyssen and the Construction of German Corporate Management* (Cambridge, MA, 2005), 21; see, more generally, 12–31.

57. Herrigel, *Industrial Constructions,* 2. My critique here of Herrigel's work draws on a fuller consideration of the strengths and weaknesses of flexible specialization as a conceptual tool for analyzing business history: see David Hamlin, "Flexible Specialization and the German Toy Industry, 1880–1914," *Social History* 29, no. 1 (Feb. 2004): 30–40.

58. Herrigel, *Industrial Constructions,* 2. The mistaken use of *than* rather than *as* in the phrase quoted suggests that Herrigel's original formulation may have been "are shaped more by the desire to cope with environmental uncertainty than by the imperatives of efficiency." Such a formulation would demonstrate the general inclination to demote economic factors.

59. Herrigel, *Industrial Constructions,* 21.

60. *Handelskammer Mittelfranken, 1883,* 120–21.

61. *Jahresberichte der Königliche Bayerischen Fabriken-Inspectoren, 1886* (Munich, 1887), 55.

62. Dorothea Schmidt, "Die 'Herren der Technik' und die 'feine Hand' der Arbeiterinnen: Mechanisierung und Geschlechterverhältnis," *PROKLA,* 93, vol. 23, no. 4 (1993): 597–98. Christopher Tilly and Charles Tilly make much the same point in *Work under Capitalism* (Boulder, 1998), 156–60.

63. See Dressel, *Entwicklung,* 1–49, 70–72.

64. See Paul Ehrenberg, *Hausindustrie und Heimarbeit in Deutschland und Oesterreich,* vol. 3, *Die Spielwarenhausindustrie im Kreis Sonneberg,* Schriften des Vereins für Sozialpolitik 86 (Leipzig, 1899), 218; Morton Wharton, "Trade between Sonneberg and the United States," *Monthly Consular and Trade Reports,* 6 Apr. 1882.

65. See Phillip Samhammer, "Urtheile über die Spielwaren-Industrie," *Wegweiser für die Spielwarenindustrie und verwandte Branche* 4, no. 45 (10 Feb. 1889): 479.

66. See Ehrenberg, *Spielwarenhausindustrie,* 224–25; Stillich, *Spielwaren-Hausindustrie,* 90–91.

67. Sax, *Hausindustrie Thüringens,* 24.

68. Dressel, *Entwicklung,* 98.

69. For a discussion of the relative value of hierarchical versus market relationships and of the value of long-term market relations, see Lamoreaux, Raff, and Temin, "Beyond Markets and Hierarchies."

70. Landes, *Unbound Prometheus,* 330–31.

71. See Dressel, *Entwicklung,* 60–61.

72. For discussions of incomes, see Rausch, *Sonneberger Spielwaren,* 77–81 (Rausch received financial support from the Sonneberg *Handelskammer*); Stillich, *Spielwaren-Hausindustrie,* 55. Stillich emphasized that the majority of the region's households did not pay the income tax, which was obligatory for those with incomes above six hundred marks per annum.

73. See Bierer, *Hausindustrielle Kindarbeit,* 52–55.

74. See Bierer, *Hausindustrielle Kindarbeit,* 21–22, 46, 76–77; Schönlank, "Haus-industrie," 12; "Heimarbeiterelend," *Die Hilfe* 10, no. 36 (4 Sept. 1904): 5.

75. See Stillich, *Spielwaren-Hausindustrie,* 58.

76. See Rausch, *Sonneberger Spielwaren,* 70–72.

77. Ehrenberg, *Spielwarenhausindustrie,* 265.

78. See Stillich, *Spielwaren-Hausindustrie,* 36.

79. See Meyer, *Erzgebirge,* 25.

80. *Handelskammer Dresden, 1877–1880,* 278–79; *Handelskammer Dresden, 1884,* 134.

81. See Westenberger, *Holzspielwarenindustrie,* 141, 143.

82. See Meyer, *Erzgebirge,* 60.

83. For the lathe works, see Meyer, *Erzgebirge,* 37–39.

84. See *Handelskammer Dresden, 1887,* 197–98.

85. See Westenberger, *Holzspielwarenindustrie,* 41.

86. See Max Schneider, "Über das Wesen und die Entwicklung des Spielzeugs," *Deutsche Spielwaren-Zeitung,* no. 1 (5 Aug. 1909): 5; "Neue Spielwaren," *Deutsche Spielwaren-Zeitung,* no. 6 (20 Mar. 1910): 137.

87. See Max Schneider, "Über das Wesen und die Entwicklung des Spielzeugs," *Deutsche Spielwaren-Zeitung,* no. 1 (5 Aug. 1909): 5; "Der Wert des modernen Spielzeugs," *Rundschau über Spielwaren* 4, no. 136 (10 June 1913): 2117–18. For a discussion of fashion and its many critics, see Schwartz, *Werkbund,* 18–43.

88. "Der Wert des modernen Spielzeugs," *Rundshau über Spielwaren* 4, no. 136 (10 June 1913): 2117–18; "Prophete rechts, Prophete links . . . ," *Deutsche Spielwaren-Zeitung,* no. 6 (20 Mar. 1911): 197–201.

89. "Spielzeug von heute und Kinder von heute," *Deutsche Spielwaren-Zeitung,* no. 11 (1 June 1911): 337; "Neuheiten in Beschäftigungs- und Gesellschafts-spielen," *Deutsche Spielwaren-Zeitung,* no. 5 (20 Feb. 1912): 7–9.

90. "Einige Leipziger Meßneuheiten der Spielwarenindustrie," *Deutsche Spielwaren-Zeitung,* no. 4 (10 Feb. 1913): 5.

91. See "Zinnspielwarenindustrie und Puppenzimmer," *Deutsche Spielwaren-Zeitung,* no. 21 (1 Nov. 1910): 521.

92. See "Deutsche Spielwaren," *Deutsche Spielwaren-Zeitung,* no. 19 (1 Oct. 1910): 463.

93. See *Münchner Neueste Nachrichten* (1 Dec. 1906): 6.

94. See "Vorbildliche Typen für Spielwaren bei der Jahrhundert feier des Münchner Oktoberfest," *Deutsche Spielwaren-Zeitung,* no. 21 (1 Nov. 1910): 515.

95. See Gustav Reder, *Mit Uhrwerk, Dampf und Strom: Vom Spielzeug zur Modelleisenbahn* (Düsseldorf, 1988), 45–48.
96. Völker-Kraemer, *Wie ich zur Teddymutter wurde,* 92–97.
97. See Rausch, *Sonneberger Spielwaren,* 42, 48.
98. "Modelldampfmaschinen und Betriebsmodelle als Spielzeug," *Der Spiel- und Holzwaren Markt* 7, no. 9 (1 May 1911): 1.
99. Huber, "Nürnbergs Spielwaren-Industrie," 112. Huber worked for Gebruder Bing, the largest toy maker.
100. See Kurtz, *Spielwaren und Puppen, 1913.*
101. See "Neue Vorbilder für Luxusspielwaren," *Deutsche Spielwaren-Zeitung,* no. 12 (15 June 1910): 279; "Deutsche Spielwaren," *Deutsche Spielwaren-Zeitung,* no. 12 (1 Oct. 1910): 463.
102. See "Die aktuelle Spielwarenindustrie," *Deutsche Spielwaren-Zeitung,* no. 24 (15 Dec. 1911): 697; *Handelskammer Mittelfranken, 1911,* 153.
103. See Hildebrandt, *Spielzeug,* 285; *Handelskammer Mittelfranken, 1904,* 217.
104. See "Soldatisches Spielzeug," *Rundschau über Spielwaren* 5, no. 167 (20 Apr. 1914): 2772; "Franzözische Spielzeug-Neuheiten," *Deutsche Spielwaren-Zeitung,* no. 1 (2 Jan. 1912): 9.
105. See "Englischer Bazar-Neuheiten," *Deutsche Spielwaren-Zeitung,* no. 9 (1 Dec. 1909): 137–39; "Roosevelt's Spielzeug und Spielzeug-Luftschiffe Populär in Paris," *Deutsche Spielwaren-Zeitung,* no. 12 (15 June 1910): 287.
106. See "Ein deutsches Nordpolentdeckungsspiel," *Deutsche Spielwaren-Zeitung,* no. 10 (15 Dec. 1909): 151; "Französische Spielwaren-Neuheiten," *Deutsche Spielwaren-Zeitung,* no. 1 (2 Jan. 1912): 9.
107. See *Handelskammer München, 1910,* 400.
108. Stillich, *Spielwaren-Hausindustrie,* 44; Rausch, *Sonneberger Spielwaren,* 42.
109. See Rausch, *Sonneberger Spielwaren,* 42; "Bericht über die Leipziger Oster-Messe," *Wegweiser für die Spielwarenindustrie und verwandte Branche* 3, no. 29 (25 Apr. 1888): 300.
110. See "Weite Gewinn," *Wegweiser für die Spielwarenindustrie und verwandte Branche* 4, no. 53 (10 June 1889): 581; "Die Mangel unseres Musterschutzgesetzes," *Wegweiser für die Spielwarenindustrie und verwandte Branche* 5, no. 82 (23 Aug. 1890): 959.
111. Rosenhaupt, *Metallspielwarenindustrie,* 124–28.
112. See "Geschäfts-Bericht der Bayerischen Celluloidwaren-Fabrik vorm. Albert Wacker A.G.," 2 Feb. 1899, BWA V5/V90; "Geschäfts-Bericht der Bayerischen Celluloidwaren-Fabrik vorm. Albert Wacker A.G.," 25 Mar. 1905, BWA V5/V90; "Prospekt über nom. Mark 4000000.-neue auf dem Inhaber lautende Aktien," Nov. 1911, BWA V5/V90.
113. Henry J. Winser, *Monthly Consular and Trade Reports,* 17 Dec. 1880, 278–80.
114. "Die Spielwaren Monat," *Deutsche Spielwaren-Zeitung,* no. 23 (1 Dec. 1911): 719.

115. Henry J. Winser, *Monthly Consular and Trade Reports,* 17 Dec. 1880, 278–80.

Chapter 3

1. "Nünberger Weihnachtsmarkt," *Daheim* 24, no. 11 (17 Dec. 1887): 174.

2. I consciously chose a male subject for this Christmas scene from the early twentieth century. It is clear from press accounts and illustrations in such weekly journals as *Daheim* and *Die Gartenlaube* that, despite all the discursive association of shopping with women, men did at least some Christmas shopping. My fictive comparative accounts of the German Christmas scene at the beginning and end of the period of change under discussion in this book are based on descriptions found in *Daheim, Die Gartenlaube, Berliner Tageblatt, Berliner Lokal-Anzeiger, Vossische Zeitung, Vorwärts, Frankfurter Zeitung, Münchner Neueste Nachrichten, Dresdner Nachrichten,* and so on.

3. See Uwe Spiekermann, *Basis der Konsumgesellschaft: Entstehung und Entwicklung des modernen Kleinhandels in Deutschland 1850–1914* (Munich, 1999); "Display Windows and Window Displays in German Cities of the Nineteenth Century: Towards the History of a Commercial Breakthrough," in *Advertising and the European City: Historical Perspectives,* ed. Clemens Wischermann and Elliott Shore (Aldershot and London, 2000).

4. For a discussion of changing evaluations of vision and the association of visibility, rationality, and truth, see Martin Jay, *Downcast Eyes: The Denigration of Vision in Twentieth-Century French Thought* (Berkeley, 1993).

5. As demonstrated in figure 4, Keilich, a toy specialty store, featured a wide variety of pictures in its ads and described its store as "worthy of seeing."

6. See Noschke and Knerr, *Bauklötze Staunen,* 51–54; Zwijnenberg, *De Geschiedenis van Richter's Anker Steenbouwdozen;* Ernst Meyer-Margreth, "Geschichte des Anker-Steinbaukastens," in *Beiträge zur Deutschen Volks- und Altertumskunde,* vol. 17, ed. Jörgen Bracker (Hamburg, 1978).

7. Cited in Alexander Tille, *Die Geschichte der deutschen Weihnacht* (Leipzig, 1893), 209.

8. Berlin's Christmas market was too large to be held in only one location, but for 90 percent of the nineteenth century, a portion of the market was on the Lustgarten and Schloßplatz around the residential palace of the Hohenzollerns; see "Der Weihnachtsmarkt," *Vorwärts* 21, no. 285 (4 Dec. 1904): 2. Beilage, 1. Dresden's Christmas market was likewise placed in direct relation to the urban residence of the Saxon monarchs; see "Der Christmarkt," *Dresdner Nachrichten* 30, no. 356 (22 Dec. 1885): 2. Hamburg's Christmas market was known as the "Dom" because of its long residence next to the Mariendom; see "Allerlei vom Dom," *Hamburger Nachrichten,* no. 288 (8 Dec. 1902): 1. Beilage, 1. Nuremberg's market was located in the central square with the Schönenbrun, below the medieval residence of the Holy Roman Emperor; see "Nürnberger Weihnachtsmarkt," *Daheim* 24, no. 11 (17 Dec. 1887): 174.

9. "Allerlei vom Tage," *Berliner Illustrirte Zeitung* 3, no. 50 (16 Dec. 1894): 2.

10. Th. von Kramer, "Spielwaren und Spielwarenindustrie," *Bayerische Gewerbe-Zeitung* 3, no. 9 (1890): 193.

11. "Allerlei vom Tage," *Berliner Illustrirte Zeitung* 3, no. 50 (16 Dec. 1894): 2.

12. In the 1850s, the locations for the Berlin Christmas market included the Lustgarten, the Schloßplatz, Breitestrasse (immediately south of the Schloßplatz), and other locations spread from Rosenthaler Tor in the west to Spittelmarkt. To prevent traffic problems, the various locations were gradually moved or closed. First Gertraudtenstrasse was closed, then Rosenthalerstasse in 1871. In either 1873 (*Vossische Zeitung*) or 1880 (*Vorwärts*), the Breitestrasse was closed. In 1884, the Neue Promenade and Burgstrasse were closed. Finally, in 1890, stalls were banned from the Lustgarten and the Schloßplatz. The Christmas market was thenceforth limited to the Petrikirche, Belle Alliance Platz, and a few streets. See "Der Weihnachtsmarkt," *Vorwärts* 21, no. 285 (4 Dec. 1904): 2. Beilage, 1; "Der Weihnachtsmarkt," *Vossische Zeitung,* no. 609 (6 Dec. 1911): 1. Beilage, 1.

13. "Eine Wanderung über den Berliner Weihnachtsmarkt," *Berliner Lokal-Anzeiger* 6, no. 302 (23 Dec. 1888): 2. The *Berliner Illustrirte Zeitung* wrote, "What was self-evident yesterday can already be today impossible—new times have new viewpoints" ("Allerlei vom Tage," *Berliner Illustrirte Zeitung* 3, no. 50 [16 Dec. 1894]: 2). *Vorwärts* added, "[A]s modern development has created new relationships in all parts of economic life, so have new forms developed for the business of Christmas" ("Ein Stück moderner Entwicklung," *Vorwärts* 18, no. 293 [15 Dec. 1901]: 1. Beilage, 1). Uwe Spiekermann (*Basis der Konsumgesellschaft*) dwells repeatedly on the biases built into the contemporary theories of the "historical school" of sociology that assumed small retailers were obsolete vestiges of earlier stages of capitalism.

14. See, for example, Philip G. Nord, *Paris Shopkeepers and the Politics of Resentment* (Princeton, NJ, 1986), 83–88.

15. "Eine Wanderung über den Berliner Weihnachtsmarkt," *Berliner Lokal-Anzeiger* 6, no. 302 (23 Dec. 1888): 2.

16. See StadtAM, Dulten und Jahresmärkte, no. 85, 4 July 1906, An das Kollegium der Gemeindebevollmächtigen; StadtAM, Dulten und Jahresmärkte, no. 85, no. 13459I Stadtbauamt, 11 Aug. 1906.

17. See StadtAM, Dulten und Jahresmärkte, no. 85, 4 July 1906, An das Kollegium der Gemeindebevollmächtigen; StadtAM, Dulten und Jahresmärkte, no. 82/2, "Vortrag des Herrn Dr. Kolbeck," *Münchner Gemeinde Zeitung* 33, no. 95 (28 Nov. 1904): 1554–57. Berlin had a similar experience. See Christa Lorenz, *Berliner Weihnachtsmarkt: Bilder und Geschichten aus 5 Jahrhunderten* (Berlin, 1987), 88.

18. See StadtAM, Dulten und Jahresmärkte, no. 82/2, "Vortrag des Herrn Dr. Kolbeck," *Münchner Gemeinde Zeitung* 33, no. 95 (28 Nov. 1904): 1554–57; "Vom Weihnachtsmarkt," *Vorwärts* 15, no. 296 (18 Dec. 1898): 1. Beilage, 1.

19. See Lorenz, *Berliner Weihnachtsmarkt,* 98–99.

20. See Lorenz, *Berliner Weihnachtsmarkt,* 86–88; "Der Weihnachtsmarkt," *Vossische Zeitung,* no. 609 (6 Dec. 1911): 1. Beilage, 1.

21. See StadtAM, Dulten und Jahresmärkte, no. 82/2, "Vortrag des Herrn Dr. Kolbeck," *Münchner Gemeinde Zeitung* 33, no. 95 (28 Nov. 1904): 1554–57; StadtAM, Dulten und Jahresmärkte, no. 85, *Pasinger Zeitung.*

22. See Robert Gellately, *The Politics of Economic Despair: Shopkeepers and German Politics, 1890–1914* (London and Beverly Hills, 1974), 30–34; Spiekermann, *Basis der Konsumgesellschaft.*

23. See Lorenz, *Berliner Weihnachtsmarkt,* 98–99.

24. "Vom Weihnachtsmarkt," *Vorwärts* 15, no. 296 (18 Dec. 1898): 1. Beilage, 1.

25. See "Der Weihnachtsmarkt," *Vorwärts* 22, no. 287 (8 Dec. 1905): 3. Beilage, 1; "Der Weihnachtsmarkt," *Vorwärts* 18, no. 289 (11 Dec. 1901): 2. Beilage, 1.

26. See Georg Tietz, *Hermann Tietz: Geschichte einer Familie und ihrer Warenhäuser* (Stuttgart, 1965), 30–31, 40–41; Simone Ladwig-Winters, *Wertheim: Geschichte eines Warenhauses* (Berlin, 1997), 20–22; Leo Colze, *Berliner Warenhäuser* (Berlin, 1989), 13–14.

27. See Johannes Wernicke, *Warenhaus, Industrie und Mittelstand* (Berlin, 1911), 16–21, 26; Alfred Wiener, *Das Warenhaus: Kauf-, Geschäfts-, Büro-Haus* (Berlin, 1912), 16–19; Colze, *Berliner Warenhäuser,* 17; Michael Miller, *The Bon Marché: Bourgeois Culture and the Department Store, 1869–1920* (Princeton, NJ, 1981); Richard Sennett, *The Fall of Public Man* (New York, 1976), 141–49.

28. Charles Baudelaire, "The Painter of Modern Life," in *The Painter of Modern Life, and Other Essays,* ed. and trans. Jonathan Mayne (New York, 1964), 9.

29. See Jürgen Schwarz, *Architektur und Kommerz: Studien zur deutschen Kauf- und Warenhausarchitektur vor dem Ersten Weltkrieg am Beispiel der Frankfurter Zeil* (Frankfurt am Main, 1995), 17, 27–32, 129.

30. See Helmut Frei, *Tempel der Kauflust: Eine Geschichte der Warenhauskultur* (Leipzig, 1997), 81. The Tietz store was intended to reach middle- and upper-class customers, though it was eventually reconfigured to be a more "popular" store after the difficulties the store experienced in its first years. The next Tietz store in Berlin, on Alexanderplatz, was built specifically for the more "popular" classes and had considerably less glass and therefore less openness than its Leipzigerstrasse sister store. This chronology would seem to bring into question Schwarz's contention (*Architektur und Kommerz,* 129–32) that the development of department stores in Germany before World War I reflected the class-bound society and customers of the stores. Roughly, he asserts that department store architecture can be read as follows: more openness when appealing to the poor, more closedness and exclusiveness in the architecture when appealing to the upper classes. See Tietz, *Hermann Tietz,* 60–62; Frei, *Tempel der Kauflust,* 82–84.

31. See Max Creutz, *Joseph M. Olbrich: Das Warenhaus Tietz in Düsseldorf* (Berlin, 1909), 14.

32. See Frei, *Tempel der Kauflust,* 93–97.

33. Creutz, *Joseph M. Olbrich,* 15.

34. Simmel, *Philosophy of Money,* 76.

35. Moritz Otto Baron Lasser, "Kaufhaus Oberpollinger, München," in *Bayerns Industrie und Handel,* ed. Adam Guttmann (Nuremberg, 1906), 192.

36. "Weihnachts-Wanderung," *Hamburger Nachrichten,* no. 290 (11 Dec. 1899): 1. Beilage, 1.

37. Gustav Stresemann, *Zeitschrift für die gesamte Staatswirtschaft* (1900), quoted in Frei, *Tempel der Kauflust,* 95.

38. See Ladwig-Winters, *Wertheim,* 31.

39. See *Berliner Lokal-Anzeiger* 6, no. 293 (13 Dec. 1908).

40. See Kurtz, *Spielwaren und Puppen, 1912; Das VEDES Buch, 1904–1954* (Nuremberg, 1954), 2–5.

41. Tille, *Geschichte der Deutschen Weihnacht,* 209.

42. For discussions of the press's construction of the modern city, see Fritzsche, *Reading Berlin;* V. Schwartz, *Spectacular Realities;* Erika Diane Rappaport, *Shopping for Pleasure: Women in the Making of London's West End* (Princeton, NJ, 2000).

43. Fritzsche, *Reading Berlin,* 128.

44. "Weihnachtshändler," *Vorwärts* 25, no. 298 (20 Dec. 1908): 5. Beilage, 1.

45. Alfred Kerr, *Wo liegt Berlin? Briefe aus der Reichhauptstadt* (Berlin, 1997), 539–41.

46. "Berliner Beobachter," *Berliner Lokal-Anzeiger* 18, no. 600 (23 Dec. 1900): 2. Beiblatt, 1.

47. "Goldener Sonntag," *Berliner Tageblatt* 32, no. 645 (20. Dec. 1903): 1. Beiblatt, 1.

48. See "Der silberne Sonntag," *Frankfurter Zeitung* 47, no. 348 (16 Dec. 1902): 2; "Weihnachtsvorzüge," *Kölnische Volkszeitung* 41, no. 1146 (19 Dec. 1900): 2; "Der Christmarkt," *Dresdner Nachrichten* 30, no. 356 (22 Dec. 1885): 2; "Der gestrige 'kupferne Sonntag,'" *Berliner Lokal-Anzeiger* 18, no. 577 (10 Dec. 1900): 2; Kerr, *Wo liegt Berlin?* 335.

49. "Der gestrige Sonntag," *Berliner Tageblatt* 28, no. 629 (11 Dec. 1899): 2.

50. "Silberner Sonntag," *Vossische Zeitung,* no. 583 (13 Dec. 1909): 2. Beilage, 2.

51. "München zur Weihnachtszeit," *Münchner Neueste Nachrichten* 41, no. 591 (24 Dec. 1888): 2.

52. As many people worked Monday through Saturday, it was difficult for numerous families to do their Christmas shopping on days other than Sunday. The regulations preventing Sunday retailing were therefore relaxed before Christmas, giving rise to the traditional "Copper," "Silver," and "Golden" Sundays in the weeks leading up to Christmas.

53. "Weihnachtsstimmung," *Berliner Tageblatt* 30, no. 649 (22 Dec. 1901): 1. Beiblatt, 1.

54. "Schaufenster-Revue über Spielwaren," *Deutsche Spielwaren-Zeitung,* no. 25 (1 Dec. 1913): 9.

55. "Weihnachtswanderung," *Berliner Lokal-Anzeiger* 26, no. 621 (6 Dec. 1908): 2. See also "Schaufenster-Revue über Spielwaren," *Deutsche Spielwaren-Zeitung,* no. 25 (1 Dec. 1913): 9.

56. Arthur Eloesser, *Die Strasse meiner Jugend: Berliner Skizzen* (Berlin, 1987), 33. For an excellent analysis of the relation between modern urbanism, commerce, and speed, see Ricahrd Sennett, *Flesh and Stone: The Body and the City in Western Civilization* (New York and London, 1994), 317–54.

57. For a thorough analysis of the emergence and professional ethos of German advertising, see Ciarlo, "Consuming Race, Envisioning Empire," 114–55; for eye-catching effects and tastefulness, see especially 117–20.

58. "Der silberne Sonntag," *Berliner Tageblatt* 31, no. 635 (15 Dec. 1902): 2; "Spielzeug auf der Strasse," *Berliner Tageblatt* 34, no. 641 (17 Dec. 1905): 1. Beiblatt, 1; "Vom silbernen Sonntag," *Berliner Tageblatt* 33, no. 631 (12 Dec. 1904): 1. Beiblatt, 1.

59. "Spielzeugverkäufer," *Die Gartenlaube* 39, no. 53 (1892): 117.

60. See De Grazia, "Changing Consumption Regimes in Europe, 1930–1970."

61. "Spielzeugverkäufer," *Die Gartenlaube* 39, no. 53 (1892): 119.

62. See "Der verflossene Sonntag," *Berliner Lokal-Anzeiger* 6, no. 297 (18 Dec. 1888): 3. Madame Boulanger was the wife of the wildly popular General Boulanger of France. The general had publicly flirted with the idea of a coup against the Third Republic to be followed by a revanchist war against Germany. At the last moment, Boulanger lost his nerve and fled France with his mistress.

63. See, for example, "Aktuelles Spielzeug," *Berliner Tageblatt* 35, no. 638 (16 Dec. 1906): 1. Beiblatt, 1. The affair involved a drifter who purchased a used captain's uniform and then, on the authority invested in him by that uniform, commandeered a squad of infantry, invaded the town hall of Charlottenberg (a rich suburb outside Berlin), and ordered the mayor to empty the city safe. No question was ever asked of the "captain."

64. Simmel, "Metropolis and Mental Life," 48–49.

65. Gluck, *Popular Bohemia,* 75.

66. Gluck, *Popular Bohemia,* 77.

67. Gluck, *Popular Bohemia,* 103.

68. Wilhelm Krieg, "Spielwaren-Industrie auf Abwegen," *Rundschau des modernen Kunstgewerbes* 9 (1912): 27.

69. "Seine Majestät das Kind," *Berliner Tageblatt* 33, no. 611 (1 Dec. 1904): 1. Beiblatt, 1.

Chapter 4

1. For general background, on John Locke and sensationalist psychology, see Ernst Cassirer, *The Philosophy of the Enlightenment,* trans. Fritz C. A. Koelln and James P. Pettegrove (Boston, 1951), 99–120; Norman Hampson, *The Enlightenment: An Evaluation of Its Assumptions, Attitudes, and Values* (London, 1968), 38–39, 75–76.

2. See Flecken, *Arbeiterkinder,* 156. On the *Philanthropen,* see Friedrich Immanuel Niethammer, *Der Streit des Philanthopinismus und Humanismus in der Theorie des Erziehungs-Unterrichts unsrer Zeit* (Jena, 1808); Herwig Blankertz, *Die Geschichte der Pädagogik: Von der Aufklärung bis zur Gegenwart* (Wetzlar, 1982), 79–82.

3. Taylor, *Sources of the Self,* 368–90; Charles Taylor, *Hegel and Modern Society* (New York, 1979), 1–14.

4. Kai Hammermeister, *The German Aesthetic Tradition* (New York, 2002), 53.

5. Friedrich Schiller, *On the Aesthetic Education of Man,* trans. Reginald Snell (New Haven, CT, 1954), 31–32. On Schiller's aesthetics, see Dieter Henrich, "Beauty and Freedom: Schiller's Struggle with Kant's Aesthetics," in *Essays in Kant's Aesthetics,* ed. Ted Cohen and Paul Guyer (Chicago, 1982); Anthony La Volpa, *Fichte: The Self and the Calling of Philosophy, 1762–1799* (New York, 2001), 218–22, 269–97; Frederick C. Beiser, *Enlightenment, Revolution, and Romanticism: The Genesis of Modern German Political Thought, 1790–1800* (Cambridge, MA, 1992), 84–110; Hammermeister, *German Aesthetic Tradition,* 42–61.

6. Taylor, *Sources of the Self,* 426. For a discussion of the role of art and creativity in defining the moral in Schiller's *Aesthetic Education,* see Taylor, *Sources of the Self,* 422–23.

7. Jean Paul Richter, *Levana; or, On the Doctrine of Education* (Boston, 1864), 83.

8. Richter, *Levana,* 84.

9. See Johann Gottlieb Herder, "Abhandlung über den Ursprung der Sprache," in *Herders Sämmtliche Werke,* ed. Bernhard Suphan, vol. 5 (Berlin, 1772; reprint, 1891); La Volpa, *Fichte;* Frederick C. Beiser, *The Fate of Reason: German Philosophy from Kant to Fichte* (Cambridge, 1987). Jean Paul was quite hostile to Fichte's "apotheosis" of the ego and to German idealism in general. Nonetheless, it seems that the basic conceptualization of ego defining itself against the nonego through the activity of the ego can be found in both Fichte and Jean Paul. For a discussion of Jean Paul's opposition to Fichte and idealism, see Theodor Ballauff and Klaus Schaller, *Pädagogik: Eine Geschichte der Bildung und Erziehung,* vol. 3 (Freiburg and Munich, 1970), 123–34.

10. Richter, *Levana,* 88.

11. For an exploration of this distrust, see Jay, *Downcast Eyes,* 106–10.

12. For a discussion of the demoralizing impact of this orthodoxy and the strenuous efforts made by German thinkers to maintain the possibility of genuine individual freedom in the face of Enlightenment determinism, see La Volpa, *Fichte.* Given his subject, La Volpa naturally emphasizes the allure of the moral autonomy posited by Immanuel Kant; but, clearly, the creative possibilities of the human imagination likewise exerted a strong attraction.

13. Voltaire, *Philosophical Dictionary,* quoted in Jay, *Downcast Eyes,* 83.

14. Richter, *Levana,* 85.

15. Richter, *Levana,* 85.

16. Richter, *Levana,* 88, 86.

17. Richter, *Levana,* 88–89.

18. Richter, *Levana,* 178–79.

19. See Bertha v. Marenholtz-Bülow, *Erinnerungen an Friedrich Fröbel* (Kassel, 1876); *Gesammelte Beiträge zum Verständniß der Fröbel'schen Erziehungsidee* (Kassel, 1877).

20. See Anne Taylor Allen, "Spiritual Motherhood: German Feminists and the Kindergarten Movement, 1848–1911," *History of Education Quarterly,* fall 1982, 319–39; *Feminism and Motherhood in Germany, 1800–1914* (New Brunswick, NJ, 1991).

21. It is telling that the article on Fröbel in the *Enzyklopädisches Handbuch*

der Pädagogik in 1905 primarily discussed Fröbel's metaphysics before dismissing them. See Friedrich Zimmer, "Fröbel, Friedrich Wilhelm August," in *Enzyklopädisches Handbuch der Pädagogik,* ed. W. Rein (Langensalza, 1905), 3:157–59.

22. See Ballauff and Schaller, *Pädagogik,* 3:103; Friedrich Fröbel, *Friedrich Froebel: A Selection from His Writings,* trans. Irene Lilley (Cambridge, 1967), 2, 7–13, 15, 17–18, 20; Robert B. Downs, *Friedrich Froebel* (Boston, 1978), 41.

23. Friedrich Fröbel, *Die Menschen-Erziehung* (Vienna and Leipzig, 1883), 4.

24. See Ballauff and Schaller, *Pädagogik,* 3:103–5. Particularly interesting in this respect is the link between Fröbel and Novalis.

25. Fröbel, *Menschen-Erziehung,* 15–16, 33–34.

26. Friedrich Fröbel, *Friedrich Froebel's Pedagogics of the Kindergarten, or His Ideas Concerning the Play and Playthings of the Child,* trans. Josephine Jarvis (New York, 1895), 24.

27. See Taylor, *Sources of the Self,* 374–77.

28. Fröbel, *Pedagogics of the Kindergarten,* 30.

29. See Fröbel, *Pedagogics of the Kindergarten,* 32–236.

30. See, for example, Julius Schaller, *Das Spiel und die Spiele: Ein Beitrag zur Psychologie und Pädagogik wie zum Verständniß des geselligen Lebens* (Weimar, 1861), 128; A. Döring, *System der Pädgogik im Umriss* (Berlin, 1894), 45–46; Eleonore Heerwart, "Fröbelsche Spiel- und Beschäftigungsmittel in der Schule," in *Enzyklopädisches Handbuch der Pädagogik,* 3:164–65; Max Reischle, "Spiel," in *Enzyklopädisches Handbuch der Pädagogik,* 8:704–5; E. Ackermann, "Spiel und Arbeit," in *Enzyklopädisches Handbuch der Pädagogik,* 8:720–23.

31. See, for example, August Köhler, *Die Praxis des Kindergartens: Theoretisch-praktische Anleitung zum Gebrauche der Fröbel'schen Erziehungs- und Bildungsmittel in Haus, Kindergarten und Schule* (Weimar, 1871), 20–22; Bertha v. Marenholtz-Bülow, *Gesammelte Beiträge zum Verständniß der Fröbel'schen Erziehungsidee* (Kassel, 1877), 8–11; Max Enderlin, "Das Spielzeug in seiner Bedeutung für die Entwicklung des Kindes," in *Beiträge zur Kinderforschung und Heilerziehung* (Langensalza, 1907), 4–9.

32. E. Ackermann, "Spiel und Arbeit," in *Enzyklopädisches Handbuch der Pädagogik,* 8:720.

33. Paul Natorp, *Sozialpädagogik* (Paderborn, 1974), 240.

34. Gustav Siegert, "Spielerisch, Spielsucht," in *Enzyklopädisches Handbuch der Pädagogik,* 8:725–26.

35. Because of the structure of the German (and Swiss) university system, most early psychologists worked from chairs of philosophy. As Thomas Nipperdey wrote, "Psychology grew in the shadow of philosophy" (*Deutsche Geschichte, 1866–1918,* 1:630–32).

36. See Karl Groos, *Die Spiele der Menschen* (Jena, 1899), 4–7. Groos rehashes his argument about the play of animals at the beginning of his book and uses it as a guide to understand the play of humans. See also Karl Groos, *Das Seelenleben des Kindes* (Berlin, 1904).

37. See Groos, *Spiele der Menschen,* 120–22.

38. See Groos, *Spiele der Menschen,* 360.

39. Schaller, *Spiel und Spiele,* 128.

40. Döring, *System der Pädagogik,* 45–46.

41. Karin Hausen, in a thought-provoking essay on the naturalization of gender roles ("Family and Role Division," 71), notes that in the course of the nineteenth century, strategies of child development increasingly aimed to foster precisely the "sexual characteristics" that were presumed to be natural to each sex. It may be added that an effort to use education to cultivate naturally occuring characteristics would be absurd unless humans were assumed to have inalienable, but deeply buried, natures—much as Jean Paul Richter and Fröbel asserted in their discussions of the "ideal man."

42. Enderlin, "Das Spielzueg in seiner Bedeutung," 17, 6.

43. Marenholtz-Bülow, *Gesamelte Beiträge,* 8–9.

44. Max Reischle, *Das Spielen der Kinder in seinem Erziehungswert* (Göttingen, 1897), 22–23.

45. Simmel, *Philosophy of Money,* 449.

46. "Durfelds Lehrmittel und Spielwaren," *Wegweiser für die Spielwarenindustrie und verwandte Branche* 4, no. 44 (25 Jan. 1889): 474.

47. "Von den Spielwaren auf der Leipziger Herbstmesse 1911," *Rundschau über Spielwaren* 3, no. 73 (10 Sept. 1911): 983.

48. "Das Spielzeug als Erzieher," *Deutsche Spielwaren-Zeitung,* no. 22 (15 Nov. 1911): 659. The title is perhaps a play on the title of Langbehn's popular nationalist book, *Rembrandt als Erzieher.*

49. Max Schneider, "Ueber den geistigen Wert des Spielzeugs," *Deutsche Spielwaren-Zeitung,* no. 3 (1 Sept. 1909): 39.

50. See "Das Spielzeug als Erzieher," *Deutsche Spielwaren-Zeitung,* no. 22 (15 Nov. 1911): 659.

51. "Ein deutsches Nordpolentdeckungsspiel," *Deutsche Spielwaren-Zeitung,* no. 10 (15 Dec. 1909): 151.

52. "Spielzeug von heute und Kinder von heute," *Deutsche Spielwaren-Zeitung,* no. 11 (1 June 1911): 339.

53. See, for example, "Pädagogik und Spielwarenindustrie," *Deutsche Spielwaren-Zeitung,* no. 4 (12 Feb. 1914): 3–5.

54. "Neuheiten," *Deutsche Spielwaren-Zeitung,* no. 7 (20 Mar. 1914): 9–11.

55. "Modelldampfmaschinen und Betriebsmodelle als Spielzeug," *Der Spiel- und Holzwaren-Markt* 7, no. 9 (1 May 1911): 1.

56. *Vossische Zeitung,* no. 624 (9 Dec. 1913): 3. Beilage, 6.

57. *Kind und Kunst,* 1904.

58. *Münchner Neueste Nachrichten* (1 Dec. 1891): 3.

59. Enderlin, "Das Spielzeug in seiner Bedeutung," 10.

60. Reischle, *Das Spielen der Kinder,* 28.

61. Döring, *System der Pädagogik,* 53–54.

62. For the cultural significance of Nietzsche, see Steven E. Aschheim, *The Nietzsche Legacy in Germany, 1890–1990.* (Berkeley, 1992), 17–127; Laird McLeod Easton, *The Red Count: The Life and Times of Harry Kessler* (Berkeley, 2002), 41–46; Maciuika, *Before the Bauhaus,* 38–42.

63. Kevin Repp, *Reformers, Critics, and the Paths of German Modernity: Anti-Politics and the Search for Alternatives, 1890–1914* (Cambridge, MA, 2000).

64. Despite Nietzsche's well-known distaste for Romanticism, this is not an absurd combination, for Nietzsche clearly shared some similar concerns with the early Romantics. See Adrian Del Caro, *Nietzsche contra Nietzsche: Creativity and the Anti-Romantic* (Baton Rouge, 1989).

65. See Gerhard Kratzsch, *Kunstwart und Dürerbund: Ein Beitrag zur Geschichte der Gebildeten im Zeitalter des Imperialismus* (Göttingen, 1969); Jennifer Jenkins, "The Kitsch Collections and *The Spirit in the Furniture:* Cultural Reform and National Culture in Germany," *Social History* 21, no. 2 (May 1996): 123–42; Repp, *Reformers, Critics, and the Paths of German Modernity,* 275–77.

66. Ferdinand Avenarius, "Vor Weihnachten," *Der Kunstwart* 16, no. 5 (Dec. 1902): 287.

67. Ferdinand Avenarius, "Dresdener Spielzeug," *Der Kunstwart* 16, no. 12 (Mar. 1903): 666.

68. Ferdinand Avenarius, "Spielzeug," *Der Kunstwart* 19, no. 6 (Dec. 1905): 303–4.

69. See, for example, Ferdinand Avenarius, "Gegen die 'Kunst im Leben des Kindes,'" *Der Kunstwart* 20, no. 5 (Dec. 1906): 303; "Gegen den Phantasiemord durch Spielzeug," *DerKunstwart* 23, no. 6 (Dec. 1909): 450–51. See also Joseph Lux, "Vom Spielzeug," *Der Kunstwart* 21, no. 6 (Dec. 1907): 424–25.

70. Oberbayern is the alpine, southern region of Bavaria.

71. Ferdinand Avenarius, "Spielzeug," *Der Kunstwart* 19, no. 6 (Dec. 1905): 303–4.

72. Ferdinand Avenarius, "Spielzeug," *Der Kunstwart* 19, no. 6 (Dec. 1905): 304.

73. Joseph Lux, "Vom Spielzeug," *Der Kunstwart* 21, no. 6 (Dec. 1907): 424–25.

74. Lux's criticism of training "specialists" before the "human" replays the conflict between *Philanthropen* and humanists, as well as between the *Realschulen* and the classical gymnasium. Were people to be trained to be useful or to be as fully human as possible?

75. Ferdinand Avenarius, "Gegen den Phantasiemord durch Spielzeug," *Der Kunstwart* 23, no. 6 (Dec. 1909): 450–51.

76. See Sigrid Randa, *Alexander Koch: Publizist und Verleger in Darmstadt; Reformen der Kunst und des Lebens um 1900* (Worms, 1990), 44–45, 87–88, 183–84.

77. "Künstlerische Kinder-Spielsachen aus München," *Deutsche Kunst und Dekoration* 13 (1904): 151.

78. Hans Boesch, "Die Puppe als Spielzeug für das Kind," *Kind und Kunst* 1, no. 3 (Dec. 1904): 102.

79. "Künstlerisches Spielzeug," *Dekorative Kunst* 9, no. 3 (Dec. 1905): 129.

80. For an excellent discussion, see Maciuika, *Before the Bauhaus,* 65–67.

81. See "Dresdner Spielzeug," *Der Kunstwart* 16, no. 12 (Mar. 1903): 666; "Künstlerische Holzspielsachen," *Dekorative Kunst* (Sept. 1903): 454.

82. "Dresdner Spielzeug," *Kind und Kunst* 1, no. 1 (Oct. 1904): 31.

83. Oskar Bie, "Kind und Kunst," *Neue Deutsche Rundschau* 15, no. 11 (Nov. 1904): 1407.

84. "Zu unseren Abbildungen," *Deutsche Kunst und Dekoration* 12 (1903): 400.

85. "Dresdner Spielzeug," *Der Kunstwart* 16, no. 12 (Mar. 1903): 667.

86. "Neue Erzgebirgische Spiel- und Gebrauchs-Sachen: Nach Entwürfen v. Geschwister Kleinhempel.," *Kind und Kunst* 1, no. 3 (Dec. 1904): 121.

87. "Spielsachen und Holzarbeiten der Geschwister Kleinhempel," *Dekorative Kunst* 7, no. 5 (Feb. 1904): 201–8.

88. "Künstlerisches Spielzeug," *Dekorative Kunst* 9, no. 3 (Dec. 1905): 129–34.

89. See W. Schölermann, "Neue Holzspielsachen," *Dekorative Kunst* (Dec. 1908): 125–27; Wilhelm Krieg, "Wie zeigt sich der künstlerische Einfluss in der Spielwaren-Industrie?" *Rundschau des modernen Kunstgewerbes* 13 (1914): 51.

90. Lux, "Vom Spielzeug," *Der Kunstwart* 21, no. 6 (Dec. 1907): 424–25.

91. "Die Zukunft der deutschen Spielwarenindustrie," *Rundschau des modernen Kunstgewerbes* 8 (1911): 31.

92. Wilhelm Krieg, "Spielwaren-Industrie auf Abwegen," *Rundschau des modernen Kunstgewerbes* 9 (1912): 27–30.

93. A. Wendt, "Neuere Spielwaren," *Rundschau des modernen Kunstgewerbes* 10 (1912): 34.

94. Wilhelm Krieg, "Wie zeigt sich der künstlerische Einfluss in der Spielwaren-Industrie?" *Rundschau des modernen Kunstgewerbe* 13 (1914): 49–52.

95. Frida Schanz, "Spielzeug aus dem Erzgebirge," *Daheim* 43, no. 11 (22 Dec. 1906): 8.

96. "Münchner Künstler-Kaulitz-Puppen," *Deutsche Kunst und Dekoration* 27 (1911): 84.

97. "Neue Puppen," *Dekorative Kunst* (Feb. 1909): 239–40.

98. See "Die Kaulitz-Puppen," *Deutsche Spielwaren-Zeitung*, no. 4 (10 Feb. 1912): 13–15.

99. "Weihnachtsfreuden und Weihnachtssorgen," *Daheim* 18, no. 10 (3 Dec. 1881): 155. For toys as a source of joy, not education, see "Eine Burg für den Weihnachtstisch," *Daheim* 23, no. 11 (11 Dec. 1886): 174–75; "Weihnachtsfreuden," *Daheim* 25, no. 12 (22 Dec. 1888): 1. Beilage, 1.

100. Friedrich Schäller, "Die Sprache des Kindes," *Daheim* 21, no. 44 (1 Aug. 1885): 694.

101. Hans von Spielberg, "Nachträgliche Weihnachtsplauderei vom Meergreis," *Daheim* 26, no. 19 (8 Feb. 1890): 294. The name *Spielberg* translates as "play mountain." In the case of this author, I am not certain if the name is merely ironic or a nom de plume.

102. "Der Nürnberger Zinnsoldat," *Daheim* 27, no. 12 (20 Dec. 1890): 186.

103. Dr. Nordenfels, "Modernes Spielzeug," *Berliner Lokal-Anzeiger* 10, no. 593 (18 Dec. 1892): 1.

104. Julius Stinde, "Der Sinn der Spiele," *Daheim* 33, no. 30 (24 Apr. 1897): 482.

105. "Haben wir noch Puppenmütter," *Daheim* 35, no. 12 (10 Dec. 1898): 7.

106. "Erfinderwitz im Spielzeug," *Berliner Lokal-Anzeiger* 18, no. 600 (23 Dec. 1900): 3. Beiblatt, 1.

107. "Weihnachtsspielzeug," *Berliner Tageblatt* 32, no. 646 (21 Dec. 1903): 2.

108. "Aktuelles Spielzeug," *Berliner Tageblatt* 35, no. 638 (16 Dec. 1906): 1. Beiblatt, 1.

109. "Weihnachtsspielzeug," *Berliner Tageblatt* 38, no. 643 (19 Dec. 1909): 1. Beiblatt, 1.

110. "Neues künstlerisches Kinderspielzeug," *Vossische Zeitung,* no. 590 (17 Dec. 1909): 1. Beiblatt, 2–3.

111. "Künstlerisches Spielzeug," *Berliner Lokal-Anzeiger* 29, no. 628 (10 Dec. 1911): 8. Beiblatt, 2–3.

112. "Die Lokomotive als Spielzeug," *Vorwärts* 28, no. 297 (20 Dec. 1911): 1. Beilage, 1.

113. Antonie Steimann, "Moderne Puppen I. Puppen von der Puppenausstellung zu Berlin," *Daheim* 45, no. 9 (28 Nov. 1908): 25–26.

114. "Charackterpuppen," *Daheim* 49, no. 9 (30 Nov. 1912): 26–27.

115. E. Müller, "Geschmack, Erziehung und Charakter," *Deutsche Kunst und Dekoration* 32 (1913): 97–98.

116. Wilhelm Krieg, "Wie zeigt sich der künstlerische Einfluss in der Spielwaren-Industrie?" *Rundschau des modernen Kunstgewerbes* 13 (1914): 52.

117. See also Rohkrämer, *Eine Andere Moderne?* 32–226. More generally, see Jeffries, *Imperial Culture,* 191–223.

118. See Edgar Beckers, *Das Beispiel Alfred Lichtwark: Eine Studie zum Selbstverständnis der Reformpädagogik* (Cologne, 1976), 26, 32, 40–41.

119. Alfred Lichtwark, "Rede auf dem 1. Kunsterziehungstag, 1901," in *Eine Auswahl seiner Schriften,* vol. 1 (Berlin, 1917), 3.

120. Konrad Lange, *Die künstlerische Erziehung der deutschen Jugend,* 2nd ed. (Darmstadt, 1900), 21.

121. Lange, *Künstlerische Erziehung,* 26–29.

122. Lange, *Künstlerische Erziehung,* 31–32.

123. Konrad Lange, "Ästhetische Bildung," in *Enzyklopädisches Handbuch der Pädagogik,* 1:291–92.

124. Konrad Lange, "Kunst und Spiel in ihrer erzieherischen Bedeutung," *Kind und Kunst* 1, no. 1 (Oct. 1904): 4–7.

125. See Maciuika, *Before the Bauhaus,* 25–68.

126. For an excellent discussion of fashion in German discourse, see Schwartz, *Werkbund,* 29–40. See also Silva Bovenschein, ed., *Die Listen der Mode* (Frankfurt am Main, 1986); Friedrich Theodor Vischer, *Mode und Cynismus: Beiträge zur Kenntniss unserer Culturformen und Sittenbegriffe* (Stuttgart, 1879).

127. Schwartz, *Werkbund,* 62–66.

128. Georg Simmel, "Das Problem des Stiles," *Dekorative Kunst* (Apr. 1908): 313–14.

129. Mark Jarzombek refers to the influence that Schiller and his aesthetic education thesis exerted on the ideology of the *Kunstgewerbereformbewegung* and the

Werkbund: "it was also around this time [1905] that the *Kunstgewerbe* first began to reflect a sense of confidence in the possibility that Schillerian ideals of an enlightened society could be transcribed onto twentieth century industrialized modernity" (Mark Jarzombek, "The Discourses of a Bourgeois Utopia, 1904–1908, and the Founding of the Werkbund," in *Imagining Modern German Culture, 1889–1910,* ed. Francoise Forster Hahn [Washington, DC, 1996], 127; see 127–45).

130. Georg Simmel, "Das Problem des Stiles," *Dekorative Kunst* (Apr. 1908); 314.

131. See Ralph Mathew Leck, *Georg Simmel and the Soul of German Culture, Geist-Politik: Fin de Siècle to the Great War* (Ann Arbor, MI, 1995), 61–65.

132. Simmel, *Philosophy of Money,* 71.

133. Simmel, *Philosophy of Money,* 73.

134. Simmel, *Philosophy of Money,* 257.

135. Simmel, *Philosophy of Money,* 460.

136. Jurgen Habermas, "Georg Simmel on Philosophy and Culture: Postscript to a Collection of Essays," trans. Mathieu Deflem, from *Texte und Kontexte* (Frankfurt am Main, 1991).

137. See Jay, *Downcast Eyes,* 149–209. See also the analysis of Karl Marx in Ward, *Weimar Surfaces,* 191–92.

138. "Die Leipziger Messe," *Deutsche Spielwaren-Zeitung,* no. 6 (20 Mar. 1910): 135; "Spielwaren auf der Leipziger Messe," *Deutsche Spielwaren-Zeitung,* no. 7 (5 Apr. 1910): 167.

139. "Die Spielzeug-Kritik von grünem Tisch und Künstlerspielzeug," *Rundschau über Spielwaren* 3, no. 84 (10 Jan. 1912): 1142.

140. "Wie man's nicht machen soll.," *Deutsche Spielwaren-Zeitung,* no. 3 (1 Feb. 1912): 7.

141. "Spielzeug, das Erwachsenen gefällt," *Rundschau über Spielwaren* 3, no. 73 (10 Sept. 1911): 988.

142. Steimann, "Moderne Puppen," *Daheim* 45, no. 9 (28 Nov. 1908): 25.

143. Gustav Rudi, "Moderne Holzspielsachen," *Rundschau über Spielwaren* 4, no. 109 (10 Sept. 1912): 1587.

144. *Handelskammer Mittelfranken, 1908,* 183. See also *Handelskammer Mittelfranken, 1910,* 234–35.

145. *Handelskammer Sonneberg, 1909,* 66–67.

146. "Spielwaren auf der Leipziger Messe," *Deutsche Spielwaren-Zeitung,* no. 7 (5 Apr. 1910): 167.

147. *Handelskammer Mittelfranken, 1911,* 205–7.

148. The *Deutsche Spielwaren-Zeitung* noted that Marion Kaulitz sold dolls to the crown princess of Romania, the queen of Bulgaria, and the German empress ("Die Kaulitz Puppen," *Deutsche Spielwaren-Zeitung,* no. 4 [10 Feb. 1912]: 13–14).

149. "Von der Thüringischen Puppenfabrikation," *Der Spiel- und Holzwaren-Markt* 7, no. 5 (1 Mar. 1911): 45–46.

150. *Handelskammer Sonneberg, 1908,* 96.

151. *Handelskammer Sonneberg, 1910,* 81; *Handelskammer Sonneberg, 1911,* 78.

152. *Handelskammer Oberbayern, 1910,* 400.

153. "Einige Leipziger Meßneuheiten der Spielwarenindustrie," *Deutsche Spielwaren-Zeitung,* no. 4 (10 Feb. 1913): 5.

154. For a description of the role played by the Café des Westens in Berlin's intellectual life, see Roy F. Allen, *Literary Life in German Expressionism and the Berlin Circles* (Ann Arbor, MI, 1983).

155. Käthe Kruse, *Das große Puppenspiel: Mein Leben* (Duisburg, 1992), 78.

156. Kruse, *Das große Puppenspiel,* 79.

157. Kruse, *Das große Puppenspiel,* 86.

158. "Kruse-Puppen," *Deutsche Kunst und Dekoration* 29 (1911): 277.

159. Kruse, *Das große Puppenspiel,* 86.

160. See Kruse, *Das große Puppenspiel,* 89–93.

161. Kruse, *Das große Puppenspiel,* 93.

162. See Kruse, *Das große Puppenspiel,* 94–99. Concerning opening a workshop, Kruse wrote: "I was suddenly a merchant [*Kaufmann*]. A woman, who is a merchant, is nonsense. The fact that the word 'businesswoman' [*Kauffrau*] could never find its way into our language shows that" (99).

163. "Charakterpuppen," *Daheim* 49, no. 9 (30 Nov. 1912): 27; "Neue Puppenmoden," *Daheim* 50, no. 10 (6 Dec. 1913): 26.

164. See Kruse, *Das große Puppenspiel,* 105.

165. "Neue Puppenmoden," *Daheim* 50, no. 10 (6 Dec. 1913): 26.

166. By way of example, my own daughter received a Käthe Kruse doll as a gift. Thank you again, Herr and Frau Hellmann.

Chapter 5

1. It is instructive to consider the numerous appearances of Friedrich Naumann in Kevin Repp's *Reformers, Critics, and the Paths of German Modernity,* a work that explicitly seeks to address reform efforts separate from Naumann's.

2. Maciuika, *Before the Bauhaus,* 14.

3. Theodor Heuß, *Friedrich Naumann: Der Mann, das Werk, die Zeit* (Stuttgart and Berlin, 1937), 258–59. See also Friedrich Naumann, *Neudeutsche Wirtschaftspolitik* (Berlin, 1902), 5; *Demokratie und Kaisertum* (Berlin, 1905), 67–79, 214; *Die wirtschaftliche und politische Folgen der Bevölkerungs-Vermehrung* (Berlin, 1903), 8.

4. See Naumann, *Demokratie,* 214–17.

5. Naumann, *Folgen der Bevölkerungs-Vermehrung,* 8. In this respect, Naumann was a forerunner of Robert Reich; see Reich's *The Work of Nations* (New York, 1991).

6. See Friedrich Naumann, *Kunst und Volk* (Berlin, 1902), 6.

7. See Maciuika, *Before the Bauhaus;* Schwartz, *Werkbund.*

8. Naumann, *Neudeutsche Wirtschaftspolitik* (Berlin, 1906), 107; see also p. 20.

9. Naumann, *Neudeutsche Wirtschaftspolitik* (1906), 104. Werner Sombart made the same point in *Kunstgewerbe und Kultur* (Berlin, 1908), 68.

10. Naumann, *Neudeutsche Wirtschaftspolitik* (1906), 370.

11. See, for example, "Ruckblick auf das I. Semester 1889," *Wegweiser für die Spielwarenindustrie und verwandte Branche* 4, no. 56 (25 July 1889): 617.

12. Heuß, *Friedrich Naumann,* 258; Sombart, *Kunstgewerbe und Kultur,* 45–48.

13. Hermann Muthesius, "Die Bedeutung des Kunstgewerbes," *Dekorative Kunst,* Feb. 1907, 182–83.

14. See Heuß, *Friedrich Naumann,* 258.

15. Theodor Fischer, "Die Veredelung der gewerblichen Arbeit in Zusammenwirken von Kunst, Industrie und Handwerk," in *Die Veredelung der gewerblichen Arbeit in Zusammenwirken von Kunst, Industrie und Handwerk: Verhandlung des Deutschen Werkbundes zu München am 11. und 12. Juli 1908* (Leipzig, 1947), 4–8.

16. Peter Jessen, "Der Werkbund und die Grossmmächte der Deutschen Arbeit," in *Jahrbuch des deutschen Werkbundes 1912* (Jena, 1912), 3.

17. See Maciuika, *Before the Bauhaus;* Hermann Muthesius, in *Die Veredelung der gewerblichen Arbeit,* 48–49.

18. See, for example, Wolf Dohrn, "Die Kulturpflicht des Käufers," *Die Hilfe* 14, no. 8 (23 Feb. 1908): 123.

19. See Kenneth D. Barkin, *The Controversy over German Industrialization, 1890–1902* (Chicago, 1970), 159–85.

20. My discussions of *Reich* financial policy are drawn from Witt, *Finanzpolitik.*

21. *Handelskammer Mittelfranken, 1909,* 31–32, 154–55.

22. *Handelskammer Mittelfranken, 1901,* 77–78; *Handelskammer Mittelfranken, 1905,* xxvii. See also *Handelskammer Mittelfranken, 1906,* 206–7.

23. *Metallarbeiter-Zeitung,* no. 28 (1911): 226, quoted in *Dokumente zur Geschichte der Arbeiterbewegung in Nürnberg,* vol. 3, *Vom Fall des Sozialistengesetzes bis zur Novemberrevolution, 1890–1918,* ed. Elfi Müller (Nuremberg, 1985), 178–80.

24. "Die Nürnberger Spielwarenindustrie vor einem Streik?" *Deutsche Spielwaren-Zeitung,* no. 14 (15 July 1911): 427–29.

25. See *Fabrik-Inspectoren, 1911,* 133; "Geschäfts-Bericht für das Jahr 1911," *Verband bayerischer Metallindustrieller,* StadtAN C7/V 1840; quote from "Lohnbewegung in der Nürnberger Blechspielwarenindustrie," *Deutsche Spielwaren-Zeitung,* no. 16 (15 Aug. 1911): 491–93.

26. See "Die Neuregelung der Lohnfrage in der Nürnberger Metallspielwaren-Industrie," *Rundschau über Spielwaren* 3, no. 70 (10 Aug. 1911): 927.

27. *Handelskammer Mittelfranken, 1911,* 67–68.

28. "Gibt es ein Mittel?" *Deutsche Spielwaren-Zeitung,* no. 23 (1 Nov. 1912): 3.

29. For a sectoral breakdown of money wages, see Desai, *Real Wages in Germany,* 109–10.

30. A minor mystery is contained in figure 12. Despite the extraordinarily high level of earnings per share indicated in figure 11, the price-earnings (PE) ratios in figure 12 are comparatively low. The PE ratio should measure market expecta-

tions of a company's future growth potential. In the case of the three toy firms publicly listed, the market appears to have discounted the remarkably high current profits in the expectation of plodding future growth. Though they were far less profitable, both Norddeutsche Lloyd (with PE ratios in 1904 and 1907 of 21.2 and 48.3, respectively) and Leipziger Gummi-Waaren Fabrik (with corresponding PE ratios of 88.2 and 69.5, respectively) registered far higher PE ratios than toy makers (based on figures in the *Handbuch der deutschen Aktien-Gesellschaften; Jahrbuch der deutschen Börsen* [Berlin u. Leipzig, 1904 and 1907]).

31. See "Geschäftsbericht für das Jahr 1913," *Verband bayerischer Metallindustrieller,* StadtAN C7/1840.

32. "Geschäftes-Bericht der Nürnberger Metall- und Lackierwaren-Fabrik vorm. Gebrüder Bing Aktiengesellschaft," 13 Feb. 1913, BWA V05/V151.

33. Planck, "Nürnberger-Fürther Metallspielwaren-Industrie," 119.

34. Gustav Rudi, "Aus der Nürnberger Schiffspielzeug-Industrie," *Rundschau über Spielwaren* 3, no. 89 (22 Feb. 1912): 1241.

35. See Planck, "Nürnberger-Fürther Metallspielwaren-Industrie," 118–19; Parry-Crooke, *Märklin,* 17.

36. See, for example, "Geschäftsbericht der Bayerischen Celluloidwaren Fabrik vorm. Albert Wacker A.G.," BWA V5/V90. Bing asserted that it was able to overcome the rising labor costs of 1904 through the introduction of new products (*Handelskammer Mittelfranken, 1904,* 201–2).

37. See "Prospekt über Mark 4,500,000.—Aktien der Nürnberger Metall- und Lackierwaren-Fabrik vorm. Gebrüder Bing Aktiengesellschaft," June 1906, BWA V05/V151; "Prospekt über M. 900,000.—neue Aktien der Nürnberger Metall- und Lackierwarenfabrik vorm. Gebrüder Bing Aktiengesellschaft," Dec. 1908, BWA V05/V151; "Prospekt über Mark 1,300,000.—neue Aktien der Nürnberger Metall- und Lackierwarenfabrik vorm. Gebrüder Bing Aktiengesellschaft," Sept. 1913, BWA V05/V151; "Prospekt. Bayerische Celluloidwaren-Fabrik vormals Albert Wacker A.-G.," Mar. 1906, BWA V5/V90.

38. The employment figures are drawn from Rosenhaupt, *Metallspielwarenindustrie,* 60.

39. The employment figures are drawn from Estelmann, "Nürnberger Spielwaren-Herstellung," 117.

40. Karl Brandstätter, "Die Produktions- und Absatzverhältnisse der Nürnberger-Fürther Spielwaren-industrie unter Berücksichtigung ihrer Zusammenschlussbestrebungen" (PhD diss., Julius-Maximilians-Universität, Würzburg, 1921), 9, StadtAN Av 6503.4.

41. See Uhlfelder, *Zinnmalerinnen,* 12.

42. See *Handelskammer Mittelfranken, 1899,* 273; *Handelskammer Mittelfranken, 1900,* 356; *Handelskammer Mittelfranken, 1904,* 217; *Handelskammer Mittelfranken, 1906,* 210; *Handelskammer Mittelfranken, 1909,* 144; "Bericht über die General-Versammlung am 23. Mov. 1911," Verband Zinnfiguren-Fabrikanten, StadtAN C7/V 3894.

43. See *Fabrik-Inspectoren, 1897,* 299–300; *Fabrik-Inspectoren, 1898,* 292–93; *Fabrik-Inspectoren, 1906,* 168–69. George Schoenner instituted a compulsory sav-

ings program for its employees. Contributions of at least fifty pfennig weekly were mandated; at the end of the year, Schoenner would match 20 percent of the employee's annual savings (*Fabrik-Inspectoren, 1898,* 293). The largest maker of tin figures, Heinrichsen, offered "individual older workers" rent subsidies of up to 120 marks (*Fabrik-Inspectoren, 1898,* 293).

44. *Handelskammer Mittelfranken, 1901,* 301.

45. See *Handelskammer Mittelfranken, 1904,* 217; *Handelskammer Mittelfranken, 1909,* 144; *Handelskammer Mittelfranken, 1911,* 153.

46. See *Handelskammer Mittelfranken, 1904,* 230, 321.

47. See "Vereinigen sich die Metallspielwaren-Fabrikanten?" *Deutsche Spielwaren-Zeitung,* no. 11 (15 Mar. 1912): 3; "Auf dem Weg zum Verband," *Deutsche Spielwaren-Zeitung,* no. 13 (15 Apr. 1912): 3–5.

48. See "Bericht über die General-Versammlung am 23. Mov. 1911," Verband Zinnfiguren-Fabrikanten, StadtAN C7/V 3894.

49. *Handelskammer Mittelfranken, 1906,* 206–7.

50. For example, in 1909, Märklin offered stripped-down toy train stations for between 7.10 and 11.70 marks. A more elaborate version cost between 23.75 and 32.50 marks. Of course, the child must already have "invested" in a toy train and a certain length of track before a toy train station was reasonable. See Höllerer, *Märklin,* 36, 154. That price did not disappear as an important fact even among technology toys can be seen by the introduction in the middle and late 1890s of stripped-down economy toy trains (colloquially named *Storchbeine* [stork legs]), starting from 7.00 marks. See Gustav Reder, *Mit Uhrwerk, Dampf und Strom: Vom Spielzeug zur Modelleisenbahn* (Düsseldorf, 1988), 30–32.

51. See Beck, "Die Fabrikindustrie Nürnbergs," 455.

52. See *Handbuch der deutschen Aktien-Gesellschaften, 1907/1908,* 869; *Handbuch der deutschen Aktien-Gesellschaften, 1911/1912,* 1089; *Handbuch der deutschen Aktien-Gesellschaften, 1912/1913,* 1118; *Handbuch der deutschen Aktien-Gesellschaften, 1913/1914,* 1124; *Handbuch der deutschen Aktien-Gesellschaften, 1914/1915,* 1049.

53. "Amerika und die deutsche Spielwarenindustrie," *Deutsche Spielwaren-Zeitung,* no. 7 (1 Apr. 1911), 223; "Spielwarenfabrikation, Exporteurverband, und Kommisionäre," *Rundschau über Spielwaren* 3, no. 56 (20 Mar. 1911): 762.

54. See *Hausindustrie und Heimarbeit in Deutschland und Oesterreich,* vol. 1, *Süddeutschland und Schlesien,* Schriften des Vereins für Sozialpolitik 84 (Leipzig, 1899), v; "Deutsche Heimarbeitausstellung," *Vorwärts* 23, no. 13 (17 Dec. 1906): 2. Beilage, 1; Edgar Jaffé, "Die Hausindustrie und ihre gesetzliche Regelung," *Süddeutsche Monatshefte* 3, no. 5 (May 1906): 563.

55. K. Marx, *Capital,* 410.

56. K. Marx, *Capital,* 465–66.

57. K. Marx, *Capital,* 473.

58. K. Marx, *Capital,* 477–78.

59. Robert Liefmann, *Über Wesen und Formen des Verlags (der Hausindustrie): Ein Beitrag zur Kenntnis der volkwirtschaftlichen Organisationsformen* (Freiburg, 1899), 16–27.

60. See "Vom Heimarbeiterschitz-Kongress," *Münchner Neueste Nachrichten* 57, no. 120 (12 Mar. 1904): 1–2.

61. *Protokoll der Verhandlung des ersten Allgemeinen Heimarbeiterschutz-Kongresses* (Berlin, 1904), 105–6.

62. *Protokoll,* 106.

63. *Protokoll,* 70.

64. *Protokoll,* 92.

65. *Protokoll,* 92.

66. "Heimarbeit-Ausstellung," *Vorwärts* 23, no. 20 (25 Jan. 1906): 2. Beilage, 1.

67. *Protokoll,* 76.

68. "Der Deutsche Heimarbeit-Ausstellung," *Vorwärts* 23, no. 11 (14 Jan. 1906): 4. Beilage, 1.

69. See Carl E. Schorske, *German Social Democracy, 1905–1917: The Development of the Great Schism* (Cambridge, MA, 1955), 1–27.

70. See *Protokoll,* 4–6, 38–41.

71. *Protokoll,* 88, 91.

72. *Protokoll,* 99.

73. *Protokoll,* 67.

74. *Protokoll,* 95, 116.

75. See "Das Hausarbeitergesetz und die Spielwarenindustrie," *Deutsche Spielwaren-Zeitung,* no. 18 (20 Aug. 1912): 13–17.

76. Zygmunt Bauman, *Post-modernity and Its Discontents* (New York, 1997). Baumann suggests that the quintessential ambition of modernity is the effort to exert control in the interests of security, whereas the quintessential ambition of postmodernity is freedom at the cost of increased risk.

77. *Protokoll,* 76–77. Braun's theses recommended that there be more female inspectors (as part of the larger argument that more inspectors were required), and it referred to female *Heimarbeiterinnen* forced into prostitution as part of the larger thesis that the nation would not be harmed should *Heimarbeit* disappear.

78. See *Protokoll,* 76–77, 92.

79. *Protokoll,* 103–5.

80. *Protokoll,* 42.

81. *Protokoll,* 41.

82. *Protokoll,* 116–17.

83. *Protokoll,* 133–36.

84. See *Hausindustrie und Heimarbeit in Deutschland und Österreich,* v, vi.

85. Liefmann, *Wesen und Formen,* 3.

86. Bierer, *Hausindustrielle Kinderarbeit.*

87. Käthe Graebel, *Die Heimarbeit: Das jungste Problem des Arbeiterschutzes* (Jena, 1913).

88. *Protokoll,* 85–86.

89. *Protokoll,* 109–11, 114. See also Edgar Jaffé, "Die Hausindustrie und ihre gesetzliche Regelung," *Südduetsche Monatshefte* 3, no. 5 (May 1906): 565–67; Eugen Katz, "Schutz den Heimarbeitern!" *Die Hilfe* 10, no. 12 (20 Mar. 1904): 4.

90. Edgar Jaffé, "Die Hausindustrie und ihre gesetzliche Regelung," *Süddeutsche Monatshefte* 3, no. 5 (May 1906): 564.

91. "Deutsche Reichstag," *Münchner Neueste Nachrichten* 64, no. 558 (29 Nov. 1911): 2.

92. E. Francke, "Die gesetzliche Regelung der Hausindustrie," *Soziale Praxis: Zentralblatt für Sozialpolitik* 15, no. 25 (22 Mar. 1906): 642–45. Francke was also a chair of the General *Heimarbeiter* Protection Congress of 1904.

93. *Protokoll,* 124–25.

94. Elizabeth Gottheiner, "Die Heimarbeiterschutz-Kongress," *Frankfurter Zeitung* 48, no. 72 (12 Mar. 1904): 1.

95. Graebel, *Heimarbeit,* 21–37. This was not an uncommon point of view; see also Wilbrandt in *Protokoll,* 109.

96. Ehrenberg, *Spielwarenhausindustrie,* 242.

97. See Sax, *Hausindustrie Thüringens,* 55–56; Meyer, *Erzgebirge,* 50; Bierer, *Hausindustrielle Kindarbeit,* 123.

98. See Eugen Katz, "Schutz den Heimarbeitern!" *Die Hilfe* 10, no. 12 (20 Mar. 1904): 4.

99. Graebel, *Heimarbeit,* 18.

100. Friedrich Naumann, "Die Not der Hausindustrie," *Die Hilfe* 16, no. 19 (15 May 1910): 297.

101. For a discussion of "colonial fantasies," see Zantop, *Colonial Fantasies,* 1–16.

102. Stillich, *Spielwaren-Hausindustrie,* 16.

103. L. Von Weise, "Was wird mit der deutschen Heimarbeitsaustellung in Berlin beabsichtigt," in *Soziale Fortschritt, Hefte und Flugschriften für Volkswitschaft und Sozialpolitik* (Leipzig, 1906), 2.

104. *Protokoll,* 125.

105. See Elizabeth Gottheiner, "Der Heimarbeiterschutz-Kongress," *Frankfurter Zeitung* 48, no. 72 (12 Mar. 1904): 1; "Was ist Heimarbeit," *Vorwärts* 23, no. 18 (23 Jan. 1908): 3–4.

106. Adolf Fleischmann, *Kathedersozialismus,* 21.

107. See *Handelskammer Sonneberg, 1900,* III; "Die Spielwarenheimarbeit," *Deutsche Spielwaren-Zeitung,* no. 18 (15 Sept. 1911): 567; Westenberger, *Holzspielwarenindustrie,* 124. Dr. Bernhard Westenberger had a very close relationship with the Dresden *Handelskammer,* and I am therefore treating him as a representative of the industry.

108. See "Heimarbeit in Mittelfranken: Referat des Herrn Kommerzienrat Seiler," June 1910, StadtAN D4/149; *Handelskammer Mittelfranken, 1910,* 158–59.

109. See Westenberger, *Holzspielwarenindustrie,* 98.

110. *Handelskammer Dresden, 1901,* 213–14. See also Westenberger, *Holzspielwarenindustrie,* 32.

111. See Bernhard Westenberger, "Die deutsche Spielwarenindustrie und der Weltmarket," *Deutsche Spielwaren-Zeitung,* no. 6 (1 Mar. 1914): 3; Westenberger, *Holzspielwarenindustrie,* 31.

112. Westenberger, *Holzspielwarenindustrie,* 31.

113. See *Handleskammer Mittelfranken, 1906,* 210.

114. Dressel, *Entwicklung,* 104.

115. See *Handelskammer Sonneberg, 1900,* IV; "Spielwarenheimarbeit und Krankenversicherung," *Deutsche Spielwaren-Zeitung,* no. 15 (1 Aug. 1911): 465–66.

116. Under Bismarck's health insurance program, employees paid 4 percent of wages into a local fund to cover health expenses, while employers paid 2 percent of wages into the fund.

117. *Handelskammer Sonneberg, 1900,* III.

118. Westenberger, *Holzspielwarenindustrie,* 112. See also "Unsere Hausindustrie," *Deutsche Spielwaren-Zeitung,* no. 11 (1 June 1910): 255–57.

119. See *Handelskammer Mittelfranken, 1905,* 179.

Conclusion

1. Quoted in James J. Sheehan, *German Liberalism in the Nineteenth Century* (Chicago, 1978), 39.

2. Detlev J. K. Peukert, *Max Webers Diagnose der Moderne* (Göttingen, 1989), 64.

3. Peukert, *Diagnose,* 5–26.

4. Gluck, *Popular Bohemia,* 7. This approach to German history may be seen, for example, in Peter Fritzsche's *Reading Berlin* and Janet Ward's *Weimar Surfaces.*

5. Gluck, *Popular Bohemia,* 83–84.

Bibliography

Archival Sources

Bayerische Wirtschaftsarchiv [BWA], V05/V151, V05/V90.
Geheimes Staatsarchiv, Preussischer Kulturbesitz [GSPK], HA Rep. 120 BB VII 1, no. 23, Part 1; HA Rep. 120 C VIII 1, no. 109.
Stadtarchiv München [StadtAM], Dulten und Jahresmärkte, nos. 82/2, 84, 85.
Stadtarchiv Nürnberg [StadtAN], Av 6381.4, 6463.4, 6503.4; C7/V 1840, 3778, 3894, 4925; D4/149, 228.

Contemporary Periodicals

Bayerische Gewerbe-Zeitung (Nuremberg), 1888–1902.
Bayerische Handelszeitung (Handelskammer Oberbayern, Munich), 1886–88, 1899, 1905, 1910–14.
Berliner Illustrirte Zeitung, 1890–1913.
Berliner Lokal-Anzeiger, 1888, 1891–92, 1899–1905, 1907–9, 1911.
Berliner Tageblatt, 1898–1912.
Daheim (Berlin), 1865–1914.
Dekorative Kunst (Verlagsanstalt F. Bruckmann, A.-G., Munich), 1900–1910.
Der Kunstwart (Munich), 1887–1914.
Der Spiel- und Holzwaren-Markt (Leipzig), 1911–14.
Deutsche Kunst und Dekoration (Verlaganstalts Alexander Koch, Darmstadt), 1889–1914.
Deutsche Spielwaren-Zeitung (Nuremberg), 1909–14.
Deutsches Handles-Archiv: Zeitschrift für Handel und Gewerbe (Reichsamt des Innern, Verlag von Ernst Siegfried Mittler und Sohn, Berlin), 1892–95.
Die Gartenlaube (Verlag von Ernst Keil, Leipzig), 1875–1910.
Die Hilfe (Berlin), 1900–1912.
Die Kinder-Gartenlaube (Verlag der Kinder-Gartenlaube, Nuremberg), 1888–91.
Dresdner Nachrichten, 1885–86.
Frankfurter Zeitung, 1895–1904.
Hamburger Nachrichten, 1899, 1902.
Innen-Dekoration (Verlag Alexander Koch, Darmstadt), 1902.
Kind und Kunst (Verlagsanstalt Alexander Koch, Darmstadt), 1904–6.

Kölnische Volkszeitung, 1889–91, 1899–1902.
Kunstgewerbeblatt (Verlag E. A. Seemann, Leipzig), 1892–1910.
Münchner Neueste Nachrichten, 1886, 1888, 1891, 1896, 1901, 1904, 1906, 1911–13.
Neue Deutsche Rundschau (Verlag S. Fischer, Berlin), 1900–1910.
Neue Preussische-Zeitung (Berlin), 1906–11.
Nordbayerische Zeitung (Verlag von F. Willmy, Nuremberg and Fürth), 1904–10.
Pädagogisches Magazin (Langensalza), 1892–1914.
Rundschau des modernen Kunstgewerbes (Verlag Trenkler, Leipzig), 1910–14.
Rundschau über Spielwaren, Sportartikel und Galanteriewaren (Nuremberg and Plauen), 1909–14.
Soziale Praxis: Zentralblatt für Sozialpolitik (Berlin), 1905–6.
Süddeutsche Monatshefte (Munich), 1906.
Technische-Industrielle Rundschau (Nuremberg), 1896.
Vorwärts, Berliner Volksblatt, 1891–1913.
Vossische Zeitung (Berlin), 1909–13.
Wegweiser für die Spielwarenindustrie und verwandte Branche (Berlin), 1886–1904.
Zeitschrift für Kinderforschung (Langensalza), 1900–1914.

Government Publications

Bericht der Handels- und Gewerbekammer zu Dresden. Dresden: Druck von S. Heinrich, 1882–1911.
Bericht der Handels- und Gewerbekammer zu Sonneberg. Sonneberg, 1890–1914.
Bericht über Handel und Industrie von Berlin nebst einer Uebersicht über die Wirksamkeit des Aeltesten-Kollegium. Berlin, 1890–93, 1898.
Berliner Jahrbuch für Handel und Industrie: Bericht der Ältesten der Kaufmannschaft von Berlin, 1903–1904. Berlin: Verlag von Georg Reimer, 1904–5.
Jahresberichte der Gewerbe- und Handelskammer Mittelfrankens. Nuremberg, 1878–1913.
Jahresberichte der Gewerbe- und Handelskammer Oberbayern. Munich, 1892–1913.
Jahresberichte der Königliche Bayerischen Fabriken-Inspectoren, 1879–1913. Munich: Theodor Ackermann, Königlicher Hof-Buchhändler, 1880–1914.
Monatliche Nachweise über den auswartigen Handel des deutschen Zollgebiets. Berlin, 1892–1914.
Monthly Consular and Trade Reports. Washington, DC: United States Department of Commerce and Labor, 1875–90.
Neue Gesetz- und Verordnungen-Sammlung für das Königreich Bayern. Vols. 38–39. Munich: C. H. Beck'sche Verlagsbuchhandlung, 1913–14.
Preussisch-deutsch Gesetz-Sammlung, 1806–1904. Vol. 1.2, *Reichs- und Staatsfinanzwesen, Kommunalabgabgen.* 4th ed. Düsseldorf: L. Schwann, Königliche Hofbuchhandlung, 1905.
Statistisches Jahrbuch für den Freistaat Bayern, 1919. Vol. 14. Munich: J. Lindauersche Universitäts-Buchhandlung, 1919.
Vierteljahrshefte zur Statistik des Deutschen Reiches. Berlin: Kaiserlichen statistischen Amt. Verlag Puttkammer und Mühlbrecht, 1898–1914.

Published Primary Sources

Ackermann, Eduard. *Die häusliche Erziehung.* 2nd ed. Langensalza: Hermann Beyer und Söhne, 1895.

Ahlers-Hestermann, Friedrich. *Pause vor dem dritten Akt.* Hamburg: Gesellschaft der Bücherfreunde zu Hamburg e.V., 1975.

Beck, L. C. *Bayerns Grossindustrie und Grosshandel.* Nuremberg: Commissions-Verlag der Sigm. Soldan'schen Hofbuch- und Kunsthandlung, 1895.

———. "Die Fabrikindustrie Nürnbergs." In *Festschrift zur 40. Haupt-versammlung des Vereins Deutscher Ingenieure in Nürnberg vom 11.–15. Juni 1899.* Nuremberg: E. Nister, 1899.

Benda, Johannes. *Puppenspiele.* 2nd ed. Marburg: N. G. Elwert'sche Verlagsbuchhandlung, 1921.

Bierer, Willy. *Die Hausindustrielle Kinderarbeit im Kreise Sonneberg: Ein Beitrag zur Kritik des Kinderschutzgesetzes.* Tübingen: Verlag von J. C. B. Mohr, 1913.

Bilder aus der deutschen Heimarbeit. Vol. 63/64, *Soziale Fortschritt, Hefte und Flugschriften für Volkswirtschaft und Sozialpolitik.* Leipzig: Felix Dietrich Verlag, 1906.

Bodelschwingh, Friedrich v. *Aus einer hellen Kinderzeit.* Bethel bei Bielefeld: Verlagshandlung der Anstalt Bethel, 1948.

Boveri, Margaret. *Verzweigungen: Eine Autobiographie.* Munich: R. Piper, 1977.

Brecht, Arnold. *Aus Nächster Nähe, Lebenserinnerungen 1884–1927.* Stuttgart: Deutsche Verlags-Anstalt, 1966.

Bunsen, Marie v. *Die Welt in der ich Lebte, Erinnerungen aus glücklichen Jahren 1860–1912.* Leipzig: Koehler und Amelang, 1929.

Die Veredelung der gewerblichen Arbeit im Zusammenwirken von Kunst, Industrie, und Handwerk: Verhandlung des Deutschen Werkbundes zu München am 11. und 12. Juli 1908. Leipzig: R. Viogtländers Verlag, 1947.

Doberer, Kurt Karl. "Der Pfennig war das Mark der Währung." In *Kindheit im Kaiserreich: Erinnerungen an vergangene Zeiten,* ed. Rudolf Pörtner. Düsseldorf: Bechtermünz Verlag, 1998.

Dokumente zur Geschichte der Arbeiterbewegung in Nürnberg. Vol. 3, *Vom Fall des Sozialisten gesetzes bis zur Novemberrevolution, 1890–1918,* ed. Elfi Müller. Nuremberg: Selbstverlag des Stadtrats zu Nuremberg, 1985.

Döring, A. *System der Pädadgogik im Umriss.* Berlin: R. Gaertners Verlagsbuchhandlung, 1894.

Ehrenberg, Paul. *Hausindustrie und Heimarbeit in Deutschland und Oesterreich.* Vol. 3, *Die Spielwarenhausindustrie im Kreis Sonneberg.* Schriften des Vereins für Sozialpolitik 86. Leipzig: Duncker und Humblot, 1899.

Eloesser, Arthur. *Die Strasse meiner Jugend: Berliner Skizzen.* Berlin: Das Arsenal, 1987. 1st ed., 1919.

Enderlin, Max. "Das Spielzeug in seiner Bedeutung für die Entwicklung des Kindes." In *Beiträge zur Kinderforschung und Heilerziehung.* Langensalza: Hermann Beyer und Söhne, 1907.

Enzyklopädisches Handbuch der Pädagogik. Ed. W. Rein. 10 vols. Langensalza: Hermann Beyer und Söhne, 1903–11.

Ermatinger, Emil. *Richte des Lebens: Geschichte einer Jugend.* Frauenfeld: Verlag Huber, 1943.

Fallada, Hans. *Damals bei uns Daheim: Erlebtes, Erfahrenes und Erfundenes.* Stuttgart: Rowohlt Verlag GmbH, 1958.

Festschrift zur 40. Haupt-versammlung des Vereins Deutscher Ingenieure in Nürnberg vom 11.–15. Juni 1899. Nuremberg: E. Nister, 1899.

Fontane, Theodor. *Cécile.* Frankfurt am Main: Verlag Ullstein, 1996.

———. *Die Poggenpuhls.* Munich: Deutscher Taschenbuch Verlag, 1974.

———. *Meine Kinderjahre.* Munich: Nymphenburger Verlagshandlung GmbH, 1985.

Formanek-Brunnell, Miriam. *Made to Play House: Dolls and the Commercialization of American Girlhood, 1830–1930.* New Haven, CT: Yale University Press, 1993.

Fröbel, Friedrich. *Die Menschen-Erziehung.* Vienna and Leipzig: A. Pichler's Witwe und Sohn, 1883.

———. *Friedrich Froebel: A Selection from His Writings.* Ed. Irene Lilley. Cambridge: Cambridge University Press, 1967.

———. *Friedrich Froebel's Pedagogics of the Kindergarten, or His Ideas concerning the Play and Playthings of the Child.* Trans. Josephine Jarvis. New York: D. Appelton, 1895.

———. *Froebel's Letters to His Wife and Others.* Ed. Arnold H. Heinemann. Boston: Lee and Shepard, 1893.

Gaulke, Johannes. *Die Ästhetische Kultur des Kapitalismus.* Berlin: Freier Literarische Verlag, 1909.

Gerhard, Adele. *Das Bild meines Lebens.* In *Das Werk Adele Gerhards als Ausdruck einer Wendezeit,* ed. Melitte Gerhard. Bern and Munich: Francke Verlag, 1963.

Glatzer, Dieter, and Ruth Glatzer, eds. *Berliner Leben, 1900–1914: Eine historische Reportage aus Errinerungen und Berichten.* Vol. 1. West Berlin: Verlag das europäische buch, 1986.

Gradl, Joann Baptist. "Als Kreuzberg noch kaiserlich war." In *Kindheit im Kaiserreich: Erinnerungen an vergangene Zeiten,* ed. Rudolf Pörtner. Düsseldorf: Bechtermünz Verlag, 1998.

Graebel, Käthe. *Die Heimarbeit: Das jungste Problem des Arbeiterschutzes.* Jena: G. Fischer, 1913.

Grassmann, Günther. "Man liebte russische Literatur und fürchtete die 'russische Dampfwalze.'" In *Kindheit im Kaiserreich: Erinnerungen an vergangene Zeiten,* ed. Rudolf Pörtner. Düsseldorf: Bechtermünz Verlag, 1998.

Groos, Karl. *Das Seelenleben des Kindes.* Berlin: Verlag von Reuther und Reichard, 1904.

———. *Die Spiele der Menschen.* Jena: Verlag von Gustav Fischer, 1899.

———. "Unser Bedürfnis nach ästhetischer Kultur." *Der Kunstwart* 19, no. 14 (Apr. 1906).

Guttmann, Adam, ed. *Bayerns Industrie und Handel.* Nuremberg: J. L. Schrag, 1906.

Handbuch der deutschen Aktien-Gesellschaften: Jahrbuch der deutschen Börsen. Berlin and Leipzig: Verlag für Börsen- und Finanzliteratur A. G., 1897–1914.

Handbuch der süddeutschen Aktien-Gesellschaften. Berlin, Leipzig, and Hamburg: Verlag für Börsen- und Finanzliteratur A. G., 1910.

Hausindustrie und Heimarbeit in Deutschland und Oesterreich. Vol. 1, *Süddeutschland und Schlesien.* Schriften des Vereins für Sozialpolitik 84. Leipzig: Duncker und Humblot, 1899.

Herder, Johann Gottlieb. "Abhandlung über den Ursprung der Sprache." In *Herders Sämmtliche Werke,* ed. Bernhard Suphan, vol. 5. Berlin: Weidmannsche Buchhandlung, 1772. Reprint, 1891.

———. "Plastik." In *Herders Sämmtliche Werke,* ed. Bernhard Suphan, vol. 8. Berlin: Weidmannsche Buchhandlung, 1891.

Hildebrandt, Paul. *Das Spielzeug im Leben des Kindes: Reichillustriertes Haus- und Familienbuch.* Berlin: S. Soehlke Nachfolger, 1904.

Hippel, Ernst von. *Meine Kindheit im kaiserlichen Deutschland.* Meisenheim am Glan: Verlag Anton Hain, 1975.

Hopf, Angela, and Andreas Hopf, eds. *Geliebtes Kind! Elternbriefe aus Zwölf Jahrhunderten.* Munich: Nymphenburger Verlagshandlung GmbH, 1987.

Jahrbuch des Deutschen Werkbundes. Berlin: Eugen Diedrichs, 1912–13.

Jeanmaire, Claude. *Bing, die Modellbahnen unserer Grossväter.* Villigen: Buchverlag für Eisenbahn- und Strassenbahnliteratur, 1972.

Kästner, Erich. *Als ich ein kleiner Junge war.* Berlin: Cecilie Dressler Verlag, 1957.

Kerr, Alfred. *Wo liegt Berlin? Briefe aus der Reichshauptstadt.* Ed. Günter Rühe. Berlin: Aufbau-Verlag, 1997.

Key, Ellen. *The Century of the Child.* New York: Arno, 1909.

Köhler, August. *Die Praxis des Kindergartens: Theoretisch-praktische Anleitung zum Gebrauche der Fröbel'schen Erziehungs- und Bildungsmittel in Haus, Kindergarten und Schule.* Vol. 1. Weimar: Hermann Böhlau, 1871.

Kruse, Käthe. *Das große Puppenspiel: Mein Leben.* Duisburg: Verlag Puppen und Spielzeug, 1992.

Kurtz, Hermann. *Spielwaren und Puppen, 1912.* Reprint, Stuttgart: Spielwaren Kurtz Stuttgart, 1983.

———. *Spielwaren und Puppen, 1913.* Stuttgart, 1913.

Lange, Konrad. "Ästhetische Bildung." In *Enzyklopädisches Handbuch der Pädagogik,* vol. 1, ed. W. Rein. Langensalza: Hermann Beyer und Söhne, 1903.

———. *Die künstlerische Erziehung der deutschen Jugend.* 2nd ed. Darmstadt: Arnold Bergsträsser, 1900.

———. "Kunst und Spiel in ihrer erzieherischen Bedeutung." *Kind und Kunst* 1, no. 1 (Oct. 1904): 4–7.

Liefmann, Robert. *Über Wesen und Formen des Verlags (der Hausindustrie): Ein Beitrag zur Kenntnis der volkswitschaftlichen Organisationsformen.* Freiburg: Verlag von J. C. B. Mohr, 1899.

Linde, Ernst. *Kunst und Erziehung.* Leipzig: Friedrich Brandstetter, 1901.

Lotter, Hans. *Gross-Industrie und Gross-Handel von Nürnberg-Fürth und*

Umgebung. Nuremberg: Selbstverlag des Herausgebers und in Commission der Joh. Phil. Raw'schen Buchhandlung, 1894.

Mann, Thomas. *Bekentnisse des Hochstaplers Felix Krull.* Frankfurt am Main: Verlag S. Fischer, 1998.

———. *Buddenbrooks.* New York: Vintage, 1961.

———. *Doctor Faustus: The Life of the German Composer Adrian Leverkühn.* New York: Alfred A. Knopf, 1975.

———. "Kinderspiele." In *Essays,* vol. 1, *Frühlingssturm 1893–1918.* Frankfurt am Main: Verlag S. Fischer, 1993.

Marenholtz-Bülow, Bertha v. *Erinnerungen an Friedrich Fröbel.* Kassel: Verlag Georg H. Wigand, 1876.

———. *Gesammelte Beiträge zum Verständniß der Fröbel'schen Erziehungsidee.* Kassel: Verlag Georg H. Wigand, 1877.

Marx, Friedrich. *Gewerbe- und Handelsgeschichte der Stadt Fürth.* Fürth: Druck und Verlag von Michael Krauß, 1890.

Marx, Karl. *Capital.* Vol. 1. In *Collected Works,* vol. 35. New York, 1996.

Moderne Kultur: Ein Handbuch der Lebensbildung und des guten Geschmacks. Vol. 1, *Die Häuslichkeit,* ed. Eduard Heyck. Stuttgart and Leipzig: Deutsche Verlags-Anstalt, 1907.

Mühsam, Erich. *Tagebücher (1910–1924).* Munich: Deutscher Taschenbuch Verlag, 1994.

Müller, Elfi. *Dokumente zur Geschichte der Arbeiterbewegung in Nürnberg.* Vol. 3, *Vom Fall des Sozialistengesetzes bis zur Novemberrevolution 1890–1918.* Nuremberg: Selbstverlag der Stadt Nürnberg, 1985.

Natorp, Paul. *Sozialpädagogik.* Paderborn: Ferdinand Schöningh, 1974.

Naumann, Friedrich. *Demokratie und Kaisertum.* Berlin: Buchverlag der "Hilfe," 1905.

———. *Die Erziehung zur Personlichkeit im Zeitalter des Grossbetriebes.* Berlin: Buchverlag der "Hilfe," 1904.

———. *Die wirtschaftliche und politische Folgen der Bevölkerungs-Vermehrung.* Berlin: Buchverlag der "Hilfe," 1903.

———. *Kunst und Volk.* Berlin: Buchverlag der "Hilfe," 1902.

———. *Neudeutsche Wirtschaftspolitik.* Berlin: Buchverlag der "Hilfe," 1902.

———. *Neudeutsche Wirtschaftspolitik.* Berlin: Buchverlag der "Hilfe," 1906.

———. *Volksschule und industrielle Entwicklung.* Berlin: Buchverlag der "Hilfe," 1902.

Niethammer, Friedrich Immanuel. *Der Streit des Philanthropinismus und Humanismus in der Theorie des Erziehungs-Unterrichts unsrer Zeit.* Jena: F. Frommann, 1808.

Planck, Ernst. "Die Nürnberger-Fürther Metallspielwaren-Industrie mit besonderer Berücksichtigung der Optischen Metallspielwaren-Industrie." PhD diss., Friedrich-Alexander-Universität, Erlangen, 1922.

Pörtner, Rudolf, ed. *Kindheit im Kaiserreich: Erinnerungen an vergangene Zeiten.* Düsseldorf: Bechtermünz Verlag, 1998.

Posener, Julius. *Fast so alt wie das Jahrhundert.* Berlin: Siedler Verlag, 1990.

Protokoll der Verhandlungen des ersten Allgemeinen Heimarbeiterschutz-

Kongresses. Berlin: Verlag der Generalkommission der Gwerkschaften Deutschlands, 1904.

Rathenau, Walter. *Zur Kritik der Zeit.* 3rd ed. Berlin: S. Fischer Verlag, 1912.

Reischle, Max. *Das Spielen der Kinder in seinem Erziehungswert.* Göttingen: Vandenhoeck und Ruprecht, 1897.

Richter, Jean Paul. *Levana; or, On the Doctrine of Education.* Boston: Ticknor and Fields, 1864.

Rosenhaupt, Karl. *Die Nürnberger-Fürther Metallspielwarenindustrie in geschichtlicher und sozialpolitischer Beleuchtung.* Stuttgart: J. G. Cotta, 1907.

Rousseau, Jean Jacques. *Emile; or, On Education.* New York: Basic Books, 1979.

Sala, George Augustus. *Notes and Sketches of the Paris Exhibition.* London: Tinsley Brothers, 1868.

Sax, Emmanuel. *Die Hausindustrie in Thüringen.* Vol. 1, *Das Meininger Oberland.* 2nd ed. Jena: Verlag von Gustav Fischer, 1885.

Schaller, Julius. *Das Spiel und die Spiele: Ein Beitrag zur Psycholgie und Pädagogik wie zum Verständniß des geselligen Lebens.* Weimar: Hermann Böhlau, 1861.

Scheffler, Karl. *Berlin—ein Stadtschicksal.* Berlin: Fannei und Walz, 1989. 1st ed., 1910.

Schenkendorf, E. von, and Dr. F. A. Schmidt. *Über Jugend und Volksspiele.* Hannover and Linden: Verlag von Manz und Lange, 1892.

Schiller, Friedrich. *On the Aesthetic Education of Man.* Trans. Reginald Snell. New Haven, CT: Yale University Press, 1954.

Schönlank, Bruno. "Die Hausindustrie im Kreise Sonneberg." *Sozialpolitische Zeit- und Streitfragen,* vol. 8. Munich, 1887.

Simmel, Georg. "Das Problem des Stiles." *Dekorative Kunst,* Apr. 1908, 307–16.

———. "The Metropolis and Mental Life." In *Classic Essays on the Culture of Cities,* ed. Richard Sennett. New York: Appleton-Century-Crofts, 1969.

———. *The Philosophy of Money.* Trans. Tom Bottomore and David Frisby. 2nd ed. London and New York: Routledge, 1990.

Sombart, Werner. *Die deutsche Volkswirtschaft im neunzehnten Jahrhundert.* 2nd ed. Berlin: Verlag Georg Bondi, 1909.

———. *Gewerbewesen.* Leipzig: G. F. Göschen'sche Verlagsanstalt, 1904.

———. *Kunstgewerbe und Kultur.* Berlin: Marquadt und Co. Verlagsanstalt GmbH, 1908.

———. *Luxury and Capitalism.* Trans. W. R. Dittmar. Ann Arbor: University of Michigan Press, 1913. Reprint, 1967.

———. *Wirtschaftspolitik und Mode: Ein Beitrag zur Theorie der Modernen Bedarfsgestaltung.* Grenzfragen des Nerven- und Seelenlebens. Wiesbaden: Verlag von J. F. Bergmann, 1902.

Tieck, Johann Ludwig. "Der Gestiefelte Kater." In *German Plays of the Nineteenth Century,* ed. Thomas Moody Campbell. New York: F. S. Crofts, 1946.

Tietz, Georg. *Hermann Tietz: Geschichte einer Familie und ihrer Warenhäuser.* Stuttgart: Deutsche Verlags-Anstalt, 1965.

Troeltsch, Walter. *Über die neuesten Veränderungen im deutschen Wirtschaftsleben.* Stuttgart: Verlag von W. Kohlhammer, 1899.

———. *Volkswirtschaftliche Betrachtungen über die Mode.* Marburg: N. G. Elwert'sche Verlagsbuchhandlung, 1912.

Uhlfelder, Wilhelm. *Die Zinnmalerinnen in Nürnberg und Fürth: Eine wirtschaftliche Studie über Heimarbeit.* Leipzig: Duncker und Humblot, 1899.

Vischer, Friedrich Theodor. *Mode und Cynismus: Beiträge zur Kenntniss unserer Culturformen und Sittenbegriffe.* Stuttgart: Verlag Konrad Wittwer, 1879.

Waentig, Heinrich. *Wirtschaft und Kunst: Eine Untersuchung über Geschichte und Theorie der Modernen Kunstgewerbebewegung.* Jena: Verlag von Gustav Fischer, 1909.

Wendt, Hans. "Als Hindenburg zum Ersatzkaiser avancierte." In *Kindheit im Kaiserreich: Erinnerungen an vergangene Zeiten,* ed. Rudolf Pörtner. Düsseldorf: Bechtermünz Verlag, 1998.

Westenberger, Bernhard. *Die Holzspielwarenindustrie im sächsischen Erzgebirge unter besonderer Berücksichtigung der Hausindustrie.* Leipzig: Otto Wigand Verlagsbuchhandlung und Buchdruckerei m.b.H., 1911.

Zinn, Clara. *Kinderspiel und Spielzeug.* Leipzig and Berlin: Teubner, 1910.

Secondary Sources

Adamson, Robert. *Fichte.* Freeport, NY: Books for Libraries Press, 1969.

Allen, Ann Taylor. *Feminism and Motherhood in Germany, 1800–1914.* New Brunswick, NJ: Rutgers University Press, 1991.

———. "Spiritual Motherhood: German Feminists and the Kindergarten Movement, 1848–1911." *History of Education Quarterly,* fall 1982, 319–39.

Allen, Roy F. *Literary Life in German Expressionism and the Berlin Circles.* Ann Arbor, MI: UMI Research Press, 1983.

Anderson, Perry. *The Origins of Postmodernity.* London: Verso, 1998.

Aschheim, Steven E. *The Nietzsche Legacy in Germany, 1890–1990.* Berkeley: University of California Press, 1992.

Auslander, Leora. *Taste and Power: Furnishing Modern France.* Berkeley: University of California Press, 1996.

Bachmann, Manfred. *Holzspielwaren aus dem Erzgebirge.* Dresden: VEB Verlag der Kunst, 1984.

Ballauff, Theodor, and Klaus Schaller. *Pädagogik: Eine Geschichte der Bildung und Erziehung.* Vol. 2. Freiburg and Munich: Verlag Karl Alber, 1970.

———. *Pädagogik: Eine Geschichte der Bildung und Erziehung.* Vol. 3. Freiburg and Munich: Verlag Karl Alber, 1973.

Barkin, Kenneth D. *The Controversy over German Industrialization, 1890–1902.* Chicago: University of Chicago Press, 1970.

Baudelaire, Charles. *The Painter of Modern Life, and Other Essays.* Ed. and trans. Jonathon Mayne. New York: Da Capo, 1964.

Baudrillard, Jean. *For a Critique of the Political Economy of the Sign.* St. Louis: Telos, 1981.

———. *The System of Objects.* Trans. James Benedict. London and New York: Verso, 1996.

Baumann, Zymunt. *Post-modernity and Its Discontents.* New York: New York University Press, 1997.
Beckers, Edgar. *Das Beispiel Alfred Lichtwark: Eine Studie zum Selbstverständnis der Reformpädadgogik.* Cologne, 1976.
Beiser, Frederick C. *Enlightenment, Revolution, and Romanticism: The Genesis of Modern German Political Thought, 1790–1800.* Cambridge, MA: Harvard University Press, 1992.
———. *The Fate of Reason: German Philosophy from Kant to Fichte.* Cambridge, MA: Harvard University Press, 1987.
———. *The Romantic Imperative: The Concept of Early German Romanticism.* Cambridge, MA: Harvard University Press, 2003.
Bell, Daniel. *The Cultural Contradictions of Capitalism.* New York: Basic Books, 1976.
Benjamin, Walter. *Selected Writings.* Vol. 2, *1927–1934.* Ed. Michael W. Jennings, Howard Eiland, and Gary Smith. Trans. Rodney Livingstone. Cambridge, MA: Belknap, 1999.
Benz, Richard. *Die deutsche Romantik: Geschichte einer geistigen Bewegung.* Leipzig: Philipp Reclam jun. Verlag, 1937.
Bergerson, Andrew. *Ordinary Germans in Extraordinary Times: The Nazi Revolution in Hildesheim.* Bloomington: Indiana University Press, 2004.
Berghahn, Volker R. *Imperial Germany, 1871–1914: Economy, Society, Culture, and Politics.* Providence, RI: Berghahn Books, 1994.
———. *Sarajewo, 28. Juni 1914: Der Untergang des alten Europa.* 2nd ed. Munich: Deutscher Taschenbuch Verlag, 1997.
Berghoff, Hartmut. *Konsumpolitik: Die Regulierung des privaten Verbrauchs im 20. Jahrhundert.* Göttingen: Vandenhoeck und Ruprecht, 1999.
———. *Zwischen Kleinstadt und Weltmarkt: Hohner und die Harmonika, 1857–1961; Unternehmensgeschichte als Gesellschaftgeschichte.* Paderborn, Munich, and Vienna: Ferdinand Schöningh, 1997.
Berlin, Isaiah. *The Crooked Timber of Humanity: Chapters in the History of Ideas.* New York: Vintage Books, 1990.
———. *Vico and Herder: Two Studies in the History of Ideas.* New York: Viking, 1976.
Betts, Paul. *The Authority of Everyday Objects: A Cultural History of West German Industrial Design.* Berkeley: University of California Press, 2004.
Betts, Paul, and Greg Eghigian. *Pain and Prosperity: Reconsidering Twentieth-Century Germany.* Stanford, CA: Stanford University Press, 2003.
Beuys, Barbara. *Familienleben in Deutschland: Neuer Bilder aus der deutschen Vergangenheit.* Reinbeck bei Hamburg: Rowohlt Verlag, 1980.
Blackbourn, David. *The Long Nineteenth Century: A History of Germany, 1780–1918.* New York and Oxford: Oxford University Press, 1998.
Blankertz, Herwig. *Die Geschichte der Pädagogik: Von der Aufklärung bis zur Gegenwart.* Wetzlar: Verlag Büchse der Pandora, 1982.
Bloom, Lisa. *Gender on Ice: American Ideologies of Polar Expeditions.* Minneapolis: University of Minnesota Press, 1993.

Borchardt, Knut. *Die Industrielle Revolution in Deutschland.* Munich: R. Piper, 1972.

Born, Karl Erich. *Staat und Sozialpoltik seit Bismarcks Sturz: Ein Beitrag zur Geschichte der Innenpolitischen Entwicklung des Deutschen Reiches, 1890–1914.* Wiesbaden: Franz Steiner Verlag, 1957.

Bourdieu, Pierre. *Distinction: A Social Critique of the Judgement of Taste.* Trans. Richard Nice. Cambridge, MA: Harvard University Press, 1984.

———. *The Logic of Practice.* Trans. Richard Nice. Stanford, CA: Stanford University Press, 1990.

Brandstätter, Karl. "Die Produktions- und Absatzverhältnisse der Nürnberg-Fürther Spielwaren-industrie unter Berücksichtigung ihrer Zusammenschluss-bestrebungen." PhD diss. Julius-Maximilians-Universität, Würzburg, 1921.

Brown, Kenneth D. *The British Toy Business: A History since 1700.* London: Hambledon, 1996.

———. "Modelling for War? Toy Soldiers in Late Victorian and Edwardian Britain." *Journal of Social History* 24 (1990–91): 237–55.

Bücher, Karl. *Von den Productionsstätten des Weihnachtsmarktes.* Basel: Schweighauserische Verlagsbuchhandlung, 1887.

Budde, Gunilla-Frederike. *Auf dem Weg ins Burgerleben: Kindheit und Erziehung in deutschen und englischen Bürgerfamilien, 1840–1914.* Göttingen: Vandenhoeck und Ruprecht, 1994.

Bürger, Peter. *Theorie der Avantgarde.* Frankfurt am Main: Suhrkamp Verlag, 1974.

Campbell, Colin. *The Romantic Ethic and the Spirit of Modern Consumerism.* New York: Blackwell, 1987.

Campbell, Joan. *The German Werkbund: The Politics of Reform in the Applied Arts.* Princeton, NJ: Princeton University Press, 1978.

Canning, Kathleen. *Languages of Labor and Gender: Female Factory Work in Germany, 1850–1914.* Ithaca, NY: Cornell University Press, 1996. Reprint, University of Michigan Press, 2002.

Carrier, James G. "The Rituals of Christmas Giving." In *Unwrapping Christmas,* ed. Daniel Miller. Oxford: Clarendon, 1993.

Cassirer, Ernst. *Freiheit und Form: Studien zur deutschen Geistesgeschichte.* Berlin: Bruno Cassirer, 1922.

———. *The Philosophy of the Enlightenment.* Trans. Fritz C. A. Koelln and James P. Pettegrove. Boston: Beacon Books, 1951.

———. *The Question of Jean-Jacques Rousseau.* Trans. Peter Gay. New Haven, CT: Yale University Press, 1963.

Chandler, Alfred D., Jr. *Scale and Scope: The Dynamics of Industrial Production.* Cambridge, MA: Belknap, 1990.

———. *The Visible Hand: The Managerial Revolution in American Business.* Cambridge, MA: Belknap, 1977.

Christadler, Marieluise. "Zwischen Gartenlaube und Genozid: Kolonialistiche Jugendbücher im Kaiserreich." In *Die Menschen sind arm weil sie arm sind: Die Dritte Welt im Spiegel von Kinder und Jugendbüchern.* Frankfurt am Main, 1978.

Ciarlo, David. "Consuming Race, Envisioning Empire: Colonialism and German Mass Culture, 1887–1914." PhD diss., University of Wisconsin–Madison, 2003.

Colze, Leo. *Berliner Warenhäuser.* Berlin: Fannei und Walz, 1989. 1st ed., 1908.

Confino, Alon, and Rudy Koshar. "Regimes of Consumer Culture: New Narratives in Twentieth-Century German History." *German History* 19, no. 2 (2001): 131–61.

Creutz, Max. *Das Warenhaus Tietz in Elberfeld von Prof. Wilhelm Kreis—Düsseldorf.* Berlin: Ernst Wasmuth A.-G., 1912.

———. *Joseph M. Olbrich: Das Warenhaus Tietz in Düsseldorf.* Berlin: Ernst Wasmuth A.-G., 1909.

Cross, Gary. *Kids' Stuff: Toys and the Changing World of American Childhood.* Cambridge, MA: Harvard University Press, 1997.

Crossic, Geoffrey, and Heinz Gerhard-Haupt. In *The Petite Bourgeoisie in Europe, 1780–1914: Enterprise, Family, and Independence.* London and New York: Routledge, 1995.

Crothers, George Dunlop. *The German Elections of 1907.* New York: Columbia University Press, 1941.

Church, Roy. "New Perspectives on the History of Products, Firms, Marketing, and Consumers in Britain and the United States since the Mid-nineteenth Century." *Economic History Review* 52, no. 3 (1999): 405–35.

Das VEDES Buch, 1904–1954. Nuremberg: Buchdruckerei August Meyer, 1954.

De Grazia, Victoria. "Changing Consumption Regimes in Europe, 1930–1970: Comparative Perspectives on the Distribution Problem." In *Getting and Spending: European and American Consumer Societies in the Twentieth Century,* ed. Susan Strasser, Charles McGovern, and Matthias Judt. New York: Cambridge University Press, 1998.

Debord, Guy. *The Society of the Spectacle.* Trans. Donald Nicholson-Smith. New York: Zone Books, 1994.

Del Caro, Adrian. *Nietzsche contra Nietzsche: Creativity and the Anti-Romantic.* Baton Rouge: University of Louisiana Press, 1989.

Desai, Ashok. *Real Wages in Germany, 1871–1913.* Oxford: Oxford University Press, 1968.

Dornseifer, Bernd, and Jurgen Kocka. "The Impact of the Preindustrial Heritage: Reconsiderations of the German Pattern of Corporate Development in the Late 19th and Early 20th Centuries." *Industrial and Corporate Change* 2, no. 2 (1993): 233–48.

Douglas, Mary, and Baron Isherwood. *The World of Goods: Toward an Anthropology of Consumption.* 2nd ed. London and New York: Routledge, 1996.

Downs, Robert B. *Friedrich Froebel.* Boston: Twayne, 1978.

Dressel, Hans. *Die Entwicklung von Handel und Industrie in Sonneberg.* Gotha: Friedrich Andreas Perthes, 1908.

Easton, Laird McLeod. *The Red Count: The Life and Times of Harry Kessler.* Berkeley: University of California Press, 2002.

Elias, Norbert. *The Civilizing Process.* Trans. Edmund Jephcott. Oxford: Blackwell, 1939. Reprint, 1994.

Endres, R., and M. Fleischmann. *Nürnbergs Weg in die Moderne: Wirtschaft, Politik und Gesellschaft im 19. und 20. Jahrhundert.* Nuremberg: Verlag W. Tümmels, 1996.

Estelmann, Georg. "Die Nürnberger Spielwaren-Herstellung von den Aeltesten Zeiten bis zur Gegenwart." PhD diss., Universität Frankfurt am Main, 1923.

Faber, Marion. "Von Dockenmachern und Wildrufdrehern." In *SCHUCO, Bing & Co.: Berühmtes Blechspielzeug aus Nürnberg,* ed. Jürgen Franzke. Nuremberg: W. Tümmels Buchdruckerei und Verlag, 1993.

Fear, Jeffrey R. *Organizing Control: August Thyssen and the Construction of German Corporate Management.* Cambridge, MA: Harvard University Press, 2005.

Fine, Ben. "From Political Economy to Consumption." In *Acknowledging Consumption: A Review of New Studies.* London: Routledge, 1995.

Fine, Ben, and Ellen Leopold. *The World of Consumption.* London and New York: Routledge, 1993.

Flecken, Margarete. *Arbeiterkinder im 19. Jahrhundert: Eine sozialgeschichtliche Untersuchung ihrer Lebenswelt.* Weinheim and Basel: Beltz Verlag, 1981.

Fleischmann, Adolf. *Die Arbeiter-Agitatoren des Katheder-Sozialismus und die Sonneberger Spielwaren-Industrie und ihr Handel.* Verlag von Leonhard Simion, Berlin, 1884.

———. *Gewerbe, Industrie und Handel des Meininger Oberlandes in ihrer historischen Entwicklung.* Vol. 1. Hildburghausen: Kesselring'sche Hofbuchhandlung, 1878.

Foucault, Michel. *Discipline and Punish: The Birth of the Prison.* New York: Random House, 1977.

———. *The Order of Things: An Archaeology of the Human Sciences.* New York: Random House, 1970.

——— "Two Lectures." In *Culture/Power/History.* Princeton, NJ: Princeton University Press, 1994.

Franzke, Jürgen. *SCHUCO, Bing & Co.: Berühmtes Blechspielzeug aus Nürnberg.* Nuremberg: W. Tümmels Buchdruckerei und Verlag, 1993.

Frei, Helmut. *Tempel der Kauflust: Eine Geschichte der Warenhauskultur.* Leipzig: Edition Leipzig, 1997.

Friedrichsmeyer, Sara, Sara Lennox, and Susanne Zantop. *The Imperialist Imagination: German Colonialism and Its Legacy.* Ann Arbor: University of Michigan Press, 1998.

Frisby, David. *Sociological Impressionism: A Reassessment of Georg Simmel's Social Theory.* London: Heinemann, 1981.

Fritzsche, Peter. *A Nation of Fliers: German Aviation and the Popular Imagination.* Cambridge, MA: Harvard University Press, 1992.

———. *Reading Berlin, 1900.* Cambridge, MA: Harvard University Press, 1996.

Ganaway, Bryan Frederick. "Toys, Consumption, and Middle-Class Childhood

in Imperial Germany, 1871–1918." PhD diss., University of Illinois at Urbana-Champaign, 2003.
Gay, Peter. *Education of the Senses.* New York: Oxford University Press, 1984.
———. *Weimar Culture: The Outsider as Insider.* New York: W. W. Norton, 2001.
Geertz, Clifford. *The Interpretation of Cultures.* New York: Basic Books, 1973.
Gellately, Robert. *The Politics of Economic Despair: Shopkeepers and German Politics, 1890–1914.* London and Beverly Hills: Sage, 1974.
Gerlach, Siegfried. *Das Warenhaus in Deutschland: Sein Entwicklung bis zum ersten Weltkrieg in historisch-geographischer Sicht.* Stuttgart: Franz Steiner Verlag, 1988.
Gerschenkron, Alexander. *Economic Backwardness in Historical Perspective.* Cambridge, MA: Belknap, 1962.
Giddens, Anthony. *Modernity and Self-Identity: Self and Society in the Late Modern Age.* Stanford, CA: Stanford University Press, 1991.
Giedion, Siegfried. *Die Herrschaft der Mechanisierung: Ein Beitrag zur anonymen Geschichte.* Frankfurt am Main: Europäische Verlagsanstalt, 1982.
Gilman, Sander, "The Figure of the Black in German Aesthetic Theory." *Eighteenth-Century Studies* (summer 1975): 373–91.
Gluck, Mary. *Popular Bohemia: Modernism and Urban Culture in Nineteenth-Century Paris.* Cambridge, MA: Harvard University Press, 2005.
Göhre, Paul. *Das Warenhaus.* Frankfurt am Main: Literarische Anstalt, 1907.
Golby, J. M., and A. W. Purdue. *The Making of Modern Christmas.* Athens: University of Georgia Press, 1986.
Green, Nancy. *Ready-to-Wear and Ready-to-Work: A Century of Industry and Immigrants in Paris and New York.* Durham, NC: Duke University Press, 1997.
Guth, Karl. "Die Rückwirkung des wirtschaftlichskrieges auf Nürnberger Spezialindustrie." PhD diss., Friedrich-Alexander-Universität, Erlangen, 1922.
Habermas, Rebekka. "Parent-Child Relationships in the Nineteenth Century." *German History* 16, no. 1 (1998): 43–56.
Hamlin, David. "Flexible Specialization and the German Toy Industry, 1880–1914." *Social History* 29, no. 1 (Feb. 2004): 30–40.
———. "Romanticism, Spectacle, and a Critique of Wilhelmine Consumer Capitalism." *Central European History* (spring 2005): 250–68.
———. "The Structures of Toy Consumption: Bourgeois Domesticity and Demand for Toys in Nineteenth-Century Germany." *Journal of Social History* (summer 2003): 857–69.
Hammermeister, Kai. *The German Aesthetic Tradition.* New York: Cambridge University Press, 2002.
Hampson, Norman. *The Enlightenment: An Evaluation of Its Assumptions, Attitudes, and Values.* London: Penguin Books, 1968.
Hardach-Pinke, Irene, and Gerd Hardach, eds. *Deutsche Kindheiten: Autobiographische Zeugnisse 1700–1900.* Kronberg: Athenäum Verlag, 1978.
Haug, Wolfgang. *Critique of Commodity Aesthetics: Appearance, Sexuality, and Advertising in Capitalist Society.* Trans. Robert Bock. Minneapolis: University of Minnesota Press, 1986.

Hausen, Karin. "Family and Role Division: The Polarisation of Sexual Stereotypes in the Nineteenth Century; An Aspect of the Dissociation of Work and Family Life." In *The German Family: Essays on the Social History of the Family in Nineteenth- and Twentieth-Century Germany,* ed. Richard Evans and W. R. Lee. Totowa, NJ: Barnes and Noble Books, 1981.

Haxthausen, Charles W., and Heidrun Suhr, eds. *Berlin: Culture and Metropolis.* Minneapolis: University of Minnesota Press, 1990.

Henrich, Dieter. "Beauty and Freedom: Schiller's Struggle with Kant's Aesthetics." In *Essays in Kant's Aesthetics,* ed. Ted Cohen and Paul Guyer. Chicago: University of Chicago Press, 1982.

Henze, Asgar. "Eisenzeit: Geschichte und Technik der Metallbaukästen." In *Eisenzeit, Geschichte des Metallbaukastens.* Museen der Stadt Nürnberg/ Spielzeugmuseum. Nuremberg: W. Tümmels Buchdruckerei und Verlag GmbH, 1995.

Hepp, Corona. *Avantgarde: Moderne Kunst, Kulturkritik und Reformbewegungen nach der Jahrhundertwende.* Munich: Deutscher Taschenbuch Verlag, 1987.

Hermand, Jost. "Artificial Atavism: German Expressionism and Blacks." In *Blacks and German Culture,* ed. Reinhold Grimm and Jost Hermand. Madison: University of Wisconsin Press, 1986.

Herrigel, Gary. *Industrial Constructions: The Sources of German Industrial Power.* New York: Cambridge University Press, 1996.

———. "Industry as a Form of Order: A Comparison of the Historical Development of the Machine Tool Industries in the United States and Germany." In *Governing Capitalist Economies: Performance and Control of Economic Sectors.* New York: Oxford University Press, 1994.

———. "Large Firms, Small Firms, and the Governance of Flexible Specialization: The Case of Baden Württemberg and Socialized Risk." In *Country Competitiveness: Technology and the Organization of Work,* ed. Bruce Kogut. New York: Oxford University Press, 1993.

Heuß, Theodor. *Friedrich Naumann: Der Mann, das Werk, die Zeit.* Stuttgart and Berlin: Deutsche Verlags-Anstalt, 1937.

Hobsbawm, Eric. *The Age of Empire, 1875–1914.* NewYork: Vintage Books, 1987.

Höllerer, Otto. *Märklin: Handbuch für Ausstattungsstücke zu den großen Spurweite, 1895–1939.* Munich: Verlag Dr. O. Höllerer, 1999.

Huber, F. H. "Nürnbergs Spielwaren-Industrie." In *Bayerns Industrie und Handel,* ed. Adam Guttmann. Nuremberg: J. L. Schrag, 1906.

Iggers, Georg. *The German Conception of History: The National Tradition of Historical Thought from Herder to the Present.* Middletown, CT: Wesleyan University Press, 1968.

Jakob, F. A. L. *Deutschlands Spielende Jugend.* 4th ed. Leipzig: Verlag von Eduard Kummer, 1896.

Jameson, Frederic. *The Cultural Turn: Selected Writings on the Postmodern, 1983–1998.* London: Verso, 1998.

Jarausch, Konrad H., and Michael Geyer. *Shattered Past: Reconstructing German Histories.* Princeton, NJ: Princeton University Press, 2003.

Jarzombek, Mark. "The Discourses of a Bourgeois Utopia, 1904–1908, and the Founding of the Werkbund." In *Imagining Modern German Culture, 1889–1910,* ed. Francoise Forster-Hahn. Washington, DC: National Gallery of Art, 1996.

Jay, Martin. *Adorno.* Cambridge, MA: Harvard University Press, 1984.

———. *Downcast Eyes: The Denigration of Vision in Twentieth-Century French Thought.* Berkeley: University of California Press, 1993.

Jeffries, Matthew. *Imperial Culture in Germany, 1871–1918.* New York: Palgrave, 2003.

Jenkins, Jennifer. "The Kitsch Collections and *The Spirit in the Furniture:* Cultural Reform and National Culture in Germany." *Social History* 21, no. 2 (May 1996): 123–42.

Jones, John Philip. *What's in a Name? Advertising and the Concept of Brands.* Lexington, MA: Lexington Books, 1986.

Kaelble, Hartmut. *Industrielle Interessenpolitik in der Wilhelmischen Gesellschaft: Centralverband Deutscher Industrieller, 1895–1914.* Berlin: Walter de Gruyter, 1967.

Kaplan, Marion. *The Making of the Jewish Middle Class.* New York: Oxford University Press, 1991.

Kind, Hansgeorg. *Das Kind in der Ideologie und der Dichtung der deutschen Romantik.* Dreden: Verlag M. Dittert, 1936.

Kitchen, Martin. *The Political Economy of Germany, 1815–1914.* Montreal: McGill-Queens University Press, 1978.

Kocka, Jürgen. *Arbeitsverhältnisse und Arbeiterexistenzen: Grundlagen der Klassenbildung im 19. Jahrhundert.* Bonn: Verlag J. H. W. Dietz Nachfolger, 1996.

Komlos, John, and Scott Eddie. *Selected Cliometric Studies on German Economic History.* Stuttgart: Franz Steiner Verlag, 1997.

Kramer, Waldemar, ed. *Die alt-frankfurter Art zu leben: Anhand von Zeichnungen der "Kleinen Presse" aus der Jahren 1885 bis 1912.* Frankfurt am Main: Verlag von Waldemar Kramer, 1974.

Kratzsch, Gerhard. *Kunstwart und Dürerbund: Ein Beitrag zur Geschichte der Gebildeten im Zeitalter des Imperialismus.* Göttingen: Vandenhoeck und Ruprecht, 1969.

Kriedte, Peter, Hans Medick, and Jürgen Schlumbohm. *Industrialization before Industrialization: Rural Industry in the Genesis of Capitalism.* Cambridge: Cambridge University Press, 1981.

Krugmann, Paul. *Peddling Prosperity: Economic Sense and Nonsense in the Age of Diminished Expectations.* New York: W. W. Norton, 1994.

La Volpa, Anthony. *Fichte: The Self and the Calling of Philosophy, 1762–1799.* New York: Cambridge University Press, 2001.

Ladwig-Winters, Simone. *Wertheim: Geschichte eines Warenhauses.* Berlin: Bra, 1997.

Lambi, Ivo Nikolai. *Free Trade and Protectionism in Germany, 1868–1879.* Wiesbaden: Franz Steiner Verlag, 1963.

Lamoreaux, Naomi, Daniel Raff, and Peter Temin. "Beyond Markets and Hierarchies: Toward a New Synthesis of American Business History." *American History Review* 108, no. 2 (Apr. 2003): 404–33.

Landes, David. *The Unbound Prometheus: Technological Change and Industrial Development in Western Europe from 1750 to the Present.* Cambridge: Cambridge University Press, 1969.

———. *The Wealth and Poverty of Nations: Why Some Are So Rich and Some So Poor.* New York: W. W. Norton, 1999.

Lasser, Moritz Otto Baron. "Kaufhaus Oberpollinger, München." In *Bayerns Industrie und Handel,* ed. Adam Guttmann. Nuremberg: J. L. Schrag, 1906.

Leck, Ralph Mathew. *Georg Simmel and the Soul of German Culture, Geist-Politik: Fin de Siècle to the Great War.* Ann Arbor, MI: UMI Research Press, 1995.

Lee, Martyn J. *Consumer Culture Reborn: The Cultural Politics of Consumption.* London: Routledge, 1993.

Liebersohn, Harry. *Fate and Utopia in German Sociology, 1870–1923.* Cambridge, MA: MIT Press, 1988.

Lorenz, Christa. *Berliner Weihnachtsmarkt: Bilder und Geschichten aus 5 Jahrhunderten.* Berlin: Berlin-Information, 1987.

Maciuika, John V. *Before the Bauhaus: Architecture, Politics, and the German State, 1890–1920.* Cambridge: Cambridge University Press, 2005.

Maiholzer, Clemens. *Die Rentabilität der bayerischen Staatseisenbahnen.* Leipzig: A. Deichert'sche Verlagsbuchhandlung, 1911.

Marcus, Sharon. *Apartment Stories: City and Home in Nineteenth-Century Paris and London.* Berkeley: University of California Press, 1999.

Matthaei, Julie. *An Economic History of Women in America: Women's Work, the Sexual Division of Labor, and the Development of Capitalism.* New York: Schocken Books, 1982.

Maynes, Mary Jo. *Taking the Hard Road: The Life Course in French and German Workers' Autobiographies in the Era of Industrialization.* Chapel Hill: University of North Carolina Press, 1995.

McKenrick, Niel, John Brewer, and J. H. Plumb. *Birth of a Consumer Society: The Commercialization of Eighteenth-Century England.* Bloomington: Indiana University Press, 1982.

Meinel, Angela. *Kinderleben und Kinderkultur in Sachsen: Versuch eines Uberblicks.* Dresden: Sachsisches Druck- und Verlagshaus GmbH, 1998.

Meyer, Gertrud. *Die Spielwarenindustrie im sächsischen Erzgebirge.* Leipzig: U. Deichert'sche Verlagsbuchhandlung Nachf., 1911.

Meyer-Margreth, Ernst. "Geschichte des Anker-Steinbaukastens." In *Beiträge zur Deutschen Volks- und Altertumskunde,* vol. 17, ed. Jörgen Bracker. Hamburg: Museum für Hamburgische Geschichte, 1978.

Mielke, Siegfried. *Der Hansa-Bund für Gewerbe, Handel und Industrie 1909–1914: Der gescheiterte Versuch einer antifeudalen Sammlungspolitik.* Göttingen: Vandenhoeck und Ruprecht, 1976.

Miller, Daniel. *Material Culture and Mass Consumption.* Oxford: Blackwell, 1987.

———. "A Theory of Christmas." In *Unwrapping Christmas,* ed. Daniel Miller. Oxford: Clarendon, 1993.

———. *A Theory of Shopping.* Ithaca, NY: Cornell University Press, 1998.

Miller, Michael. *The Bon Marché: Bourgeois Culture and the Department Store, 1869–1920.* Princeton, NJ: Princeton University Press, 1981.

Mitchell, Timothy. *Colonising Egypt.* Berkeley: University of California Press, 1988.

Möckl, Karl. *Die Prinzregentenzeit.* Munich and Vienna: R. Oldenbourg Verlag, 1972.

Mosse, George. *Nationalism and Sexuality: Respectability and Abnormal Sexuality in Modern Europe.* New York: H. Fertig, 1985.

Neuhouser, Fredrick. *Fichte's Theory of Subjectivity.* Cambridge: Cambridge University Press, 1990.

Nipperdey, Thomas. *Deutsche Geschichte, 1800–1918.* Munich: Verlag C. H. Beck, 1992.

Nissenbaum, Stephen. *The Battle for Christmas.* New York: Alfred A. Knopf, 1997.

Nord, Philip G. *Paris Shopkeepers and the Politics of Resentment.* Princeton, NJ: Princeton University Press, 1986.

Noschke, Annette, and Günter Knerr. *Bauklötze Staunen: Zweihundert Jahre Geschichte der Baukästen.* Munich: Hirmer Verlag and Deutsche Museum, 1986.

Nussbaum, Helga. *Unternehmer gegen Monopole: Über Struktur und Aktionen antimonopolischer bürgerlicher Gruppen zu Beginn des 20. Jahrhunderts.* Berlin: Akademie-Verlag, 1966.

Parry-Crooke, Charlotte. *Märklin, 1895–1914.* London: Denzs Ingram, 1983.

Pascal, Roy. *The German Sturm und Drang.* Manchester: Manchester University Press, 1951.

Perry, Joseph B. "The Private Life of the Nation: Christmas and the Invention of Modern Germany." PhD diss., University of Illinois at Urbana-Champaign, 2001.

Peukert, Detlev. *Inside Nazi Germany: Conformity, Opposition, and Racism in Everyday Life.* New Haven, CT: Yale University Press, 1987.

———. *Max Webers Diagnose der Moderne.* Göttingen: Vandenhoeck und Ruprecht, 1989.

———. *The Weimar Republic: The Crisis of Classical Modernity.* New York: Hill and Wang, 1989.

Pine, B. Joseph, II. *Mass Customization: The New Frontier in Business Competition.* Boston: Harvard Business School Press, 1993.

Piore, Michael J., and Charles F. Sabel. *The Second Industrial Divide: Possibilities for Prosperity.* New York: Basic Books, 1984.

Pollard, Sidney. *Peaceful Conquest: The Industrialization of Europe, 1760–1970.* Oxford: Oxford University Press, 1981.

Porter, Michael E. *The Competitive Advantage of Nations.* New York: Free Press, 1990.

———. "How Competitive Forces Shape Strategy." *Harvard Business Review* 57, no. 2 (Mar.–Apr. 1979): 137–45.

Prater, Donald. *Thomas Mann: A Life.* Oxford: Oxford University Press, 1995.

Randa, Sigrid. *Alexander Koch: Publizist und Verleger in Darmstadt; Reformen der Kunst und des Lebens um 1900.* Worms: Wernersche Verlagsgesellschaft, 1990.

Rang, Martin. *Rousseaus Lehre vom Menschen.* Göttingen: Vandenhoeck und Ruprecht, 1965.

Rausch, Ernst. *Die Sonneberger Spielwaren-Industrie und die verwandten Industrieen der Griffel- und Glasfabrikation unter besonderer Berücksichtigung der Verhältnisse in der Hausindustrie.* Berlin: Siemenroth und Troschel, 1901.

Reder, Gustav. *Mit Uhrwerk, Dampf und Strom: Vom Spielzeug zur Modelleisenbahn.* Düsseldorf: Alba Publikation Alf Teloeken GmbH, 1988.

Reid, Roddy. *Families in Jeopardy: Regulating the Social Body in France, 1750–1910.* Stanford, CA: Stanford University Press, 1993.

Reidel, Peter Anselm. *Kandinsky.* Hamburg: Rowohlt Taschenbuch Verlag, 1983.

Repp, Kevin. *Reformers, Critics, and the Paths of German Modernity: Anti-Politics and the Search for Alternatives, 1890–1914.* Cambridge, MA: Harvard University Press, 2000.

Riasanovsky, Nicholas V. *The Emergence of Romanticism.* Oxford: Oxford University Press, 1992.

Ridley, Hugh. *The Problematic Bourgeois: Twentieth-Century Criticism on Thomas Mann's "Buddenbrooks" and "The Magic Mountain."* Columbia, SC: Camden House, 1994.

Ritter, Gerhard A. *Sozialversicherung in Deutschland und England: Entstehung und Grundzüge im Vergleich.* Munich: Verlag C. H. Beck, 1983.

Roberts, Mary Louise. "Gender, Consumption, and Commodity Culture." *American Historical Review,* June 1998, 817–44.

Roche, Daniel. *A History of Everyday Things: The Birth of Consumption in France, 1600–1800.* Cambridge: Cambridge University Press, 2000.

Rockmore, Tom, and Daniel Breazeale, eds. *New Perspectives on Fichte.* Atlantic Highlands, NJ: Humanities Press, 1996.

Rohkrämer, Thomas. "Antimodernism, Reactionary Modernism, and National Socialism: Technocratic Tendencies in Germany, 1890–1945." *Contemporary European History* 8, no. 1 (Mar. 1999).

———. *Eine andere Moderne? Zivilisationskritik, Natur und Technik in Deutschland, 1880–1933.* Paderborn: Ferdinand Schöningh, 1999.

Röhl, J. C. G. *Germany without Bismarck: The Crisis of Government in the Second Reich, 1890–1900.* London: B. T. Batsford, 1967.

Rosenbaum, Heidi. *Formen der Familie: Untersuchungen zum Zusammenhang von Familienverhältnissen, Sozialstruktur und sozialem Wandel in der deutschen Gesellschaft des 19. Jahrhunderts.* Frankfurt am Main: Suhrkamp Verlag, 1982.

Sabel, Charles F., and Jonathan Zeitlin, eds. *World of Possibilities: Flexibility and Mass Production in Western Industrialization.* Cambridge: Cambridge University Press, 1997.

Sadji, Amadou Booker. *Das Bild des Negro-Afrikaners in der Deutschen*

Koloniallieratur (1884–1945): Ein Beitrag zur literarischen Imagologie Schwarzarfrikas. Berlin: Dietrich Reimer Verlag, 1985.
Safranski, Rudiger. *E. T. A. Hoffmann: Das Leben eines skeptischen Phantasten.* Munich: Carl Hanser Verlag, 1984.
———. *Schopenhauer and the Wild Years of Philosophy.* Trans. Ewald Osers. Cambridge, MA: Harvard University Press, 1987.
Sauermann, Dietmar, ed. *Weihnachten in Westfalen um 1900: Berichte aus dem Archiv für westfälische Volkskunde.* Münster: Volkskundliche Kommission fur Westfalen, 1976.
Saul, S. B. *The Myth of the Great Depression, 1873–1896.* London: Macmillan, 1969.
Schmidt, Dorothea. "Die 'Herren der Technik' und die 'feine Hand' der Arbeiterinnen: Mechanisierung und Geschlectsverhältnis." *PROKLA* 23, no. 4 (1993): 597–98.
Schmölders, Claudia. *Deutsche Kinder: Siebzehn biographische Porträts.* Berlin: Rowohlt, 1997.
Schoenbaum, David. *Zabern 1913. Consensus Politics in Imperial Germany.* London: George Allen and Unwin, 1982.
Schorske, Carl E. *German Social Democracy, 1905–1917: The Development of the Great Schism.* Cambridge, MA: Harvard University Press, 1955.
Schulin, Ernst. *Walther Rathenau: Repräsentant, Kritiker und Opfer seiner Zeit.* Göttingen: Musterschmidt Verlag, 1979.
Schwartz, Frederic J. *The Werkbund: Design Theory and Mass Culture before the First World War.* New Haven, CT: Yale University Press, 1996.
Schwartz, Vanessa. "The Public Taste for Reality: Early Mass Culture in Fin de Siècle Paris." PhD diss., University of California, Berkeley, 1993.
———. *Spectacular Realities: Early Mass Culture in Fin de Siècle Paris.* Berkeley: University of California Press, 1998.
Schwarz, Jürgen. *Architektur und Kommerz: Studien zur deutschen Kauf- und Warenhausarchitektur vor dem Ersten Weltkrieg am Beispiel der Frankfurter Zeil.* Frankfurt am Main: Kunstgechichtliches Institut der Johann Wolfgang Goethe-Universität, 1995.
Scranton, Phillip. *Endless Novelty: Specialty Production and American Industrialization, 1865–1925.* Princeton, NJ: Princeton University Press, 1998.
Sennett, Richard. *Classic Essays on the Culture of Cities.* Englewood Cliffs, NJ: Prentice-Hall, 1969.
———. *The Fall of Public Man.* New York and London: W. W. Norton, 1976.
———. *Flesh and Stone: The Body and the City in Western Civilization.* New York and London: W. W. Norton, 1994.
———. *The Uses of Disorder.* New York: Alfred A. Knopf, 1970.
Senst, Otto. *Die Metallspielwarenindustrie und der Spielwarenhandel von Nürnberg und Fürth.* Erlangen: Universität Buchdruckerei von Fr. Junge, 1901.
Sharpe, Lesley. *Schiller's Aesthetic Essays: Two Centuries of Criticism.* Columbia, SC: Camden House, 1995.

Sheehan, James J. *German Liberalism in the Nineteenth Century.* Chicago: University of Chicago Press, 1978.

Slater, Don. *Consumer Culture and Modernity.* London: Polity, 1997.

Smith, Woodruff D. "Colonialism and Colonial Empire." In *Imperial Germany: A Historiographical Companion,* ed. Roger Chickering. Westport, CT: Greenwood, 1996.

Spiekermann, Uwe. *Basis der Konsumgesellschaft: Entstehung und Entwicklung des modernen Kleinhandels in Deutschland 1850–1914.* Munich: Verlag C. H. Beck, 1999.

———. "Display Windows and Window Displays in German Cities of the Nineteenth Century: Towards the History of a Commercial Breakthrough." In *Advertising and the European City: Historical Perspectives,* ed. Clemens Wischermann and Elliott Shore. Aldershot: Ashgate, 2000.

Spindler, Max, ed. *Bayerische Geschichte im 19. und 20. Jahrhundert, 1800–1970.* Vol. 2. Munich: Verlag C. H. Beck, 1975.

Stargardt, Nicholas. "German Childhoods: The Making of a Historiography." *German History* 16, no. 1 (1998): 1–15.

Stearns, Peter. *Consumerism in World History: The Global Transformation of Desire.* New York: Routledge, 2001.

Stillich, Oskar. *Die Spielwaren-Hausindustrie des Meiningen Oberlandes.* Jena: Verlag von Gustav Fischer, 1899.

Sutton-Smith, Brian. *Toys as Culture.* New York and London: Gardner, 1986.

Taylor, Charles. *Hegel and Modern Society.* New York: Cambridge University Press, 1979.

———. *Modern Social Imaginaries.* Durham, NC: Duke University Press, 2004.

———. *Sources of the Self: The Making of the Modern Identity.* Cambridge, MA: Harvard University Press, 1989.

Tester, Keith, ed. *The Flaneur.* London and New York: Routledge, 1994.

Tille, Alexander. *Die Geschichte der deutschen Weihnacht.* Leipzig: E. Keil, 1893.

Tilly, Charles. *Big Structures, Large Processes, Huge Comparisons.* New York: Russell Sage Foundation, 1984.

Tilly, Christopher, and Charles Tilly. *Work under Capitalism.* Boulder, CO: Westview, 1998.

Tilly, Richard. *Vom Zollverein zum Industriestaat: Die wirtschaftlich-soziale Entwicklung Deutschlands, 1834–1914.* Munich: Deutscher Taschenbuch Verlag, 1990.

Toni, Eckert. *Ignaz Bing: Sein Leben in Streitberg.* Forschheim: Fränkische Schweiz-Verein, Verlag Forschheimer, reihe F. Streit, 1995.

Twentieth-Century Continental Philosophy. Ed. Richard Kearny. London and NewYork: Routledge, 1991.

Ullmann, Hans-Peter. *Der Bund der Industriellen: Organisation, Einfluß und Politik klein- und mittelbetrieblicher Industrieller im Deutschen Kaiserreich, 1895–1914.* Göttingen: Vandenhoeck und Ruprecht, 1976.

Völker-Kraemer, Sabine. *Wie ich zur Teddymutter wurde: Das Leben der*

Margarete Steiff nach ihren eigenen Aufzeichnungen. Stuttgart: Quell Verlag, 1996.

Ward, Janet. *Weimar Surfaces: Urban Visual Culture in 1920s Germany.* Berkeley: University of California Press, 2001.

Warmbold, Joachim. *Germania in Africa: Germany's Colonial Literature.* New York: Peter Lang, 1989.

Weber-Kellermann, Ingeborg. *Das Weihnachtsfest: Eine Kultur- und Sozialgeschichte der Weihnachtszeit.* Lucerne: Bucher, 1978.

———. *Die deutsche Familie: Versuch einer Sozialgeschichte.* Frankfurt am Main: Suhrkamp Verlag, 1974.

———. *Die Kinderstube.* Frankfurt am Main: Insel Verlag, 1991.

———. *Die Kindheit: Eine Kulturgeschichte.* Frankfurt am Main: Insel Verlag, 1979.

Wehler, Hans-Ulrich. *Bismarck und der Imperialismus.* Cologne: Kiepenheuer und Witsch, 1969.

———. *Deutsche Gesellschaftgeschichte, 1849–1914.* Munich: Verlag C.H. Beck, 1995.

Weitowitz, Rolf. *Deutsche Politik und Handelspolitik unter Reichskanzler Leo von Caprivi, 1890–1894.* Düsseldorf: Droste Verlag, 1978.

Wenzel, Georg. "Die Geschichte der Nürnberger Spielzeugindustrie." PhD diss., Friedrich-Alexander-Universität, Erlangen and Nuremberg, 1967.

Wernicke, Johannes. *Warenhaus, Industrie und Mittelstand.* Berlin: Verlag von Emil Ebering, 1911.

Wiener, Alfred. *Das Warenhaus: Kauf-, Geschäfts-, Büro-haus.* Berlin: Ernst Wasmuth A.-G., 1912.

Williams, Rosalind H. *Dream Worlds: Mass Consumption in Late Nineteenth-Century France.* Berkeley: University of California Press, 1982.

Witt, Peter-Christian. *Die Finanzpolitik des deutschen Reiches von 1903 bis 1913: Eine Studie zum Innenpolitik des Wilhelmischen Deutschland.* Lübeck and Hamburg: Matthiesen Verlag, 1970.

Wittke, Volker. *Wie enstand industrielle Massenproduktion? Die diskontinuierliche Entwicklung der deutschen Elektroindustrie von Anfängen der "großen Industrie" bis zur Entfaltung des Fordismus (1880–1975).* Belin: Edition Sigma, 1996.

Wolfgang, Heger. *Das Tor zur Kindheit: Die Welt der Margarete Steiff.* Giengen an der Brenz: Arbeitskreis für Stadtgeschichte, 1997.

Zantop, Susanne. *Colonial Fantasies: Conquest, Family, and Nation in Precolonial Germany, 1770–1870.* Durham, NC: Duke University Press, 1997.

Zwijnenberg, Peter. *De Geschiedenis van Richter's Anker Steenbouwdozen.* Alphen aan den Rijn, 1982.

Index